Wills of Delaware County, Pennsylvania 1789-1835

Compiled by
Robert G. Swift

Willow Bend Books
Westminster, Maryland
2001

Willow Bend Books

65 East Main Street
Westminster, Maryland 21157-5026
1-800-876-6103

WB1494

Source books, early maps, CDs -- Worldwide

For our listing of thousands of titles offered
by hundreds of publishers, see our website
at
www.WillowBendBooks.com

Visit our retail store

©1998 F. Edward Wright
Second Printing, Willow Bend Books, 2001

All rights reserved. No part of this book may be reproduced or transmitted in any form or by any means, electronic or mechanical, including photocopying, recording or by any information storage and retrieval system without written permission from the author, except for the inclusion of brief quotations in a review.

International Standard Book Number: 1-58549-464-X

Printed in the United States of America

INTRODUCTION

These wills were abstracted by Robert G. Swift and his notes were later copied under the auspices of the Genealogical Society of Pennsylvania in the early 1900s. Copies of these abstracts were made available to various libraries in Pennsylvania and microfilm copies made by the Genealogical Society of Utah (LDS). Recently bound photostat copies of the abstracts were offered for sale by the Genealogical Society of Pennsylvania.

We extend our appreciation to the staffs of the Historical Society of Pennsylvania (1300 Locust Street, Philadelphia, PA 19107) and encourage use and support of its facilities and to the Genealogical Society of Pennsylvania whose collections are housed in the Historical Society Library. We also encourage membership in the Genealogical Society of Pennsylvania (1305 Locust Street, Philadelphia, PA 19107-5699).

> F. Edward Wright
> Westminster, Maryland
> 1998

WILLS OF DELAWARE COUNTY, PENNSYLVANIA. 1789-1835

CHAMBLERLIN, SUSANNAH, widow, Concord.
Nov 5, 1774 - Oct 17, 1789.
County of Chester, Pennsylvania. Granddaughters Mary FAIRLAMB, Abigail PENNELL and Ledah PENNELL, grandson Thomas PENNELL. To Hannah, daughter of grandson Joseph PENNIL. To Susannah, daughter of sd. Joseph PENNEL. To Hannah, wife of Jonathan HAYCOCK. To Caleb PYLE.
Exr: Sd. grandson Joseph PENNEL.
Wits: Thomas HOWELL, Stephen MENDENHALL, Robert MENDENHALL and Benjamin RYLE. #1.

TAYLOR, ISRAEL, Tinicum Island, Ridley Township, Chester County.
_____.
Plantation leased to Jacob RINALS to his brother Thomas SMITH. Legacies to sisters Margaret SMITH and Rebecca SMITH when they reach age of eighteen years. Plantation leased to Jos. PENROSE and also the meadow land on the Darby Creek by the Ferry to brother Luke SMITH he paying the above sisters £100 a piece at above age. Probated Nov 2, 1789 on application of William WORRALL and Phoebe WORRALL.
Wits: William WORRALL, Phoebe WORRAL and Joseph KING. #2.

FAWKES, RICHARD, Newtown, yeoman, County of Chester.
Feb 13, 1789 - Nov 29, 1789.
Gives to wife (Rebeccah) lot 8 1/2 acres 10 perches of land where his son John formerly lived, during her natural life. Daughter Rebacah to live with mother and if unmarried to have the lot after the mother's decease, if she marries, lot to be sold by executors. Gives to wife certain household furniture and the rest to daughter Rebacah, gives to son John FAWKES five shillings and to have no more of estate, 100 acres where his son John lives in Newtown, Chester County adjoining estates of Thomas WILLING, David LEWIS, David MORRIS and the David MORRIS road, the line to be as many perches on Morris Road as on David ALEXANDER'S line, this land to remain in name of executors for the bringing up of John's children born of the body of his wife Sarah LANE until the youngest child arrive at the age of 14. Executors to put on interest for support of son Thomas during life £250. After death of wife and son Thomas £20 to granddaughter Elise and daughter Sarah to have £20 less. Wife and daughter Rebacah to be

executrix and son in law Caleb MORIS and Joseph WOOD to be executors.
Codicil Feb 15, 1789, son Richard FAWKES to assist the executors and to be paid for trouble.
Wits: George DARBY, Emily HORTON (X).
Codicil Feb 23, 1789.
Wits: George DARBY and Emily HORTON (mark).
Codicil Nov 12, 1789, 80 acres to be set off instead of 100 acres.
Wits: Bernard VALNEER, Jr. and Joseph FAWKES.
Exrs: Wife, daughter Rebacah, Caleb MORIS and Joseph WOOD.
Wits: J. MARIS, Daniel BURTNITT and John DARBY. #3.

HAWORTH, JOHN, yeoman, Haverford Twp., Chester County.
Oct 7, 1776 - Jan 6, 1790.
Son George 50 acres, to start 1 perch from the line of William LAWRENCE'S land and begin at the creek, leaving 16 1/2 feet roadway to creek, rest of land to wife Mary with all personal effects if she does not marry, but if she does, two thirds to the children, except that George and Hannah shall have one child's share.
Exrs: Wife Mary, son George and brother David HALL.
Wits: John GRACY, Lewis DAVIS, Jr. and Samuel GRACY. #4.

HALLOWAY, SARAH, Philadelphia.
June 4, 1785 - Jan 21, 1790.
Names cousin Deborah daughter of her brother William GRISCOM, cousin Deborah BOLTON daughter of brother Samuel GRISCOM. To the two daughters of same Sarah and Rachel all her pewterware, to Elizabeth daughter of her sister Mary HIBBERD, to two sisters Abigail PARISH and Mary HIBBERD, to brother Samuel GRISCOM. After decease of sisters, estate to go to children of Mary HIBBERD namely, John, Joseph and Elizabeth.
Exrs: Brother in law Hezekiah HIBBERD and cousin John HIBBERD, both of Darby.
Wits: Jonathan OWEN and Elizabeth HOOPS. #5.

JONES, DAVID, husbandman, Radnor, Delaware County.
Jan 1, 1790 - Jan 25, 1790.
Cousin Morgan DAVID, moneys and personal estate to wife forever, real estate to her for life, afterwards to be in charge of his friends Thomas GEORGE and Evan LEWIS for the use of Radnor particular meeting, residue to children of his sisters Sarah and Hannah EVANS,

except that Sarah's daughter Amy and Nathan son of Hannah shall have a double portion.
Exrs: Elinor JONES.
Wits: Philip SHEAF, Henry LEWIS and Henry LAWRENCE, Jr. #6.

HAYS, ELIZABETH, Darby, Chester County.
Sept 7, 1787 - Jan 26, 1790.
To friends Elizabeth GRIME and Alice ASH. To nieces Ann SMITH and Rachel SMITH, sister Mary SPEAKMAN, cousins Ann SMITH, Rachel SMITH, Henry Hays SMITH and Samuel Sharp SMITH, friend Hugh LLOYD, sole executor.
Exrs: Hugh LLOYD.
Wits: Nicholas DIEHL and Tristin COX. #7.

VANLEER, BARNHERD, physician, Marple Twp., Chester County.
Feb 10, 1786 - Feb 12, 1790 (Probated as Branson VanLEER).
Wife Christian, sons George, Branson, Samuel and Benjamin each 5 shillings, these being already provided for, son Isaac, daughter Mary wife of Moses MOORE, messuages and land in Tradyfrin including the Blue Ball Tavern, purchased of Cunrod YOUNG and Thomas HUBBERT during her life and afterwards to her heirs who die leaving lawful issue. To daughter Hannah, property on the east side of Front Street in the District of Southwark, to daughter Catharine house and lot in Moyamensing Township bought of John EVANS, to daughter Christian ground rents of 4 lots on Arch Street purchased of Benjamin COOPER, son Barnherd, homestead and heirlooms reserving certain rights for mother during life.
Exrs: Sd. wife and son Barnhard VANLEER.
Wits: Henry LAWRENCE and Thomas TUCKER. #8.

REECE, WILLIAM, Newtown Twp., Delaware County.
Jan 26, 1790 - April 10, 1790.
Wife's name not given - mentions Mordecai LEWIS his wife's father, as having left property in Philadelphia to her, also in Newtown and Edgemont which will descend to his son Mordecai as heir entail, to eldest daughter Sidney the homestead. Orders executors to sell tract in London Grove township purchased of Nathaniel WALLACE and the net proceeds to be given to his daughter Orpah - mentions property on High Street, Philadelphia.
Exrs: Son Mordecai.
Wits: Jesse REECE, Nathl. GRUBB and Thomas GEORGE. #9.

EVANS, MARY, Darby.
March 2, 1790 - April 24, 1790.
Leaves certain heirlooms to the following persons: son Thomas EVANS, sisters Ann MORRIS, Sarah WARNER, Hannah SERRILL, Elizabeth ASH, nieces Mary MORRIS, Sarah HANSELL, Mary WARNER, Hannah LLOYD, Hannah OVERLY. To Lydia TOWNSEND daughter of Benjamin TOWNSEND, Deborah EVANS, mother in law and Esther TOWNSEND, to son Thomas all real estate - mentions a brother Thomas PEARSON, and Sarah LLOYD, John PEARSON a brother to be executor and guardian of son Thomas.
Exrs: Brother John PEARSON.
Wits: Jacob SERRILL and Thomas LLOYD. #10.

HAYES, ANN, widow, Delaware County.
Oct 14, 1789 - April 24, 1790.
Homestead and furniture to niece Mary LLOYD, the wife of Thomas LLOYD - mentions nephew George and nieces Sarah, Ann and Tacey WOOD children of brother Jonathan WOOD, also nieces Hannah and Margaret WOOD and nephew Henry, children of brother George, sisters Jane SELLERS and Sarah PEARSON and niece Rebecca SERRILL. To children of sisters Jane and Sarah.
Exrs: Friend Hugh LLOYD.
Wits: Margaret PEARSON, Jonathan PEARSON and John PEARSON. #11.

GREEN, ROBERT, yeoman, Birmingham Twp., Chester County.
Sept 21, 1789 - May 11, 1790.
Mentions wife, brothers in law John BALDWIN and Isaac STARR, son Jesse to have 106 acres in township of Concord, sister Margaret CHALFANT. Leaves son Amos tract of six hundred acres in Harrison County, Virginia purchased of Thomas PENNELL (son of Robert), son Silas, property in Wilmington oc. by Solomon FUSSELL, son Robert, plantation in Goshen Twp. bought of George PIERCE, son Lot GREEN 1200 acres in Virginia, daughters Abigail HOLLINGSWORTH, Rachel GREEN, Rebecca GREEN, Robert, Hannah and Aaron HOLLINGSWORTH, children of daughter Abigail.
Exrs: Sons Jesse and Robert GREEN.
Wits: Thomas CHANDLER, William HICKLEN and Isaac STARR. #12.

McCALL, THOMAS, yeoman, Concord Twp.
March 16, 1787 - May 31, 1790.

Names nephews: Joseph McCALL, William McCALL, George McCALL, John McCALL, also Thomas McCALL son of William.
Exrs: Nephews William and George.
Wits: Isaac EYRE, H.H. GRAHAM and James DILWORTH, Jr. #13.

ELLIOTT, RUTH, widow of Christian ELLIOTT, Kingsees Twp., Philadelphia.
May __, 1790 - June 11, 1790.
Names sister in law Abigail MERRION, cousins Ruth MERRION and Thomas MERRION, brother Joseph MERRION, granddaughter Mary ELLIOTT, son Israel ELLIOTT and daughter in law Mary ELLIOTT.
Exr: Brother Joseph MERRION.
Wits: Benjamin RICHARDS and John TORTON. #14.

CRAWFORD, JOHN, Lower Chichester, Chester County.
Aug 29, 1788 - Aug 26, 1790.
Appoints son John CRAWFORD and sons in law Thomas GRUBB and Samuel TRIMBLE executors, four children: John CRAWFORD, Margaret GRUBB, Hannah TRIMBLE and Samuel Crawford.
Exrs: Son John CRAWFORD, sons in law Thomas GRUBB and Samuel TRIMBLE.
Wits: Melchior LOVEN, Thomas WALLACE and Thomas POWER. #15.

BONSALL, HANNAH, Upper Darby.
Aug 21, 1790 - Sept 16, 1790.
Interest of certain money to sister Sarah at her decease to seven cousins: George BONSALL and Mary PALMER children of brother Isaac, dec'd., Esther and Benjamin, children of brother Benjamin, Levi, Isaac and Jonathan, children of brother Jonathan, other children of Jonathan, John Caleb, Reuben, Ann, Charles. To children of brother Enoch, dec'd.: William, Enoch, Moses, Samuel, Ann and Rachel. To children of brother Joshua, dec'd., Joshua and Joel, Sidney and Hannah. To children of brother Joseph, Margaret, Martha, James, Susannah, Lydia, Sarah and Joseph. To sisters in law Rachel BONSALL, Margaret BONSALL (widow), Elizabeth BONSALL, Rachel BONSALL, Hannah GRACY, Lydia BONSALL, Margaret BONSALL and Margaret wife of brother Jonathan BONSALL.
Exr. Brother Joseph BONSALL.
Wits: John ASH, A. C. BONSALL and Hezekiah HIBBERD. #16.

YARNALL, JOSHUA, Philadelphia.
Jan 5, 1784 - Oct 22, 1790.
Mentions brothers Ephraim and John and sister Edith SHARPLESS, brother Samuel and Ellis, also Middletown Meeting, brothers Eli YARNALL, Benjamin YARNALL and Aunt Lydia MENDENHALL.
Exrs: Brothers Eli and Ellis YARNALL.
Wits: Thomas EVANS, Jane EVANS and Hannah YARNALL. #17.

SHARPLESS, SAMUEL, yeoman, Middletown Twp, Chester County.
Jan 24, 1785 - Dec 21, 1790.
Wife Jane, son Joel, and in Middletown Township bought of Thomas GRIZEL, sons Thomas and John also four married daughters, Mary, wife of Cornelius WOOD, Hannah wife of William EDDINS, Susannah wife of Jacob TALBERT, Phebe wife of Peter SMEDLEY and Lydia, Abigail and Rachel single.
Exrs: Sons John and Thomas.
Wits: Daniel SHARPLESS, John PENNELL and William SHARPLESS. #18.

GRUBB, ADAM, Borough of Chester.
March 9, 1790 - Jan 10, 1791.
Wife Mary, niece Rachel SAUNDERS (daughter of sister Hannah), niece Mary MAUL, daughter of sister Mary, dec'd., nephew John GRUBB, son of brother Samuel, dec'd., nephew William GRUBB of Virginia and his son Adam GRUBB, cousin Susannah GRUBB daughter of Aaron GRUBB, George and Richard GRUBB, sons of brother Richard, cousin Susannah PEDRICK daughter of John PEDRICK, nieces Rachel GOODING, Lydia GIBSON and Mary GAMBLE, nephew Richard FLOWER, his son Henry Hale FLOWER, also cousins John GRUBB, Sr., Isaac GRUBB and cousin John GRUBB, Jr.
Exrs: Cousins John GRUBB, Sr., and Isaac GRUBB, Jr.
Wits: Isaac EYRE, W. M. GRAHAM and Zedekiah Wyatt GRAHAM. #19.

HUNT, JOHN, yeoman, Darby, Chester County.
March 21, 1783 - Feb 8, 1791.
Provides for wife ____ - mentions cousins Rebecca HOWELL, Mary KENDLE, Ruth HOWELL, Rebecca McCLEES and Elizabeth MACKEMSON, daughters Sarah BUNTING wife of Josiah BUNTING of Kingsessing land adjoining Adam GUIRE'S land, Rebecca HUMPHREYS, wife of Daniel HUMPHREYS, land purchased of

George MORTON at Calcoon Hook, also at Darby occupied by Hugh LLOYD, Hannah BUNTING wife of Samuel BUNTING land in Kingsessing purchased of John HOOD adjoining Matthew JONES'S and late belonging to Benjamin BONSALL. Elisabeth BARTRAM land purchased of John HOOD, Thomas HOLLOWAY and Jehu JONES in tenure of Matthew JONES. Son John receives large part of estate.
Codicil Feb 29, 1788 - mentions nephews Samuel MARSHALL and James GLEAVE and niece Rebeckah McCLEES, Elizabeth MACHEMSON, land purchased of Joseph BONSALL.
Wits: Rebecca JESS (X) and Zachariah JESS.
Exrs: Sd. wife, sons in law Josiah BUNTING, Samuel BUNTING and Benjamin BARTROM and son John HUNT.
Wits: Aaron OAKFORD and James IDDINGS. #20.

TURNER, JAMES, Upper Providence, Chester County.
Jan 26, 1787 - March 4, 1791.
George MILLER, the son of cousin George MILLER, house and lot in Providence called Blue Hill, provision being made for the society of Protestants called Quakers. Residue of estate to Jacob MINSHALL in trust for a school subject to Chester monthly meeting.
Exr: Jacob MINSHALL.
Wits: Israel TAYLOR and Sarah MILLER. #21.

SMEDLEY, SAMUEL.
Jan 12, 1791 - March 4, 1791.
Leaves to brother William one third of his lands, residue to other brothers and sisters, namely Peter, George, Joseph and Mary.
Exr: Brother William SMEDLEY.
Wits: James EMLEN and Sarah SMEDLEY. #22.

PRICE, ELISABETH, widow of John PRICE, Springfield, late of Chichester.
May 2, 1791 - Not Probated.
Daughter Elisabeth BUSH wife of David BUSH, bond of J. KNOWLES of Ridley Twp, son John PRICE to be provided with clothes at expense of estate.
Exrs: Elisabeth BUSH.
Wits: John CROZIER and Mary CROZIER. #23.

DAVIS, JOSEPH, Birmingham Twp.
Jan 5, 1791 - June 14, 1791.

Son William to have money after the decease of Elizabeth CHADS, daughter Perthenia MARSH, daughter Sarah and husband Nathan HAYES, daughter Elizabeth BALDWIN and Amey DAVIS daughter of Elizabeth. Sons Joseph and Benjamin plantation bounded by land of Joseph PYLE, Edward SIMONSON, Micaijah SPEAKMAN and Elizabeth CHADDS and on west by Brandiwine Creek, also a lot bounded by the great road near CHADE'S Ford, westward by land of Elizabeth CHADS, eastward by Micaijah SPEEKMAN to be equally divided between them both in quantity and value. All obligatory writings against my three sons to be null and void.
Bequeaths to Amey DAVIS (for some years his housekeeper) various pieces of furniture such as six pillow cases, six pewter porringers, a big and little spinning wheel, a real, a warming pan and frying pan, considerable stock and provision.
Wits: Margaret DAVIS and William WEST.
Exrs: Benjamin DAVIS, Joseph DAVIS and Nathan HAYES.
Wits: Amos CHANDLER, William HARVEY, Jr. and William WEST. #24.

CHEYNEY, RICHARD, Thornbury Twp.
June 14, 1791 - June 25, 1791.
Wife's name not given. To children: Jane CHEYNEY, John CHEYNEY, William, Elizabeth and Mary CHEYNEY, to son Charles one hundred pounds of gold to remain until he is twenty one in charge of Bank of North America. Executors to sell land and give two thirds to sons John and William and one third to three daughters Jane, Elizabeth and Mary. Action to be brought against Jacob BROOM, Esq. for remainder of purchase money of the mill property in tenure of Joseph TATNALL - mentions partnership in land in Huntingdon with John WANNISON.
Exrs: Sons John and William.
Wits: John CHEYNEY, Abraham WILLIAMSON and Jno. MARSHALL. #25.

KERNS, ANN, Ridley Twp.
June 20, 1791 - ____
Moneys arising from sale to be placed at interest until youngest daughters Ann and Martha arrive at the age of 21 years being twins - mentions also daughter Elizabeth and her son Hugh, also sons Benjamin, John and George, daughters Margaret and Mary.
April 13, 1791 John KERNS renounced executorship.

April 13, 1791 adjudged a good nuncupative will on testimony of
Thomas McCULLOUGH, Hannah McCULLOUGH, William McCARTY,
Benjamin KERNS and George KERNS.
Exrs: Son John KERNS and friend and kinsman Mr. William
McCARTY.
Later William McCARTY made sole executor. #26.

WORRALL, JOSEPH, Upper Providence Twp.
April 2, 1791 - July 26, 1791.
Bequeaths to wife Margaret WORRALL the lower room of my dwelling house next to the road and such other privileges as she may need in the oven and spring house, son Elisha £100 which he now owes; Isaiah the plantation in the Township of Marple bought of Walter JESS; also plantation in Providence bought of James and Mary LEE; also an acre bought of John PARK. Son Owen WORRALL the plantation bought of John WORRALL; also land of Charles McMICHAEL and Evan PENNEL.
Exrs: Owen.
Wits: Joseph RHOADS and George G. ASHBRIDGE. #27.

NUZUM, THOMAS, Nether Providence Twp., Chester County.
Witnessed April 7, 1789 - July 28, 1791.
Son Richard NUZUM the plantation on which he lives, except the stone house, smith shop &c, willed to grandson Thomas NUZUM; also gives Thomas fifty acres bought of Andreas JOHNSTON, James KERR (weaver) to have the weaver's shop as long as he pleases, he to have free egress &c. to and from the same without any hindrance or molestation.
Exr: Grandson Thomas NUZUM.
Wits: Isaac TAYLOR, William WALTON and Jacob DINGEE. #28.

MATHER, JOHN, Radnor Twp.
March 3, 1791 - Aug 9, 1791.
Wife not mentioned, bequeaths to son John £100, granddaughter Mary MATHER, who lives with him, furniture, other children of son John viz. Deborah, John, Joseph, Sarah, Elizabeth and Jane MATHER the sum of £5 a piece, as they arrive at twenty one years. To my daughter Mary TAYLOR'S children viz. John TAYLOR, Thomas and Robert TAYLOR £20 each. To son Robert MATHER all the rest of estate, he to be sole executor.
Exr: Robert MATHER.

Wits: Isaac DAVIS, Jesse BROOKE and Susannah MATSON. #29.

CHADDS, ELIZABETH, widow, Birmingham Twp., Chester County.
March 7, 1790 - Aug 27, 1791.
Bequeaths to sister Mary BALDWIN'S three daughters, viz. Catharine BENTLY, Sophia ROGAN and Martha JOHNSON, John and Robert BALDWIN sons of Robert BALDWIN dec'd., and his daughter Mary BENTLY, William and James JOHNSON sons of Henry JOHNSON; sister Martha STEWARD and her children; Job HARVEY son of Kaziah HARVEY; Phebe BROOMER, Susanna HOUSE and Martha HOUSE daughters of cousin Amos HOUSE by his wife Sarah; also Mary, Jehu and Benjamin by his wife Martha. Mentions Mary wife of David REYNOLDS and her two daughters Elizabeth and Lydia, cousin John PARKER son of Abraham PARKER and Kaziah WICKERSHAM daughter of same; Betty PARKER daughter of John, George and Ann STEWART children of John STEWART, dec'd., Keziah SMITH daughter of David and Phebe SMITH.
Exrs: John PARKER and Amos HARVEY.
Wits: John TOWNSEND and William TOWNSEND. #30.

WORRALL, HANNAH, Upper Providence Twp.
Oct 4, 1791 - Oct 31, 1791.
Leaves heirlooms and furniture to granddaughters Sarah NUZUM, Phebe NUZUM and Martha WORRALL, to grandsons Benjamin KIRK and John KIRK. Sons Jonathan, Thomas and Benjamin each to get one shilling; the rest of estate to daughters Hannah NUZUM and Ester KIRK and son Joshua KIRK.
Exr: Grandson John NUZUM.
Wits: Lewis TRIMBLE and Richard NUZUM. #32.

RUSSELL, JAMES, Birmingham Twp.
Nov 16, 1791 - Dec 23, 1791.
Wife Isabella, three sons: Samuel, James and Ephram get the homestead adjoining land of Joseph PIRA, Ralph PYLE, Marcey SHIELDS, Daniel GREEN and others, to be divided so that Samuel gets one half. Daughter Martha the wife of William SIMONSON and grandchildren James RUSSELL, Samuel MACEY and Jane RUSSELL children of son John RUSSELL, dec'd.
Exrs: Sons Samuel and James.
Wits: Amos CHANDLER, John MIDDLTON and William MAXWELL. #33.

BURN, WILLIAM, Marple Twp.
May 19, 1791 - Dec 3, 1791.
Wife Jane to have all personal estate during life and then to be disposed of as she shall order it, also most of the plantation except 10 acres in possession of son Joseph, to son Isaac during life, land purchased of Richard FAWKS and after his death to his children if any, if not, to Rachel DUNWOODY (a daughter) - mentions lines of David LEWIS and Elizabeth MORRIS - mentions son William BURN, dec'd., and his daughters Ann and Jane BURN and son William. Samuel McCLENAN to get £6 on death of wife.
Exrs: Son Isaac and daughter Rachel DUNWOODY.
Wits: Lewis LEWIS, Mary LEWIS and Hannah LEWIS. #34.

GARRETSON, JOSEPH, Upper Providence.
Dec 12, 1791 - Feb 25, 1792.
Wife Hannah, one third of estate, the residue to support and educate my children.
Exrs: Wife and brother in law Thomas CALVERT.
Wits: Israel TAYLOR, Joseph BISHOP and George MILLER, Jr. #35.

COWEN, WILLIAM, Ridley Twp., Chester County.
May 4, 1786 - March 5, 1792.
To son Ephraim, the dwelling house together with the land from the great road down to the long stump in the road leading to Darby Creek ferry &c. - mentions land of John HOOF. Reserves the weaving shop and loom for son Jonas while he behaveth, son Ephraim to make up £15 to be paid to daughter Ann COWEN when she arrives at eighteen years, she being allowed to live with him without hinderance, son William to get tenement occupied by William SMITH and ground to the above mentioned stump. Daughter Mary COWEN to get 40 shillings annually and be found in clothing.
Exrs: Son Ephraim.
Wits: James CROZER, William SMITH and Michael TRITES. #36.

FELL, WILLIAM, Springfield Twp.
June 17, 1790 - March 20, 1792.
To my relation Edward FELL all my real estate together with my right in 84 acres in lower Providence held in joint tennancy with John HENCOCK, Jr. Interest of £350 to be paid by him to my sister Ann during her life, also the interest of £50 to his sister Hannah FELL, also one hundred pounds to Henry and Mary HOLLAND, children of Henry

HOLLAND, under care of Warrington Meeting and in case of their death, to surviving children of Henry HOLLAND. Thomas HOLLAND, son of Thomas HOLLAND, dec'd., to have £75 when he arrives at 21 years, also to William son of William MARSHALL £75 - mentions Joseph RHOADS and Hugh LOWNES as trustees for £50 toward the promoting of a school near Springfield Meeting House. Relation Deborah, wife of William McMULLIN and Deborah wife of David HALL and her sister Sarah wife of Benjamin TAYLOR. To Joseph GREEN (wife's name Lydia), also Hannah and Sushanah ROBINSON (relations) of Cocker mouth in the county of Cumberland in Great Britton, also Ithamar HOLLAND grandson of Henry HOLLAND, dec'd., and other grandchildren of same, descended from his daughter Deborah McMULLN. Relations David HALL and Edward FELL to be executors, receiving for services a lot in the Borrow of Wilmington. Codicil Feb 28, 1792.
Wits: William WEST and Joseph RHOADS.
Exrs: David HALL and Edward FELL.
Wits: Joseph RHOADS, Roger DICKS and John POWELL, Jr. #37.

McMINN, JOHN, yeoman, Aston Twp.
Dec 17,1791 - March 29, 1792.
Leaves wife Isabella, all personal estate, interest on real estate, use of new house and lot. Sons James, John and Thomas and daughters Mary, Martha and Ann to have sums for service. Grandchildren Isabella BLACK and James McMINN son of James McMINN.
Exrs: Wife and son in law Aaron MATSON.
Wits: Samuel BLACK and Joseph THATCHER. #38.

WORRALL, PHEBE, Marple Twp.
Feb 9, 1792 - March 31, 1792.
Leaves to son John WORRALL all residue of estate after debts are all paid and appoints him sole executor.
Exrs: Son John WORRALL.
Wits: Joseph BOND, Jr. and Jonathan MORRIS. #39.

HARRISON, CALEB, Sr., Delaware County.
Nov 17, 1790 - April 21, 1792.
To wife Eleanor, daughter Mary, son Joshua and daughter Hannah wife of John MERIDITH. Grandchildren: Mary EVANS daughter of David EVANS and Vincent, Caleb, Isaac, Elenor, Mary and Phillip BONSALL. Son Caleb the plantation part in township of Middletown

and part in Chester, also one acre known as the grave yard bounded by lands of James BARTON. Property in Union Township, Berks County to be sold to John BARDE.
Exrs: Sons John and Caleb HARRISON.
Wits: Thomas TUCKER, Frederick FAIRLAMB and John FAIRLAMB. #40.

LINDSAY, JAMES, Aston Twp.
May 2, 1791 - May 2, 1792.
Wife Elizabeth, daughters Margaret PORTER and Elizabeth MEHAFFY, grandsons James McCLELEN, James LINDSAY, Jr. and James MEHAFFY. Son James if it conveniently can be done, to be settled on the place and pay the others their legacies, he to be sole executor.
Exr: Son James.
Wits: James ANDERSON and Levi MATSON. #41.

PANCOST, SETH, Springfield Twp., Chester County.
March 6, 1783 - May 15, 1792.
Wife the plantation in Springfield that she may educate his three daughters, Hannah, Elisa and Ester, after death of mother, the same to be held in common by them. Leaves to his two sons Samuel and Seth PANCOST, the plantation in Marple to be divided as to quantity and quality equally between them. Married daughters Sarah LEWIS, wife of Thomas LEWIS and Phebe LEWIS, wife of Isaac LEWIS.
Codicil March 6, 1792 mentions John POWELL, Jr. and Joseph RHOADS.
Exrs: Wife Ann PANCOAST and friend Joseph RHOADS of the township Marple.
Wits: Nathaniel HOLLAND, Jesse MARIS and Edward FELL. #42.

CEAZAR, labourer, Middletown.
May 7, 1791 - June 2, 1792.
Bequeaths to his daughters Jin and Milleigh each five shillings, friend James HARPER, melatto, five pounds &c., friend Isaac BROOMEL 5£. All overplus to be equally divided between the said Isaac BROOMALL and James HARPER.
[Note: Ceasar probably a freed slave with no other name.]
Exr: Thomas WOOD, of Newlin.
Wits: Amos SHARPLESS and Samuel SHARPLESS. #43.

BRINTON, GEORGE, Birmingham.
May 11, 1792 - June 4, 1792.
Wife Esther, four sons: Amos, Edward, William and Joseph, daughter Jane wife of John THATCHER.
Exrs: Gideon GILPIN and William GIBBONS.
Wits: James DILWORTH and Edward DARLINGTON. #44.

DEHAVEN, HANNAH, Radnor Twp.
March 3, 1792 - June 14, 1792.
Gives to daughter Edith, interest in legacy due from her father's estate and all other estate, real and personal.
Exr: Uncle Peter DEHAVEN.
Wits: Margret HOLMAN, Isaac MATSON and Rachel MATSON. #45.

THOMPSON, JOHN, Springfield Twp.
Aug 11, 1792 - Aug 11, 1792.
Plantation purchased of Ezekiah LEONARD, Esq., sheriff, to be sold. All other real and personal estate to wife Ann during widowhood. All goods and money previously given to son Isaac to be deemed a part of his share.
Exrs: Wife Ann THOMPSON and sons Jonah and Joshua.
Wits: William PENNOCK and Mary GRAHAM. #46.

NOBLIT, WILLIAM, Aston Twp.
Aug 3, 1792 - Oct 9, 1792.
Leaves to his father Joseph NOBLIT all wearing apparel and to his mother Mary NOBLIT all rest of estate for her support and relief, anything remaining at their death, to brothers and sisters (names not given).
Exr: Joseph PENNELL.
Wits: Eli FEW and Nathan PYLE. #47.

PRESTON, MARY.
May 1, 1791 - Oct 18, 1792.
Leaves to daughters Abigail GRAHAM and Hannah PUSEY, grandchildren, Ann PENNELL, Mary GRAHAM, Joseph PENNELL, Mary Ann, Jemima, Daniel and John CORBITT, Pennell, Edward and Thomas CORBITT - mentions her own four children: Abigail GRAHAM, Hannah PUSEY, Thomas LEA and Jonas PRESTON. Bequest to friends free school in Nottingham.
Exrs: Son Jonas and grandson William GRAHAM.

Wits: William GRAHAM, Elizabeth LINDSAY and Dorothea GRAHAM. #48.

PENNELL, SUSANN, wife of Robert PENNELL, Middletown Twp.
April 2, 1791 - Oct 22, 1792.
Being entitled to certain monies and estate by will of daughter Susanna FAIRLAMB, leaves the same as follows: to son Frederick FAIRLAMB; daughter Catherine wife of Peter HILL; and to children of her son Samuel FAIRLAMB namely: John, Samuel and Maria and Francis FAIRLAMB; Susanna PEDRICK daughter of John PEDRICK and to her daughter Ann; daughter Eleanor; son John; daughter Mary wife of Joseph CLOUD and son Nicholas.
Exr and guardian: son Frederick FAIRLAMB.
Wits: Caleb HARRISON and Mary HARRISON. #49.

MOORE, THOMAS, mariner, Lower Chichester, Chester County.
Sept 11, 1789 - ____.
Leaves wife Hannah MOORE entire charge of estate including lot of land at Marcus HOOK until son John arrives at age of 21 years, after that, on half proceeds from sale of same, gives son Thomas £10.
Estate settled and accounts filed.
Exrs: Wife Hannah and John CROZER. #50.

SWAYNE, THOMAS, yeoman, Darby, Chester County.
Aug 2, 1775 - April 24, 1793.
Daughter Phebe HORNE wife of William HORNE the sum of 5£, only son George SWAYNE all residue of estate, he to be executor.
Exrs: Son George SWAYNE.
Wits: Josiah BUNTING, Abraham BONSALL and John HUMPHREYS. #51.

GROVER, ELIZABETH, widow, Radnor Twp.
____, 1790 - July 15, 1793.
After distributing heirlooms &c. orders the plantation in Radnor to be sold and equally divided between all her children, namely: John, Hugh, George and Robert, Mary DERRICK and Elizabeth and Margaret GROVER, they to divide their shares equally among their own children, granddaughter Elizabeth GROVER, daughter of son John; and Christopher GROVER son of Hugh; granddaughters Elizabeth DERRAH and Elizabeth GROVER daughter of George.
Exrs: Sons John and Robert.

Wits: Hugh JONES, Nathan EVANS and John JARMAN. #52.

BISHOP, GEORGE, yeoman, Edgemont.
June 11, 1793 - Sept 28, 1793.
Wife Mary, certain rights and privileges and £10 per year as long as she remains his widow, son Joseph to be paid sixty pounds by his other sons George and Thomas BISHOP who are to have the plantation at Edgemont and also land purchased of William RUSSELL, another tract of James HOWARD and one of John WILLIAMSON. Daughter Phebe, wife of Oliver PHARO £60 and daughter Margaret BISHOP £100. Daughters Mary and Sarah BISHOP and granddaughter Jane PHARO also mentioned. Grandson Samuel Bishop GRUBB son of deceased daughter Jane.
Exrs: Sons Joseph, George and Thomas.
Wits: James HOWARD, Abraham FARR and Josiah LEWIS. #53.

FERGUSON, ROBERT, Delaware County.
Dec 16, 1790 - Nov 16, 1793.
Wife Elizabeth, all estate in Cumberland County and elsewhere, she to be executrix.
Exrs: Wife Elizabeth.
Wits: William GRAHAM, John Jonas PRESTON. #54.

LOWNES, GEORGE, blacksmith, Springfield Twp.
Jan 8, 1791 - Nov 19, 1793.
Property to be divided into eight equal shares, one of which for the children of his deceased son Slater, namely Clarisa, Mary, Jane and George LOWNES; the other seven share to children Jane, Burns, Sarah HIBBS, Elizabeth LEWIS, Mary and Rebeckah LOWNES, Curtis LOWNES and George Bolston LOWNES.
Exrs: Sons Curtis and George Bolston LOWNES and friend John HIBBERD.
Wits: John LOWNES, David RICHARD and James CALDWELL. #55.

ELLIS, HUMPHREY, fuller, Haverford Twp.
Sept 25, 1793 - Nov 21, 1793.
Wife Mary to have all goods belonging to her before we were married also interest of estate toward bringing up and educating my children until they come of age, daughter Elizabeth eighteen years and son Isaac, twenty one. Son to be put to some useful trade. When of age 1/3 of estate to daughter and 2/3 to son, they to pay wife £10 yearly.

Should children die, wife to have one half and the other half to children of his brothers Isaac, William and Amos and sister Elizabeth.
Exrs: Sd. wife and brother Amos.
Wits: John DANIEL and Jacob HUMPHREYS. #56.

SWAFFER, WILLIAM, surveyor, Borough of Chester now called Delaware.
May 8, 1792 - Dec 11, 1793.
Wife Abigail, law books and instruments to nephew Roger DICKS, other nephews and nieces: Catherine DAVIS, Jane wife of John PEIRCE, Daniel HUMPHREYS, Rachel ELLIS, Hannah ELLIS wife of Abraham DAVIS and children of his sister Ann ELLIS, dec'd., Phebe daughter of sister Hannah HUMPHREYS now wife of Michael MINEAR and Eleanor widow of Nehemiah DAVIS - mentions being executor of Peter DICK'S estate - mentions the Jacob GILES affair and gives one third his share of commissions to his wife Abigail SWAFFER and to his wife's children, namely: John WORRALL, Sarah wife of Levis MATSON, Rachel wife of Nehemiah MATSON, Abigail wife of Joseph THATCHER and Mary wife of Samuel Richards, Jr. Gives wife property in Chester purchased by John OWEN, for life, then to William DAVIS, son of nephew Nehemiah DAVIS, dec'd., land purchased of William CROSBY in Ridley - mentions six daughters of Nehemiah DAVIS namely: Mary, Sarah, Elizabeth, Eleanor, Dorothy and Susanna, also Benjamin BURK and Rachel CHERRY seemingly as servants receiving legacies, land purchased of Daniel JAMES to go to his wife Abigail.
Exrs: Wife and Roger DICKS.
Wits: Thomas SHARPLESS and Daniel SHARPLESS. #57.

JONES, EDWARD, Esq, Radnor Twp.
April 28, 1792 - Dec 23, 1793.
One half profits on estate to wife Abigail until her death. Abigail MILES daughter of Richard MILES of Tredifferin to have property in Radnor and Tredifferin townships and now in possession of Richard MILES, also to Sarah sister of Abigail 20£, a tract formerly owned by Timothy DAVIS to Edwin PUGH son of John PUGH of Radnor. Five pounds to Mary HOULSTON, daughter of Peter HOULSTEIN - mentions Edward SITERS, son of Adam SITERS of Philadelphia as great grandson of his father Edward JONES and leaves to him his plantation of 130 acres in Radnor, he to pay certain bequests to niece Mary WALTS, Evan WALTS son of Mary and to Dinah daughter of

same. Legacies to Dr. John DAVIS and Ann wife of Aaron ASHBRIDGE of Philadelphia and Hannah SITERS. Legacies to Evan, Samuel and John, children of Richard MILES and Joseph, Amelia, Elijah, John and Mary, children of John PUGH.
Exrs: Dr. John DAVIS and Richard MILES. All legacies to paid in spanish silver milled dollars at seven shillings and six pence each and weighing seventeen pennyweights and six grains each or other gold or silver of like value.
Wits: H. DeHAVEN, John GEORGE, Sarah DeHAVEN and John DAVIS. #58.

REID, CLOTOWORTY, Haverford Twp.
April 22, 1793 - March 11, 1794.
Clothing marked E. R, F. R. and H. R. to daughters Elizabeth, Frances and Hannah. Son Paul a suit of wearing apparel, silver knee buckles and gun; any accounts in favor of estate to be divided equally.
Exrs: Jacob LITZENBERG, Martin WISE and Henry CLINE.
Wits: John LINDSEY and Richard TIPPINGS. #59.

COBORN, THOMAS, yeoman, Chester Twp.
April 19, 1790 - April 2, 1794.
Wife Rachel to have one third of all personal estate forever and one third of real estate for life, the residue to son Thomas, his share to wife in case he dies without lawful issue, should she die first then estate goes to nephew Israel COBURN his heirs and assigns. Son Thomas to be clothed and educated out of legacy to him until twenty one.
Exr: Wife Rachel.
Wits: William GRAHAM, Catherine GRAHAM and Jno. PRICE. #60.

CROSBY, ELEANOR, widow, Ridley.
March 3, 1792 - Aug 15, 1793.
Legacies to Elizabeth, daughter of son Richard CROSBY, dec'd., and to Eleanor daughter of son John CROSBY. Residue to daughter Susanna, wife of Caleb PHIPPS.
Proved before Christopher QUIGLEY and certified Oct 1, 1794 by William LYON. Prothonotary - probated in Delaware County April 14, 1794.
Exrs: Grandson Elisha PHIPPS.

Wits: William PRICE, at probate, he was of Delaware County, and Sarah PRICE, at probate, she testifies before Justice of the Peace, Cumberland County, Pennsylvania, as Sarah BRYAN.
Admin. Account names legacy to Elizabeth LONG. #61.

SMEDLEY, ANN, widow, Edgemont Twp.
April 10, 1794 - April 23, 1794.
Orders plantation in Willistown, Chester County called the Rising Sun Tavern to be divided into two parts, the southerly part to Ann SKOT, wife of John SKOT except ten acres purchased of William GIBBONS to kinsman Fransis SMEDLEY son of George and Hannah SMEDLEY. Cousin Mary SMEDLEY wife of Jesse SMEDLEY to have part north of division line she to pay £100 gold or silver to executors - mentions Isaac MASSEY, Benjamin HIBBERD, George SMEDLEY, dec'd., Charles WILLING, Caleb HIBBERD, William GARRETT and Amos GARRETT as holding adjacent land. Bequests to Friends Meeting, Priscilla GREEN wife of George GREEN, Sarah SMEDLEY daughters of George SMEDLEY, Elizabeth and Esther LEWIS daughter of Isaiah LEWIS, Samuel Mucl. DUFF son of Ann SKOT, Martha BARRINGTON wife of Charles BARRINGTON, William HART (apprentice), brother in law Thomas and his sons Daniel, Joseph and Thomas SMEDLEY, cousin Sarah STARR daughter of John MINSHALL. Heirlooms to her brothers George HUNTER and Jonathan HUNTER and cousins children Mary, daughter of Hannah SCHOPHEL and Ann daughter of Ann SCOT. Residue of estate to cousins Richard HUNTER, George HUNTER, Elizabeth wife of Nathaniel ERWIN, George MATLACK, Jesse MATLACK, Jonathan MATLACK, Hanna wife of Nathaniel SCHOFEL and Ann wife of Richard FOX children of brother Peter HUNTER, dec'd., and sister Mary MATLACK dec'd., and cousin Samuel Muccl. DUFF and Martha wife of Charles BARRINGTON.
Exrs: Josiah LEWIS of Edgemont and Jesse SMEDLEY of Willistown.
Wits: William YARNALL, Abel GREEN and Jane YARNALL. #62.

WILSON, JOHN, practitioner of physick, Astown Twp., Chester County.
May 1, 1781 - April 28, 1794.
To sister Mary 20 s. and to step brother Thomas WILSON 5 s. Residue to wife Mary WILSON she to be sole executrix.
Exrs: Wife Mary WILSON.
Wits: Robert HALL, Abraham MARTIN and Daniel SHARPLESS. #63.

ALLEN, THOMAS, yeoman, lately of the Kingdom of Great Britain but now of the township of Springfield in Delaware County in the Commonwealth of Pennsylvania and the United States of America.
March 10, 1794 - April 30, 1794.
Estate to wife Sarah with power to sell, if she wishes to return to England, equal division of estate to children at her death.
Exrs: Sd. wife.
Wits: Passmore WEST, Thomas NEW and Jesse BICKERTON. #64.

SMITH, SAMUEL, Darby.
July 2, 1792 - June 17, 1794.
Wife Elizabeth all estate during life, to be equally divided among children at her death.
Exrs: Sd. wife and friend John PEARSON.
Wits: Cadr. MORRIS and William HANSELL. #65.

MOORE, THOMAS, mariner, Lower Chichester, Chester County.
Sept 11, 1789 - ____.
Personal estate to wife Hannah MOORE, also all profits of certain land in Marcus Hook purchased from Joseph MOULDER until son John is twenty one, then property to be sold and each receive half, son Thomas MOORE legacy of 10£.
Will recorded but no witnesses mentioned and no probate (same as Will 50).
Exrs: Wife Hannah and friend John CROZIER. #66.

CROSBY, ELEANOR (duplicate of will 61).
 #67.

EVANS, JOHN, Radnor.
July 25, 1784 - Oct 20, 1794.
Sawmill properties purchased of George FETTERMAN and Samuel HARRY containing 47 acres, adjoining lands of John JONES, to son David EVANS, on payment of legacies to following: daughters Ruth, wife of Abraham FREE, Amey and Margaret and son Acquilla.
Exrs: Sd. son David.
Wits: Thomas TEMPLE, Jr., James DILWORTH and Charles DILWORTH. #68.

McILVAIN, HUGH, Ridley Twp.
June 24, 1793 - Nov 25, 1794.

Leaves to negro woman Lemon sixty pounds cash and my dwelling
house __ during her natural life, she to be a free woman.
Registers' Court held and will proved on testimony of Richard
BARNARD, James McILVAIN and John CROSBY.
Wits: Richard BARNARD. #68B.

LEVIS, SAMUEL, Springfield.
Aug 22, 1793 - Nov 25, 1794.
Provides for wife Mary as follows: sons Samuel, William and Joseph to
pay certain sums from profits of plantation in Upper Darby purchased
of James SPRAY. To son Samuel, tract on southwest side of Darby
Creek adjoining Nathan DAVIS'S land and Isaac LOBB'S land
containing 118 acres of mill property also meadow land on Calcon Hook
purchased of Peter and George MATSON. Son William 80 acres on
north side of Darby Creek purchased of father Samuel LEVIS, land on
Tinicum Island purchased of John MORTON, and on west side of
Darby Creek. Son Joseph the upper and western division of the
plantation. Daughter Elizabeth, plantation where Joseph now dwells
bought of Jesse MARIS and conveyed to me by John HALL. To
grandson Samuel GARRETT land purchased of James SPRAY -
mentions children: Isaac, Hannah, Mary, Joshua, John, Elizabeth and
Martha, the wife of James HUNTER, son William to have residue of
estate.
Exrs: Sons Samuel and William LEVIS.
Wits: William WEST and William PENNOCK. #69.

WILLIAMSON, JOHN, yeoman, Newtown.
Aug 13, 1794 - Dec 2, 1794.
To wife Elizabeth and her heirs certain part of land devised to him by
his father John WILLIAMSON, dec'd., and also of the 85 acres
purchased from heirs of Henry CALDWELL adjoining property of John
and Edward HUNTER and George DUNN, also right to certain
moneys &c. during widowhood - mentions conditions controlled by
brother Daniel's decease; his son Enos's duty in caring for his mother;
his son Adam to have 40 acres in Brandywine Hundred purchased of
William GRUBB stating provision made for him by his grandfather
Adam BUCKLEY, dec'd., - mentions mother Sarah WILLIAMSON, son
John remaining portion of tracts mentioned above, except saw mill
property and homestead on Crum Creek which he gives to Enos. Son
Walter £70 and release on notes for money borrowed. Daughters Sarah

PRATT, Ann WILLIAMSON, Elizabeth GARRETT, Ester GARRETT and Jane WILLIAMSON, small legacies, they having been provided for.
Exrs: Sd. wife and son Enos.
Wits: John BALDWIN, Edward HUNTER and John HUNTER. #70.

HEACOCK, JOHN, Middletown.
Nov 16, 1791 - Dec 3, 1794.
Plantation in Middletown to be sold and money equally divided among his five children: Hannah, Ann, Jonathan, Nathan and John.
Exr: Son in law Jacob MINSHALL.
Wits: Thomas PEIRCY, Caleb YARNALL and James EMLEN. #71.

REECE, DAVID, Newtown Twp.
Aug 30, 1787 - Dec 4, 1794.
Provides for wife Sarah she to have control of Esther BEERY an indentured servant. Certain furniture to be sold proceeds to three daughters Sarah GRUBB, Elizabeth DOWNING and Hannah CALEY, son Jesse to have plantation, he to provide for mother, son William REECE, grandson Lewis REECE, his watch.
Exrs: Sons in law, Nathaniel GRUBB of Willistown and Richard DOWNING of East Caln.
Wits: Isaac MASSEY and Caleb HIBBERD. #72.

BYERS, ELIZABETH, yeoman, Concord Twp.
June 30, 1791 - Dec 6, 1794.
Legacies to sons in law John BOWERS and Uriah FORTNER and Sarah MATSON wife of John MATSON. Residue to friend Levi MATSON for settling estate.
Wits: Joseph THATCHER and Morris RATTAW. #73.

WILDAY, OBADIAH, yeoman, Haverford.
Dec 12, 1794 - Jan 2, 1795.
Provides for wife Hannah WILDAY, son Jonathan and daughters Mary and Elizabeth WILDAY, younger son Obadiah to be raised by Jonathan under supervision of George HAYWORTH.
Exrs: Son Jonathan WILDAY.
Wits: Isaac DAVIS, William LLEWELYN and Mordecai LEWIS. #74.

SUTTON, BARTHOLOMEW, Chester County.
March 11, 1786 - Jan 2, 1795.

Estate to wife Deborah after paying legacies to the following: her son
William DOYLE, her daughter Mary Ann WADE, grandchildren
Elizabeth and Deborah WADE, to the poor, to Reverends Messieurs
Ferdinand FARMER and Robert MOLYNEAUX, Thomas ALLEN,
shoemaker, Tombstone to be placed over the body of Barnaby DOYLE
and another over his own. Wearing apparel to Thomas SLATERY of
Chester County.
Exrs: Sd. wife and brother in law Mark WILLCOX.
Wits: Robert PENNELL and Ezekiel LEONARD. #74B.

LEWIS, DAVID, yeoman, Radnor. Chester County
May 20, 1788 - Jan 6, 1795.
Grandson David LEWIS, minor, to have westernmost tract in Newtown
and pay his brother Allixander and his sisters Siscela and Mary £150
for the three. Son Henry 60 acres bought of John MORRIS, about 20
acres adjoining land of Richard FAWKES and John JONES and 54
acres in Newton he paying daughters Mary and Hannah each 20£, wife
Jane and daughters while single to have use of homestead, son Lewis
the rest of the plantation, he to have all right and title to land in
Cumberland County - mentions daughter Rachel as widow of Isaac
DAVIS.
Exrs: Sons Henry and Lewis LEWIS.
Wits: Owen SKELTON, Lewis LEWIS, Jr. and Nathan EVANS. #75.

THOMAS, BENJAMIN, Upper Providence Twp.
Nov 1, 1784 - Feb 10, 1795.
Estate to wife Susanah THOMAS and at her death to my children.
Exrs: Sd. wife and sons Owen and Thomas.
Wits: Richard NUZUM and James DIZER. #76.

DUTTON, RICHARD, yeoman, Upper Chichester.
Dec 1, 1793 - May 4, 1796.
Son Jonathan, plantation in U. Chichester and Aston purchased of
William HAY, Edward WHITEKER, Joseph BROWN and Kingsman
DUTTON, son Jonathan, land purchased of John WILLIAMSON, Isaac
LAWRENCE and John COUBOURN on River Delaware, adjoining
David JOHNSON and Edward RICHARDS of Lower Chichester. To
sons of son Thomas DUTTON, dec'd., (Richard and Thomas) land
bounded by land of Aaron MATSON, Edward GRISSEL and by
Chester Creek, they paying their sisters Sarah, Hannah, and Susannah
£10 each. Land in Bradford Township to be sold. Mentions legacies to

daughter Rebeckah PILKINGTON, Thomas, Jehu, Jonathan, Joseph, Richard, Josiah and Lucy RICHARDS, children of daughter Hannah, Hannah PLOWMAN and Lydia RICHARDS, five grandchildren, children of son Thomas viz. Richard, Thomas, Sarah, Hibbard, Hannah and Susanna DUTTON, other grandchildren, not named - mentions Jacob DERIBERKER and his son Eli and Chichester Meeting.
Exrs: Son Jonathan and James BARNARD.
Wits: James BARNARD and Jacob DERIBERKER. #77.

MIERS, HENRY, Concord Twp.
May 22, 1795 - May 5, 1796.
Gives son John MIERS the plantation in Concord subject to certain incumbrances, also in New Castle Hundred lies a part of the legacies to be paid to four daughters hereafter named. Personal property and real estate near Reading to be sold. Son Henry, plantation and saw mill in Thornbury subject to payment of 242£. Legacies to daughters Rebeckah HOOPES, Elizabeth PEIRCE, Phebe and Sarah MIERS with home privileges on John's plantation until married.
Exrs: Son John and my friend Thomas MARSHALL of Concord.
Wits: M. SPAKMAN and Thomas MARSHALL. #78.

GARRETT, ANN, widow of William GARRETT, Darby Twp.
March 29, 1793 - May 5, 1796. signed April 4, 1795.
Legacies and heirlooms to sons William, Oborn and John, daughters Elizabeth LEVIS and Ann GARRETT.
Exrs: Son William GARRETT and daughters Elizabeth LEVIS and Ann GARRETT.
Wits: Benjamin BRANNON and John HORNE. #79.

RINEHEART, SIMON, Upper Chichester.
June 28,1795 - May 5, 1796.
Estate to son Samuel (minor), he to be in care of grandfather Joseph NOBLIT till spring then to be apprenticed by guardian Jacob DERIBARKER.
Wits: James HENDERSON and Jacob DERIBERIKER. #80.

RHOADS, ELIZABETH, Marple Twp. Chester County.
July 28, 1788 - June 13, 1795.
House and lot in Philadelphia to son Joseph, plantation in Springfield to son Owen, Legacies to daughters Hannah, Rebeckah and Tacy - mentions grandson John Owen RHOADS and other grandchildren:

George and Joseph RHOADS (Elizabeth RHOADS), James, Elizabeth
and Nathan GARRETT, Joseph LOWNES and Elizabeth DAVIS.
Codicil April 10, 1795 (recorded May 6, 1796) mentions decease of
daughter Hannah, her legacy to her children: James, Elizabeth and
Nathan GARRETT.
Wits: Daniel RIDGWAY and Mary M. FERGUSON.
Exrs: Sons Joseph and Owen.
Wits: Mordicai MARKWARD and George MASSEY. #81.

BONSAL, OBADIAH, Birmingham.
April 6, 1795 - May 6, 1796.
Provides for wife (name not given), one third to sons Samuel and
Obadiah, the other two thirds to the rest of his children, to wit:
Elizabeth GREGG, Sarah HANNUM, Joseph BONSAL, Hannah
BONSAL, Jane TAYLOR, Tacy BONSAL and Rebecah BONSAL.
Exrs: Sons Samuel and Obadiah.
Wits: Jesse OWENS and Thomas GIBSON. #82.

RUDOLPH, MARY, Darby.
Attested: April 23, 1795 - Recorded: May 6, 1796.
Executors to sell all real estate in Darby bounded by lands of Jacob
SERRILL and Darby Creek, also that bounded by lands of John
PEARSON, Benjamin PASCHALL and Nathaniel NEWLIN. Leaves to
four children: Joseph and Jacob RUDOLPH, Ann PASCHALL wife of
Benjamin PASCHALL and Hannah MITCHELL wife of John
MITCHELL equal shares from the proceeds of sales.
Exr: Friend Hugh LLOYD.
Wits: William SMITH, Charles PEARSON and Jno. PEARSON. #83.

MOORE, SAMUEL, farmer, Radnor.
March 25, 1795 - May 7, 1796.
Provides for wife Alice, she to bring up son (unnamed). Later mentions
two sons and two daughters (all unnamed), sons shares as two to one.
Register gives James MOORE as executor; this is incorrect by
reference to will.
Exrs: Brother in law James JONES.
Wits: Joshua THOMAS and Simeon MATLACK. #84.

WORRALL, JOSEPH, Haverford.
Aug 13, 1795 - May 7, 1796.

Property of 45 perches &c.to kinsman Maris WORRALL to reward him for care he hath had of me.
Wits: Jno. SHELLINGTON and William MARKWORTH. #85.

TRIMBLE, WILLIAM, Concord Twp.
Aug 15, 1795 - May 7, 1796.
To son William, premises in West Whiteland that adjoins his saw mill and north of the Lancaster Road, son John had all intended except legacies to be paid by Daniel and by grandson William. Son Samuel £175 and what he has already received. Son Daniel plantation in Thornbury. To daughter Hannah wife of Isaac JACOBS, land in Whiteland west of Lancaster Road. Daughters Rachel and Ann TRIMBLE each £250 and use of homestead until married. Sons Joseph and Samuel right to saw wood at my saw mill during residence. Grandson William son of John, dec'd., plantation in Concord purchased of Thomas WEST and Joseph NICKLIN. Daughter Hannah JACOBS £25. Granddaughter Lydia, daughter of William £10. Residue to five of his children: Joseph, Samuel, Hannah, Rachel and Ann share alike.
Exrs: Son Samuel and son in law Isaac JACOBS.
Wits: Peter HALTON, Abraham SHARPLESS and Thomas MARSHALL. #86.

VERNON, ABIGAIL, Nether Providence.
May 16, 1794 - May 9, 1796.
Leaves all estate to daughter Mary VERNON.
Exr: Grandson Isaac ENGLE appointed Aug 19, 1795.
Wits: Ja. STEPHENSON and Moses VERNON. #87.

CARTER, LYDIA, widow, Chester Twp.
Dec 25, 1794 - May 9, 1796.
To daughter in law Margaret wife of son Joseph CARTER, sons Daniel and Joseph.
Exrs: Sd. sons David and Joseph. Exrs. affirm March 2, 1796.
Wits: William BURNS, Jr., John SLAWTER and Nathaniel SQUIB. #88.

PENNELL, JOSEPH, Philadelphia.
May 1, 1763 - May 10, 1796.
Executors to sell all estate in Chester County, proceeds as per agreement with mother, brother and sisters dated April 25, 1763. Legacies to Pennsylvania Hospital, Abigail GRIFFITTS widow of

William, merchant, of Philadelphia, niece Eleanor GRAHAM, Jr., daughter of sister Abigail (to father for her use), brother John PENNELL Int. Rights and Title to Darby Library, one fourth all other estate to sister Abigail GRAHAM, the other three quarters to brother John and sister Mary PENNELL, minors, executors to pay £15 yearly to mother Mary PRESTON.
Exrs: Uncle Robert PENNELL and brother in law Henry Hall GRAHAM.
Wits: Jno. FAIRLAMB, dec'd., Jeremiah CLOUD (absent) and ___ Price (affirmed). #89.

HOOPES, ABRAHAM, yeoman, Elder of Edgemont.
Dec 12, 1792 - Oct 10, 1795.
Legacies to sons Benjamin and George HOOPES, to son John and his sons: Abraham and Daniel HOOPES, to son Jacob, daughter Abigail wife of William REGESTER and then to her children by present husband, daughter Jane wife of Joseph ROBINS, sons Abraham and Isaac HOOPES grandson Abraham WILLIAMSON, granddaughters Phebe HUNT, Lydia YARNALL and Mary ROBINS.
Exrs: Son in law Joseph ROBINS and grandson Daniel HOOPES.
Wits: Francis WISELEY, John MEGOWIN and Edward CHURCHMAN. #89B.

VERNON, MOSES, yeoman, Nether Providence, Chester County.
Aug 22, 1785-Mar 21, 1796.
Provides for wife Elizabeth for life or widowhood, then to two nephews John ENGLE son of Frederick ENGLE (dec'd.) and Moses VERNON son of brother Gideon VERNON.
Exrs: James HAMM, Jr. (renounced) and wife Elizabeth.
Wits: Joshua ELY and Roger DICKS. #90.

HOLSTON, JOHN, Edgemont.
March 11, 1795 - Apr 14, 1796. Recorded May 11, 1796.
Wife Martha HOLSTON to have home privileges and annuity charged on 3 sons John, Benjamin and Joseph who get the plantation share and share alike, son George HOLSTON (minor) 200£, daughter Ann CALVART wife of Daniel land in Middletown. Legacies to daughters Mary SILL, Sarah McCARTY and Phebe HARDIN. Residue of estate to three sons first mentioned subject to payment of these legacies, James GIBBONS, John EDWARDS, Jacob MINSHALL, James SILL and Thomas BISHOP trustees for dividing plantation.

Exrs: Sd. wife and friend John EDWARDS.
Wits: William YARNALL, Caleb YARNALL and Jno. EDWARDS. #91.

CRIPS, JACOB, Middletown.
April 7, 1796 - April 21, 1796, Recorded May 12, 1796.
Executors to sell plantation in Middletown, wife Sarah to have all personal property and proceeds of sale, she to bring up son William.
Exrs: Sd. wife and Nicholas Fairlamb.
Wits: Frederick FAIRLAMB, William SHARPLESS and John MANCILL. #92.

WORRALL, JAMES, Marple Twp.
Feb 9, 1792 - April 25, 1796. Recorded May 13, 1796.
Legacies to children Elizabeth WORRALL, Hannah RAY, Isaac WORRALL, James WORRALL, Rebecka BALL, Lydia HOOPS, Rachel WARNER and all residue to son Daniel, he to be executor.
Exrs: Son Daniel.
Wits: John WORRALL, Evan MORRIS and Jonathan MORRIS. #93.

BROWN, JOSEPH, Upper Chichester.
Feb 29, 1796 - April 28, 1796.
Son Daniel to have use of the land until his son William is 21, then to his heirs forever less debt of £11, to Sarah DAY and in case of William's death during minority then to his brother Caleb and heirs, son Jeremiah £19 and money paid to John HIBBARD on his note and to pay his step mother £5. Proceeds from sale of other property to 4 daughters Agnes SMITH, Elizabeth TALLEY, Susannah MARTIN and Hannah HARTLEY.
Exr: Son Daniel.
Wits: Jacob D. BARKER and James BARNARD. #94.

PEIRCE, JOHN, Concord Twp.
June 11, 1795 - April 27, 1796.
Son John the home plantation also that formerly John WALTER'S, also gold watch, silver spurs &c., plantation subject to 2/5 interest to daughter Mary wife of John JAMES, yearly during life, she to have use of plantation purchased of Ezekiel LEONARD and also that formerly Israel PYLE'S purchased of Sheriff GARDNER, also house and land farmed by her husband, old house rented to James CROSLEY and fence timber from near Joseph PENNALLS triangular field. To sons of Mary, namely John and Joseph plantation on the Delaware purchased

of David BEVEN subject to payment of £600, £200 being to Mires,
Worrall, Sarah and John PEIRCE, £400 to other children of daughter
Mary.
Exrs: Stephen MENDENHALL (who renounced) and son John.
Wits: Micajah SPEAKMAN, Joseph FINCH and Caleb PEIRCE. #95.

EFFINGAR, HENRY, Marple.
May 11, 1790 - May 23, 1796.
Legacies to children (not named), all residue of estate to wife Agnes
EFFINGAR and her heirs, she to be executrix.
Exrs: Wife Agnes EFFINGAR.
Wits: Samuel FARRA and Daniel WORRELL. #96.

GREEN, SILAS, Concord.
June 12, 1796 - July 26, 1796.
Wife, all personal estate and use of real estate until youngest child is
twelve, plantation then to be sold and interest of proceeds to be 1/3 for
widow and 2/3 for children.
Exrs: Sd. wife and John BALDWIN.
Wits: Lot GREEN, James JEFFERIES and Jos. McCALL. #97.

GRANTHAM, GEORGE, Ridley.
July 9, 1791 - July 26, 1796.
Bequests to Rebecka SMITH, Christiana WILSON, Margaret
WILSON, Ester WILSON and Dinah WILSON. All residue to brother
Charles GRANTHAM, whom he appoints executor.
Exrs: Charles GRANTHAM.
Wits: George MADDOCK and William MADDOCK. #98.

HOLLAND, NATHAN, Marple.
April 16, 1792 - July 27, 1796.
Son Thomas to have plantation in Marple subject to certain provisions
for his wife Catharine including £400 to be placed in the hands of
brother Samuel POTTS, interest for her benefit. To other children
namely: Mary, Sarah, Samuel, Nathaniel and Johannah. Legacies to
sisters Sarah MAY and Joannah POTTS and to Providence Monthly
Meeting.
Exrs: Wife Catharine and brother in law Samuel POTTS.
Wits: William PAIST, Joseph WEST and Edward FELL. #99.

GIBBONS, JOSEPH, Springfield Twp.

Nov 8, 1795 - Aug 18, 1796.
Provides for wife (not named), to grandson John Haysham GIBBONS of Philadelphia, when of age, grandson Mifflin by name, to sons James Mifflin GIBBONS, Jos. and George W. and to daughters Jane wife of Robert MALCOM, Mary wife of Matthew ASH, Hannah wife of Enock HARLON, Ann, Elizabeth, Sarah and Rebecca GIBBONS.
Exrs: Sons James M. & Joseph and son in law Matthew ASH.
Wits: John HIBBERD, Isaac HIBBERD and Nathaniel SMITH. #100.

SHARPLESS, SAMUEL, farmer, Delaware County.
Sept 2, 1796 - Sept 23, 1796.
Provides for support of his mother, after her death legacies to be paid brothers Joshua and Aaron and sister Esther cousin Benjamin (only son of brother Isaac, dec'd.), and aunt Lydia MENDENHALL and balance to brother Aaron, sisters Amy DARLINGTON, Ester SHARPLESS and Sarah POOLE and to the children of sister Hannah YARNALL dec'd., James EMLEN, trustee for his mother.
Exrs: Jesse DARLINGTON and William POOLE.
Wits: John SHARPLESS and Thomas SHARPLESS. #101.

PRITCHET, WILLIAM, Edgmont Twp., Chester County.
Nov 15, 1786 - Oct 1, 1796.
During life sister Elizabeth PRITCHET to have all profits of home plantation #1 and also that in Upper Providence #2 formerly David MALIN'S. Plantation on Crum Creek #3 bounded by land of George MILLER and Abraham CALVERT to sister Phebe HAMET during life. #1 at Elizabeth's decease, to Jesse PRITCHET son of brother John on payment of 3/4 of valuation to Sarah BISHOP, Lydia RICHARDS and Phebe PRITCHET (#2 and #3) at Phebe HAMETS decease, to John PRITCHET son of brother John on same conditions as #1. Legacy to Mordecai YARNALL as in service of sister Elizabeth to whom he gives personal estate.
Exrs: Joseph BISHOP and Isaac MASSEY.
Wits: James HOWARD and Abraham FARR. #102.

HAZARD, ORAM, Middletown, Delaware County.
____ - Dec 24, 1796.
Province of Pennsylvania to wife (not named) 8 pounds, son Joel 10£, daughter Jane HAZARD 3 pounds, daughter Mary HAZARD 5 shillings, daughter Phebe HAZARD £6 if it is to spare, son Ely HAZARD £6 -

mentions that Richard BLACKHAM left £10 to be divided among children.
Exr: Ambrose SMEDLEY.
Wits: Joseph STARR and Aquila STARR. #103.

HALL, JOHN, Springfield.
Sept 12, 1796 - Jan 3, 1797.
To daughter Mary RHOADS, her heirs and assigns all plantation. Legacies to grandchildren William LEWIS, Sarah LOBB and George LOBB children of daughter Hannah wife of Benjamin LOBB. Residue of estate to son in law Owen RHOADS, daughter Mary RHOADS, grandchildren Sarah and George LOBB except cost of clothing for William LEWIS according to indentures. Provisions in case of death of any minor legatee.
Exrs: Son in law Benjamin LOBB.
Wits: Mary RHOADS and Jonathan PENNELL. #104.

KIRK, JOHN, Upper Darby.
April 18, 1796 - Feb 13, 1797.
To cousin Isaac KIRK 16 acres north side of Lancaster Road adjoining lands of James WILLIAMSON and Richard WILLING, the same to descend to his son John his heirs and assigns. Evan EVANS of Upper Darby, taylor, 4 acres on south west side of road from Darby to Haverford and adjacent to lands of Richard WILLING and Ann PARCLE, nephew Thomas LEWIS 5 acres adjoining land of William GARRETT and heirs of Thomas LEWIS, nephew Mordecai LEWIS 5 acres next to Thomas, sister Hannah POLLING 20 acres next to land of John ROSS and on decease to her daughter Elizabeth. Nephews Nathan and William POLLING each 4 acres, Joseph KIRK son of cousin Samuel KIRK 20 acres. Thomas KIRK son of cousin Samuel KIRK, residue of estate, he paying out of same all debts, claims &c. against estate.
Exr: John PEARSON of Darby.
Wits: Oborn GARRETT, James PYOTT and James WILLIAMSON. #105.
#106 - No 106 on file or Register.

WORRALL, SAMUEL, Upper Providence.
April 24, 1794 - March 14, 1797.
Wife Eleanor WORRALL to have seven acres bought of Joseph SWAFER and to heirs if she remains widow, if not, to be sold and

money distributed - mentions brother Seth, then sons Jonathan and Samuel, daughters Martha WORRALL and Sarah PILKINTON and distributes one half among them. The other half into five parts for sd. wife, daughters Eunis MADDOCK, Eleanor, Lois and Eliza WORRALL.
Exrs: Wife Eleanor and brother Jacob WORRALL taking special care of Martha.
Wits: Joseph WORRALL, Abel WORRALL and John RILEY. #107.

BROOKE, SAMUEL, Radnor.
Jan 2, 1797 - April 25, 1797.
Mentions wife Margaret, to son David the plantation bought of Rev. William CURRIE, son John the plantation in Radnor, bought of Moses ROBERTS. Bequeaths money to pay deceased son Samuel's debts. Speaks of Samuel's five children receiving their shares on their arrival at age except Margaret and Samuel spoken of as weak in mind and body, other three being Jehu, Charles and Elijah. To son Jesse the mills and plantation in Radnor bought of Benjamin DAVIS. Makes John executor to be aided by Jesse BROOKE.
Exrs: John and Jesse BROOKE.
Wits: Simeon MATLACK, Mordecai MOORE and George MOORE. #108.

MILEY, MARY, Borough of Chester.
April 16, 1707 - May 22, 1797.
All income of estate to sisters Hannah WEST and Ann JONES during life, then to nephew Pasmore WEST, then his son Samuel WEST and heirs forever.
Exrs: Brother in law William WEST and Abraham LEWIS.
Wits: John WOOD and Abraham DICKS. #109.

HIBBERD, ISAAC, Upper Darby.
Feb 27, 1795 - May 23, 1797.
Devises to son Joseph and heirs west end of plantation as per agreement of April 1783 touching land of Nathan DAVIS and great road, also meadow next to John HOBBERD'S with certain rights and restrictions. Son Isaac all remainder of estate, he paying legacies amounting to three hundred pounds - mentions daughter Elizabeth DAVIS, grandsons Isaac and Benjamin DAVIS and James and Hervey PENNELL as receiving legacies.
Exrs: Son Isaac and cousin John HIBBERD.
Wits: Matthew ASH, David LOWNES and John DAVIS. #110.

MILLER, GEORGE, Upper Providence.
Jan 12, 1794 - May 25, 1797.
To son George and his heirs all plantations on south side of Providence Road in townships of Providence and Middletown also woodland north side adjoining land of William PRITCHETT and John CALVERT, dec'd. Daughter Phebe profits of certain land north side of sd. road during life the same to go to George and heirs at her death. To friend Jacob MINSHALL of Middletown 1 acre of ground called Blue Hill in trust for a school for Chester Monthly Meeting.
Codicil of Dec 14, 1794.
Wits: Israel TAYLOR, Mahlon PARSONS and Mary PARSONS.
Exrs: Son George and daughter Phebe MILLER.
Wits: Israel TAYLOR, Ezekiel YARNALL and Thomas HAMOR. #111.

WORRALL, BENJAMIN, Marple.
March 9, 1797 - Oct 5, 1797.
Mentions Joseph WORRALL of Marple and a step son Moses THOMPSON, estate to daughter Frances WORRALL, should she die under age or without issue, estate to go to brother Elija's son William. To Peter TAYLOR £100 and Joseph WORRALL and Moses THOMPSON the residue.
Exrs: Edward HUNTER of Newtown and Joseph RHOADS of Marple.
Wits: Jonathan MORRIS and Joseph WORRALL. #112.

SHARPLESS, MARTHA, widow, Borough of Chester.
Sept 27, 1797 - Oct 19, 1797.
To eldest son William SHARPLESS and heirs the property by deed of gift from her father Jonas PRESTON, also adjoining marsh purchased from Joseph RUSSELL and wife, sd. William to pay to other children £260 - mentions land on Chester Creek adjoining Isaac EYRE, also lot given by her father. Daughter Jane SHAW'S share to be in hands of executors. Legacies to grandchildren Thomas SHARPLESS and Martha SHAW, and son Preston owner in mill at St. George's Hundred, N. Castle County.
Exr: Son William SHARPLESS.
Wits: Rebecca HOWARD and William MARTIN. #113.

HALL, ROBERT, Aston Twp.
Oct 15, 1797 - Oct 30, 1797.
Wife Sarah to have plantation bought of Jesse WORRALL to use during life. Orders sale of mill property &c. - mentions his two

granddaughters Ann REDDER and Margaret Hall STARR, both minors.
Exrs: Sd. wife and son Robert.
Wits: Richard DUTTON and Thomas DUTTON. #114.

SHOTTEN BREAM, mariner, Chester Twp.
Feb 18, 1794 - Nov 23, 1797.
Wife Mary executrix and sole legatee.
Exr: Wife Mary.
Wits: Lewis EYRE and Abraham DICKS. #115.

CROSBY, JOHN, labourer, Ridley Twp.
Nov 3, 1797 - Nov 23, 1797.
Makes will in favor of Hannah McCULLY wife of Thomas McCULLY for her attention to him in his distressed state - mentions indebtedness to Davis BEVAN, Esq. and Jonathan BONSALL, settlement with Ann KERN'S estate and money recovered from Jacob WORRALL, money due from William PYWELL of Ridley.
Exr: Sd. Hannah McCULLY.
Wits: James ARMSTRONG and Hugh FREED. #116.

GREEN, JANE, relict of Abel GREEN, Edgmont, dec'd.
March 17, 1796 - Dec 25, 1797.
Daughters Lydia MINSHALL, Esther McGOWING, Jane BAKER, Sarah SMEDLY, and Margret BURNS, granddaughters Jane GREEN, daughter of Robert GREEN, Jane GREEN daughter of Abel GREEN, Abigail BAKER and Jane BAKER, daughter in law Hannah, son Daniel REGISTER, sons Abel, Robert and George.
Exrs: Son Daniel REGISTER and two sons in law Edward BAKER and Daniel McGOWING.
Wits: Robert GREEN, Ann YARNALL and George RUSSELL. #117.

ELLIS, THOMAS, yeoman, Haverford.
March 26, 1781 - Dec 25, 1797.
Wife Sarah, daughters Hester and Mary (minors), sons Isaac and Amos under ten years, sons David, Jonathan and Thomas to be apprentices. Estate to be equally divided.
Exrs: Friend John PRICE and sd. wife. Wife Sarah ELLIS then deceased.
Wits: Jacob BURY and Jacob HUMPHREYS. #118.

SHARPLESS, SARAH, Nether Providence Twp.
Oct 27, 1796 - Feb 3, 1798.
Grandchildren: Sarah EYRES, Rebecca EYRES, Beaulah EYRES children of son in law John EYRE, Isaac SHARPLESS, Enos SHARPLESS, John SHARPLESS and Sarah SHARPLESS, children of son Daniel, Caleb, Abigail and Phebe MERCER children of daughter Abigail Mercer.
Exrs: Sd. Abigail and Daniel.
Wits: Roger DICK and Ellis ROBERTS. #118.

LEWIS, JOSIAH, Edgmont.
Jan 17, 1798 - Feb 13, 1798.
Wife not mentioned, children Samuel, Elizabeth LEWIS, Abraham, William, Phebe wife of Joseph BAKER and Esther wife of Jesse BAKER, grandson Josiah son of William and Josiah son of Abraham. Samuel 2/3 and Elizabeth 1/3 of plantation along county line from Aaron GARRETT'S to William HAYMAN'S Ford - mentions Rising Sun Tavern, Chester Great Road, Moses MEREDITHS and James SILLS. Son Abraham southern part of plantation. Josiah rest of estate.
Exrs: Sons Samuel and Josiah.
Wits: Thomas JOHNSON and Joseph McAFEE. #119.

DAVIS, JOHN, Chichester.
Jan 9, 1798 - Feb 23, 1798.
Plantation to be sold, 1/3 interest to wife Rebecca, residue to son John.
Exrs: Friend Joseph TALBOT and sd. wife.
Wits: Charles DINGEE, Jeremiah DUTTS and John HIBBERD. #120.

WILLING, RICHARD.
March 1, 1792 - Feb 20, 1798.
Wife Margaret and her heirs to have household furniture, negroes and legacy. Residue of estate to Thomas WILLING, Tench FRANCIS, Samuel POWELL and Robert HARE. Grandson Richard WILLING son of Charles WILLING of Chester County. Mother Ann WILLING. Richard Willing BYRD. Sisters Francis, Byrd, Powell, Hare; Brother James WILLING, nephews Charles WILLING, Thomas M. WILLING, John FRANCIS, Thomas FRANCIS, Charles FRANCIS, Charles HARE, Robert HARE, Richard W. BYRD, friend Sallie GREENWAY, Andrew HALL.
Exrs: Tench FRANCIS, Samuel POWELL and Thomas M. WILLING.
Wits: Michael FIMPLE and George FIMPLE. #121.

BRINTON, GEORGE, yeoman, Thornbury.
Dec 22, 1796 - Feb 27, 1798.
Wife Christianna and eight children viz: Joseph, Caleb, Thomas, John, Mary JACOBS, Phebe BRINTON, Hannah BRINTON and Jane BRINTON, Joseph tract in Chester County bought of Richard EAVENSON, tract bought of Joseph PIERCE trustee of Isaac YEARDSLEY (dec'd.), Caleb, tract in east Bradford purchased of Joseph GEST, Thomas the home farm in Thornbury inherited from father Joseph BRINTON, dec'd., John, moneys &c.
Exrs: Sd. wife, Joseph and Caleb.
Wits: Thomas TEMPLE, Caleb TEMPLE and Edward TEMPLE. #122.

BEAUMONT, JOSEPH, Newtown.
March 3, 1798 - March 12, 1798.
Estate to wife Margaret, son George W. - mentions father and mother then living.
Exr: Uncle Joseph DAVIS.
Wits: Samuel CALEY, Joseph FAWKES and David PRATT. #123.

GRAHAM, ABIGAIL.
May 15, 1796 - Dec 8, 1797.
Son William to have double share, homestead and Market lot, oldest daughter Eleanor HOSKINS, other daughters Mary HOSKINS, Henrietta FLOWER, Dorothea GRAHAM, Catherine ROBINSON and Abigail GRAHAM - mentions brother Joseph PENNELLS natural son Joseph PENNELL, also niece Abigail PENNELL, sister Dorothy SMITH.
Codicil explanatory Sept 26, 1797.
Wits: Benjamin CHEW and Edward TILGHMAN.
Exrs: William GRAHAM.
Wits: Susanna TREVILLS, Henrietta FLOWER and Dorothea GRAHAM. #124.

CROZER, JAMES, yeoman, Springfield.
Aug 4, 1793 - April 12, 1798.
Estate to be valued and son John to have a chance to hold same by paying sisters their share at appraisement viz.: Mary wife of John CALDWELL, Elizabeth, Sarah, Rebecca BRINTON and three unmarried Rachel, Martha and Esther. Grandsons David CALDWELL and James CROZER.
Codicil Decease of daughter Rebekah without issue April 26, 1794.

Wits: John LEWIS and James CALDWELL.
Exrs: John and Rachel CROZER.
Wits: Joseph GIBBONS and Jno. PRICE. #125.

SIDERS, ADAM, tanner, Radnor.
Feb 20, 1790 - April 30, 1798.
Property in Radnor to be sold, after death of wife Elizabeth and proceeds to sons: Adam, George, John, William and Jacob. Legacies to daughters Elizabeth, Mary and Sarah.
Exrs: Sons George and John.
Wits: John MORGAN and Samuel HAVORD. #126.

DAVID, AMOS.
Wife not named, eight children viz: John, Amos, Samuel, Joseph, Mary, George, Amer and Sarah to have equal shares.
Exrs: Joseph DAVIS and son Amos by decision of Registers Court held at Chester Feb 27, 1798. #126B.

BOND, BENJAMIN, Chester.
Nov 16, 1792 - May 16, 1798,
Plantation to be sold, proceeds to wife Rosanna, sons Abraham and Amos and daughter Elizabeth BARTON.
Codicil Nov 27, 1797.
Wits: Deborah HENVIS and Joseph RHOADS.
Exrs: Friend Daniel SHARPLESS of Nether Providence.
Wits: Samuel ASTON, Joseph RHOADS and Deborah HENVIS. #127.

MARIS, ISAAC, Marple.
Marcy 8, 1794 - May 16, 1798.
Plantation in Springfield to be sold, proceeds divided. Wife Elizabeth, son James, other children: Mary LAWRENCE, Elizabeth WEST, Isaac and Eliza MARIS.
Exrs: Sd. wife, James and Isaac.
Wits: Sarah YOKUM, Lewis PENNELL and Joseph RHOADS. #128.

MATLACK, NATHAN, yeoman, Radnor.
June 5, 1797 - July 19, 1798.
Late wife's will to be fulfilled. Children: Phebe wife of Dydemus LEWIS, William, George, Tacy, Hannah wife of Jacob TRACEL, Nathan, Thomas and Simeon. Plantation in Radnor to George on payment of £450 to executors Simeon, Nathan and Thomas.

Exrs: Simeon, Nathan and Thomas.
Wits: Ann NORTON and John BROOKE. #129.

LINDSEY, SAMUEL, Aston.
July 9, 1798 - July 20, 1798.
Wife Joice LINDSEY to have one half the land and two daughters each to have one fourth.
Exrs: Sd. wife and daughter Ann.
Wits: Samuel RUSSEL, James RUSSEL and James RIGBY. #130.

REYNOLDS, BENJAMIN, Upper Chichester.
Aug 3, 1795 - Aug 6, 1798.
To wife Phebe and kinsfolk, Margaret REYNOLDS, daughter of Samuel and Jane, Isaac TOWNSEND, son of Joseph and Hannah TOWNSEND and George MARTIN'S two sons George and John, also to Mary SWAYN, Alice SEEDS, Lydia WEBB, William WHITE and Sarah HASTINGS.
Exrs: Sd. wife and John TALBOT.
Wits: Charles DINGEE and Sarah WELCH. #131.

VERNON, JOSHUA.
March 14, 1798 - Sept 14, 1798.
Wife Ann to have all during life unless she marries, then to have one third and daughters Lydia and Ann VERNON two thirds of estate.
Exrs: Wife sole executrix.
Wits: William HEWES and Isaac KIMBER. #132.

BECKERTON, JESSE, yeoman, Chester.
Aug 25, 1798 - Sept 6, 1798.
Estate to wife Elizabeth and her heirs.
Exrs: Sd. wife and her brother James SHAW.
Wits: William SIDDONS and E. PRICE. #133.

BICKERTON, ELIZABETH, widow, Chester.
Sept 7, 1798 - Sept 18, 1798.
Brother James SHAW sole executor. Legacy to Shaw BURNS son of William BURNS, Jr. Residue to John and Samuel SHAW sons of brother Samuel SHAW and to Jesse and Joseph BICKERTON sons of Samuel BICKERTON, dec'd.
Exrs: Brother James SHAW.
Wits: Elizabeth PRICE, A. MUSGRAVE and Ea. PRICE. #134.

MOULDER, JOHN.
Sept 27, 1798 - Oct 22, 1798.
Mentions wife, sister and aged father (not named). Letters of administration granted to Margaret MOULDER on testimony of Peter EVANS and Charles HEWES. #135.

SILL, JAMES, yeoman, Edgmont.
May 23, 1798 - Oct 22, 1798.
Children: James, Aaron, Nehemiah, William, Ann and Elizabeth. Plantation to sons Aaron and James (minor) and in case of his death before he is 21, to Nehemiah (minor).
Wits: Joseph McAFEE and Benjamin YARNALL. #136.

HATTON, PETER, yeoman, Concord.
Aug 23 1793 - Oct 29, 1798.
Provides for wife Sarah, son Joseph to have plantation in Concord, son Peter plantation purchased of Elizabeth SAWYER already in his possession, son Thomas previously provided for, daughters Rachel WILSON, Hannah ASKEW and Elizabeth MERCER.
Exrs: Sd. wife and son Joseph.
Wits: Gideon GILPIN, Samuel PAINTER and Isaac G. GILPIN. #137.

EMLEN, JAMES.
Sept 22, 1797 - Nov 9, 1798.
Mentions housekeeper Sarah DAVIS, £100 in trust to cousin Thomas FISHER for general school at West Town. "Friend Nathan YEARSLEY preference as a miller to run my mill." Estate to six children (not named).
Exrs: Miers FISHER of Philadelphia and Abraham PENNELL of Middletown, brother in law John PIERCE, friend Thomas STUARTSON and Jonathan EVANS of Philadelphia to be guardians of children.
Wits: Not named. #138.

JACOBS, LYDIA, Concord.
Aug 20, 1798 - Nov 19, 1798.
Children: Hannah and Thomas both minors, appoints William GARRET of Willistown and aunt Hannah RITTENHOUSE as guardians of their education. John JACOBS a brother in law, Mary PENNEL, daughter of brother Thomas PENNEL. Mentions land in Westmoreland County, patented by husband Thomas, another tract in Middletown inherited

from father Robert PENNEL bounded by lands of Robert PENNEL, Sr. and Jr. both to be sold and proceeds to two children. In case of their decease the children of brothers Thomas and Joseph, sisters Mary FAIRLAMB and Abigail NEWLAND to receive fifths, residue to uncle Isaac JACOBS, sister Phebe HOBSON and uncle Jesse JACOBS.
Exrs: Brother Thomas PENNEL and friend John UMSTAD.
Wits: Eli FEW, George PALMER and Ann BIGLAR. #139.

MORGAN, MAGDALANE, Radnor.
April 30, 1798 - Nov 24, 1798.
Executors son John and grandson Joseph JOHNSON, other children Sarah JOHNSON, Rachel MORGAN, Ruth MORGAN, Hannah BELFORE and her two children James and Ann BELFORE. Legacy to negro girl Cloe.
Exrs: Son John and grandson Joseph JOHNSON.
Wits: William THOMAS and Amos THOMAS. #140.

SMITH, DOROTHY, widow, Chester.
____ - Nov 7, 1798.
Cousin Elizabeth Wyatt WINNEY of Old England, step daughters Sarah NEWLAN, Elizabeth SMITH, Martha SMITH, nieces Eleanor HOSKINS, Mary GRAHAM (HOSKINS), Henrietta FLOWER, Dorothy GRAHAM, Catharine GRAHAM (ROBINSON) and child (not named), nephew William GRAHAM*. [Part of this will was evidently written before Mary and Catharine GRAHAM were married, spelling and ink both different. No real estate given.]
*Inventory mentions Zedkiah W. GRAHAM.
Exr: Brother William GRAHAM.
Wits: Nicholas NEWLIN, Joseph WHARTON and Sampson MOORE. #141.

HARRISON, JOHN, Borough of Chester.
July 19, 1798 - Nov 30, 1798.
Provides for wife Mary, children: Joseph, Ann and Elizabeth share alike after wife's death. Brother in law William PAUL to assist wife, Joseph and Ann in executing.
Exrs: Brother in law William PAUL, wife, Joseph and Ann.
Wits: Jonas EYRE and James BARNARD. #142.

GRAHAM, ZEDEKIAH WYATT.
Sept 28, 1798 - Dec 18, 1798.

Sister Dorothy SMITH to have income of estate during life, then in six
shares, two to William GRAHAM residue at interest for Eleanor and
Mary HOSKINS, Henrietta FLOWER and Catherine ROBINSON,
signed in the presence of Dorothy SMITH.
Exr: William GRAHAM.
Wits: Thomas PEDRICK and James SHAW. #143.

NEIDE, JOSEPH.
May 19, 1796 - Dec 29, 1798.
Children: John the eldest son, Mary, Rebecka, Elizabeth, Abegal,
Jacob, Benjamin, Sarah's children, Joseph (not married),
granddaughter Elizabeth EVANS, mulatto boy Tom, land bought of
Elizabeth CLAXTON, 4 acres between the Bristo field and
SHARPLESS land, also marsh and quarry rights. Benjamin 20 acres of
Bristo field to begin at William SWAFFER'S line. Residue of real estate
to Joseph's heirs.
Exrs: Joseph NEIDE.
Wits: William KERLIN, John CALDWELL and Pearce POWERS.
#144.

POWELL, GEORGE, Haverford.
Jan 18, 1799 - March 12, 1799.
Eldest three children: John, Joseph and Patience DICKERSON and a
younger daughter Sarah POWELL to have legacies, wife Hannah and
younger children: George, Nathan, Mary, Hannah, Abraham and
Thomas estate in fee forever.
Exrs: Sd. wife and brother in law John BALL.
Wits: Amos LUKENS and Joseph BALL. #145.

McCALL, JOSEPH, Concord.
March 9, 1799 - March 30, 1799.
Estate to brother William McCALL'S children viz: Mary, William and
James.
Exr: Sister in law Isabel McCALL.
Wits: Samuel RUSSELL and James RUSSELL. #146.

RICE, DANIEL, Darby.
May 23, 1798 - April 8, 1799.
Estate equally to children: Jacob, Elizabeth and Daniel, provided no
claims are made for services.
Exr: Friend John PEARSON.

Wits: Joseph SHALLCROSS and Richard LLOYD. #147.

PEDRICK, THOMAS, Chester.
Dec 18, 1798 - May 7, 1799.
William GRAHAM and James SHAW to sell all real estate and pay interest of same to daughter Elizabeth during life. Legacies after her death, to Caleb BIRCHALL, Daniel PEDRICK'S son Thomas, Ann BUCKLEY, Thomas PARSON, James BIRCHALL and each of the children of Caleb BIRCHALL, residue to sd. James and Caleb BIRCHALL, their heirs and assigns.
Wits: Tristram SMITH and Aaron COBOURN. #148.

ARNOLD, JAMES, Springfield.
April 8, 1799 - May 15, 1799.
Plantation to be sold, proceeds to wife Martha. Provides for Martha HORN daughter of Edward HORN and Orpha RIGHT daughter of Rachel OGDEN.
Exrs: Sd. wife and brother in law John OGDEN.
Wits: John CALDWELL and Joseph RHOADS. #149.

EFFINGER, HENRY, Ridley.
____ - June 12, 1799.
The following are the minutes of the last will and testament of Henry EFFINGER of Ridley Township in Delaware County taken by me Abraham DICKS, this twelfth day of the second month Anno Domini, one thousand, seven hundred and ninety eight. The same after being penned was read and approved by him the said Henry EFFINGER. Provides for wife Rachel, son Henry a minor, sons Jacob and Henry to have the plantation according to certain division which mentions Charles GRANTHAM'S line, Ridley Creek, Delaware River and John CROSBY'S land. Daughters Agness, Margaret, Sarah and Rebecca or their lawful issue to have profits of plantation till Henry comes of age.
Wits: Elizabeth DICKS and Abraham DICKS. #150.

CROZER, ESTHER, Springfield.
Sept 16, 1798 - Sept 24, 1799.
Executors brother John CROZER and sister Rachel CROZER, two unmarried sisters Rachel and Martha. Gives all her share in division of her late father's land to brother John CROZER, sisters Mary CALDWELL, Elizabeth BERCHAL, Sarah OGDON, Rachal CROZER and Martha CROZER except legacy to Mary's children viz: Jeames,

David, Elizabeth and Sarah CALDWELL. Mary's and Elizabeth's share to be kept from control of their husbands.
Exrs: Brother John CROZER and sister Rachel CROZER.
Wits: John LEWIS and Ann LEWIS. #151.

DAUGHERTY, SUSANNAH, Nether Providence.
March 3, 1792 - Oct 8, 1799.
To brother's daughters: Martha SANKEY, Margaret SANKEY, Abigail RICHARDS and Susannah LANGUIN. Brother's son William SANKEY, real estate, and he to be sole executor.
Exr: William SANKEY.
Wits: Daniel SHARPLESS and Roger DICKS. #152.

ARMENT, JOHN, Concord.
June 3, 1798 - Oct 25, 1799.
Provides for wife Cathren ARMENT; at her decease real and personal estate to be sold. Legacies to sons Isaac and William, residue to Isaac, William, Elizabeth CROS, Hannah HALL and Nansy BISHOP.
Exrs: Sd. wife and son Isaac ARMENT.
Wits: Joseph MORRISON, Joseph PALMER and Asher PALMER. #153.

DAVIS, RUTH, Radnor.
June 26, 1799 - Oct 29, 1799.
To Benjamin DAVIS of Radnor, Sarah GUYGER wife of Jesse GUYGER, sister Rebecca ELLIS, after her death the following legatees: brother Edward DAVIS, Ruth PEIRCE, Rebecca REECE, Hannah DAVIS, wife of Benjamin DAVIS, Tacy DAVIS, Edith DAVIS, Edward DAVIS (son of Edith), Hannah DAVIS, (daughter of Edith), Tacy ELLIS, Guinn ELLIS, Griffith ELLIS. Mentions two daughters of sister Rebecca, Bridget and Guinn.
Exrs: Joshua THOMAS and Bridget ELLIS.
Wits: Samuel TAYLOR and Jno. ELLIOTT. #154.

ELLIS, JESSE, Haverford.
Jan 2, 1799 - Oct 29, 1799.
To wife Hannah ELLIS, son in law John FREE and daughter Mary FREE, if no issue, heirs to be children of niece Esther BOND wife of Joseph BOND, other bequests to Lydia and Mary GRIFFITHS nieces of wife, Elizabeth FIELD daughter of Nathan FIELD, Friends Meeting House, Friends Burial Ground. Residue to daughter Mary.

Exrs: John FREE and Benjamin Hayes SMITH.
Wits: Abraham FREE and Amos LUKENS. #155.

BONSALL, SAMUEL, Concord.
Aug __ , 1799 - Nov 23, 1799.
To nephew Robert BONSALL son of sister Rebekah (minor). Residue to brothers and sisters viz: Joseph BONSALL, Sarah HANNUM, Hannah BONSALL, Jane TAYLOR, Tacy BONSALL, Obadiah BONSALL, Rebeckah BONSALL.
Drs. MONRO, James TELTON, SMITH and SAYRES mentioned in Administrators account.
Exrs: Thomas MARSHALL of Concord.
Wits: Joseph TRIMBLE and Thomas NEWLIN, Jr. #156.

MEREDITH, MOSES, yeoman, Edgemont.
June 1, 1786 - Nov 30, 1799.
Wife Mary left in care of son Joseph he to have the home plantation in Edgemont and Willistown, son John, plantation where he now lives in Plymouth, Montgomery County on payment of certain bequests. Daughter Sarah PENNELL wife of Joseph PENNELL, granddaughter Sarah MEREDITH daughter of dec'd. son David, David, Mary and Sarah HARREY (or HARVEY) children of daughter Alice HARREY (or HARVERY).
Exrs: Sd. wife and sons Joseph and John.
Wits: Josiah LEWIS, Samuel LEWIS and David REGISTER. #157.

RICHARDS, LUCEY, Aston.
Dec 3, 1799 - Dec 20, 1799.
Bequests to sisters Hannah PLOWMAN and Lydia PRICE, brothers Thomas, Jehu, Jonathan, Joseph, Josiah, Richard and Dutton RICHARDS, Josiah RICHARDS'S daughter Sarah Ann RICHARDS, cousin Sarah HIBBERD, Susanna RICHARDS and her two daughters Hannah and Mary Ann.
Exrs: Jehu and Joseph RICHARDS.
Wits: Jonathan DUTTON, John DUTTON and Susanna DUNN. #158.

THOMAS, OWEN, Springfield.
Oct 10, 1799 - Dec 25, 1799.
Estate to mother Susanna THOMAS for life, then to brothers and sisters James, George, Jonathan, Rebecca, Benjamin and Seth.
Exrs: Mother and brother George.

Wits: Henry GARNER and William PENNOCK. #158B.

NORRIS, MARY, Borough of Chester, Delaware County.
Feb 15, 1794 - Jan 7, 1800.
Son Isaac, daughter Deborah LOGAN, tract in Gloucester County, N.J. which my grandfather conveyed to my mother, messuage where I now dwell and three lots in Borough of Chester which father bought of John YEATES and Isaac WILLIAMS, all my upland and marsh situated there, father bought of James SANDELAND, Rebecca MADDOX, James CLAXTON, David SANDELAND and Isabella BACKHOUSE. Son Joseph P. NORRIS plantation and two tracts in Chester purchased of Jno. WRIGHT and Nineveh CARTER. Son Charles NORRIS lots on Norris Count adjoining ground of George LOGAN, MIFFLIN'S, Drs. KHUNS and William KINLEY, William BINGHAM, south east corner 5th and Chestnut purchased of James ASH, Esq., High Sheriff. Mentions Jno. WADE, William KERLIN, Price TREVILLO and John POWELL and housekeeper Phebe CHANDLER, cousins Mary DICKENSON, Hannah GRIFFITHS, Hannah THOMPSON, Joseph ASKEW, Mary SHAW and Agnes MINSHALL, friends Dorothy SMITH, Ann DAVIS, her daughter Jane DAVIS, Abigail GRAHAM, Mary GRUBB, Mary KENNY, Mary WELSH, James CROSS and Margaret ____.
Exrs: Son Joseph and daughter Deborah LOGAN.
Wits: Jonas PRESTON, William GRAHAM and Jno. PRICE. #159.

WORRALL, JOHN, Edgmont.
May 16, 1799 - Jan 14, 1800.
Rights and privileges to wife Sarah during widowhood, son Isaac the home tract as described in father's will, less about 40 acres to his brother Samuel for life, being the portion described as lying along the Edgmont Road to Thomas WORRALL'S, then to the Mill Road. Daughters Mary THOMPSON and Lydia WILLIAMS, grandson John WILLIAMS, granddaughter Priscilla HOOPES, grandson Samuel WILLIAMS. Daughters Elizabeth HOOPES and Lydia WILLIAMS to have proceeds of sale of 84 acres in Edgmont bounded by land of Robert GREEN, George GREEN and others.
Exrs: Son Isaac, son in law Abraham HOOPES and nephew John WORRALL.
Wits: Eli YARNALL, John MENDENHALL and Joshua FOX. #160.

GILPIN, SARAH, Upper Providence.

Feb 12, 1793 - Feb 17, 1800.
Daughters Mary CROSLEY, Abigail GILPIN and Lydia PORTER, daughter in law Mary WOODWARD wife of son Edward WOODWARD, grandchildren Sarah WOODWARD, Alice WOODWARD, Edward WOODWARD, All real estate to son Edward.
Exr: Son Edward.
Wits: David PRATT and Thomas CALVERTE. #161.

SHAW, MARY, relict of Anthony.
Dec 21, 1797 - March 7, 1800.
Land in Chester township to be sold for benefit of surviving children of sister Agnes MINSHALL, viz: Jacob, Margaret, Phebe, Ann, Mary and Grace. Legacy to Chester Monthly Meeting.
Exrs: Nephew Jacob MINSHALL and friend James EMLEN.
Wits: Isaac HOOPES and Eli HOOPES. #162.

COURTNEY, THOMAS, Newtown.
Dec 31,1792 - April 12 1800.
Estate to wife Ann during widowhood. Legacies after her death to Leah RHOADS, daughter of Joseph RHOADS, Newtown, Springfield and Grange Meetings, the last near Charlymont in Ireland.
Exrs: Levy LEWIS and Edward HUNTER.
Wits: John LEWIS, Jehu GARRETT and Unity GARRETT. #163.

WOOLLEY, SARAH, widow, Springfield.
June 15, 1792 - May 19, 1800.
Daughters Jane DENNIS and Ann PANCOAST; estate to Ann, she to be executrix.
Exr: Ann.
Wits: Edward FELL, John POWELL, Jr. and Joseph RHOADS. #164.

PANCOAST, HANNAH, Springfield.
____ - May 25, 1800.
Sister Eliza HARRISON and her children to have one half and sister Esther LEWIS the other half right in father's plantation, nephews and nieces John PANCOAST, Rebekah PANCOAST, brother Seth's four children: Hannah, Anne, Ester and Stephen, Caleb HARRISON, Kitty HARRISON, Anne P. LEVES. Makes provision for Ann WOOLLY and an indentured black girl Elisa BALLARD, "unless my mother is willing to keep her."
Exrs: "My bros. Samuel PANCAST and William LEWIS"

Wits: Samuel PANCOAST and Edward FELL. #165.

BOON, REBECCA, Ridley.
Feb 20, 1795 - June 6, 1800.
Bequests to daughters Lydia DAVIS and Elizabeth HALL, lands &c. to son William BOON.
Exr: Sd. son William.
Wits: Peter LONGACRE and John CULIN. #166.

MILLER, JOHN, Ridley.
May 28, 1800 - June 23, 1800.
Estate in Fayette County to be sold for use and education of daughters Margaret and Jane. Estate in Ridley to be sold on death of wife (not named) for use of children.
Exrs: Friend James CARSON and nephews Benjamin and James MILLER.
Wits: Elizabeth MORTON, Mary CARSON and James CARSON. #167.

LEWIS, LEWIS, Radnor.
June 6, 1800 - July 29, 1800.
Estate to mother Jane LEWIS and at her death to sisters Mary and Hannah LEWIS, they to pay to brother Henry LEWIS £1000. Provides for children of brother Abner and sister Rachel - mentions Lewis DAVIS as one of her sons.
Exrs: Brother Henry LEWIS and cozen Lewis LEWIS.
Wits: Lewis LEWIS and John FAIRLAMB. #168.

HUNTER, JONATHAN, yeoman, Edgemont.
Sept 18, 1783 - Aug 5, 1800.
Rights in home property on death of brother George to Richard and George HUNTER sons of brother Peter HUNTER, tract of land formerly Daniel REGESTER's to cousin Samuel MICKLEDUFF and his sister Martha wife of Charles BARRINGTON. Bulls Head Tavern on Strawberry Alley, Philadelphia one half ownership to cousins Richard and George HUNTER, Ann wife of John SCOTT, Elizabeth wife of Nathaniel ERWIN, all children of dec'd., brother Peter HUNTER; George MATLACK, Jesse MATLACK, Jonathan MATLACK, Hannah wife of Nathan SCHOPPELL (or SCHOPHELL), Ann wife of Richard FAWKES and Mary wife of Jesse SMEDLEY children of sister Mary the wife of Isaiah MATLACK equal tenths. Other half ownership belongs to brother George HUNTER. Land in

Appoquinimy, St. George's Hundred, N. Castle County to be sold. Land in Whiteland, Chester County also in borough of Chester to Samuel MUCKELDUF son of Ann wife of John SCOTT. Remainder of property to aforesaid eight cousins.
Exrs: Jonathan MATLACK of Goshen and Richard FAWKES of Newtown.
Wits: Joseph CHEYNEY, Abel GREEN and Josia LEWIS. #169.

OTTEY, JOHN, Middletown.
May 18, 1798 - Oct 11, 1800.
Provides for wife Ann, she to support and bring up younger children - daughters Sarah, Ann, Lydia and Hannah, sons Philip, John, Thomas, Richard and Eli.
Exrs: Sd. wife.
Wits: Robert PENNELL, Robert PENNELL, Jr. and Abraham PENNELL. #170.

GRUBER, JOHN, wheel wright, Darby.
June 19, 1789 - Oct 20 1800.
Tract in Darby on highway to Chester adjacent to land of Daniel HUMPHREYS, Joseph BONSALL and others, to son George. Wife (name not given) to be cared for by sd. son. Legacies to children: George, Mary, Elizabeth wife of Michael TRITES, Catharine, Margaret wife of Samuel SHAW also equal shares in final settlement of residue.
Wits: Jno. PEARSON, George SWAYNE and Charles PEARSON. #171.

YARNALL, CALEB, Edgmont.
Oct 17, 1799 - Nov 25, 1800.
Wife Phebe. Children: Owen, Agnes, Caleb, Phebe and John. To Owen land adjoining Benjamin HOUSTON and Phebe HAMMILL'S lines. Son John all other land in Edgmont and Middletown.
Exrs: Sd. son John.
Wits: William YARNALL, Jacob MINSHALL and George YARNALL. #172.

CLIME, PHILIP, shoemaker, Ridley.
Feb 13, 1799 - Jan 6, 1801.
Legacy to Sarah WHITEMAN.
Exrs: Thomas HALL and James MADDOCK, Elizabeth WALTON, Sarah WHITMAN, Israel MORTON and Mary MORTON.

Wits: Thomas BOWMAN and William SHOEMAKER. #173.

HALL, SARAH, widow, Aston.
Sept 20, 1800 - Jan 9, 1801.
Daughters Elizabeth JONES, Ann VERNON, Mary RICARD. Granddaughters Ann REEDER and Margaret H. STARR. Sons Robert one third and Joseph two thirds of residue.
Exrs: Son Robert.
Wits: Jno. TALBOT and Edward GRISSELL. #174.

BONSALL, MARY, Darby.
Sept 8, 1794 - Feb 30[?], 1801.
Property in Upper Darby on Haverford Road, adjoining James TYSON'S and John and Joseph BALL'S land to daughter Hannah. Rest of Upper Darby tract to daughter Mary. Legacies to Benjamin BRANNON, Esq., and to Darby Monthly Meeting. Legacies to grandchildren Abraham OWEN, Elizabeth OWEN and Mary HIBBERD (both minors), son in law Joseph HIBBERD, brother John HIND.
Exrs: Sons in law Jonathan OWEN and Joseph HIBBERD.
Wits: James TYSON, Joseph BALL and John HIBBERD. #175.

GAMBLE, PATRICK, Concord.
June 3, 1797 - March 6, 1801.
Plantation to grandson Robert Nossit GAMBLE. Legacies to nephews John and Peter GAMBLE.
Exrs: William HANNUM and John PEIRCE, Sr.
Wits: Joseph MORRISON, Joseph PALMER and Caleb PEIRCE. #176.

CLOUD, MORDICAI, yeoman, Upper Chichester.
April 28, 1800 - March 6, 1801.
Legacies to wife Agnes, granddaughter Susanna GILL, son Harlin, 100 acres of plantation to son Benjamin - mentions land of Caleb EYRE. Daughter Ann PETERS to have about 80 acres where she now dwells in Lower Chichester adjoining lines of Martha SMITH and Samuel ARMER. Rest of home plantation partly in Bethel to be sold proceeds to sd. son Harlin and Ann PETERS.
Wits: Isaac PENNELL and Caleb EYRE.
Exrs: Harlan and Joseph LARKIN.
Wits: William EYRE and Jonathan DUTTON.
Codicil Jan 22, 1801. #177.

VAUGHAN, CHRISTIANA, Haverford.
April 2, 1800 - March 30, 1801.
Five acres at upper end of land at now in tenure of Samuel WRIGHT also legacy to son Joshua, the rest of plantation to son Jacob, he to pay legatees. Legacies to sons Johnson and Jonathan, also to Martha STANDLY.
Exrs: Jacob and Joshua VAUGHAN.
Wits: Adam LITZENBERG and Philip LITZENBERG. #178.

MARTIN, JONATHAN, Middletown.
Oct 20, 1798 - April 27, 1801.
To daughter Mary, wife of Wm. SHARPLESS, the plantation bounded by lines of Frederick FAIRLAMB, Ridley Creek, Joshua HARRISON and Chester and Edgmont Road, also land in Chester Twp. bounded by lands of Caleb COBURN, commonly known by name of the *Invention*. To daughter Mary for life then to Lydia's heirs. To daughter Lydia, wife of Joshua CLAYTON, home plantation adjoining lines of Jonathan DUTTON, Chester Creek, John SHARPLESS and aforesaid Road.
Exrs: Brother Abraham MARTIN and sons in law.
Wits: Nichs. FAIRLAMB [or Richd. Fairlamb?] and Jonathan DUTTON. #179.

TAYLOR, NATHAN, Upper Providence, Chester County.
Jan 20, 1787 - April 30, 1801.
Legacies to daughters Hannah WILKINSON and Ruth BAKER, son Evan TAYLOR and wife Amy, housekeeper Mary BRAINARD (or BRANON), son Enoch TAYLOR to have residue of estate in Providence and to be executor.
Exrs: Son Enoch TAYLOR.
Wits: John TAYLOR and Peter TAYLOR, Jr. #180.

PARKER, JOHN, yeoman, Middletown.
April 9, 1801 - May 16, 1801.
Legacies to children viz: Abraham, Elizabeth WIDENER, Mary LOWAIN, Robert and Ralph. Grandchildren Thomas and John, sons of son Robert, Evins PARKER and John PARKER, sons of son Ralph.
Exrs: John SHARPLESS, of Middletown and John MENDENHALL.
Wits: Stephen HALL, Nathaniel WALTER and Nathaniel WALTER, Jr. #181.

EVANS, LYDIA, Radnor, Chester County.

April 1, 1801 - ... 1801. Registered May 25, 1801.
Kinsman Robert ANNELSEY to see that three granddaughters Lydia HAWORTH, Rachel HAWORTH and Ann HAWORTH get furniture. Right and title to house and lot in Radnor to niece Hannah HARRY of Philadelphia. Residue for the education of grandson Musgrave EVANS in care of Robert ANNESLEY.
Exrs: Son Samuel EVANS.
Wits: William GOVELL, Jr. and Mord. CHURCHMAN. #182.

MINSHALL, SARAH, Middletown.
Feb 23, 1799 - May 21, 1801.
Legacies to daughters Mary HALL, Jane LONGSTRETH, Sarah STARR, granddaughter Sarah YARNALL and to Phebe YARNALL for use of poor friends of Middletown Meeting. Residue to son Thomas MINSHALL, he to be executor.
Wits: Thomas BISHOP and Thomas STEELE. #183.

FRANCIS, PHILIP, Upper Darby.
Feb 17, 1794 - June 10, 1801 on file. Inventory dated Jan 12, 1801.
After death of wife Henrietta Maria, estate to children John and Maria.
Exrs: Sd. wife.
Wits: Nathan GARRETT, Jr., Thomas GARRETT and Sarah GARRETT. #183B.

FAIRLAMB, ELEANOR, Newtown.
March 30, 1801 - July 28, 1801.
Brother John FAIRLAMB executor and sole legatee.
Wits: Joseph HOOD and Richard FAWKES. #184.

SLATER, PRUDENCE, Borough of Lancaster.
May 2, 1799 - Aug 5, 1801.
Granddaughter Prudence, daughter of son John. Seven children: Thomas, John, James, Ann, Elizabeth, Mary and Sibby or Libby. Husband Thomas SLATER to have an annuity.
Exrs: Son Thomas and John WILCOX of Delaware County and brother in law Mark WILCOX.
Wits: Joseph PENNELL and Benjamin PALMER.
The inventory taken Aug 14, 1801 distinctly states that the same was taken by "us freeholders in the city of Philadelphia and district of Southwark." Will signed SLETER. #185.

EDWARDS, WILLIAM, Nether Providence.
July 1, 1801 - Aug 6, 1801.
Son Jacob to have tract bought of James WOOD and wife, lot in Chester, also share with Seth THOMAS bought from John CHALLIS and wife. Home tract to son James for life then mentions William GRAHAM of Chester and his heirs, but says that he devises the land to the child or children of son James. Jacob to inherit in case James dies without issue. Legacies to three daughters Margaret EDWARDS, Prudence THOMAS, wife of Seth THOMAS, and Sarah BARTON. Also land in Providence near Fells on the saw mill lane between home tract and Edward TILGHMAN to sd. sons, grandson William son of son William EDWARDS, dec'd.
Exrs: Sons James and Jacob EDWARDS.
Wits: Edward TILGHMAN and Parke SHEE. #186.

LITZENBERGER, SIMON, cooper, Haverford.
Aug 13, 1794 - Aug 18, 1801.
To wife Dorothy and sons George and John - mentions grandchildren (names not given).
Exrs: Sons Adam, Jacob and Simon.
Wits: Richard TEPPINGS and Jacob STANDLEY. #187.

VERNON, MARY, Nether Providence.
May 25, 1799 - Aug 19, 1801.
To Woodward VERNON son of brother Elias VERNON, 11 3/4 acres, bounded by lands of Reuben ROBERTS, Isaac ENGLE and Providence Street.
Exrs: Friend Joshua ELY.
Wits: Jno. STEPHENSON and (John) Yahn VALENTIN. #188.

YOUNG, GEORGE, mariner, Philadelphia.
Nov 4, 1800 - Sept 9, 1801.
Daniel McNULTY executor and sole legatee.
Wits: Alexander TOD and Hugh BOYLE. #189.

TAYLOR, ENOCH, Upper Providence.
Aug 7, 1800 - Sept 21, 1801.
Estate in Newlin Township, Chester County, in Euclin Township and all in Upper Providence to be valued and divided. Wife Elizabeth, sons Nathan, Ezra and Maris and daughters Eliza, Mary, Hanah, Jemima and Gula.

Exrs: Sd. wife and sons Nathan and Ezra.
Wits: Parke SHEE and William ROBINSON. #190.

PALMER, JOHN, Concord.
Sept 17, 1801 - Sept 29, 1801.
Wife Hannah, children: Benjamin PALMER, Abigail COFFMAN, Lydia HALLOWELL, Abraham, Thomas, Moses, Hannah, Norris and John PALMER -mentions saddler's shop.
Exrs: Sd. wife and son John.
Wits: Nathaniel WALTER and Wm. HANNUM. #191.

FORREST, WILLIAM, Nether Providence.
Feb 16, 1801 - July 14, 1801.
Estate to wife Jane for life, then to son Henry less certain legacies to other children: Elizabeth, James, Jane, Andrew, Nancy and William.
Exrs: Sd. wife and son Henry.
Wits: Thomas TRIMBLE and Wm. SHEPHERD. #192.

WEAVER, JEREMIAH, Birmingham.
Sept 24, 1801 - Oct 15, 1801.
Wife Margaret and children: Joseph, Bernard, Abigail, Jeremiah and Margaret.
Exrs: Jesse GREEN and Asher PALMER.
Wits: Joseph MORRISON and George BALDWIN. #193.

MENDENHALL, BENJAMIN, Concord.
Aug 19, 1800 - Oct 27, 1801.
Legacies to children: Joel, Betty wife of Thomas KENNY, Elijah, Ruth and Mary wife of Abner PYLE. Grandchildren Beulah MENDENHALL, Orpha MENDENHALL and Phebe the daughter of Joseph PYLE. Residue to wife Phebe, she and son Elijah to be executors.
Wits: Jas. GIBBONS and William GIBBONS. #194.

PEIRCE, HENRY, Concord.
Oct 19, 1801 - Nov 30, 1801.
Estate to wife Marget and children: Jacob, Henry, Mary and Charles.
Estate to be divided at majority of youngest child.
Exrs: Uncle John PEIRCE.
Wits: William PEIRCE and John PEIRCE. #195.

BRITTON, RICHARD, yeoman, Tinicum.

Dec 22, 1810 - Feb 25, 1802.
Legacies to children: Ezekiel, Richard, Amy wife of John FERMAN, Ann wife of Wm. GEORGE for her children, Mary wife of Isaac STIDHAM, Catherine wife of Caleb T. BENNETT and Sarah.
Exrs: Sons in law Isaac STIDHAM and William GEORGE and daughter Sarah.
Wits: Sarah BRITTON and John CULIN.
Sarah BRITTON renounced right to estate of her father before being sworn as witness. Personal property per inventory $4094.25. #196.

McLAUGHLIN, WILLIAM, Ridley.
Feb 23, 1799 - Jan 28, 1802.
House and lot on "Plunb Street," Philadelphia to be sold, moneys for schooling and support of children. Wife Margaret, children to be bound to trades.
Exrs: Peter HILL and Aaron MORTON.
Wits: William PRICE and Abijah PRICE. #197.

SITERS, GEORGE, Newtown. *In body of will "Siter."*
April 5, 1801 - Feb 4, 1802.
Wife Sarah to have estate and at her death to children: John, Hannah, Adam, Nathaniel, Joseph, Clerica and George.
Exr: Sd. wife.
Wits: James JONES, Thomas THOMAS and Joseph LEWIS. #198.

RUSSELL, WILLIAM, saddler, Edgemont.
July 10, 1801 - March 15, 1802.
Wife Lydia, children: Jesse, Obed, John, William, Hannah wife of Evan EACHUS and Sarah REJESTER, wife of Joseph REJESTER. Sons Obed and John joint ownership of plantation on north side of Ridley Creek - mentions PRITCHARD'S line, mouth of Joseph BISHOP'S Run, BISHOP'S lane, Jas. HOWARD'S corner and Providence Road. John as minor. To son Jesse the home plantation. Lines of Elizabeth PRITCHARD, George BISHOP, Joseph PRATT, Daniel MEGOWEN, George GREEN, Joseph BISHOP and the aforesaid tract subject to payment of legacy to William when of age.
Exrs: Obed and Jesse RUSSELL.
Wits: George GREEN, Abraham HOOPES and Daniel MEGOWEN. #199.

SHAW, JAMES, Delaware County.

*May 12, 1802 - *April 10, 1802.
Estate to wife and his own to be added and valued. Wife Martha and Samuel each to have one third. Exrs: Sd. wife and brother in law Ephraim PEARSON.
Wits: Arthur MAY, James BIRCHALL and Wm. GRAHAM.
*On the oaths and affirmations of the witnesses to the foregoing will the date of the said will was the 12th day of March. Jas. BARNARD, Register. #200.

HUMPHREYS, ANN, Delaware County.
Nov 17, 1796 - No date of probate; inventory dated March 26, 1802 and filed July 28, 1802.
Heirlooms to Aaron OAKFORD and wife Ann, Ann CLEMENT daughter of John CLEMENT, Hannah daughter of Benjamin Webber OAKFORD, Ann OAKFORD daughter of Benjamin W. OAKFORD, Samuel HUMPHREYS son of Joshua HUMPHREYS, Sarah HUMPHREYS and Isaac OAKFORD. Residue to Benjamin Webber OAKFORD, he to be executor.
Wits: Jno. PEARSON, Richd. LLOYD and Nathan PEARSON. #201.

PRICE, JOHN, Esq., Lower Chichester.
Dec 12, 1770 - [See below.]
Wife Elizabeth, children: Ann EYRE, Samuel, Hannah, Sarah, (minor), John (minor), Elizabeth, (minor), sister Sarah PRICE, Rev. Geo. CRAIGE to be guardian of John and Elizabeth. House and lot in town of Chester purchased of Richard LAWRENCE adjacent to James ROWAN'S land to wife during life. Plantation in Brandywine Hundred, New Castle County, adjoining Naaman's Creek to dau. Ann, wife of Robert Eyre (not subject to control of her husband), and to her children. To son Samuel, the home farm purchased of Charles NORRIS, John CLOUD and Moses MOORE, with grist mill, saw mill and extension to river Delaware purchased of John PIERCE. To John the LAWRENCE parcel, the Thomas CLAYTON tract to lines of Elisha PRICE, Hannah and Adam CLAYTON, woodland bought of Richard LAWRENCE; also legacies to Hannah, Sarah, John and Elizabeth.
Exrs: Friend Elisha PRICE and son Samuel PRICE.
Wits: John SMITH, Richard RILEY and Levi LLOYD.
The docket gives this as from a certified copy from the Chester County Docket, the original being lost. Certified Sept 20, 1784. Letters of administration granted to John CROZER April 27, 1802. #202.

BULLOCK, ISAAC, Concord, Chester County.
Sept 19, 1797 - June 11, 1802.
Wife Margery, land from the old shop door to a certain large willow tree. To sons Thomas and Moses - mentions Joseph MORRISON'S and Thomas SPEAKMAN'S lines. Residue of land to son John. Legacies to daughters Mary HALL and Jane.
Exrs: Sd. three sons.
Wits: William FOULK and Stephen FOULK. #203.

PYLE, RALPH, Birmingham.
May 28, 1802 - June 12, 1802.
Wife Hannah, her thirds during life. Sons Ralph, Samuel, William and David, daughters Elizabeth, Sarah and Susannah. To sons land in equal shares, daughters legacies. "But if in case my will of said land should be dislowd of by my father, then my will is that my four sons above named take an equal share of the personal estate with the girls."
Exrs: Brothers William PYLE and Samuel EACHO.
Wits: Robert FRAME, Henry WASSON and Phins. CARY.
[Note: This man seems to have been a tanner as per inventory of partly tanned skins.] #204.

WALTER, RACHEL, Concord.
Sept --, 1801 - Aug 7, 1802.
Children: Lydia widow of James PENNELL, Nathaniel, Isaac, William. To Deborah, wife of son John. Great grandchildren: Ruth and Ann CROSBY children of Charles CROSBY. Grandchildren John Taylor and Hannah Grizle, children of daughter Elizabeth ---. Children of daughter Hannah, dec'd., William and Benjamin JONES, Mary, Rachel, Elizabeth and Hannah REED. Mentions children of son Thomas WALTER, dec'd., and William son of Isaac WALTER.
Exrs: Sons William and Nathaniel.
Wits: Stephen HALL, John PALMER, Jr. and John TRIMBLE.
Codicil of June --, 1802 mentions the possible decease of son John and share to go to his widow (no witnesses). #205.

ELY, SARAH, Nether Providence.
June 16, 1801 - Dec 27, 1802.
To daughter Esther and heirs, a house and land inherited from father; also lot purchased of John DARLINGTON and Esther his wife. To son Joshua in satisfaction of any demands gives two lots adjoining above one bought of brother John DICKS, the other of Peter DICKS.

Exrs: James HINKSON son of John HINKSON and Esther ELY my daughter.
Wits: Roger DICKS and Frederick DICKS.
[Note: Signature if "ELLY" also in probate gives "Esther ELLY."] #206.

KERLIN, MATTHIAS, Lower Chichester.
Nov 25, 1791 - Dec 27, 1802.
Legacies to son William, daughters Ann VANDEVER, Sarah FLOWER, Susannah GRUBB, Hannah McKEE and Rebeccah SHELLEY; grandsons Benjamin FORD, Philip FORD, Mathias FORD, David Kerlin McKEE. Son Matthias to have plantation in Upper Chichester, also tract in Bethel purchased of Joseph BOOTH, also tenement and lot in Marcus Hook purchased of William EYRE and any residue.
Exrs: Sd. son Matthias and friend William BURNS.
Wits: Thos. DICK, William FORD and James BURNS, Jr. #207.

TAYLOR, PETER, Upper Providence.
Nov 11, 1802 - Dec 22, 1802.
Sons Ambrose and Joseph all land in Virginia paying one third of proceeds to children of deceased son Peter. John, Moses and Francis, sons of sd. son Peter, the home tract in Upper Providence subject to the payment of legacies to children, Ambrose, Joseph; children of daughter Mary SMEDLEY or SMEDLY, dec'd.; Sarah THOMAS wife of Joshua THOMAS; Grace TAYLOR widow of son Peter - rights in the homestead.
Exrs: Son in law Joshua THOMAS and friend Luke CASSIN.
Wits: Joseph NEWLIN, Martha CROMWELL and Luke CASSIN. #208.

EVANS, ANN (or ANNE), relict of CADWALLEDER (or CADWALADER) EVANS, Edgmont. Jan 15, 1799. March 5, 1803.
Daughter Alice MORRIS wife of Jonathan MORRIS, son Robert, granddaughter Jane LAD daughter of son Robert, niece Rachel JORDAN, granddaughter Sarah COWPLAND, grandson Cadwalleder EVANS, granddaughter Sarah SAVERY and Alice MORRIS, grandchildren: Ann, Catharine, Samuel, Evan and Alice children of daughter Alice MORRIS; grandsons Caleb and David COWPLAND. Legacy to Sarah EVANS a black woman, sd. legacy to be in care of Jacob MINSHALL. Abram, son of son Robert. Residue to Sarah and David COWPLAND.
Exr: Sd. Jacob MINSHALL.

Wits: Isaac HOOPES [HOOPS], Eli HOOPES [HOOPS] and Abraham HOOPES [HOOPS]. #209.

GARRETT, NATHAN, yeoman, Upper Darby.
Aug 17, 1798 - March 9, 1803.
Sons Nathan and Thomas, grandson Samuel, daughters Jane JONES and Ann PASCHALL to be legatees.
Exrs: Sons Nathan and Thomas.
Wits: Hezekiah HIBBERD, Benjamin LOBB and Joseph HIBBERD.
Codicil Oct 9, 1801 mentions grandson Thomas GARRETT.
Wits: Hezekiah HIBBERD and Joseph HIBBERD. #210.

BURN, JANE, Marple.
Dec 1, 1798 - March 14, 1803.
Children: Joseph; Isaac and his children William, Isaac and Jane; William deceased and his children: Wm., Ann and Jane; daughter Rachel DUNWOODY, Jane DUNWOODY daughter of James DUNWOODY. Isaac to have plantation on which he now lives for life.
Exrs: Son Joseph and Edward HUNTER.
Wits: Jonah TAYLOR, Martha TAYLOR and Philip MOORE. #211.

PENNELL, ROBERT, Middletown.
March 4, 1797 - March 18, 1803.
Children: Joseph and his son Robert; Thomas; Abigail NEWLIN and her son Robert NEWLIN; Lydia JACOBS and her son Thomas; Mary FAIRLAMB and her husband Frederick. Legacies to the above named excepting Mary and her heirs who get residue of estate.
Wits: John OTTEY, Job VERNON and Nicholas FAIRLAMB. #212.

LEWIS, MARY, Radnor.
Feb 11, 1803 - March 19, 1803.
Cousin Mary VAULT, Mordicai LEWIS son of Lewis LEWIS; Mary CITER daughter of Adam CITER; Agnes LEWIS; niece Sarah CITER; Hannah LEWIS, daughter of Evan LEWIS; Lydia LEWIS, daughter of Evan LEWIS; Elizabeth, Ann and Mary CITERS, daughters of Adam CITERS £15 in trust with Edward CITER until they are eighteen.
Exr: Step son Lewis LEWIS.
Wits: Evan ROBERTS and Henry LEWIS. #213.

ANDREWS, JAMES, Darby.
Dec 6, 1802 - April 11, 1803.

One half estate to wife Martha, proceeds from the rest to be placed at interest for support of children: Hannah, Josiah, John, James, Sarah, Rebecca and if another, sd, child to have equal share with those above named.
Exrs: Wife Martha and brother in law Josiah BUNTING, Jr. and John BUNTING.
Wits: Aaron OAKFORD, John BROOKS and Benj. W. OAKFORD.
Inventory March 28, 1803. #214.

JONES, JOHN, Radnor.
Nov 19, 1801 - April 21, 1803.
Provides for wife Alice. Legacies to sisters Elizabeth LEWIS and Jane BERRY; nephews Joseph, Abel and John LEWIS (sons of Elizabeth); nephews John, Standish, Richard, Levallin and niece Mary (children of daughter Jane BERRY); eldest male child of nephews John and Standish BERRY; nephew Nathaniel MILES (son of sister Hannah, dec'd.); Sarah SITERS (daughter of Hannah); Sarah YARNALL and Tabitha DENNIS.
Exrs: Wife Alice and friends Edward and William HUNTER.
Wits: Evan ROBERTS, Evan EVANS and Benjamin H. SMITH.
Codicil of March 6, 1703 changes Sarah SITER'S legacy to an annuity.
Wits: James MORGAN and John BROOKE. #215.

PARKS, RICHARD, Thornbury.
March 29, 1803 - May 24, 1803.
To wife Sarah and her son Samuel PAINTER' son Jacob PARKS and his eldest son Richard; grandchildren Vernon PARKS, half brother of Richard; Sarah PARKS; daughter in law Hannah, wife of Jacob to have an annuity should she survive her husband.
Exrs: Sd. wife, son Jacob and friend John PEIRCE.
Wits: Robert PENNELL and James HICKMAN. #216.

SNEIDER, MATHIAS, Haverford.
April 6, 1803 - May 27, 1803.
To wife Mary and eight children: Elizabeth, Leonard, John, Catherine, David, Thomas, Margaret and Sarah (some of them minors).
Exrs: Mordecai and Clement LAWRENCE.
Wits: George HAWORTH and Joseph RHOADS. #217.

BOON, JOSEPH, Darby.
April 23, 1802 - June 25, 1803.

Three children: Rebecca, Joseph and John BOON, to share alike. Legacy to granddaughter Elizabeth PAINTER - mentions plantation and meadow adjoining the thoroughfare lands of Robert CALVIN.
Wits: George GRUBER and Isaac LODGE. #218.

GUYGER, GEORGE, Radnor.
July 29, 1803 - April 10, 1803*
Wife Margaret; children: Jacob, Susanna BEALE and Mary WHITE; Jacob to have the estate on Lancaster Road and lines of Thomas PAUL, Joseph HOSKINS and the late John SMITH.
Exrs: Sd. son Jacob.
*Dates taken from will same as docket. Inventory is dated Sept 9, 1803 - from comparison of other probates this should probably be August not April.
Wits: Jonathan RICHARDS and Joseph HOSKINS. #219.

ASKEW, JOSEPH, Upper Chichester.
May 24, 1801 - Oct 17, 1803.
Wife Elizabeth; children: John, William, Benjamin, Parker, Samuel, Mary HALL and Joseph. To son Samuel subject to annuity to Mary, the lower place, lines of Joseph TALBOT, John EYRE, Mathias KERLIN, Isaac PENNELL and Jonathan DUTTON. The home plantation to Joseph, lines of Joseph TALBOT, Caleb EYRE and others.
Exrs: Sd. son Joseph.
Wits: Samuel EVANS and Jonatn. DUTTON. #220.

HARMON, JOHN, Upper Providence. Nuncupative.
Oct 24, 1803 - Oct 24, 1803.
Property should go to the children of Charles BETTLE he expressing himself that they had done the most for him. (Died Oct 13th.)
Wits: Luke CASSIN and Ezra TAYLOR. #221.

HUNTER, HANNAH, Newtown.
May 12, 1802 - Dec 3, 1803.
To grandson Peter HUNTER, plantation in Radnor whereon son James now lives, subject to care of James and his wife Martha and the payment of £1000. To executors to distribute; great grandchildren Morgan and Elizabeth HUNTER (children of grandson Samuel HUNTER, dec'd.). Rest to granddaughters (children of son James): Ann, Hannah, Mary, Sarah, Rachel, Martha and Sidney. Legacies to

own children: John, George, Sarah LEWIS (wife of Evan LEWIS) and Mary JONES. Grandchildren James JONES, Hannah BROOKS, James HUNTER (son of John); Ann HUNTER, daughter of James HUNTER; Agnes, Hannah and Lydia LEWIS, daughters of Evan LEWIS; Hannah, daughter of John; George Morgan HUNTER; Martha, Emily and Albert Gallatin HUNTER, children of George HUNTER. Mentions names of deceased husband James and deceased father John.
Inventory Nov 28th.
Exrs: Son George and kinsman Edward HUNTER.
Wits: David READ and Benjamin H. SMITH. #222.

HALL, DAVID, yeoman, Marple.
Sept 5, 1801 - Dec 13, 1803.
To son David, portion of plantation adjoining Marple Street Road line of Richard MARIS, also a piece of woodland touching Benjamin TAYLOR'S land. To son Edward, plantation purchased of Jacob and Ellenor WORRALL in Upper Providence. To son Joseph, the home plantation in Marple. Daughters Sarah LEVIS, Beulah and her husband William BROMWELL.
Exrs: Sons David and Joseph.
Wits: Roger DICKS, Abraham PENNELL and Joseph RHOADS. #223.

JOHNSON, PETER, Concord.
Oct 10, 1803 - Dec 30, 1803.
Estate to two children: Cato and Jacob.
Exrs: John PEIRCE.
Wits: James MARSHALL and Joseph CLOUD. #224.

GEST, WM., house carpenter, Bethel.
Dec 8, 1802 - Jan 6, 1804.
Two sons Benjamin and Abraham, plantation they to pay certain legacies. To son John rents and profits of 90 acres in Fawn Twp., York County, to be laid off from whole tracts of 300 acres. Sons Henry and Samuel rest of tract. Daughters Susanna WILLIS, Rachel CLOUD, Mary PEIRCE, Hannah PEIRCE and deceased daughter Sarah PRINCE'S two sons Adam and Isaiah and dec'd. daughter Alice MARTIN'S children, Lewis, Eliza and John. Residue to sd. nine children.
Exrs: Sons Benjamin and Abram and friend Isaac STEVENSON of Wilmington.
Wits: Isaac LARKIN and Thomas BOOTH, Sr. #225.

PEARSON, JOSEPH, yeoman, Ridley.
May 14, 1803 - Jan 12, 1804.
Wife Elizabeth; son John L. the plantation subject to payment of legacies to daughters Hannah, Martha, Ann, Elizabeth and Susanna, grandson Levi PEARSON, lots in Darby, Marsh in Calcon Hook near Darby Creek, Marsh on Tinicum Island all to be sold.
Exrs: Sd. wife and son John PEARSON.
Wits: John HORNE, Jonathan SMITH and John SMITH. #226.

REED, THOMAS, yeoman, Radnor.
Oct 6,1799 - March 26, 1804.
Wife Margaret; son John all the plantation, other children: Mary, James, Davis and Ann, daughter in law Susannah REED, granddaughter Martha QUIN.
Exrs: Son John.
Wits: Lewis LEWIS, Moses PALMER and Henry LEWIS. #227.

WORRALL, JOHN, farmer, Ridley.
June 21, 1803 - April 2, 1804.
"My will is that I may be decently buried in my Rockfield near a cherry tree." Wife may live with Eunice MADDOCK wife of Jesse MADDOCK. Personal estate in Ridley and Springfield to Edward LANE, my nephew, now of Philadelphia except four acres purchased of John MODLIN which he gives to his molatto man, Phillip COLINS, his heirs and assigns.
Exrs: Edward LANE.
Wits: William WORRALL and David BEVAN. #228.

ISAAC LOBB, Upper Darby.
Sept 17, 1802 - March 26, 1804.
Plantation between Springfield Road and Darby Creek to son Israel except one lot for building on, also six acres of woodland; the rest to son Josiah and his lawful issue. To son Isaac the plantation on which he now lives in Upper Darby subject to payment of £400 (one year after mother's decease). To sisters Jane, Ann, Elizabeth, Esther, Phebe and Amy, plantation between Isaac's and Darby Creek to son Ephraim.
Exrs: Two eldest sons Israel and Isaac.
Wits: John DAVIS, Peter YARNALL and John HIBBERD.
An unsigned codicil dated Aug ___ 1803 mentions decease of Jane. #229.

DAVIS, LEWIS, Haverford.
Sept 3, 1796 - Feb 28, 1804.
Sons Benjamin and Joseph, daughters Mary ASHBRIDGE and Ann LEWIS. Mary to have legacy, Ann, annuity during husbands life, then legacy, Joseph plantation in Haverford and pay legacies to his mother in law Hannah DAVIS and others.
Exrs: Sd. son Joseph.
Wits: Mordecai LAWRENCE, Abraham FREE and Thomas PHILLIPS. #230.

WOOD, WILLIAM, blacksmith, Chester.
Dec 13, 1803 - March 10, 1804.
Father John WOOD premises formerly owned by mother Sarah WOOD.
Exrs: Father and unkle Matthew WOOD of Edgemont.
Wits: Jon. POWELL, Jr. and David THOMAS. #231.

SELLERS, JOHN, Upper Darby.
Sept 13, 1803 - March 19, 1804.
Wife Ann; two granddaughters Ann GARRETT and Sarah RHOADS; sons Samuel, Nathan and David; last two to get four acres adjoining land previously given them on COBB'S Creek. Son John the grist and merchant mills and land beginning over the middle of COBB'S Creek and a bridge on the West Chester Road - mentions line of John CLAUGUS. Son George residue, subject to care of mother, he to be sole executor.
Wits: James STEEL, Abraham JOHNSON and Robert STEEL. #232.

BOON, REBECCA, Darby.
Oct 6, 1803 - April 24, 1804.
Cousin Andrew BOON, son of Hans BOON; Robert CALVIN, Jr.; Elizabeth NOBBIT, daughter of friend John NOBBIT. Last two mentioned all my part of father John BOON'S plantation, lines of Edward HORNE, Jacob and Daniel RICE, George SWAYNE and brother Joseph BOON.
Exr: John PEARSON.
Wits: Jon. PEARSON, George SWAYNE and John NOBBIT. #233.

MORRIS, DAVID, Radnor.
Jan 8, 1799 - April 30, 1804.

Wife Mary to have life interest in plantation then to son George and heirs. Children: John, George, Ann, Phebe RUTHERFORD.
Exrs: Sd. son George.
Wits: Henry LEWIS and Lewis LEWIS. #234.

ROGGERS, LIDYA, Concord.
April 13, 1804 - May 7, 1804.
Signed by mark Lyda RODGERS.
Three sisters: Deborah ROGERS, Ann BARRET and Amy JOHNSON. Brother Abner's two oldest sons John and Thomas.
Exrs: Brother John ROGGERS and brother in law Charles BARRET.
Wits: Asher PALMER and Joseph PALMER. #235.

MERIN, JOSEPH, farmer, Darby.
June 1, 1803 - June 4, 1804.
To be buried at Elliott's burring ground in Kingsessing. Wife Abigail and children: Thomas, Ruth HOOPER, Rebecca and Mary, grandson Joseph HOOPER.
Exrs: Thomas SMITH.
Wits: Jonathan ADAMS and John JOHNSTON.
Codicil of June 1st leaves watch in care of wife for grandson. Same witnesses. #236.

BLACK, JAMES, Upper Providence.
June 18, 1804 - July 16, 1804.
Provides for mother (name not given). All land to brothers Joseph and Thomas and their heirs. Legacies to sisters Mary COCHRAN, Christian BLACK, Eliza BLACK.
Exrs: Thomas BISHOP and George MILLER.
Wits: Ezekiel YARNALL and Abel MINSHALL. #237.

ROGERS, DEBORAH, Upper Darby.
June 15, 1804 - Aug 25, 1804.

Sister Amy JOHNSON and daughter Ann. Nephews John and Samuel
H. TAYLOR, nieces Elizabeth and Deborah TAYLOR, children of sister
Mary TAYLOR, dec'd.
Exr: Brother in law Joseph JOHNSON.
Wits: Joseph HIBBERD and Ephraim LOBB. #238.

WALTERS, JOSEPH, Haverford.
July 9, 1804 - Aug 28, 1804.
Brother Jonathan WALTERS, sisters Margaret COLBERT, wife of
John, Sarah LOBB wife of Edward and Mary PRICE wife of Joseph.
Property to be sold proceeds to sisters.
Exrs: Friend Benjamin Hayes SMITH.
Wits: William BITTLE and Joshua THOMPSON. #239.

CROSBY, JOHN, JR. Ridley.
Aug 16, 1804 - Aug 29, 1804.
Plantation to son John at twenty one, he to pay £1200 to his sisters
Ann, Rebecca, Sarah and Eliza. Executor to sell marsh and upland on
the river adjoining lands of EYRE and TRIMBLE, plantation and
quarries to be leased during son's minority for use of wife (name not
given) and children.
Administrators account mentions Sarah CROSBY, widow.
Exr: Father.
Wits: Charles GRANTHAM and James MADDOCK. #240.

CHEYNEY, JOSEPH, Thornbury.
Aug 15, 1804 - Sept 8, 1804.
To brother Curtis CHEYNEY and heirs all estate except £100 in
legacies to brothers and sisters, Esther STRODE, Mary GREEN,
Samuel, Jesse, Ann, Abel, Elizabeth, Hannah, Phebe, Waldron, Jane
CHAMBERLIN. Inventory indicates trade of cooper.
Exrs: Sd. brother Curtis.
Wits: William YARNALL, Joseph JAMES, Jr. and William CHEYNEY.
#241.

WILLIAMSON, THOMAS, Aston.
Dec 3, 1803 - Sept 11, 1804.
Wife Abigail, children: Gidion, Thomas and Emor, plantation purchased
of John McMINN, Elizabeth wife of Enos HOOPS, Abigail widow of
son William, and George lessee for life of plantation in Goshen and
Westown 53 acres, then to be sold, proceeds to children of son Thomas,

daughter Elizabeth and son Emor, he to have residue of estate. *The farm sold in 1817 for $5975.20.*
Exrs: Sd. wife and son Emor.
Wits: Benjamin PALMER, William TURNER and John PENNELL. #242.

WORRALL, THOMAS, Middletown.
Dec 20, 1790 - Oct 9, 1804.
Estate to four sons: Thomas, Peirce, Peter and George, they to provide for wife (name not given).
Codicil April 22, 1795.
Wits: John H. CHEYNEY and James EMLEN.
Exrs: Sd. sons.
Wits: James EMLEN and Virgil EACHES. #243.

McLAUGHLIN, ROBERT, Radnor.
Feb 21, 1804 - Oct 11, 1804.
To Alexander GREGORY, son of John and Elizabeth GREGORY all stock in my name in the Books of the treasury of the United States.
Legacy to Samuel NOWLIN (or NEWLIN) minor.
Exrs: John GREGORY and Edward SITER.
Wits: John SITER and Edward PUGH. #244.

GRUB, MARY, Borough of Chester. (Signed Mary GRUBB)
Aug 15, 1803 - Oct 5, 1804.
Legacies to Friends Meeting of Chester, Jamima SMITH daughter of brother Joseph RUSSELL, dec'd., Mary RUSSELL, daughter of same, Joseph EVANS son of Benjamin EVANS and grandson of brother Joseph.
James SMITH, husband of Jamima, Mary RUSSELL and Joseph EVANS.
Wits: David BEVAN and Isaac EYRE, Jr. #245.

EVANS, ELIZABETH, Aston.
May 5, 1801 - Nov 1, 1804.
Daughter Ruth, wife of William HANNUM, Hannah wife of Thomas VERNON, son Samuel residue of estate. Black woman Sylvia to have her freedom immediately. Grandchildren John BUTLER, Mary EVANS, Elizabeth EVANS.
Exrs: Son Samuel.
Wits: James GIBBONS, Robert Hall and Hugh CALDWELL. #246.

HOLMES, THOMAS, mariner, Ridley.
Sept 11, 1804 - Nov 6, 1804.
Provides for wife Susannah on conditions that she supports the child (unborn) and gives it a trade. Land in Union Twp, Erie County.
Exrs: David REY, dealer, of Philadelphia.
Wits: Lewis MOREY, Richard HOLMES and Joseph SHALLCROSS. #247.

TYSON, JOHN, Upper Darby.
June 7, 1804 - Dec 4, 1804.
Wife Ann, Mary TYSON daughter of son William, Margaret TYSON daughter of son John TYSON, dec'd. Estate to be sold proceeds to children: William, Mathias, Levi, Isaac, Jacob, Margaret SIMMONS, children of Benjamin dec'd.
Exrs: Sons Levi and Jacob.
Wits: Amos PENEGAR, Benjamin BONSALL, Jr. and Peter STEELE. #248.

CARTER, MARTIN, Chester.
Oct 4, 1801 - Jan 10, 1805.
Wife Jane, children: Thomas, Sarah BRANNER, Prudence LINN, Moses, Grace BABB and Theron.
Exrs: Edward CARTER, farmer and son Thomas CARTER.
Wits: John GILL, Patrick M. CANN and James BIRCHALL. #249.

KERLIN, WILLIAM, Borough of Chester.
Nov 28, 1804 - April 29, 1805.
Provides for wife Catharine. Plantation in Nether Providence bought of James WITHY, lot on Chester Creek bought of James SPARKS, Isaac TUCKER tenant? 14 acres bounded by Chester Creek, Concord Road and land of Jonathan PENNELL and Isaac EYRE, Esq., called the Mazard Lot all to be sold. Son William lot purchased by Eleazer OSWALD, son Abraham lot and tenements in possession of Valentine DICK and John BEATTY, 8 acres of John EYRE also tract bought at Sheriff's sale, estate of Edward VERNON called Fairfield. Son John the barn lot bounded by lands of William SHARPLESS and Jonas EYRE, he to have the home after wife's death. Daughter Sarah PIPER the Tavern property corner of Free and High Streets. Grandson Kerlin BURNS and Mathias BURNS to have frame messuage north east corner of Middle and West Streets subject to life interest for their

mother Margaret BURNS, grandsons John and William ODENHEIMER and George Henry KIRLIN (minor).
Exrs: Sd. wife, son William and son in law John PIPER.
Wits: John LUNGREN and Thomas B. DICK. #250.

SPECKMAN, MICAJAH, (signed Speakman), Concord.
Feb 28, 1805 - May 8, 1805.
Provides for wife Phebe SPEAKMAN also giving her land purchased of Abraham JOHNSON for life. Grandchildren Esther SPEAKMAN, Nathaniel SPEAKMAN, other part of JOHNSON tract to grandson John SPEAKMAN also land in Birmingham bounded by Wilmington Road. Joseph MORRISON, Concord Twp. line he to pay brothers Micajah and Nathaniel (minors) £400. Micajah the remainder of land in Birmingham paying legacy to sister Mary JACKSON. Son Micajah land purchased of Joseph DAVIS and Ely HARVEY, he to pay certain moneys to wife Phebe and granddaughter Mary JACKSON. Legacy to son Thomas.
Exrs: Wife and son Micajah.
Wits: Thomas MARSHALL, Thomas SPEAKMAN and Joseph CLOUD. #251.

WILLIAMSON, DANIEL, Marple.
April 3, 1805 - April 17, 1805.
Estate to niece Ester GARRETT.
Exrs: Jonah GARRETT.
Wits: John GRIM and Mary BRADLEY. #252.

ART, JAMES, mariner, Lower Chichester.
Jan 1, 1803 - May 27, 1805.
James ART son of brother William to be educated. All other estate to wife Ann ART, she to be executrix.
Exrs: Wife Ann.
Wits: John BURNS and John HARDING. #253.

CHERRY, JAMES, Bethel.
July 4, 1805 - July 29, 1805.
Legacies to Hannah GOSSET, Ann GOSSET, Elizabeth GOSSET and Pompey GOSSET. Sister's son Jesse GIBBONS.
Exrs: Jesse GREEN of Birmingham and Thomas NEWLIN of Concord.
Wits: Benjamin JOHNSON, Thomas NEWLIN and Thomas SPEAKMAN. #254.

SHARPLES, JOHN, yeoman, Middletown.
Sept 9, 1801 - July 30, 1805.
Brother Thomas and nephews and nieces viz. Lydia, daughter of brother Joel, dec'd., Joshua son of same, Phebe IDDING, Samuel IDDING son of sister Hannah IDDING, Samuel son of Joel SHARPLES, dec'd., sister Mary WOOD, Lydia RUSSELL, Abigail SHARPLES, Hannah IDDING, Susanna TALBOT wife of Jacob, Phebe SMEDLEY and Rachel WALTER wife of Nathaniel. Plantation to Joshua (minor) son of Joel adjoining Jesse DARLINGTON, Daniel SHARPLES, Abraham PENNELL and heirs of Joel.
Exrs: Brother Thomas SHARPLES and cousin Nathan SHARPLES of Middletown.
Wits: John BROOMALL, James BROOMALL and Samuel JOBSON. #255.

WILLIAMSON, ELIZABETH, widow of John, Newtown.
June 20, 1805 - Aug 12, 1805.
Sons Adam, John, Enos, books which were his brother George's, daughters Ann, Esther GARRETT wife of Jonah, Sarah PRATT, Elizabeth GARRETT and Jane HIBBERD, grandchildren John and Rebecca WILLIAMSON children of son Walter), Eliza GARRETT, Elizabeth HIBBERD and Elizabeth GARRETT.
Exrs: Sons in law Abraham PRATT and William HIBBERD.
Wits: John HUNTER and Enos HOOPER. #256.

ELY, JOSHUA, Nether Providence.
July 1, 1805 - Aug 17, 1805.
Executrix and sole legatee George ELY son of Esther ELY.
Exrs: George ELY.
Wits: George ELY and Esther ELY. #257.

WOODWARD, EDWARD, Middletown.
Sept 6, 1805 - ____.
Wife ____, son Edward (minor) land in Middletown on East side of Edgmont Road lines of Frederick FAIRLAMB, Ridley Creek, Abraham SEYES and Patrick MULVANEY. Daughters Sarah, Alice, Jean, Mary and Betty and heirs all West of same. Last three minors.
Codicil Sept 26, 1805 - same witnesses.
*Election of Mary WOODWARD to take her dower of the estate of Edward WOODWARD October 14, 1805. NOT IN DOCKET.
Exrs: Joseph ENGLE and Frederick JAMES.

Wits: Isaac G. GILPIN, Jonathan BONSALL, Jr. #258.

GARRETT, OBORN, Upper Darby.
April 25, 1804 - Nov 19, 1805.
Release of brother John of all sums of money owing also an annuity, brother William £500 for heirs, sister Ann JONES (the James PYOTT tract lines of same, Jonathan EVANS, Samuel KIRK and William GARRETT) and to her children William and Mary Ann JONES, nephews Samuel and Oborn LEVIS sons of sister Elizabeth the mansion, mills and tract lines of Hezekiah HUBBERD, Nathan and David SELLERS and Benjamin BRANNON subject to payment of £1000 to executors and annuity to sister Elizabeth LEVIS also a tract, lines of William GARRETT, John BROOKS and Thomas LEWIS, nephew William LEVIS son of sd. sister Elizabeth and his sisters Nancy wife of Thomas LEVIS and Mary wife of John LEVIS, nieces Margaret, Sarah and Henrietta LEVIS, daughters of sd. sister Elizabeth, Elizabeth daughter of niece Nancy LEVIS, Hannah GARRETTSON, the Elder, Lydia GARRETTSON, Charles BEVAN, Samuel GARRETT (son of Thomas), George SELLERS, daughter Lydia use of Old House, niece Margaret LEVIS. Residue to Lydia GARRETSON, Sarah LEVIS, Henrietta LEVIS and Hannah GARRETTSON the younger.
Codicil of Oct 22, 1805 holds John responsible for debts and mentions death of Hannah GARRETTSON.
Wits: Margaret SMITH, Benjamin H. SMITH and William WRIGHT, Nov 23, 1805.
Exrs: Brother in law Samuel LEVIS and kinsman Samuel GARRETT.
Wits: Benjamin H. SMITH and Samuel ASH. #259.

PRICE, PETER, Borough of Chester.
Dec 10, 1805 - Dec 16, 1805.
Estate to children: Peter, Charles, Hannah and Charlotte. Hannah to remain with William ANDERSON till she is 18 years, he to be sole executor.
Exrs: William ANDERSON.
Wits: John L. HAM and Jonathan MORRIS. #260.

DAVIS, EDWARD, Radnor.
Oct 8, 1801 - Dec 25, 1805.
Sister Rebecca ELLIS, brother Samuel DAVIS, dec'd. and children (names not given), niece Rebecca REESE, Tacey ELLIS daughter of

Thomas ELLIS, dec'd., Edith DAVIS, widow of nephew Edward DAVIS, dec'd., Edward and Hannah children of same. Residue to Edward and Hannah DAVIS.
Exrs: David PHILLIPS and Lewis LEWIS.
Wits: John JONES, Alice JONES and Edward HUNTER. #261.

WALTER, NATHANIEL, Concord.
Feb 1, 1805 - Dec 28, 1805.
Wife Rachel, children: Nathaniel and Thomas, Sarah SALYARDS, Lydia CLOUD, Ann STARR, Mary, Elizabeth and Jesse WALTER, Nathaniel the plantation, subject to payment of annuities he to be executor.
Exrs: Nathaniel.
Wits: Thomas NEWLIN and John PALMER. #262.

DUNN, GEORGE, Radnor.
Feb 25, 1805 - Feb 25, 1805.
Wife Mary, children: Martha DUNN, Margaret SMITH, Robert and George.
Exrs: Son Robert and son in law Benjamin H. SMITH.
Wits: George WHITE and Abraham FREE. #263.

BARNARD, JAMES, Chester.
Feb 16, 1806 - Feb 25, 1806.
Wife* (name not given), children: James D. BARNARD, Elizabeth, Isaac and Thomas .
*Nov 19, 1807 Letters of administration to Susanna BARNARD.
Exrs: Thomas B. DICK and Jacob D. BARKER.
Wits: William BROWN and Jonathan PENNELL. #264.

MILLER, ROBERT, yeoman, Newtown.
March 6, 1806 - April 28, 1806.
Children: William, James, Martha and Mary.
Exrs: Son James MILLER and Hugh CALDWELL
Wits: Samuel BLACK and James LINDSAY. #265.

HOULSTON, MARTHA, widow of John, Edgmont.
Feb 8, 1806 - May 27, 1806.
Children: John, Benjamin, Joseph, George, Ann CALVERT, Mary SILL, Sarah McCARTY and Phebe Harden.
Exrs: Son in law William McCARTY.

Wits: Thomas BISHOP and Owen YARNALL. #266.

HUNTER, GEORGE, yeoman, Edgmont.
March 6, 1803 - July 21, 1806.
Nephew George HUNTER, cousin George IRWIN and Richard IRWIN sons of Nathaniel and Elizabeth 100 acres at south east and of the home estate lines of John BAKER and Abel GREEN. Housekeeper Hannah GRIFFITHS and heirs the John MULLIN house and lot also woodland adjoining the Forge Road on the north west side of same. Richard SCOTT son of John and Ann, of Willistown, rest of home plantation subject to payment of certain legacies. Charles BARRINGTON and heirs of Philadelphia, land in Edgmont called Hunting Hill formerly property of brother Jonathan HUNTER, dec'd., Executors to sell lands in Honey Brook Twp. Chester County tenanted by Nathaniel IRWIN and title to property known as the Bull's Head Tavern and two lots in Burrow of Chester also formerly brother Jonathan's, cousin Mary wife of Jesse SMEDLY, Elizabeth and Ann daughters of John and Ann SCOTT, Eli YARNALL in trust for Friends Middletown Meeting, Hunter SMEDLEY son of Jesse and Mary, cousin Martha wife of Charles BARRINGTON.
Exrs: Friends John HUNTER and Edward HUNTER of Newtown and Benjamin YARNALL of Willistown.
Wits: Cassell GRIFFITHS, Amos YARNALL and Lewellin GRIFFITHS. #267.

LEWIS, ANTHONY, Upper Darby.
June 21, 1799 - Aug 18, 1806.
Legacies to nieces Elizabeth MORRIS and Hannah LEWIS, Henry TRIMBLE and Lewis the younger, sons of Lewis the elder, Jacob WARNER, Isaac WARNER and Mary WEST children of sister Elizabeth WARNER and Rachel WARNER widow of nephew Anthony WARNER. To nephew Abram LEWIS the plantation in Upper Darby lines of Benjamin BONSALL, John BALL and Benjamin BRANNAN also one in Haverford lines of Lewis DAVIS, Elisha WORRALL, Darby Creek, William DAVIS and line of Upper Darby and Haverford.
Wits: William WEST and Levis MARIS. #268.

BARTON, JAMES.
July 17, 1806 - Sept 1, 1806.
Son Isaac and heirs the Thomas MORGAN tract subject to payment of legacies to children: Jane, Ziba, Adam, son in law Peter LONGACRE.

To daughter Sarah LONGACRE and heirs 6 1/4 acres part of Thomas
COBURN tract. Daughter Elizabeth wife of Robert SNEATH and her
heirs 20 acres of Thomas COBOURN tract, lines of John POWELL and
Caleb COBOURN.
Exrs: Sons Abner BARTON and Eden BARTON.
Wits: Nich FAIRLAMB and John POWELL. #269.

WARNER, JACOB.
Sept 16, 1797 - Sept 5, 1806.
Wife Mary executor and sole legatee.
Exrs: Wife Mary.
Wits: John DOUGHERTY and Henry BARTELSON. #270.

EVANS, DAVID, Radnor.
Sept 12, 1806 - Oct 4, 1806.
Legacies to children Mary and Hannah. Two plantations in Radnor to
three sons John, David and Cadwalader on arrival of twenty one,
division be made by Joseph HOSKINS, John SITER and John
ELLIOTT.
Exrs: Joseph HASKINS and John ELLIOT.
Wits: Robert MATHER, William McCLURE and James CROWLEY.
#271.

CHEYNEY, JOHN, Thornbury.
Sept 20, 1805 - Oct 13, 1806.
To nephew William son of brother Thomas half of land in Thornbury
purchased of Mary CHEYNEY, land bounded by land of Mary
CHEYNEY, William YARNALL, Thomas HALL, land, lines of M.
CHEYNEY, J. MARSHALL, T. CHEYNEY and late Joseph CHEYNEY
also woodland along William YARNALL's north west line and Street
Road, nephew Curtis woodland to extend to YARNALL'S line, nephew
Waldron CHEYNEY reminder of land, sister Mary wife of Richard
RILEY, Betsy wife of nephew William, nephews William, Samuel,
Curtis and Jesse, niece Mary JOHNSON wife of Abraham, Persifor
MacCULLUM, children of brother Thomas: Ann, Richard, Mary, John,
Alice and Betsy and of his dec'd. daughter Lucy HICKMAN and his
grandchildren the children of his son Thomas. To children of brother
Joseph, dec'd: Samuel, Jesse, Abel, Esther, Mary, Ann, Jane, Elizabeth,
Hannah and Phebe; children of sister Mary RILEY: John and Margaret
CONRO, Curtis to be guardian for Abel.
Exrs: Nephews William and Curtis CHEYNEY.

Wits: Caleb JAMES, Stephen MARSHALL and Emmor VERNON. #272.

MORRIS, GEORGE, Radnor.
Nov 5, 1806 - Dec 11, 1806.
To wife Sarah all estate unless without issue, in that case to brother John MORRIS.
Exrs: Sd. wife and brother in law Isaac YARNALL.
Wits: Henry LEWIS, Nathan GIBSON, William SMITH and Michael SILL, Jr. #273.

WILLIAMSON, ABRAHAM, Thornbury.
April 19, 1799 - Feb 16, 1807.
Wife Esther and heirs to have home plantation purchased by Jesse JAMES and self, of Jacob VERNON and Sarah his wife, James and wife Elizabeth being paid off, also woodland in Goshen, Chester County, lot of Aaron JAMES. Legacies to father William WILLIAMSON, Sarah, Passmore, Phebe, William, Thomas and Cheyny all father's children, uncle Thomas WILLIAMSON.
Exrs: Wife.
Wits: Thomas HICKMAN, Sr., John HICKMAN and Thomas HICKMAN, Jr. #274.

THATCHER, WILLIAM, yeoman, Thornbury.
Feb 27, 1804 - Feb 25, 1807.
Wife Sarah in care of son William who inherits plantation in Thornbury and Concord townships. Other children: Joseph, Elizabeth, Hannah, Sarah, Phebe. Grandson William GREEN; Sarah, William and Robert children of son Richard dec'd.
Exrs: Sd. wife and son William.
Wits: Lydia GARRETT, Nathan SMITH and Isaac G. GILPIN. #275.

EVANS, ROBERT, Edgmont.
Nov 20, 1804 - March 19, 1807.
Bequests to nephew Joseph EVANS and his sister Mary, also to nephew Paul PENNINGTON. Cousins: Catherine widow of Evan EVANS of Newtown, John EVANS of East town, Evan ROBERTS, Jacob ROBERTS. Friends Joseph MEREDITH of Edgmont and John MEREDITH of Plymouth, John GARRETT of Willistown. In trust to Jacob MINSHALL for Middletown Meeting and to John EVANS for N. Wales Meeting.

Exrs: John MEREDITH of Plymouth, John GARRETT of Willistown and Edward EVANS of Newtown.
Wits: Isaac YARNALL, Richard OTTEY and Benjamin YARNALL. #276.

FENTHAM, PRISCILLA, Darby.
Dec 15, 1803 - March 27, 1807.
Granddaughter Priscilla and Sarah FENTHAM, residue to daughter Ann FEW and Mary PRICE.
Exrs: Sd. Mary PRICE.
Wits: Philip PRICE, Joseph PENNALL and Jonathan TYSON. #277.

ORMSBY, GEORGE, Darby.
April 1, 1807 - May 14, 1807.
Wife Sarah to bring up small children, son John to have estate at her death paying legacies to three sisters (names not given). Two other boys (names not given).
Exrs: Sd. wife and John.
Wits: John ATTMORE and John MARSHALL. #278.

CHAMBERLAIN, ANN, Birmingham.
July 24, 1805 - June 1, 1807.
Sons John and William and their heirs, plantation subject to payment of legacies, children: Joseph, Robert, James, Hannah HICKMAN and Mary GREEN, friends Isaac G. GILPIN, Gideon GILPIN, Joseph BENNETT and William THATCHER, Jr. to divide land.
Exrs: Sons John and William.
Wits: William THATCHER, John BEALE, Jr. and Isaac G. GILPIN.
Codicil July 25, 1805.
Wits: Same. #279.

TALBOT, JOSEPH, yeoman, Upper Chichester.
June 16, 1807 - Aug 3, 1807.
Wife Hannah, son John part of plantation, mentions road from Bethel to Chester, lines of Joseph ASKEW, Jacob RICHARDS, Sawmill Dam etc. Son Joseph rest of plantation estate partly in Aston, lines of Jacob RICHARDS, John TAYLOR, Jonathan DUTTON subject to certain claims etc. Other children Ruth and Rachel.
Exrs: Son Joseph.
Wits: George MARTIN and Jonathan DUTTON. #280.

PRITCHET, ELIZABETH, Edgmont. Signed Elizabeth PRICHETT.
March 9, 1807 - Sept 18, 1807.
Legacy to sister Phebe HAMMEL, residue to her daughter Sarah BISHOP.
Exrs: Joseph BISHOP.
Wits: James HOWARD, John RUSSELL and Jonathan HOWARD.
#281.

YARNALL, WILLIAM, Edgment.
Aug 25, 1807 - Sept 18, 1807.
Wife Mary, son George, part of plantation, line of Phebe HAMMILS at Ridley Creek to John YARNALL'S line up the courses of the creek to beginning, son Enoch, part on line between Middletown and Edgment to lane etc. to John YARNALL'S line etc., son Ezekiel residue of plantation, son William all book accounts etc.
Exrs: Sons Ezekiel, George and Enoch.
Wits: Jacob MINSHALL, Ambrose SMEDLEY and Hannah McCLESTER. #282.

BLACK, ANN, Edgment.
Dec 9, 1797 - Sept 25, 1807.
Legacies to three children: Margaret BISHOP, Mary McMIN and Samuel BLACK. Inventory gives "late of Marple".
Exrs: Abraham HOOPES, Elizabeth HOOPES and Priscilla HOOPES.
#283.

HAYWORTH, GEORGE, Haverford.
Sept 9, 1807 - Oct 12, 1807.
Wife Patience, children: John, Rebeccah, Deborah and Mary. Plantation, son John and sd. wife for life or widowhood, then equal shares to second daughter.
Exrs: Son John and John GRACY.
Wits: Mordecai LAWRENCE, Henry LAWRENCE and Amos LUKENS.
#284.

KIRK, SAMUEL, Upper Darby.
Dec 29, 1800 - Oct 28, 1807.
Legacies to sons Joseph and Thomas, grandson William KIRK (minor) son of Joseph, 5 acres lines of Thomas GARRETT and Samuel LEVIS, grandson John KIRK (minor) son of Thomas 5 acres adjoining William's and Samuel LEVIS'S, granddaughter Elizabeth (minor) child of

Thomas 5 acres next to John's. Joseph's daughters Martha, Lydia, Elizabeth and Mary Ann legacies. Son William's, dec'd., child Hannah all residue of estate.
Exrs: John PEARSON of Darby.
Wits: Bevan PEARSON and Joseph HIBBERD. #285.

MEREDITH, MARY, Edgmont.
March 20, 1805 - Nov 11, 1807.
Legacies to children John, Sarah, Pennell and Joseph, granddaughters Mary FAIRLAMB, Ellinor WELLS, Sarah DILWORTH and all residue to Joseph.
Exrs: Joseph and John.
Wits: Samuel LEWIS, Abraham LEWIS and Benjamin YARNALL. #286.

MOORE, NATHAN, yeoman, Radnor.
March 1, 1800 - Nov 16, 1807.
Wife Elizabeth, seven children: Jesse, William, Jacob, Nathan, Mary, Ely and Samson.
Exrs: Sd. wife and son in law George BONSALL.
Wits: Evan LEWIS and Abner LEWIS. #287.

IRETON, ANTHONY, cordwainer, Ridley.
Oct 28, 1807 - Nov 23, 1807.
To wife Mary, she and her father David TREINOR to be executors.
Exrs: Wife Mary and David TREINOR.
Wits: J. L. PEARSON, Joseph HIBBERD and David TRENOR. #288.

FLOWERS, JOHN, Marcus Hook.
Nov 2, 1803 - Nov 23, 1807.
Mother Sarah MARSHALL property fronting the Delaware River extending to Discord Lane, N. by David MARSHALL and S. by Isaac LAWRENCE &c. to sister Hannah HANNON.
Exrs: Mathias KERLIN, Esq.
Wits: Thomas B. DICK, James BURNS, Jr. #289.

DAY, JAMES, Middletown.
Aug 17, 1804 - Dec 7, 1807.
To children: John, Samuel and Margaret RICHARDS wife of Isaiah RICHARDS, plantation next to Thomas TRIMBLE.
Exrs: Son James.

Wits: Frederick FAIRLAMB and Nicholas FAIRLAMB. #290.

BATES, RICHARD, Concord.
Dec 12, 1807 - Jan 8, 1808.
Bequests to Lydia BARRETT, Charles BARRETT and Martha HIGHFIELD.
Exrs: William HANNUM and John LARKIN.
Wits: Joseph TRIMBLE and Thomas MARSHALL. #291.

BONSALL, BENJAMIN, Upper Darby.
Jan 8, 1806 - Jan 22, 1808.
Son Benjamin the home plantation subject to care of his sister Esther, also a lot in Kingsessing lines of James BONSALL, daughter Esther to have third part of Messuage in Darby held by Hezekiah HIBBERD and self.
Exrs: Sd. son Benjamin.
Wits: Thomas GARRETT, Joseph HIBBERD and Jonathan OWEN. #292.

JONES, JAMES, Newtown.
Oct 3, 1804 - Feb 20, 1808.
Estate to wife Jennis for life. To Joseph LEWIS son of sister Susanna the plantation on death of wife, he to pay legacy to his mother or her children William, Jenkin and Jane, also his brother's son James Jones LEWIS (minor), Jennis MOORE daughter of Jonathan MOORE, John MOORE (minor) son of Samuel MOORE.
Exrs: Joseph LEWIS.
Wits: Thomas THOMAS and Israel YARNALL. #293.

LEWIS, EVAN, Radnor.
Feb 15, 1806 - March 8, 1808.
Wife Jane use of plantation &c. during life. Sons Enoch, Elijah and Evan the part of plantation inherited from father, son Abner remainder of plantation subject to certain payments, to son Thomas tract in Berks County bought of Edward BONSALL, son Evan capital stock in company for erecting a permanent bridge across Schuylkill at or near Philadelphia. Other children Sarah, weak minded and Jane, niece Tacy DAVIS.
Exrs: Sons Enoch and Elijah.
Wits: Simeon MATLACK, Benjamin MAULE and Simon MEREDITH. #294.

BROWN, GEORGE, black man, Nether Providence.
March 4, 1808 - March 24, 1808.
Executors Amor WILLIAMSON and Joseph THATCHER to sell property and invest proceeds for wife and children (no names).
Exrs: Amor WILLIAMSON and Joseph THATCHER.
Wits: Jacob EDWARDS and Joseph McMINN. #295.

SMITH, HANNAH, Derby.
Dec 10, 1807 - March 25, 1808.
Legacies to children: Samuel and wife Rebecca, Davis, Sarah URIAN and husband Samuel*, Eliza LYKIN and Nathaniel and Lydia SMITH, daughter of same.
*Administration account gives Samuel URIAN.
Exrs: Son and son in law Samuel URIAN.
Wits: Matthew ASH and John HIBBERD. #296.

WOOLLAS, NICHOLAS, Edgmont.
May 11, 1808 - June 3, 1808.
Wife Sarah, children: Sarah MENDENHALL, Mary MATSON, Rachel MENDENHALL, Phebe and William HART and John (minor). To Phebe north east of Enkurius BEATY tract in Catawissa Twp, Northumberland County. To son John the homestead, should he die before majority then to four daughters.
Exrs: Wife and son in law Aaron MENDENHALL.
Wits: Edward BAKER, Anthony BAKER and Benjamin YARNALL. #297.

NEIDE, SARAH, Borough of Chester.
Feb 29, 1808 - June 10, 1808.
Children: Joseph, Amelia and Orpah NEIDE. Wearing apparel of Joseph NEIDE dec'd., $14.00, wearing apparel of Sarah NEIDE dec'd., $20.00.
Exrs: Edon BARTON and Jonas SHARPLESS.
Wits: Joseph BISHOP, John CALDWELL and Joseph PYLE. #298.

CLOUD, SARAH, Concord.
Oct 15, 1805 - Aug 15, 1808.
Son Joshua and wife Ann life estate in messuage and lot of land, also interest in land in occupancy of William ALLISON and lease of 999 years with provision for Joshua's heirs. Other sons Joseph and James. Four children of Joshua: Sarah, Martha, Mary and ___ (blank).

Exrs: Stephen MENDENAHLL.
Wits: James GIBBONS and William GIBBONS. #299.

BROWN, WILLIAM, Ridley.
Aug 3, 1808 - Sept 17, 1808.
Wife Mary and children: William, George Washington, Archibald, dec'd., Jane, dec'd., and Nancy WRIGLEY. Son William all lands in Luzerne County, other legacies [called Captain in administration account. Money to Mary, George and John BABE, also Maria BROWN, granddaughter, William PENNOCK guardian of William BROWN, John BABE, Kitty BABE and George BABE.]
Exrs: Thomas B. DICK and Clement HUMPHREYS, lumber inspector of Philadelphia.
Wits: Maria BURD and Samuel ANDERSON. #300.

NEWLIN, ANN, Concord.
Sept 2, 1807 - Sept 22, 1808.
Estate to six children: Richard, Elizabeth THORPE wife of Thomas, Jane RANDEL wife of Abraham, Joseph, Rachel ARMETT wife of Isaac and John.
Exrs: Son John and friend Thomas NEWLIN of Concord.
Wits: William TRIMBLE, Mary TRIMBLE.
Thomas NEWLIN renounced. #301.

MOORE, THOMAS, Newtown.
Oct 9, 1808 - Nov 7, 1808.
Wife Mary and children: Thomas, Jonas, Mordecai, Mary LEWIS, Elisha, James, Elizabeth REECE and Jennis, grandchildren: Isaac LEWIS, Tabitha MATLACK and Mifflin (probably son of Mordecai). In case of wife's death or marriage, home plantation to Thomas and Jonas. Land bought of brother Samuel to sons James, Thomas and Jonas.
Exrs: Sons Mordecai and Elisha.
Wits: John BROOKE and William KENNEY. #302.

ELLIOT, ANN, Nether Providence.
Dec 8, 1807 - Nov 18, 1808.
Sons Hugh Linn and William Elliot, daughters Sarah DOYLE, wife of William and Mary ELLIOTT.
Exrs: William DOYLE, Mary ELLIOT and Luke KERSON.
Wits: James HINKSON and William WORRALL.

William DOYLE renounced Nov 19, 1808 and Luke CASSIN was appointed. #303.

HAMMEL, PHEBE, Edgment.
Sept 27, 1807 - Dec 16, 1808.
Tract of land bought of Abraham HOOPS, twp. of Edgment to grandson George BISHOP, daughter Sarah BISHOP and grandchildren: William, George, Sarah, Jesse, Phebe, Joseph and Mary. Legacy from Elizabeth PRITCHET estate $800.
Exrs: William and George.
Wits: Thomas BISHOP and Jonathan HOWARD. #304.

WEST, WILLIAM, farmer, Upper Darby.
May 7, 1808 - Jan 4, 1809.
Wife Hannah, children: Samuel and daughter Mary, William, Rebecca, Hannah PUSEY, Hannah, widow of son Passmore and Samuel son of same, John, James, Benjamin and Sarah. Land in Loudon County, Va. to son John, to James for life house and lot east side of Del. Front St. between Mulberry and Sassafras then to Mary daughter of Samuel. Benjamin rest of houses in same square. Residue to wife and 5 children excepting John and James.
Wits: Israel ELLIOTT, Mary ELLIOTT and Daniel FLETCHER.
Exrs: Wife, Sarah, William and Samuel.
Wits: Jno. THOMSON, Joseph LEVIS and P. THOMSON.
Codicil of May 30, 1808 revokes legacy to Samuel son of Passmore and gives it to Sally Ann, daughter of same. #305.

DICKS, ROGER, Nether Providence.
Aug 3, 1803 - Jan 11, 1809.
Wife Rebecca, cousin Daniel Humphrey for life, 4 acres where Peter WORRALL lately lived. To nephew Eli Dicks PEIRCE and Sarah PEIRCE plantation subject to claims of wife.
Exrs: Wife and brother in law John PEIRCE.
Wits: Abram SHARPLESS and Cheyney JEFFERIS. #306.

TYSON, MARY L., widow, Darby.
Dec 9, 1804 - Jan 5, 1809.
To daughter Lowry HILL (minor) should she die under lawful age then in trust to Amos SHARPLESS for Darby monthly meeting and to mother, brothers and sisters.

Exrs: And guardians, Nathan SELLERS of Philadelphia and John HUNT of Darby. Executors refused to act, William HUMPHREYS appointed by court Feb 2, 1808.
Wits: Ann TOWNSEND and Jno. Elliott CRESSON. #307.

BARR, JOANNA, Darby.
March 16, 1808 - April 5, 1809.
Daughters Mary, Ann and Tacy.
Exrs: Joseph WALN and Joseph SHALLCROSS.
April 5, 1809 Joseph WALN renounced.
Wits: Nathaniel SMITH, John ATTMORE and George SMITH. #308.

MARIS, ANN, widow, Marple.
April 23, 1809 - April 29, 1809.
Children: Joseph, John, Tacey HARRISON, Ann MACE, Hester McGUIRE, Rebecca FRAME and William. Granddaughter Ann FISS and friend Elenor FRAME.
Exrs: Son William.
Wits: Lewis MORRIS, John FRAME and Nathan GIBSON. #309.

PYLE, CALEB, Thornbury.
Nov 13, 1804 - June 1, 1809.
Sole legatee wife Mary.
Exrs: Wife Mary.
Wits: Proved on testimony of Joseph BRINTON, Esq., Levi PYLE and John JAMES. #310.

MALIN, WILLIAM, Providence.
Dec 8, 1888* - June 3, 1809.
Brothers and sisters: Joel, Abner, Samuel, Hannah MARTIN wife of Joseph MARTIN and George, Hannah daughter of Joel.
*50 given in will.
Exrs: Brother Samuel MALIN.
Wits: James SMEDLEY and Abner MALIN. #311.

RHOADS, JOSEPH, Marple.
Aug 17, 1801 - June 16, 1809.
To wife Mary, half plantation on east side of Marple Street where I dwell except the Tan Yard and building also house and lot in Church Alley, Philadelphia and then to seven children: James, George, Joseph,

Elizabeth, Rebeckah, Phebe and William residue to be divided each daughter two thirds as much as each son.
codicil Jan 17, 1805.
Wife renounced.
Exrs: Sd. wife, brother Owen and brother in law Joseph DAVIS.
Wits: George G. ASHBRIDGE and William WETHERILL. #312.

PASSMORE, ABIGAIL, Edgmont.
Nov 23, 1808 - June 24, 1809.
Brother Richard and 4 daughters: Mary PASSMORE, Abigail, ____, ____, sister Phebe WILLIAMS dec'd., and two daughters Phebe and Sarah, nephew Abijah PASSMORE, Abigail YARNALL daughter of George YARNALL, of Middletown, Amy GRIFFITHS daughter of Evan of Goshen, Chester County, niece Mary PASSMORE. Residue to executors brother Richard and nephew Everet PASSMORE.
Exrs: Brother Richard and nephew Everet PASSMORE.
Wits: Henry BOWMAN and Enoch YARNALL. #313.

HATTEN, SARAH, Concord.
April 29, 1800 - Aug 11, 1809.
Children: Thomas, Joseph, Peter, Rachel WILSON, Hannah ASKEW and Elizabeth WILSON.
Exrs: David MERCER.
Wits: George EAVENSON, John Polis SEAL and Robert SHIPPEN. #314.

EFFINGER, AGNES, widow of Henry EFFINGER, Marple.
Oct 15, 1805 - ____.
Children: Malachi EFFINGER and Agnes HOPPERSETT, grandchildren Jacob EFFINGER and Henry EFINGER, Sarah, Agnes, Margaret and Rebecca daughters of son Henry EFFINGER. Residue in three shares to Malachi, Agnes and children of Henry.
Codicil same date, cares for Rachel, widow of Henry.
Exrs: Edward HUNTER, of Newtown and David PRATT of Marple.
Wits: James MANLEY, William HILL and Joseph RHOADS. #315.

SMITH, REBECAH, relict of William SMITH, Tinicum.
Dec 11, 1807 - Nov 13, 1809.
Son Thomas, daughter Rebecah BRITTON and children, other relations mentioned, grandson William KING (minor), granddaughter Rebecah SMITH, niece Rebecah wife of Israel HELMN, of Darby.

Exrs: Son Thomas.
Wits: Sarah CAZZEL and Nathanl. NEWLIN. #316.

PRESTON, ORPAH R., Newtown.
Aug 25, 1809 - Nov 28, 1809.
To aunt Elizabeth DOWNING all plantation now occupied by John GOODWIN. Legacies to aunts Sarah GRUB and Hannah CALEY. To Townsend THOMAS in trust for Newtown Preparative Meeting.
Exrs: Uncle Richard DOWNING.
Wits: Jonas PRESTON, William GRAHAM and Abigail EVANS. #317.

KERLIN, JOHN, Chester.
May 3, 1807 - Dec 11, 1809.
Mother Catharine KERLIN, sisters Margaret BURNS and Sarah PIPER, brothers William and Abraham, brother George's widow Margaret, nephews William KERLIN, Mathais BURNS, George Henry KERLIN, John and William ODENHEIMER, also a Mary BRADFORD. Land in Borough of Chester adjoining lines of Jonas EYRE, Chester Creek and Concord Road also house and lot in Borough willed by father.
Exrs: Brother William and Jonathan PENNELL.
Wits: Joseph ENGLE and Mary ENGLE. #318.

MENDENHALL, STEPHEN, in the fifty ninth year of my age, Concord.
Oct 23, 1809 - Dec 21, 1809.
Children: James, Ann wife of John MEREDITH, Phebe, Rebecca wife of Samuel TRIMBLE and Robert. Land adjoining son James and John MEREDITH and north by PENNEL'S line, east and south by William MENDENHALL to be sold and shared equally.
Exrs: Son Robert and neighbor Thomas NEWLIN.
Wits: William MENDENHALL and Robert PENNELL. #319.

WITTY, MARY, Borough of Chester.
Nov 15, 1809 - Jan 13, 1810.
Son James, daughter in law Betsey, granddaughters Elizabeth Ewin BIOREN and her daughter Mary, Sarah, Hannah, Polly, dec'd., and Mary - mentions friend Mary LEONARD. Legacies to all, residue to son James he and John BIOREN to be executors.
Exrs: Son James and John BIOREN.
Wits: W. M. GRAHAM and ROBINSON.

Thomas ROBINSON and James WITTY renounced. #320.

RETTEW, JOHN, Aston.
Jan 1, 1810 - March 10, 1810.
John to have home plantation, daughter Eleanor 1/3 of plantation occupied by brother Aaron RETTEW in Middletown, grandson James, Beau Clark HEATH (minor) to have legacy, all other estate to son John.
Exrs: Wife Esther, son John and John LUNGREN.
Wits: David LEWIS, James LINDSAY and William LUNGREN. #321.

SEAL, MARY, Chester.
March 8, 1810 - March 13, 1810.
My niece Sarah the wife of Abner BARTON all my estate.
Exrs: Abner BARTON.
Wits: Eden BARTON and Samuel SLAWTER. #322.

SMITH, WILLIAM, Concord.
June 4, 1805 - March 22, 1810.
Son James SMITH all plantation lying east side of Wilmington Road and other "peese" of the west side of the said Rode beginning at the corner of Nathaniel NEWLIN land in said Rode thence along said Rode to a stone which Thomas and James SMITH put in for a corner for them etc. NEWLIN line etc, Thomas the remainder in Concord, also a piece in Birminham which he now lives on. Daughters Susanah TAYLOR and Hannah SMITH.
Exrs: Sons Thomas and James.
Wits: Joseph MORRISON and John PEIRCE. #323.

MALIN, PHEBE, Upper Providence.
March 31, 1804 - March 31, 1810.
Interest of estate to daughter Mary MALIN, at her decease, to daughter Susanna and son Gideon, he to be executor.
Exrs: Son Gideon.
Wits: James SMEDLEY, Benedict MALIN and Tacey MALIN.
[Note: Daughter Mary lived till 1821.] #324.

WELCH, THOMAS, Newtown.
April 11, 1810 - April 17, 1810.
Revokes Letter of Attorney given Samuel CALEY. Legacies to nurse Martha McCONNELL, wife of Joseph, Thomas Welch MARTIN

(minor) and Commissioners of Delaware County for a stone bridge
across Derby Creek at William HAYMAN'S land. Niece Mary wife of
William VANDERBECK of New Jersey heir to estate.
Exrs: Friends Mordecai DAVIS and Abner MOORE.
Wits: Rees THOMAS and James MOORE. #325.

RING, NATHANIEL, Birmingham.
March 21, 1810 - April 24, 1810.
Wife (no name given), seven children: William, James, Joseph,
Chambles, Ann and Mary to have legacies. Son Caleb to have
plantation subject to certain payments, he to be sole executor.
Exrs: Son Caleb.
Wits: Gideon GILPIN and Isaac G. GILPIN. #326.

LYONS, DAVID, Haverford.
Oct 17, 1809 - May 26, 1810.
Wife Elizabeth plantation for life, at her decease to son David, he to
pay legacies to brothers and sisters: William, James, each of sisters.
Exrs: Sd. wife and David.
Wits: Henry FORREST and William JOHNSON. #327.

MARIS, WILLIAM, Marple.
Aug 22, 1809 - June 1, 1810.
Brother Joseph and his sons Jonathan and William. Names mother's
will and leaves property to brothers and sisters. Niece Ann FISS,
sisters Rebecca FRAME and Tacey HARRISON, nephew William
(minor) the home tract with legacy to niece Ann HARRISON.
Exrs: Brother Joseph and neighbor Benjamin LOBB.
Wits: Nathan GIBSON, Nathan MATLACK and Reuben LEWIS. #328.

ATKINSON, ELIZABETH, Providence.
April 7, 1810 - June 8, 1810.
Estate to nieces Jannet and Sarah SHAW.
Exrs: Friend Daniel SHARPLESS and cousin John STAPLER.
Wits: Ellis ROBERTS and John SHARPLESS. #329.

FREE, JOHN, Haverford.
Aug 17, 1810 - Sept 6, 1810.
Mother in law Hannah ELLIS widow of Jesse ELLIS, sister Sarah
McKEE and brothers Abraham, Samuel and David, nephew James C.
CROMWELL son of sister Ann.

Exrs: Abraham and Samuel and friend Samuel DAVIS.
Wits: Mordecai LAWRENCE and Amos LUKENS.
Abraham FREE renounced. #330.

WILLIAMSON, ABIGAIL, Aston.
May 15, 1805 - Sept 19, 1810.
Children Gidion and his children: James and Abigail HOOPS, George, Emor and his children Joshua, Thomas and Abigail, Elizabeth wife of Enos HOOPS and her son James.
Joseph PENNELL renounced.
Exrs: Joseph PENNELL and son Emor.
Wits: James MARSHALL, Joseph PENNELL and Sarah PENNELL. #331.

MAULE, DANIEL, Radnor.
Aug 7, 1810 - Oct 13, 1810.
Sister in law Margaret GRAHAM, mother in law Rachel ATMORE, five minor children: Caleb, Jonathan, Margaret, Lydia and Elizabeth. Older children Joshua, Israel and Lillah MORGAN.
Exrs: Sons Joshua and Israel and friend Benjamin DAVIS.
Wits: Benjamin MAULE and Abner LEWIS.
Admin. Account April 1, 1811. Property sold to Richard KIMBER and Samuel STARKES and brothers. #332.

ASHFORD, WILLIAM, Chester.
Jan 14, 1810 - Oct 29, 1810.
Wife ____ and daughter Susan ARMSTRONG and heirs.
Exrs: John VAUGHAN, merchant of Philadelphia and John TAYLOR of Delaware County.
Wits: Samuel WEST and Thomas COBOURN. #333.

FAWKES, SARAH, Newtown.
June 11, 1810 - Nov 24, 1810.
Children: Samuel, Nathaniel, John, Richard, Rebecca, Mary, Joseph and Ann FAWKES.
Exrs: John HUNTER the elder and Richard HOOD.
Wits: Joseph FAWKES, Isaiah FAWKES and Nathan GIBSON. #334.

WORRAL, TECY, Newtown.
Aug 14, 1810 - Nov 27, 1810.

Sons Curtis and Isaiah, niece Seeneth DARBY, sister Ann WORRALL.
Signed by mark Teacy X WORRELL. Executors account gives Tacy
WORRALL.
Exrs: Edward HUNTER.
Wits: Richard FAWKES and Joseph HOOD. #335.

WOOD, JAMES, Newtown.
Dec 27, 1806 - Dec 14, 1810.
Lot by WORRALL lane adjoining line of Jacob EDWARDS in
Providence Twp. now occupied by son James to grandson James
WOOD, hatter, chargeable with care of his father and mother. Three
daughters Mary PARSONS, Sarah GILLINGHAM and Rebeckah
WATERMAN, grandson William WOOD son of William dec'd.,
granddaughter Sarah COATES. Final distribution mentions 4 sons
Mathew, John, Aaron and Septimus.
Exrs: Sons Mathew and John.
Wits: Townsend THOMAS, Beulah E. THOMAS and Jacob WOOD. #336.

WORRALL, ELEANOR, Ridlay.
Aug 29, 1810 - Dec 25, 1810.
Daughters Martha, Sarah YARNALL, Unis MADDOCK, Loas DYLE,
Eleanor JAMES and Eliza STARR, sons Jonathan and Samuel.
Grandchildren Joseph James and Eleanor STARR, son in law Joseph
STARR to be executor.
Exrs: Joseph STARR.
Wits: Susanah McILVAIN and William WORRALL. #337.

MARTIN, ABRAHAM, Aston.
Dec 17, 1808 - Feb 2, 1811.
*Wife (name not given), children: Benjamin, Hannah Palmer, Mary
BRINTON wife of Joseph, Elizabeth TURNER, Phebe wife of John
HUEY, grandson Thomas BOOTH, son Benjamin to have part of home
plantation bounded by Aston Road. Wilcox's Lane, lines of Nathaniel
WALTER, Stephen HALL, John PALMER, a branch of Chester Creek
and William PETERS.
*Ad. account names Susan MARTIN.
Exrs: Sd. son Benjamin.
Wits: Joseph TRIMBLE, Thomas PENNELL and Charles PENNELL.
#338.

WATSON, MARGARET, Thornbury.

WATSON, MARGARET, Thornbury.
Feb 17, 1804 - Feb 16, 1811.
Son William YARNALL wife Sarah, Mary BAKER husband Joseph, grandchildren: Margaret HALL, Margaret YARNALL, William HALL, Norris HALL, Thomas HALL, John HALL and Robert HALL.
Exrs: William YARNALL and Joseph BAKER.
Wits: Joseph CHEYNEY and Curtis CHEYNEY. #339.

WORRALL, OWEN, Upper Providence.
Jan 27, 1811 - Feb 26, 1811.
Nephew Joseph WORRALL property east of the road leading from Providence Road to Jones Mill subject to life estate of Catharine CLEMMONS Testator's house keeper. Nephew David WORRALL son of Elisha all property situate on west side of the same road, also land and meadow in Marple. Catharine CLEMMONS to have and keep bound boy Thomas WORRALL otherwise Thomas BENNETT. All other estate to children of brother Elisha WORRALL.
Exrs: Elisha WORRALL and his son David.
Wits: George MILLER and George MALINE. #340.

DICK, THOMAS B., attorney at law, Borough of Chester.
April 6, 1810 - May 1, 1811.
Grandfather James BRINTON, wife Phebe DICK, Grandfather BRINTON to provide for children and step children.
Exrs: Sd. wife.
Wits: Jonas SHARPLESS and Samuel LYTLE. #341.

BROOKE, DAVID, yeoman, Radnor.
July 22, 1808 - June 17, 1811.
Son James plantation which he now occupies subject to annuity etc., to daughter Sarah OGLEBE [also Ogleby], daughter Ruth WILLIS and her children, other children Nathan BROOKE and Margaret MANLOVE. Wife Rachel to have money now in possession of her brother Laurence EGBERT, granddaughter Jane WILLS. House & lot in Germantown to be sold.
Appraisement May 16, 1811, - mentions William OGLEBY'S bond.
Exrs: Samuel MAULSBY of Whitemarsh, Montgomery County.
Wits: George PEIRCE, Samuel MAULSBY and Isaac PEIRCE. #342.

REECE, MARY, Newtown.
May 15, 1811 - July 22, 1811.

Elizabeth wife of Richard DOWNING, cousins Edward GEORGE, Elizabeth PEARSON, Rebecca GEORGE widow of Amos GEORGE, four daughters of cousin John LEWIS of Springfield and Edward GEORGE, Franklin, William and Mordecai sons of same, Mordecai Reece LEWIS son of Phineas LEWIS, Mordecai LEWIS son of Lewis LEWIS dec'd., Enos REECE'S son William, Mary MENDENHALL widow of Robert, Abigail EVANS, Jehu GARRETT in trust for Newtown Meeting. Enos REECE house and lot West Chester Road joining George HUNTER and Jane NEWLIN, cousin John LEWIS of Springfield part of farm in Edgemont now occupied by William THOMAS lines of Abram FARR, George ENTREKIN and Crum Creek. Remainder to John son of same. Plantation in Newtown to son in law Jonas PRESTON lines of John HUNTER, Enos WILLIAMSON, Didimus LEWIS and Crum Creek now occupied by Matthew WOOD, John EVANS and others.
Exrs: Edward HUNTER, Esq. and Joseph PRESTON.
Wits: William GRAHAM and Joseph DAVIS. #343.

MORRIS, SUSANNAH, Kingsessing Twp. Philadelphia.
___ - Aug 3, 1811.
Nuncupative will pronounced July 12, 1811.
Died suddenly at house of Swan BOONE of Ridley while on a visit.
Names sisters Mary and Catharine SWAN, BOONE'S wife Mary - mentions brothers, not named.
Notice of hearing served on David, Jno. and Samuel MORRIS, Catharin AMBER and Mary BOONE (sister of Susannah MORRIS).
Wits: William BOON, Mary HAND and Elen BOON. #344.

PEARSON, SUSANNA, Ridley.
July 22, 1811 - Aug 6, 1811.
Sisters Martha HALL and Elizabeth HUNTER. Cousin Jane LEWIS, daughter of sister Elizabeth.
Exrs: Cousin John PEARSON.
Wits: Ann SMITH and Anna B. GARRETT. #345.

MENDENHALL, PHILIP.
April 22, 1811 - Sept 16, 1811.
Daughters Phebe wife of George CHALFONT and Mary wife of Jacob PYLE and son Thomas MENDENHALL, grandchildren Edward and Philip MENDENHALL and Thomas, Philip and Robert CHALFONT.
Sister in law Margaret MENDENHALL.

Exrs: Son Thomas MENDENHALL and Joseph PENNELL of Ashton.
Wits: Thomas PEIRCE, Joseph PENNELL and Allice YARNALL. #346.

PRICE, PHILIP, Darby.
Feb 11, 1807 - Sept 30, 1811.
Son in law Edward GARRIGUES and his present wife Margaret, meadow ground in Kingsess, 9 1/2 acres purchased of executors of Danniel RICHARDS. Other children: Sarah GARRETT, children Charles and Margaret, Philip PRICE and children Isaac, Hannah and William, Benjamin PRICE and his present wife Ruth, Isaac PRICE children Ann and Henry (orphans), Rachel PRICE and Mary PRICE, daughter in law Mary PRICE, granddaughter Martha SHARPLESS and Elizabeth PRICE, friends Sammuel RICHARDS, Jr., silversmith, of Philadelphia, Isaiah KIRK of E. Nantmill - mentions Jonathan TYSON, George TERRALL and Sammuel PRICE, daughter in law Mary PRICE to have house and lots in Darby for herself and children. To grandchildren Ann and Henry PRICE house and lots in Darby bought of Jonathan TYSON, shop occupied by George SERRILL. Tract in Greenwood Twp. Cumberland County and two other houses on Lombard Street to be sold.
Exrs: Son Philip PRICE, sons in law Thomas GARRETT and Edward GARRIGUES.
Wits: John H. BUNTING, George SERRILL [Terrill?] and Solomon HUMPHREYS.
E. GARRIGUES renounced. #347.

ELLIS, BRIDGET, Radnor.
Feb 23, 1811 - Sept 30, 1811.
Mother Rebecca ELLIS profits of lands on Old Lancaster Rd., lines of Benjamin DAVIS and Jacob MAULE for life also privileges for brother Griffith ELLIS. On death of mother this property to go to David DAVIS son of Benjamin DAVIS, subject to occupancy by said brother and payment of £50 to Ralph DAVIS. Other legatees Margaret ELLIS, Hannah MORGAN, Sarah ELLIOT, Mary Ann and Harriot WINING, Frances and Benjamin DAVIS, Ruth Ann daughter of Samuel DAVIS, Rebecca HORTON daughter of Thomas HORTON, Ann CRAWFORD and Tacey daughters of Benjamin DAVIS, Lydia DAVIS. Residue to Lydia and Mary DAVIS.
Exrs: Benjamin and Lydia DAVIS.
Wits: Jno. ELLIOTT and James ELLIOTT. #348.

HUNTER, HANNAH, Eastown, Chester County.
March 3, 1808 - Oct 18, 1811.
Three children: Alice JONES, Edward HUNTER and William HUNTER, grandchildren Mary, Margaret, John, Thomas, Hannah and Elizabeth daughters of son Edward, Tamzin daughter of son William.
Exrs: Sd. son William.
Wits: Jesse REECE and Mordecai DAVIS. #349.

JONES, ALICE, Radnor.
Jan 7, 1806 - Oct 30, 1811.
Brothers Edward and William HUNTER plantation in Newtown as tenants in common forever. Rebecca PECHIN, Margaret HUNTER, William HUNTER, Alice, Hannah, Edward Jr. and Elizabeth children of Edward, Hannah MARIS, Mary, Alice HIBBERD, Sarah, Elizabeth, John, Thomas and Tamasin children of William, children of John BERRY of Baltimore, Maryland. Nathaniel MILES and Abel LEWIS nephews of late husband. Jacob GUYGER son of George GUYGER, Sarah YARNALL wife of Ezekiel, Tabitha DENNIS.
Codicil Nov 26, 1808 gives William's share to two sons John and Thomas, he being dec'd.
Wits: John BROOKE and Philip SHEAF.
Exrs: Sd two brothers.
Wits: Philip SHEAF, Deborah SHEAF and Benjamin H. SMITH. #350.

NEWLIN, THOMAS, Concord.
July 20, 1810 - Nov 16, 1811.
Grandchildren: Eliza, John, Martha and Thomas children of son Nicholas dec'd., lower grist mill now in possession of John - mentions lines of Joseph TRIMBLE, Concord Meeting Road, Thomas PENNELL and William TRIMBLE. To friends Moses PALMER, Thomas MARSHALL, tanner, and William TRIMBLE in trust, the upper mill property and lot adjoining, now occupied by William WALTER for sons Nathaniel and Thomas. Portion of plantation to son Benjamin and daughter Sarah Ann MIFFLIN. Provides for Rachel ATKINSON housekeeper - mentions plantations in Newlin.
Exrs: Benjamin NEWLIN, Thomas MARSHALL and Moses PALMER.
Wits: William HUEY and John PEIRCE. #351.

GRACEY, SAMUEL, Haverford.
Nov 11, 1802 - Nov 28, 1811.
Estate to daughter Patience WILLIAMSON and son John GRACEY.

Exrs: Sd. son.
Wits: George BONSALL and Amos LUKENS. #352.

SHARPLES, THOMAS, Middletown.
Aug 22, 1809 - Nov 30, 1809.
Five sisters: Mary WOOD wife of Cornelius, Lydia RUSSELL widow of William, Hannah IDDINGS wife of William, Phebe SMEDLEY wife of Peter and Rachel WALTER widow of Nathaniel - mentions tract in Monongahaly County and in Wilmington. Names nephews Joshua and Samuel sons of Joel and niece Lydia and brother John.
Exrs: Cousins Jesse DARLINGTON and Nathan SHARPLES of Middletown.
Wits: John MENDENHALL, Nathan YEARSLEY and John HILL, Jr. #353.

THOMPSON, MARY, Middletown.
April 30, 1811 - Dec 4, 1811.
Children: Elizabeth BENNETT, Sarah DAVIS, Priscilla SHIPPEN, Isaac, William, James and Robert THOMPSON, Mary REECE and Amor THOMPSON.
Exrs: John WORRALL.
Wits: Peter WORRALL, Nathan YEARLEY. #354.

PERKINS, HANNAH, Bethel.
April 6, 1811 - Dec 5, 1811.
Natural daughter Sarrah QUIGLY, plantation in Concord, lines of Joel HATTEN, Moses PALMER and others, and to her son Joseph QUIGLY he to pay his sisters Hannah, Margaret and Mary and his brother Moses £10 each.
Exrs: Friend John LARKIN.
Wits: Thomas NEWLIN and Samuel NEWLIN. #355.

CROZER, RACHEL, Springfield.
Oct 1, 1811 - Dec 5, 1811.
Sisters Martha CROZER and Mary CALDWELL, nieces Elizabeth and Sarah CALDWELL, nephew John CALDWELL, brother John and his children: Elizabeth, James, Sarah, John and Samuel, sisters Elizabeth BIRCHALL and Sarah OGDEN and her children Elizabeth, Mary, James, Eliza, Hannah, Martha and John.
Exrs: Sister Martha and brother in law John OGDEN.
Wits: Debby PRICE and William PENNOCK. #356.

JONES, JENNIS, Newtown.
Jan 1, 1812 - March 17, 1812.
Brother Samuel MOORE and son John, niece Jennis DAWSON and daughters Martha and Elizabeth.
Exrs: Kinsman Joseph LEWIS and nephew John MOORE.
Wits: Elijah LEWIS and Daniel GUEST. #357.

COLVIN, ROBERT, Ridley.
March 7, 1812 - March 21, 1812.
Reputed son Robert COLVIN, brother Alexander and sister Mary COLVIN, sister in law Jane COLVIN, names also Thomas ORR and William ORR, Jr., sons of William and Elizabeth ORR, nurse Elizabeth MILLER and trustees of Middletown Meeting.
Exrs: Elisha PHIPPS and John L. PEARSON.
Wits: John CULIN, J. L. PEARSON and Elisha PHIPPS. #358.

SWAFFER, ABIGAIL, Delaware County.
Nov 7, 1811 - April 2, 1812.
Daughter Mary RICHARDS of Philadelphia and daughter Mary, son John WORRALL, daughter Rachel MATSON of Ohio, granddaughters Cidney SHARPLESS, Beulah, Sarah and Abigail THATCHER daughters of Joseph THATCHER and Sarah MATSON daughter of Levi MATSON. Also granddaughter Hannah MASSEY and grandson Peter WORRALL.
Exrs: Son John WORRALL.
Wits: John POWELL and Robert GREEN. #359.

CLAYTON, ABIGAIL, widow, Bethel.
Jan 25, 1802 - April 2, 1812.
Two daughters Hannah and Elizabeth. Son in law John TWEED to be executor.
Exr: John TWEED.
Wits: Robert PYLE and Powell CLAYTON. #360.

RING, JOSEPH, Birmingham.
Feb 14, 1812 - April 23, 1812.
Mother Hannah RING, sister Mary GREGG and her daughter Julian RING and son Lesson RING, sister Ann RING and brothers William, James, Caleb and Chamless RING. Peter HARVEY to be trustee.
Exrs: Caleb RING and friend Peter HARVEY.
Wits: Joseph HARVEY and Phebe BRINTON. #361.

LEWIS, LEVI, Radnor.
Feb 21, 1810 - April 25, 1812.
Daughter in law Hannah LEWIS one third of estate, residue to her son Levi LEWIS.
Exrs: Doctor John DAVIS and brother Azariah LEWIS.
Wits: Edward HUNTER and John BROOKE.
Azariah LEWIS renounced April 25, 1812. #362.

CLEMENT, JOHN, grazier, Darby.
May 28, 1812 - June 11, 1812.
Estate to wife Elizabeth and five children: Aaron, Isaac, Ann, John and Eliza.
Exrs: Sd. wife, son Aaron and brother in law Isaac OAKFORD.
Wits: Hugh LLOYD and John HUNT. #363.

EYRE, JOHN, Upper Chichester.
Oct 20, 1811 - June 12, 1812.
to wife Isabella home and property conveyed by Caleb EYRE, etc., daughter Maryann, heirship to all real estate if she survives her mother, otherwise to heirs of wife Isabella.
Exrs: Wife and Joseph HENDERSON.
Wits: Joseph ASKEW and Joseph TALBOT. #364.

GRIFFITH, JOSEPH, Jr., Edgmont.
June 18, 1812 - July 9, 1812.
Father Joseph GRIFFITH, sister Sarah FORRESTER and her son Ralph, sister Margaret GRIFFITH, brothers Castle GRIFFITH, William GRIFFITH and Llewelin App GRIFFITH.
Exrs: Uncle Joseph BISHOP and Jesse RUSSELL.
Wits: George BISHOP and George MILLER.
Ad. account gives Margaret CAMPBELL late Margaret GRIFFITH. #365.

BROWN, NATHANIEL, farmer, Upper Chichester.
June 29, 1812 - July 20, 1812.
Wife Esther, children: Nathaniel, Collet, Jerremiah, Rebekah ENOCHS, Elizabeth, Sarah and Susannah TRUMAN - mentions property where Samuel GOODLY dwells also house and lot in Marcus Hook.
Exrs: Biasor LAMBLUGH*.
Wits: Thomas MARSHALL and Jno. ROWAN.

*As appraiser signs his name Bezer LAMPLUGH. #366.

BRIGGS, SAMUEL, Sr., Haverford.
Feb 7, 1809 - Aug 10, 1812.
Estate to wife Mary.
Exrs: Wife Mary, son in law William GARRIGUES of Philadelphia and son Isaac BRIGGS of Montgomery County, Maryland.
Wits: William LEWELYN and Samuel GARRIGUES, Jr. #367.

YARNALL, ELI, Edgmont.
July 29, 1812 - Aug 31, 1812.
Wife (name not given), son Eli the home plantation in Edgmont and Middletown subject to care of mother, etc., granddaughters Priscilla PENNELL and Thamzin PENNELL children of daughter Sarah, dec'd., son Walker plantation in Westtown, Chester County, subject to legacies, brother Ellis and Emmore KIMBER in trust, all right in grist mill on land belonging to Yearly Meeting of Friends held in Philadelphia - mentions Martin MESSENGER and Mary LEWIS as bound children.
Exrs: Sons Walker and Eli with Abraham SHARPLESS and Abraham PENNELL to assist them.
Wits: John MENDENHALL, Peter WORRALL and Jonas PRESTON. #368.

LAWRENCE, JOSEPH, Marple.
Sept 4, 1812 - Oct 8, 1812.
Estate to brother Mordecai LAWRENCE, brother Joshua and son Clement, Samuel son of brother Henry, dec'd., sisters, the wives of Abraham LEWIS and George B. LOWNES, Mary LEWIS daughter of sister Rebecca.
Exrs: Mordecai LAWRENCE.
Wits: Bernard VANLEER and Nathan GIBSON. #369.

OLIVER, MARY, Darby.
Dec 27, 1811 - Oct 2, 1812.
Children: Samuel and Martha OLIVER, daughter Martha to be placed with niece Martha INSLEY.
Exrs: John RIVELY of Darby and Samuel DAVIS the son of Nathan of Upper Darby.
Wits: Richard LLOYD and John BUNTING. #370.

PENNELL, JOSEPH, yeoman, Lower Chichester.
Sept 5, 1812 - Oct 5, 1812.
Wife Jane PENNELL, son Jonathan, minor, home property in Marcus Hook bought of widow GRAHAM, also lot bought of Preston EYRE. If Jonathan dies before maturity then sisters Esther and Lydia and brother John PENNELL to inherit after wife's death.
Exrs: Sd. wife and father Isaac PENNELL.
Wits: Joseph R. CONNELL and Richard RILEY. #371.

SHARPLES, MARTHA, Middletown.
May 30, 1812 - Oct 26, 1812.
Children: Edith FERRIS, Joshua, Isaac and Aaron SHARPLES, Amy DARLINGTON, Hannah SHARPLES, Esther GARRETT and Sarah POOLE. Names also Rhoda, Martha and Samuel DARLINGTON, Lydia SHARPLES wife of grandson Nathan SHARPLES, Benjamin SHARPLES son of Isaac, sister Lydia, Joshua YARNALL and son Samuel.
Exrs: Joshua SHARPLES.
Wits: Francis WISELEY and Thomas THATCHER. #372.

MERCER, RICHARD, yeoman, Thornbury.
May 26, 1809 - Dec 3, 1812.
Wife Elizabeth, children: Euclid, Caleb, Isaac, Richard, Zackeriah, Ann wife of William TAYLOR, Hannah wife of Stephen TAYLOR, Elizabeth wife of Thomas COX (her share in trust of Hugh REED), Mary and Sarah MERCER.
Exrs: Wife Elizabeth and son Euclid.
Wits: Hugh REED and John KING. #373.

LEWIS, MARY, single woman, Radnor.
Jan 5, 1807 - Dec 11, 1812.
Estate to sister Hannah LEWIS, she and David LEWIS of West Bradford, Chester County to be executors.
Exrs: Hannah LEWIS and David LEWIS.
Wits: James LEWIS, Lydia EVANS and Rebecca EVANS. #374.

REECE, JESSE, Newtown.
April 1, 1810 - Dec 19, 1812.
Son Lewis and heirs the plantation inherited from father David REECE subject to payment of $5000 to son Enos and £500 to daughter Debby REECE, same to Mary wife of William BAKER.

Exrs: Son Lewis REECE.
Wits: Mordecai DAVIS and Robert LEWIS. #375.

WILSON, THOMAS, Lower Chichester.
Nov 9, 1812 - Dec 22, 1812.
Home plantation bought of Thomas DICK to be sold at death of wife - mentions dower from former husband and that which is due from son Richard DUTTON, weakly son George to be under care of executors. Grandchildren: Ruth Bostick, Nancy BOYS and Sarah BOSTICK children of Sarah, dec'd., Joseph H., John, James and Mary WILSON children of son James WILSON, dec'd. Residue to children Ezekiel, John, Mary PIERCE and Thomas WILSON.
Exrs: Sd. sons Ezekiel and John.
Wits: John BROOMALL and John HEWES. #376.

MARSHALL, ANN, wife of Joseph MARSHALL, Lower Chichester.
Dec 3, 1812 - Dec 29, 1812.
Legacies to children John, Amor, Ann ENTRIKIN and David. Estate in Brandywine hundred, New Castle County to children Joseph, Hannah, William, Thomas and Mary.
Husband's certificate of approval Dec 3, 1812. Joseph MARSHALL.
Exrs: Sd. son David.
Wits: Eliza CONNELL and Thomas NOBLIT. #377.

HOSKIN, WILLIAM, Edgmont.
Nov 8, 1812 - Jan 9, 1813.
Children: Frances SHELLY, Joseph, dec'd., William, Rebecca MOULDER, Caleb, John, Nathaniel, Hannah SMITH, Elizabeth MORRISON and Martha BOOTH.
Exrs: Sd. son John and son in law Joseph SMITH.
Wits: George GREEN and John HAWS. #378.

CULIN, WILLIAM, Upper Providence.
Dec 16, 1812 - Feb 4, 1813.
Mother Alice CULIN, all right to real estate during life then to brother Daniel and heirs. Legacy to niece Margaret CULIN (minor).
Exrs: Brothers John and Daniel.
Wits: George MILLER and Jane EDWARDS. #379.

MINSHALL, AGNES, Middletown.
May 1, 1801 - Feb 5, 1813.

Children: Margaret MARSHALL*, Phebe YARNALL, Ann MALIN, Mary THOMAS, Grace MALIN and Jacob MINSHALL.
Exrs: Sd. son Jacob MINSHALL.
Wits: Enos PAINTER and Enoch YARNALL.
*Notice that a MARSHALL married a MINSHALL. #380.

KNIGHTS, HANNAH, Middletown.
March 11, 1813 - April 19, 1813.
Niece Elizabeth EDWARDS and nephew James EDWARDS.
Exrs: Friend Issacher EDWARDS.
Wits: William SMEDLEY and Virgil EACHUS. #381.

ROBINSON, WILLIAM, Upper Providence.
April 19, 1813 - May 13, 1813.
Wife Sarah ROBINSON and eight children: viz, William, Margaret NUZUM, Sarah NUZUM, Elizabeth, Hannah YARNALL, John, Esther and Joseph ROBINSON.
Exrs: Friends John WORRALL and Isaac MALIN.
Wits: Isaac MALIN and Isaac SMEDLEY.
J. WORRALL renounced. #382.

BENTLEY, RUTH, Birmingham.
Sept 21, 1796 - May 14, 1813.
Children: Robert FRAME, Rebecca McKINLY, John, Thomas and James FRAME, grandchildren: Enos FRAME, Heini CONNOLLY, Sarah WILSON, Ruth PYLE, daughters of daughter Rebecca McKINLY.
Exrs: Sons Robert and Thomas FRAME.
Wits: Samuel RUSSEL and James RUSSEL. #383.

CUMMINGS, JAMES, Upper Darby.
March 5, 1813 - June 14, 1813.
Estate to wife Elizabeth CUMMINGS, brother Thomas CUMMINGS.
Exrs: Sd. wife Elizabeth.
Wits: Samuel DAVIS and William ROBERTS. #384.

SMEDLEY, FRANCIS, Delaware County.
May 11, 1813 - June 29, 1813.
Estate to brother Clinton and sister Sarah SMEDLEY.
Exrs: Friend George GREEN.
Wits: George GREEN and Mary Ann SMEDLEY. #385.

KIBLER, JACOB, Chester.
June 15, 1813 - July 1, 1813.
Names grandchildren: Elizabeth and Mary KIBLER, daughters son John dec'd., and Hannah GREEN daughter of Mary dec'd. Seven children: Daniel, Jacob, Samuel, David, Joseph, Barbary HOFFMAN and Elizabeth KIBLER.
Exrs: Sons Joseph and Daniel KIBLER.
Wits: Jonas SHARPLESS and Elizabeth CHARLES. #386.

MOORE, PHILIP, Marple.
Aug 19, 1813 - Aug 20, 1813.
Wife Mary, children: William, Elizabeth wife of Joseph VOGDES, John and Phebe. William, North east end of plantation Darby Creek and John CRAIG'S line, Mary NECOR's line etc. also woodland south west side of Chester Road, lines of Phebe and Hannah MORRIS'S heirs subject to annuity to stepmother Mary. Elizabeth land in her possession lines of Hugh LOWNES, William SHELDRON and Phebe and Hannah MORRIS, etc. also to pay annuity to stepmother. John, the home tract beginning at Chestnut tree in West Chester Road and lines of Jno. CRAIG and Mary MOOR dec'd. Phebe land adjoining Elizabeth's, John's, Jno. CRAIG'S, Hugh LOWNES, etc., also annuity to stepmother.
Exrs: Sd. sons William and John MOORE.
Wits: John CRAIG, George THOMAS and Nathan GIBSON. #387.

DONNE, NATHAN, Aston.
April 4, 1813 - Sept 11, 1813.
Children: John, Evelina and Charlotte DONNE (minors). Said son John A. DOONE to collect debts, etc.
Exrs: Friends Richard DUTTON and Henry MOORE.
Wits: James M. MOUNTAIN and Benjamin BURK. #388.

MARTIN, SUSANNA.
June 8, 1811 - Sept 29, 1813.
To four children of sister Hannah WILSON, Sarah HIBBERD, Hannah BROMALL, Thomas DUTTON and Susanna STEEL.
Exrs: Jacob HIBBERD and Andrew STEEL.
Wits: William SMEDLEY and Thomas HIBBERD. #389.

HIBBERD, JOHN, blacksmith, Upper Darby.
Sept 16, 1813 - Oct 1, 1813.

Half brother Abraham HIBBERD plantation in Upper Darby, also lot on Providence Road lines of Thomas SHIPLEY and others. Half brother Jacob HIBBERD marsh on Tinicum Island, names daughters of deceased brother Samuel: Ann, Rachel, Mary, Martha and Elizabeth, children of sister Mary SHARPLESS, child of sister Ann, Amy JOHNSON, Alse Rogers wife of nephew Abnor ROGERS, also James ROADS son of Joseph ROADS, dec'd., also treasurer of fund for schooling poor children of Westown.
Exrs: Kinsmen Israel LOBB and Isaac LOBB.
Wits: Nathaniel NEWLIN and John RIVELY. #390.

BUNTING, JOSIAH, farmer and graizer, in the seventy fourth year of my age, Darby.
May 7, 1808 - Oct 15, 1813.
Daughter Elizabeth BUNTING stone house and lot on east side of High Street line of Richard LLOYD, daughter Martha also house on High Street, daughter Hannah house adjoining the above, started son Josiah BUNTING in business, daughter Ann a legacy, son Joseph two lots W. side of High Street beginning at Richard LLOYDS, etc. to Jos. MORGAN'S also meadow lot line of Mathue JONES, etc. Strip of land offered to the Meeting for right of way, and if not accepted, to go to John as also the south west end of plantation, lines of HEACOCK'S lot according to BLUNSTON'S Deed, MORGAN'S, James and William BUNTING'S and BONSAL'S land to a corner of Elizabeth's, etc. Samuel Land adjoining James and William BUNTING'S land running from their land to land of Joseph MORGAN, etc. Executors to sell land in Kingsessing willed to wife Sarah by her father.
Exrs: Sons Samuel, Josiah, Joseph and John.
Wits: Isaac SULLINDER, Samuel BUNTING and William BUNTING.
Codicil of Dec 22, 1810. Gives Martha ANDREWS and Hannah BUNTING more land. Sons Samuel and Joseph renounced Dec 21, 1813. #391.

BRINTON, JOHN, Thornbury.
Oct 25, 1797 - Oct 19, 1813.
Wife Margaret to occupy premises willed to son Joseph, he to pay annuity to daughter Mary MESTON so long as she remains widow of William MESTON. Other children Esther TRIMBLE, grandchildren Margarett DUTTEN, Esther LARKIN and John BRINTON.
Exrs: Sd. son Joseph BRINTON.

Wits: Abram SHARPLES, Thomas SPEAKMAN and Joseph PEIRCE. #392.

SIMPSON, RICHARD, Edgmont.
Sept 3, 1809 - Oct 30, 1813.
Estate to Rebecca MORGAN wife of John MORGAN, for kindness received in old age.
Exrs: Sd. John MORGAN.
Wits: William YARNALL and Samuel PLANKINTON. #393.

ELLIS, HANNAH, Haverford.
Aug 8, 1813 - Oct 20, 1813.
Brother John GRIFFITH and his daughters Lydia and Mary MORGAN, Mary GRIFFITH wife of Amos and Hannah, Sarah, Elizabeth and William children of Amos, friends Joshua McMIN, William SHAKESPEAR and Elizabeth WHITE.
Exrs: Friend Samuel DAVIS of Haverford.
Wits: Simon LITZENBERG and Andrew LINDSAY. #394.

ROWAN, JAMES, yeoman, Upper Chichester.
Aug 5, 1813 - Nov 27, 1813.
Wife Rebecca, son John, daughter Martha LINDSEY and son James ROWAN (minor). In case of death of son James, estate to John, granddaughter Rebecca ROWAN daughter of John and Ann.
Exrs: Aaron HUSTON and son James ROWAN.
Wits: William BUCKNELL and James BRATTON.
Aaron HUSTON renounced Jan 1, 1814. #395.

LEWIS, HENERY*, yeoman, Radnor.
Feb 17, 1813 - Dec 27, 1813.
Son Enos plantation in Marple lines of David LATCH and others subject to legacy to mother Mary LEWIS and to sister Hester LEWIS. Legacy to daughter Mary PRATT wife of Joseph, son Henery home plantation lines of James DUNWOODY also tract in Newtown lines of Evan LEWIS.
*Will signed Henry LEWIS.
Exrs: Sons Henery and Enos LEWIS.
Wits: John READ, Lewis MORRIS and Nathan GIBSON. #396.

DAVIS, ISAAC, yeoman, Radnor.
Aug 12, 1807 - Jan 3, 1814.

Sister Margaret WILLIAMS all profit of plantation let on shares to
Jacob FISHER. Legacies to John GODFREY, Ann TAYLOR, Margaret
DAVIS, Jane FOLK, Jacob FISHER, Wardens of Radnor Church and
William VAUGHAN son of John VAUGHAN. Residue to nephews and
nieces as named: Evan ROBERTS, Davis ROBERTS, Mary SMITH
wife of James, Margaret DAVIS wife of David, Jan FOLK and Mary
GEORGE wife of David.
Exrs: Nephew Evan ROBERTS and cousin Isaac DAVIS of Earl
Township, Lancaster County.
Wits: David HUMPHREYS and Jno. ELLIOTT. #397.

MINSHALL, THOMAS, Middletown.
Feb 8, 1813 - Jan 6, 1814.
Wife Lydia, son Abel part of plantation to STARRS'S Line Jacob
MINSHALL'S, Ambrose SMEDLEY'S, George MILLER'S and Ridley
Creek. Legacy to William BAKER, husband of daughter Sarah he to
pay widow annuity. Son John remainder of plantation in Middletown
and Providence.
Exrs: Sons Abel and John and son in law William BAKER.
Wits: Jacob MINSHALL, George MILLER and Amor BISHOP. #398.

DAVID, EVAN, Radnor, County of Chester, Province of Pennsylvania.
Wife Thamer, grandchildren; Evan ROBERTS, Mary, Margret,
Sussanna* and David ROBERTS, Hannah ____, Jane, John and Mary
GODFREY. Children: Sussannah ROBERTS, Margret WILLIAMS,
Isaac and helpless son David - mentions bonds from George HINGLE.
*The docket gives Susanna and Susannah, the will as above.
Exrs: Sd. son Isaac DAVID.
Wits: Anthony C. MORRIS, Daniel EVANS and Jacob BEERY. #399.

VAUGHAN, WILLIAM, carpenter, Haverford.
Jan 21, 1814 - Feb 7, 1814.
All property to wife Ann VAUGHAN, she to be executor.
Exrs: Wife Ann VAUGHAN.
Wits: Nathaniel SMITH and Jno. KINZIE. #400.

MORRIS, JONATHAN, Chester.
Jan 17, 1814 - Feb 18, 1814.
Estate to wife (name not given) and six children: Hannah, Mary, Anna,
Margaret, Samuel R. and Cadwalader.
Exrs: Jonathan PENNELL.

Wits: William GRAHAM and Benjamin TILGHMAN. #401.

HILL, JOHN, Middletown.
Aug 10, 1812 - Feb 23, 1814.
Provides for wife Mary HILL and one eleventh part of residue to each child now living, grandson John Howard HILL, children of daughter Rachel SHARPLESS, dec'd. and of late daughter Mary STEEL.
Nathan SHARPLESS renounced Dec 26, 1827.
Exrs: Sons in law Nathan SHARPLESS and Ralph* MARSH.
Wits: Peter WORRALL and Enos PAINTER.
*Signs himself as Rolph E. Marsh in Ad. account. #402.

McCLURE, SAMUEL, weaver, Marple.
May 11, 1809 - March 7, 1814.
Wife Martha and children: Elizabeth, Nancy and Thomas.
Exrs: Sd. son Thomas McCLURE.
Wits: Joseph LAWRENCE and Joshua LAWRENCE. #403.

LAWRENCE, HENRY, Haverford.
May 29, 1810 - March 7, 1814.
Sons William, Thomas and Mordecai all estate when William is of age subject to provision for wife Mary LAWRENCE. Appoints brother Joshua LAWRENCE and brother in law Abram LEWIS guardians - mentions interest in Carding factory with brother Clement, stock in hands of Jesse PENNELL, etc.
Exrs: Brothers Joshua and Mordecai LAWRENCE and sd. wife Mary LAWRENCE.
Wits: Abraham PENNELL, Joseph LAWRENCE and Clement LAWRENCE. #404.

BARTLESON, BARTLET, Radnor.
Feb 1, 1814 - March 8, 1814.
Wife Ann BARTLESON to educate children George, Rachel and Mark. Other children named Jonathan, Cephas, Hannah Lee and Lydia.
Exrs: Jesse GYGAR and neighbour Edward SITER.
Wits: Jesse GYGER and John QUARLL. #405.

LOBB, ESTHOR, Upper Darby.
Aug 22, 1813 - March 11, 1814.
Children: Amy and two sisters at home and three sons Israel, Isaac and Josiah - mentions presents given to married daughters.

Exrs: Sd. sons Israel, Isaac [blank].
Wits: Robert ANDERSON and John HIBBERD. #406.

YARNALL, SAMUEL, Concord.
Feb 18, 1810 - March 21, 1814.
Wife Mary, children: Nathan, Elizabeth, Ellis and Rachel to have tract purchased of John HUMPHREY and Mary his wife subject to annuity to widow.
Exrs: Nathan and Elizabeth YARNALL.
Wits: Nathan SHARPLESS and James HATTON. #407.

CULIN, JOHN, Ridley.
March 8, 1814 - March 24, 1814.
Wife Ann real estate during widowhood except wheelwright tools to son Israel. Sons Israel, Justis and John.
Exrs: Sd. wife Ann CULIN.
Wits: David DUNBAR and J. L. PEARSON. #408.

MATLACK, NATHAN, Newtown.
March 15, 1814 - April 2, 1814.
Wife Rachel, children: Reuben, Josiah, Nathan, Susanna and Isaiah.
Exrs: Two nephews, Nathan LEWIS and Eli LEWIS.
Wits: John SMITH and George HUNTER.
Eli LEWIS renounce April 2, 1814. #409.

FOREMAN, JOHN, Haverford.
Dec 4, 1813 - April 4, 1814.
Wife Amy and children to have estate.
Exrs: Son Thomas FOREMAN.
Wits: Caleb BITTLE and William JOHNSON. #410.

CRAIGE, JAMES, Upper Chichester.
Dec 5, 1808 - April 9, 1814.
Son John tract in Chester Township whereon he now lives subject to legacies to daughters Mary DUTTON and Jane VINCENT, son James tract in Upper Chichester whereon he now lives subject to legacies to daughters Ann BOYD, wife of Martha [sic] BOYD and Elizabeth LINSEY, wife of William LINDSEY.
Wits: Bezer LAMPLUGH and Joseph TALBOT.
Exrs: Sd. sons John and James CRAIGE.
Wits: Bezer LAMPLUGH, Joseph TALBOT and Isaac PENNELL, Jr.

Codicil Aug 28, 1809 mentions Jane VINCENTS children, also Isaac PENNELL to be joynt executor. #411.

EVANS, NATHAN, yeoman, Radnor.
March 21, 1814 - April 11, 1814.
Estate to cousin Hannah BAYLEY wife of James BAYLEY and at her death to her children, should she die without children, then estate to cousin Hannah EVANS, youngest daughter of cousin David EVANS, dec'd. Bequest to cousin William EVANS, son of cousin Acquilla EVANS, Jane SOLEY, daughter of Edward SOLEY, Lydia BROOK, Hannah THORNBURY.
Exrs: Jesse BROOKE and Clement LAWRENCE.
Wits: John BROOKE and Alexander BROOKE. #412.

TAYLOR, BENJAMIN, Marple.
Nov 9, 1808 - April 18, 1814.
Estate to wife Sarah, during widowhood, then to daughter Bulah TAYLOR. Legacies to granddaughters Sarah MADDOCK and Ann GRIMM James RHOADS renounced April 18, 1814.
Exrs: Sd. wife and friend James RHOADS of Marple.
Wits: David HALL and James RHOADS. #413.

REECE, LEWIS, Newtown.
Feb 23, 1814 - May 7, 1814.
Provides for wife Rebecca, daughter Elizabeth L. REECE to have plantation inherited from father Jesse REECE, brother Enos REECE plantation in Tredyffren, Chester County, lines of David MAXWELL, John HENRY less 5 acres of quarry, etc., also lot adjoining Adam RICKABOUGH bought of Rebecca and Elizabeth LOWELLIN subject to $2000 to sister Debby REECE and annuity of $60 to sister Mary BAKER and $1000 at her decease to her children, £50 in trust to William LATTY, for use of Presbyterian Congregation in the Valley. Daughter Elizabeth L. REECE the Limestone Quarry, should she die without issue then her share to brother Enos REECE he paying sister Debby REECE $5000 and $5000 to heirs of sister Mary BAKER.
Exrs: Brother Enos REECE and friend Elijah LEWIS.
Wits: Mordecai DAVIS and Robert LEWIS. #414.

YARNALL, EZEKIEL, Edgmont.
March 7, 1814 - May 18, 1814.

Son John (minor) all real and personal estate allowing his mother and sisters what is left them. Wife Sarah and other children Mary HUTTON, Alice ESBEN, Phebe and Sarah.
Exrs: Brothers William and Enoch YARNALL.
Wits: George YARNALL and Israel YARNALL. #415.

LEWIS, JANE, Radnor.
April 5, 1814 - June 16, 1814.
Legacies to children: Evan, Jane and Abner LEWIS and step children Sarah and Thomas LEWIS, residue to four sons: Enoch, Elijah, Abner and Evan.
Exrs: Sons Enoch and Elijah.
Wits: Benjamin MAULE and Joseph LEWIS. #416.

SMITH, WILLIAM, Chester.
Aug 13, 1814 - Aug 22, 1814.
Legatees, Catharine JACKSON and John DEMSEY. Sale of residue of estate for education of John DEMSEY, Jr.
Exrs: Thomas KILLE.
Wits: Jonas SHARPLESS and Joseph WEAVER, Jr. #417.

VOGDES, ELIZABETH, Willistown.
Oct 16, 1813 - Sept 10, 1814.
Children: Benjamin, Joseph, Rachel MASSEY, Hannah JAMES, Israel, Jacob, Aaron, Sarah WORTHINGTON and Martha TUSSEY, granddaughters Hannah JAMES, Elizabeth VOGDES, daughter of Joseph, grandson Jacob VOGDES, son of Jesse. Residue to sons Joseph and Jesse they to executors.
Exrs: Sons Joseph and Jesse.
Wits: Benjamin YARNALL and Jesse YARNALL. #418.

WITHY, JAMES, Borough of Chester.
July 28, 1811 - Sept 12, 1814.
Children: Elizabeth BIOREN and Sarah STILLE, wife of Thomas. All residue in U. S., Great Britain or else where to wife Elizabeth WITHY and her children.
Judge CROSBY renounced Sept 14, 1814.
Exrs: Sd. wife and friend Judge John CROSBY.
Wits: Samuel EDWARDS and William GRAHAM. #419.

BAKER, ESTHER, Middletown.

Sept 20, 1814 - Oct 6, 1814.
Names Margret BAKER, Margret NEWLIN and Ann KING, then their mother Mary NEWLIN, Susannah BAKER and Mary KING, then her sisters Mary NEWLIN, Elizabeth BAKER and ---, Margret BAKER, then Sally Ann BAKER, Nathan BAKER, John NEWLIN, Samuel BAKER and Ruth GARRET. Residue to brothers and sisters.
Exrs: Nehemiah BAKER, Sr.
Wits: Esther BAKER, Joseph BAKER, Jr. and Nehemiah BAKER. #420.

FAWKES, JOSEPH, Newtown.
June 16, 1814 - Oct 8, 1814.
Legacy to Eliza PINESET. Residue to wife Alice FAWKES and her heirs, she to be executor.
Exrs: Wife Alice FAWKES.
Wits: Jesse LEWIS and Joseph LINDSAY. #421.

YARNALL, ELI, Edgment.
Aug 27, 1812 - Oct 24, 1814.
Wife Alice and her issue by me begotten, should she die without heirs then estate to sister Sarah's and brother Walker's children.
Exrs: Sd. wife and her father Joseph PENNELL.
Wits: Jno. H. CHEYNEY and Rolph C. MARSH.
Suit brought as to validity of this will Oct term 1812 given in favor of Alice YARNALL, April 16, 1814.
Joseph PENNELL renounced Oct 24, 1814. #422.

RING, SUSANNA, Birmingham.
July 8, 1803 - Dec 2, 1814.
Grandchildren Kesiah RICHARDSON, wife of Thomas, Susanna SMITH, wife of Thomas SMITH, Joseph CHANDLER, Elizabeth CHANDLER'S son Thomas, she and Joseph to have personal estate.
Exrs: Grandson Joseph CHANDLER.
Wits: Amor CHANDLER, Jesse GREEN and John TWADDELL. #423.

BURNS, WILLIAM, Marcus Hook.
Aug 28, 1814 - Dec 6, 1814.
Estate to wife Hannah and children: David, James and Henrietta and heirs.
Exrs: Sd. wife.

Wits: Joseph TURNER, J. W. ODENHEIMER and John KERLIN.
#424.

EYRE, WILLIAM, Bethel.
June 6, 1805 - Dec 12, 1814.
Estate to Jonas EYRE son of Isaac EYRE, Esq., of Chester, he to be sole executor.
Exrs: Jonas EYRE.
Wits: William GRAHAM, James HAVISTER and Deborah THATCHER. #425.

GIBBONS, MARGERY, Springfield.
Aug 5, 1813 - Dec 21, 1814.
Orders sale of home mansion and three lots also plantation adjoining, proceeds to children: Jane MALCOM, Mary Ash LLOYD, Sarah CLARKSON and George W. GIBBONS, also children of daughter Rebecca CLARK and granddaughter Sarah PENNELL. Legacies to other grandchildren James Mifflin LEWIS, Hannah HARLAN, Elizabeth LLOYD and Sarah DINNELL.
Codicil Oct 18, 1814.
Wits: James M. GIBBONS and James OGDEN.
Exrs: Sons in law Mathew ASH and Abisha CLARK.
Wits: Hannah Harlan, William PENNOCK and James OGDEN. #426.

VERNAN, EMMOR, Thornberry.
Aug 9, 1814 - Dec 27, 1814.
Nuncupative Will, gives mother Sarah VERNON all estate.
Wits: Jno. H. CHEYNEY and William CHEYNEY. #427.

ROBERTS, JOHN, blacksmith, Radnor.
Feb 25, 1813 - Feb 1, 1815.
Legacies to three daughters Ann, Elizabeth and Ellinor, daughter Hannah remainder of estate.
Exrs: Nathan EVANS, of Radnor, and daughter Hannah.
Wits: William BROOKE and Jonathan HOOD. #428.

MALIN, JACOB, yeoman, Middletown.
Oct 8, 1814 - Feb 3, 1815.
Wife Ann all estate during life, then to brother Thomas MALIN'S son Abner, he to pay his brothers and sisters, Jacob, Minshall, Agnes, Ann, Elizabeth, William and Randel MALIN each fifty dollars.

Jacob MINSHALL renounced Oct 8, 1814.
Exrs: Wife Ann and brother in law Jacob MINSHALL.
Wits: William FAIRLAMB and Sarah SHARPLESS. #429.

ROBERTS, REUBEN, Nether Providence.
Nov 2, 1804 - Feb 11, 1815.
Oldest son Ellis and wife Ann lower part of plantation formed by extending line of Roger DICKS field adjoining Providence Road running through Barbers Run lines of Daniel SHARPLESS, William WATERHOUSE, Thomas LEIPER, etc. Legacy to daughter Teacy, wife of John BARKER, to daughter Abigail, wife of Isaac ENGLE the adjacent woodland along lines of Moses VERNON, etc., son John, remainder lying above aforesaid division line. Legacies to Ann and grandchildren: Liza, Algernoon, Keziah and Julian CECIL children of daughter Alice by Charles CECIL.
Exrs: Son Ellis ROBERTS and son in law Isaac ENGLE.
Wits: Roger DICKS and William SANKEY. #430.

BROOKE, NATHAN, Radnor.
Jan 2, 1815 - Feb 27, 1815.
Estate to wife Mary and children: Jones, Mark, Benjamin and Mary BROOKE. Legacy to Warden of Radnor Church.
Exrs: Sd. wife and father Benjamin BROOKE.
Wits: James BROOKE and Jonathan DAVIS. #431.

JAMES, HANNAH, West Whiteland, County of Chester.
Oct 19, 1783 - Feb 28, 1815.
Three step sisters Elizabeth YARNALL, Rachall RING and Magdelen JOHNSON. Rachall all my part lot in Wilmington belonging to late father's estate. Legacies to sister Sarah HUMPHREYS, Margaret EVANS, niece Rebeca HUMPHREYS, niece Margeret HUMPHREYS, Jane WALKER, brother James, Samuel JAMES estate in possession of Jacob HUMPHREY. Residue to sister Sarah HUMPHREYS and her children: Samuel, Rebeca and Margeret.
Exrs: Relations Henry LAWRENCE and Charles HUMPHREYS.
Wits: John BOYERS and Elizabeth BOYERS. #432.

PEIRCE, CALEB, Thornbury.
May 13, 1813 - March 13, 1815.
Provides for wife ____, son Thomas to have plantation. Other children: Mary IDDINGS, Caleb PEIRCE, Rebecca CHURCHMAN, wife of

Edward, Thomas, Ann WEST (widow), Hannah, wife of Joseph CHURCHMAN and Joshua, also six grandchildren; Anne wife of Walter FRANKLIN, Joshua EMLEN, Mary wife of George NEWBOLD, Samuel, Phebe and James EMLEN descendants of James and Phebe EMLEN - mentions eldest sons John and Joseph having been helped and wills residue to before mentioned nine children.
Wits: Abram SHARPLES, Moses PALMER and Nathan SHARPLES. #433.

ROBESON, SAMUEL.
March 29, 1815 - April 11, 1815.
Request to be buried next to his wife. Legacies to friends Edward FELL, Lewis DAVIS, Maris WORRELL, Owen DAVIS, Samuel SHARPLES, names Abraham LEWIS.
Exrs: Lewis DAVIS and Maris WORRELL.
Wits: Joseph DAVIS and Abel WORRELL. #434.

WORRALL, SARAH, Edgmont.
Jan 17, 1814 - April 15, 1815.
Legacies to Lydia WILLIAMS wife of Joseph WILLIAMS, Abigail DAVIS wife of Abraham DAVIS, niece Rebeckah HALL, Sarah FOX wife of Joshua, Hannah IDDINGS widow of William IDDINGS, John WILLIAMS son of Joseph, Alice FOX wife of Joseph FOX, Hannah BROOMALL daughter of Daniel, Jr., Mary HAWES wife of John, Alizabeth WILLIAMS, Mary PEW, Prissila WORRALL. Residue to sister Jane's five daughters and Rebeccah's three daughters and brother Nahaniel's daughter.
John WORRALL renounced April 14, 1815.
Exrs: John WORRALL.
Wits: Peter WORRALL and Nathan YEARSLEY. #435.

DUNWOODY, JAMES, Marple.
Jan 29, 1815 - April 18, 1815.
Provides for wife Rachel, son William west end of tract in West Whiteland Twp. Chester County, which father David purchased of George HINKLE bounded by Richard THOMAS's line and Chester Road. Son John, home plantation in Marple and Haverford subject to care of mother and bequest to Joseph and annuity to Sarah Ann WOLLEY. Son Joseph, east end of tract in west Whiteland division from line between Samuel JEFFREYS and self.
Exrs: Sd. three sons.

Wits: John CRAIG and Henry LEWIS.
Codicil Jan 4, 1804.
Wits: Thomas EVANS, Gideon RUSSELL. #436.

THOMAS, HEZEKIAH, yeoman, Newtown.
Oct 26, 1802 - April 29, 1815.
Sons Ezra, Gideon and Thomas to have plantation in Newtown along lines of Uriah THOMAS, Levi LEWIS, Gideon THOMAS and Evan LEWIS, each subject to legacy to their sister Pricilla. Grandchildren: Sarah, Robert and Ann and uncle Solomon.
Codicil Jan 4, 1804.
Wits: Thomas THOMAS, Uriah THOMAS and John BROOKE.
Wits: Thomas EVANS and Gideon RUSSELL.
Exrs: Sd. son Thomas. #437.

ALLEN, AARON, Nether Providence.
March 4, 1814 - May 2, 1815.
Wife Mary and five children: Thomas, Elizabeth, Orasher, Alfred and Harriet.
Executors resigned Oct 20, 1818.
Exrs: Friends Henry FORREST and Isaac MALIN.
Wits: Isaac MALIN and Hy. FORREST. #438.

GARDNER, ARCHIBALD, Darby.
Nov 30, 1813 - June 8, 1815.
Estate to wife Hannah, she and friend Isaac OAKFORD to be executors.
Exrs: Wife Hannah and Isaac OAKFORD.
Wits: Jacob GIBBONS and Nathan RICHARDS. #439.

VANLEER, CHRISTIANAH, Marple.
Jan 1, 1808 - June 14, 1815.
Children: Isaac and Bernard, Mary MOORE, Hannah MARKWARD and Catherine BLACK small legacies, daughter Christianna LINDSAY all dower of £6 yearly in two tracts in Tredyffren now in possession of daughter Mary MOORE also all residue.
Exrs: Son in law Andrew LINDSAY and wife.
Wits: Martin WISE and John LINDSAY, Jr. #440.

BEAUMONT, WILLIAM.
Feb 9, 1810 - July 1, 1815.

Daughters Mary WEAVER, Elizabeth GRIFFITH, Hannah
CARPENTER and Sarah SUPPLEE to have legacies, annuity to
daughter Ann MOORE, grandson George Washington BEAUMONT.
Residue to son Davis BEAUMONT, he and brother in law Joseph
DAVIS to be executors.
Exrs: Davis BEAUMONT and Joseph DAVIS.
Wits: David PRATT, Jr. and Edward HUNTER.
441.

PYLE, JOSEPH, Concord.
June 22, 1815 - July 23, 1815.
Provides for wife Martha. Legacy to daughter Phebe, residue to
daughters Sally Ann, Lydia and Malissa, John SHARPLES trustee for
wife's annuity.
Exrs: William MENDENHALL and John SHARPLESS.
Wits: Stephen PYLE and Moses PYLE.
[*Note: Isaac MERCER intermarried with Phebe PYLE.*] #442.

HUNT, SUSANNA, Concord.
Nov 18, 1808 - ____.
Granddaughters Susanna, Hannah, Sarah and Edith daughters of John
SHARPLES, grandson John ROGERS son of Abner ROGERS, son
Jacob YEARSLY and children: Nathan, Mary, Sarah, Esther and Davis,
Nathan and Jesse sons of John SHARPLES.
Exrs: Jacob YEARSLEY and John SHARPLES.
Wits: Thomas PENNELL and Charles PENNELL.
Codicil of Nov 18, 1808 - to children of late husband William HUNT,
Ann SHARPLES, Mary SEAL and Rebecca TAYLOR £5 each.
Wits: The same.
*Ad. account mentions Susanna HICKMAN, Edith TAYLOR, Hannah
LEWIS, Sarah SEAL.* #443.

HALL, STEPHEN, Concord.
April 18, 1815 - Aug 7, 1815.
Wife Elizabeth all estate during widowhood. Son George, west end of
plantation corner of William HANNUM'S land and John PALMER'S to
Concord Road, also east end joining John PALMER and Benjamin
MARTIN'S land. Daughters Ann and Elizabeth, land fronting on Road
from Concord to Ashtown. Residue to be sold, proceeds to three
daughters Phebe HOLLINGSWORTH, Susannah PENNEL and Mary
PALMER - mentions six grandchildren: Susannah TAYLOR, Elizabeth

NEAL, William NEAL, Ann HAMBLETON and Lydia NEAL children of James and Lydia NEAL and Ruth, daughter of William, dec'd.
Exrs: Sd. wife and Joseph PALMER
Wits: John PALMER and Nathaniel WALTER.
Ad. account by *Ruth M. HALL.* #444.

LEWIS, HANNAH, Marple.
July 31, 1815 - Aug 19, 1815.
Sister Elizabeth MORRIS for use of Abraham MORRIS £100 - mentions Lewis MORRIS, Rebeca widow of Nathaniel FAWKES, Mary, Sarah, Elizabeth and Ann daughters of Rebecca FAWKES.
Exrs: Lewis MORRIS and Rebecca FAWKES.
Wits: Nathan GIBSON, Abner WILLIAMS and George MILES. #445.

OAKFORD, AARON, Darby.
July 15, 1815 - Aug 31, 1815.
Wife Ann, daughter Elizabeth CLEMENT - mentions Jonathan HAYCOCK'S land, Haliday JACKSON, Thomas GLASCOE, John OAKFORD and John PEARSON. Children of son Benjamin W., dec'd., Elizabeth to have a roadway through son Isaac's land to Anthony's rock, with free use of landing.
Exrs: Sd. wife, son Isaac and grandson Aaron CLEMENT.
Wits: Nathal NEWLIN, Halliday JACKSON and Isaac CLEMENT. #446.

SUTTON, DEBORAH, Aston.
Nov 22, 1811 - Oct 2, 1815.
One dollar to son William DOYLE. the income of plantation bought of David WADDLE, to daughter Mary Ann WADE, her husband Peter WADE and their daughters Elizabeth and Deborah WADE. To granddaughter Deborah PENNELL, judgment note of son William DOYLE.
Exrs: Brother Mark WILLCOX.
Wits: Charles LUNGREN, Samuel LUNGREN and Mark WILLCOX. #447.

BOWMAN, ANN, Upper Providence.
Dec 20, 1812 - Oct 9, 1815.
Estate to nieces Susannah MALIN and Tacy MALIN.
Exrs: Sd. Susannah MALIN.
Wits: Isaac COCHRAN and George LITZENBERG. #448.

ROBINSON, RACHEL, now of Edgmont.
Nov 5, 1815 - Jan 1, 1816.
Sister in law, Margaret PEARCE, nephews Edward, Cromwell and Joseph PEARCE, children of brother Cromwell PEARCE, dec'd., for their schooling. Niece Frances B. WEAVER, daughter of the same and wife of Isaac WEAVER, Rachel, Cromwell, Ann and John PEARCE, children of dec'd. nephew John PEARCE, Rebecca, wife of Henry BARRINGTON.
Exrs: Nephew, Cromwell PEARCE.
Wits: Joshua WEAVER and Jacob NEILER. #449.

TOWNSEND, JOHN, Upper Chichester.
Dec 26, 1815 - Jan 3, 1816.
Wife Catharen, the place where he now lives.
Exrs: James CRAIG.
Wits: Bozer LAMPLUGH and Daniel LIKENS. #450.

PEDRICK, ELIZABETH, Chester.
Jan 5, 1816 - Jan 12, 1816.
Estate to cousins James and Caleb BIRCHALL.
Letters of Administration to sd. cousins.
Wits: Mary COTTER and Elizabeth TAYLOR. #451.

COBOURN, CALEB, Chester.
April 24, 1815 - Jan 20, 1816.
Children: Thomas, Lazarus, Abraham, Caleb, Eliza, Susannah and Esther COBOURN and Elizabeth FIELD - mentions property joining that of Mary SHARPLES, dec'd., Thomas COBURN, George SNEATH, John POWELL and the Edgmont Road.
Exrs: Sd. son Caleb COBOURN.
Wits: John PEIRCE and Nathan SUPLEE. #452.

BAKER, AARON J., yeoman, Birmingham.
Jan 15, 1816 - Jan 31, 1816.
Wife Hannah, son Dilworth (minor) right in undivided tract willed by father Richard BAKER, situated in Edgmont, in case of sons death without issue equal shares to my brothers and sisters, Jesse MERCER, guardian.
Exrs: Friend John BRINTON.
Wits: Joseph BENNETT and William DILWORTH. #453.

LUNGREN, JOHN, paper maker, Aston.
Dec 11, 1815 - March 9, 1816.
Wife Sarah, children: Elizabeth BLACK and her daughter Sarah BLACK, Sarah HAYS, Samuel, William and Charles. Sd. daughter Sarah $4000 on interest so as to be independent of husbands debts. Son Samuel, plantation bought of Capt. John RICKER, $50 to Bible Society in Sweden to be in care of Thomas DOBSON, of Philadelphia. Names William FRY of Germantown.
Exrs: Sd. sons William and Charles.
Wits: William FAIRLAMB and Joseph HANNUM. #454.

LOWNES, HUGH, of Springfield.
Sept 1, 1811 - March 29, 1816.
Children Joseph, "Benanwell," Elizabeth & Sidney and heirs. Land to be divided by Committee of 5 or 7 friends and Joseph to have first choice. Mentions Elizabeth Redmond. Brother in law Owen Rhoads and kinsman George B. Lownes, trustees for Benanwell.
Exrs: Son Joseph and bro. in law Owen Rhoads.
Wits: Wm. Pennock, Geo. B. Lownes.
Codicil: Nov 6, 1811. Same wits. #455.

LEEDOM, SAMUEL, of Haverford.
March 9, 1814 - April 8, 1816.
Wife Hannah; children Edmund Leedam, Elizabeth Kirk, John and Daniel Leedom.
Exrs: Son John, of Merion, Montgomery Co. and Samuel Davis, of Haverford.
Wits: David Lyons, Wm. Johnson.

CUMMINGS, ELIZABETH, Upper Darby.
March 14, 1816 - April 8, 1816.
Estate to only daughter Jane HERBISON (minor), next claimant to be sister Ann HERBISON.
Exrs: Samuel DAVIS of Haverford.
Wits: Thomas KIRK and William EVANS. #457.

LAMPLUGH, BEZER, yeoman, Upper Chichester.
Jan 10, 1814 - May 1, 1816.
Wife Phebe, children: Lydia and Samuel. Names Elizabeth CROZER daughter of Elizabeth TALLEY, son Samuel home tract bought of Joseph BROWN.

Exrs: Son Samuel and friend Joseph JOHNSON.
Wits: Isaac PENNELL and Joseph TALBOT. #458.

McLEER, PATRICK, store keeper, Marple.
April 27, 1816 - May 1, 1816.
Wife Jane, natural son James HAMPTON son of the then Elizabeth HAMPTON. Final disposition 1/4 proceeds to son, 3/4 to brothers and sisters in Tyrone County, Ireland: Arthur, Daniel, Hugh, Margaret, Eleanor and Catarine McLEER.
Exrs: Samuel CARR and George THOMAS.
Wits: Jno. KERNS, Samuel CARR and Nathan GIBSON. #459.

WILSON, THOMAS, Thornbury.
Feb 24, 1816 - May 3, 1816.
Wife Sarah, daughter Mary M. WILSON.
Exrs: Sd. wife and brother Ezekiel WILSON.
Wits: Thomas PEIRCE and William T. PEIRCE. #460.

CROZER, JOHN, yeoman, Springfield.
Aug 11, 1803 - May 11, 1816.
Wife Sarah all estate in trust. All children to heir alike at their mother's decease except they disoblige her so much that she may think fit to cashier any of them, then her will be done. Second part of will mentions sons John and Samuel.
Wits: William PENNOCK and Robert CALDWELL. #461.

JOBSON, JOSEPH, Middletown.
Dec 12, 1809 - May 21, 1816.
Wife Susannah, children, Hannah and John and the heirs of daughter Mary THOMPSON and sons Samuel and John, plantation in Greenwood Twp., Mifflin County, Pennsylvania.
Exrs: Sd. wife and son Samuel.
Wits: Isaac YARNALL and Joseph PENNELL, Jr. #462.

BONSALL, LYDIA, Upper Darby.
Oct 6, 1807 - June 11, 1816.
Names five daughters: Margaret, Martha, Susannah, Lydia and Sarah, sons James, Joseph; each of my lawful grandchildren.
Exrs: Sd. son Joseph.
Wits: Jonathan BONSALL, William MATTHEWS and John HIBBERD. #463.

SHARPLESS, GRACE, Middletown.
June 3, 1816 - June 17, 1816.
Heirlooms to granddaughter Phebe SHARPLESS, child of son Samuel, Samuel, son of Joel SHARPLESS of Middletown to keep them until Phebe is eighteen, her sister Emeline to inherit in case of Phebe's death.
Exrs: Samuel SHARPLESS.
Wits: Isaac BOND and Nathan SHARPLESS. #464.

RICHARDS, JONATHAN.
March 5, 1803 - June 17, 1816.
Seven sons: Thomas, Jehu, Jonathan, Joseph, Richard, Josiah and Dutton, daughters Hannah and Lydia, son Josiah's daughter Hannah, to Lydia CLOUD who served her time in the family.
Exrs: Sons Jehu and Richard.
Wits: Preston EYRE and William GRAHAM. #465.

SHARPLESS, DANIEL, Nether Providence.
Jan 27, 1815 - June 24, 1816.
Wife Sarah, sons: John, Isaac, Enos and Henry SHARPLESS - mentions property on Ridley Creek joining land of Peirce CROSBY, Reuben ROBERTS, Woodward CROSBY, Joshua HARLAN, also property purchased of Jonas SHARPLES, of George SHARPLES and of Nathan PEIRCE. Daughters Beulah THATCHER, wife of William and Hannah SHARPLESS.
Exrs: Sons John, Henry and Enos SHARPLESS.
Wits: John PEIRCE and Ellis ROBERTS.
Codicil Nov 25, 1815 mentions grandfather's deed of April 16, 1726 and will of March 22, 1737 in regard to strip of land along line of John and Moses VERNON. This adjoining land given to son John.
Wits: Same as will. #466.

TAYLOR, JOHN, Upper Providence.
June 10, 1816 - June 22, 1816.
Brother in law George IRWIN, he and friend Isaac POWELL to be executors.
Exrs: George IRWIN and Isaac POWELL.
Wits: Philip RUDOLPH and Benjamin KIRK. #467.

QUIGG, JOHN, Ridley.
June 10, 1816 - July 3, 1816.

Estate to wife Fanny, she to be sole executor.
Exrs: Wife Fanny.
Wits: James MADDOCK and J. H. TERRILL. #468.

ELLIOTT, BENJAMIN, Darby.
Dec 29, 1808 - July 9, 1816.
Wife Sarah 68 acres; lines of Darby Creek, John HUNT, Great Road, 33 ft. Road and Hugh LLOYD. Daughters Elizabeth GROVER and Hannah MOORE, grandchildren: Benjamin Elliott MORE, Eliza MORE, Sarah GROVER and Hannah GROVER, daughter Elizabeth's other children, plantation in Kingsessing willed by father Enoch ELLIOTT, division not to exclude children of any dec'd daughter.
Exrs: Sd. wife, Benjamin W. OAKFORD and Gibbons HUNT.
Wits: Benjamin PEARSON, Richard LLOYD and William HUMPHREYS. #469.

BONSALL, JONATHAN, Upper Darby.
April 3, 1815 - Aug 14, 1816.
Orders sale of marsh meadow in Kingsessing and Darby. Wife (Margret), children: Reuben, Ann and Charles, plantation in Upper Darby.
Exrs: Sd. wife and children.
Wits: Jno. PEARSON, Morris C. SHARPLESS and Joshua BONSALL. #470.

PENNELL, SUSANNA, Upper Chichester.
Sept 8, 1816 - Oct 23, 1816.
Children: Nathan, John, James, Joseph, William, Susanna wife of Isaac HALL, Rachel wife of Jonathan DUTTON, Hannah wife of David HALL and Sarah wife of Salkeld LARKIN.
Exrs: Sd. son Nathan.
Wits: Jno. TALBOT and Mordecai LARKIN. #471.

BRINTON, CHRISTIANNA, widow, Thornbury.
Aug 19, 1810 - Oct 25, 1816.
Names children and grandchildren: Joseph and daughters Christianna, Rebecca and Sarah, Caleb, John and son George, Thomas and sons George and Hill, Mary JACOBS and children Phebe KERSEY, Elizabeth and Brinton, Phebe DILWORTH and children Christianna and Brinton, Hannah NORRIS and children Maria Jane, Hannah,

Thomas, George and Isaac, Jane TRIMBLE and daughters Harriet, Ann and Phebe.
Exrs: Sd. sons Joseph and Thomas.
Wits: William YARNALL and Thomas YARNALL. #472.

JENKINS, JABEZ.
June 3, 1816 - Signature proved on testimony of Osborn ALSTON, Aug 9, 1816; and Jonathan ALSTON, Nov 18, 1816.
Wife Tabitha, children: Jonathan, Jabez, Elizabeth, Joseph and Joshua (a minor) equal shares with certain exceptions. Jonathan, title to a lot near the forest landing in Murderkill Hundred, Kent county, Delaware, willed testator by Samuel Osburn BLACKMAN. Jabez $210 willed to testator by David McCall BLACKMAN, Nathan WHEALDON son of Rebecca WHEALDON, dec'd., believed to reside in Ohio.
Exrs: Sd. wife and grown children.
Wits: Jonathan JENKINS, Jabez JENKINS and Elizabeth JENKINS. *Heirs not accepted as witnesses.* #473.

COX, ANDREW, Darby.
Jan 16, 1816 - Feb 14, 1817.
Sons Isaac Newton COX (minor) and William COX speaks of appointment of guardian.
Exrs: Friends Charles JUSTIS, John M. JUSTIS and Thomas SERRILL.
Wits: Benjamin PEARSON and JOHN M. JUSTIS. #474.

EVANS, JONATHAN, Upper Darby.
March 6, 1807 - Feb 19, 1817.
Children: William, Jonathan, Eunice WILLIAMSON, Ann McCLELLAN, Sarah WILLIAMSON and Martha JINNINGS - mentions land joining that of William THOMPSON, Samuel KIRK and James PYOTT.
Exrs: Son William and son in law Joel McCLELLAN.
Wits: Thomas GARRETT, Thomas LEWIS and Samuel GARRETT. #475.

YARNALL, JAMES, Edgemont.
Nov 22, 1816 - March 8, 1817.
Wife Jane, all incomes until Alben is of age, children: Mary PENNELL, Isaac, Sidney, Rachel, Rheuben, James and Alben - mentions property

occupied by David COWPLAND - mentions a joint road with Abraham PENNELL.
Exrs: Sd. sons Isaac and James.
Wits: Thomas SMEDLEY and Nehimiah BAKER. #476.

DUNN, ROBERT, Ridley.
March 4, 1817 - March 13, 1817.
Wife Mary, children: Catharine, Thomas and Andrew.
Exrs: Friend George G. LEIPER and guardian during minority of children.
Wits: Christopher NOBLE and William BURNSIDE. #477.

HATTON, HANNAH, Concord.
Feb __, 1813 - March 15, 1817.
Names daughters Elizabeth and Sarah wife of ____ and their son James Prior HATTON. Wills that Elizabeth shall have all estate subject to entire control of Sarah's son James Prior HATTON until he is of age. If they interrupt her in her care of him she shall be released from all care and enjoy all my estate.
Wits: Levi MATSON and Levi MATSON, Jr. #478.

BROOMALL, DANIEL, Thornbury.
June 14, 1816 - April 8, 1817.
Children: James, John, Isaac, Nehemiah, Jacob, Joseph, Nathan and Rachel widow of Caleb TEMPLE, Hannah SMITH, dec'd., wife of John and her children: Jane WAY widow of Jacob, Joseph, Sarah ENTRIKIN wife of Samuel, David, John, Isaac, Martha BAKER wife of Nathan and Enoch; Elizabeth FRAME late wife of Isaac and her son Daniel, son James home plantation bounded by lines of John EDWARDS and Thomas HEMPHILL subject to comfortable maintenance of blind son David.
Exrs: Sons John and Nehemiah BROOMALL and friend Nehemiah BROOMALL.
Wits: Joseph BAKER, Elizeth. BAKER and Thomas HEMPHILL. #479.

FRAME, ROBERT, Birmingham.
May 10, 1817 - May 26, 1817.
Wife Eleanor, children: Robert (James, uncertain, Rebecca McKINLEY), Margaret SMITH, Ruth CRAIG, Mary HICKMAN, Elizabeth MILES, Orpah, Jane and Sarah. Wife to have use of land

bounded by lines of James RUSSELL, Nathaniel NEWLIN with privilege for life of James and Rebecca. After death of wife, James and Rebecca's land to be valued and Robert may take it at valuation, proceeds to seven daughters - mentions land along lines of Samuel RUSSELL, John BULLOCK, Thomas BULLOCK and others. Samuel RUSSELL'S land formerly James RUSSELL'S. John BULLOCK'S land formerly William SMITH'S.
Exrs: Son Robert FRAME and son in law William SMITH.
Wits: James SMITH of Concord and Benoni SHIELDS. #480.

LOBB, BENJAMIN, Upper Darby.
June 21, 1816 - May 26, 1817.
Being blind - wife Mary, children: Thomas, John, Jesse, Benjamin, Hannah TYSON, wife of Isaac and Martha, dec'd. wife of Samuel MECTEER.
Exrs: Sons Thomas and John.
Wits: Benjamin PEARSON, Thomas THOMAS and Isaac LOBB. #481.

PALMER, ASHUR, Concord.
March 3, 1815 - June 5, 1817.
Wife Allice, children: Morris, Susannah MALIN, Joseph and Allice. William TRIMBLE to see to Morris's welfare.
Exrs: Wife Allice and son Joseph.
Wits: John PALMER and Nathaniel WALTER. #482.

STURGIS, JONATHAN, Bethel.
Nov 9, 1813 - July 5, 1817.
Wife Sarah, she to execute will for her use and subsistence.
Wits: None.
George PALMER and William PETERS testified to handwriting of Jonathan STURGIS. #483.

HUNTER, EDWARD, Newtown.
July 19, 1817 - Aug 31, 1817.
Children: William, Rebeca PECHIN, Margaret, Allice CORNOG, Hannah and Elizabeth, son William west end of my plantation, lines of Robert MINDINGHALL, George HUNTER, John HUNTER and Jane NEWLIN, son Edward the rest of plantation, lines of Jane NEWLIN, Joseph HOOD, township line road and others, also lot lately purchased of William BEAUMONT, also lot on E. side of Delaware Tenth Street between Mulbery and Sasefrace Street, Philadelphia.

Exrs: Son William and sons in law Peter PECHIN and Thomas CORNOG.
Wits: George W. THOMAS and David PRATT. #484.

DUNN, WILLIAM, Haverford.
March 25, 1817 - Aug 4, 1817.
Daughter Susanna HALEY, brother David DUNN and one dollar of daughter Phebe TAGGERT.
Exrs: Patrick HALEY.
Wits: Samuel DAVIS and Ludwick KNOLL. #485.

MORGAN, JOSEPH, Darby.
April 16, 1813 - Sept 8, 1817.
Wife Mary, children: Joseph, Sarah COOPER, Mary BUNTING and Elizabeth BUNTING, grandson Joseph M. BUNTING, plantation bought of ____ LAYCOCKS, daughter Sarah COOPER, Cedar Swamp in West North Jersey on Adquoadqus branch. Three daughters, meadow bought of Israel ELLIOT lying in Gingressing Twp., Philadelphia.
Exrs: Sd. son Joseph MORGAN.
Wits: Isaac SULLENDER and John BUNTING. #486.

VERNON, SAMUEL, Aston.
Sept 2, 1817 - Sept 8, 1817.
Property along lines of Dr. William PENNELL and Thomas GRIFFITH to be sold next to Concord Road. Wife Ann and daughters Lydia and Margaret. To children of dec'd., daughter Sidney, share of daughter Elizabeth wife of John WOOD to be in hands of a trustee.
Exrs: Brother in law Robert HALL and son in law Isaac BARTEN.
Wits: Joseph JOHNSON and Jos. FOX. #487.

MARIS, ELIZABETH, Marple.
Oct 7, 1805 - Sept 27, 1817.
Children: Isaac, James, Mary LAWRENCE, Elizabeth WEST and Eliza DAVIS - mentions property joining land of Joseph RHOADS to Darby Creek to include plantation willed by grandfather James BARTRAM.
Exrs: Sons in law Joshua LAWRENCE, Thomas WEST and Samuel DAVIS.
Wits: James RHOADS and Joseph RHOADS, Jr. #488.

GRIFFITH, HANNAH, Aston.

Sept 14, 1817 - Sept 30, 1817.
Estate to niece Priscilla GRIFFITH daughter of brother in law Abner GRIFFITH.
Exrs: Brother Thomas GRIFFITH.
Wits: Jos. FOX and Lettice McCLEAVE. #489.

HUSTON, THOMAS, Thornbury.
July 24, 1817 - Nov 17, 1817.
Wife Mary, three children: Ann James HUSTON, Samuel Jones HUSTON, and Thomas Steel HUSTON, the shop and half lot on north side of road running through my land. Names a cousin John MOLDON.
Exrs: Samuel Jones HUSTON.
Wits: William YARNALL, John KING and Brinton JONES. #490.

PENNELL, WILLIAM, Aston.
Dec 31, 1813 - Dec 1, 1817.
Wife not named but initials of her maiden name on silver plate D.S.G., brother Samuel's supposed son Samuel PENNELL and his children: Aaron, Mary and William, brother Jesse's children: Mary and William. Wife's niece Dolly HOSKINS daughter of Joseph and Mary HOSKINS, wife's sister Henrietta FLOWER, friend Jacob RICHARDS. Children of sisters Rachel, Ester and Mary.
Exrs: Brother Robert PENNELL and nephew Isaac SHARPLESS.
Wits: Jacob RICHARDS and John RICHARDS.
*Ad. account *Dorothea HOSKINS, and wife possibly Dorothea S. GARRETT as Dorothea HOSKINS got the silver plate.* #491.

MANLY, THOMAS, Marple.
Aug 23, 1817 - Dec 4, 1817.
Wife Elizabeth, children: Benjamin, Elizabeth wife of John NEWLIN, Thomas, Charles, Susanna wife of Robert DUNN and Lydia.
Exrs: Son William to have plantation, pay legacies and maintain mother.
Wits: Nathan GIBSON, Enos LEWIS and Esther LEWIS. #492.

PALMER, AARON, Darby.
March 11, 1817 - Dec 4, 1817.
Wife, all estate during widowhood. Son Joseph, estate received from testators others estate by inheritance, lines of Cobbs Creek, Moses PALMER and others also part of the Widow ASH tract. Other land to

daughters Hannah JONES, Mary PALMER and Eliza PALMER joining that mentioned.
Exrs: Son Joseph and brother in law John BONSALL.
Wits: Thomas THOMAS and Isaac PALMER. #493.

KITTS, MICHAEL, Ridley.
Sept 2, 1817 - Jan 14, 1818.
To brother John KITTS until his sons John, Jacob and Michael come of age.
Exrs: James MADDOCK.
Wits: Charles GRANTHAM and Isaac CULIN. #494.

STEEL, ANDREW, Radnor.
Dec 8, 1817 - Jan 21, 1818.
Wife Susanna to maintain and educate children: Mary, Thomas, Hannah, Susanna, Margaretta, Andrew and Ann.
Exrs: Brother in law Joseph DAVIS and friend Jesse BROOKE.
Wits: Evan ROBERTS and David EVANS. #495.

THOMSON, HESTER (ESTHER), Ridley.
Jan 22, 1818 - Feb 13, 1818.
Nieces Jane BIRD, Elizabeth CALDWELL and Maria BIRD, niece Jane and cousin Edmond CALDWELL all title to estate of late sister Mary THOMSON, brother Jonah THOMSON, niece Ann THOMSON, nephews Levis P. THOMSON and John E. THOMSON and niece Mary A. THOMSON, Martha HELMS and Mary Ann CARPENTER.
Exrs: Brothers Jonah and John THOMSON and friend Samuel DAVIS.
Wits: Mary GARDINER and Benjamin THOMAS. #496.

HUNTER, JOHN, Thornbury.
Dec 30, 1817 - Feb 25, 1818.
Wife Martha, children: James, Robert, Joseph, Thompson, John and William, grandchildren: John son of James, Martha daughter of Robert, Sarah daughter of Joseph.
Exrs: Hugh REED and Thomas PEIRCE.
Wits: Joseph EAVENSON and Joseph JAMES. #497.

MITCHELL, JOHN, (at present) of Darby.
Jan 26, 1818 - April 11, 1818.
Natural daughter Edith FOULK interest of estate for life also her daughter Elennor FOULK $300 at death of mother. Residue to

Charles, Ann, Jane, William, Isaac, Joseph, Morris and George, children of George FOULK.
Exrs: John OAKFORD.
Wits: Charles OAKFORD and Elizabeth OAKFORD. #498.

BEVAN, DAVIS, Chester.
Aug 30, 1814 - Codicil Sept 13, 1815 - April 14, 1818.
Children: Ann LAWLES wife of Matthew, Tacy Anna STACY and her sons James G. and Davis B. STACY, Isabella and Matthew L. BEVAN. To sd. son Matthew L. land of the late Francis RICHARDSON conveyed by Robert E. GRIFFITH, also lot bought of Cadwallader EVANS bounded by High Street, lines of Mary RICHARDSON, Frances RICHARDSON and Owen MARIS, dec'd., also house on Front Street bought of Elisha PRICE'S administrators, also lot in Charleston, Maryland. Sd. Isabella, lot in Chester lines of Providence and Middletown Roads and Jos. ENGLE. BAZIN, a black man, recommendation, etc.
Exrs: Son Matthew L. and Tacy.
Wits: Peter DESHONG and Samuel EDWARDS. #499.

LUNGREN, SARAH, Aston.
March 10, 1817 - May 18, 1818.
Other children: Samuel and his son John (minor), Sarah HAYS and Elizabeth BLACK and daughters Sarah, Harriot and Susan, also William's eldest son Edwin LUNGREN.
Exrs: Sons William and Charles.
Wits: William FAIRLAMB and Abraham TAYLOR. #500.

WORRALL, HANNAH, widow, Edgmont.
Aug 18, 1816 - May 28, 1818.
Children: Mary HAWES and eldest son (name not given), Sarah BROOMALL wife of Daniel and her daughter Hannah, Hannah SMITH, Lydia MINSHALL, and a daughter Susanna BAKER who gets only five dollars and a gown. Right in plantation bought of George GREEN to Sarah in own right, profits on same subject to Samuel WORRALL'S annuity and at Daniel's death the title.
Exrs: Nephew John FOX and cousin Thomas HEMPHILL to hold certain property in trust during D. BROOMALL Jr.'s life.
Wits: Samuel HEWES and Hugh CALDWELL. #501.

TRIMBLE, SAMUEL, hatter, Concord.

March 19, 1818 - Aug 7, 1818.
Wife Esther, children: Joseph, Samuel, Margaret PIERCE and Ann WILLIAMS.
Exrs: Sd. wife, Joseph and Samuel.
Wits: Nathan SHARPLES and Micajah SPEAKMAN. #502.

ROBERTS, ISRAEL, Upper Darby.
Dec 29, 1812 - Aug 14, 1818.
Wife Abigail and appoints her executrix.
Exrs: Wife Abigail.
Wits: Hugh LLOYD and Richard P. LLOYD. #503.

LEWIS, CATHARINE, Upper Darby.
March 15, 1810 - Oct 1, 1818.
My desire is that my husband Thomas LEWIS'S will shall stand good in all its parts. Land to sons Thomas and Mordecai. Other children: Jane TYSON, Sidney WILLIAMSON, Demaris BITTLE, Sarah COCHRAN and Elizabeth LEWIS, also grandchildren Thomas TYSON and Thomas COCHRAN - mentions children (not named) of Elizabeth and of Rachel MARLOW.
Exrs: Son Thomas and son in law John COCHRAN.
Wits: William JOHNSON and Margret HOOVER. #504.

WORRALL, PETER, Upper Providence.
Nov 9, 1818 - Nov 16, 1818.
Son Elias, children of ____ WORRALL, Frazer, Charles, Mary, Peter, Lydia and Jonah. Other children Abigale DIZER, Sarah, ____ RICHARDS and her children Hannah, Nathaniel, Mary, Lydia, Joseph and Sarah, ____ BRANNEN child George, ____ RIGBY child Hannah.
Exrs: Isaac MALIN and Enos WORRALL.
Wits: Isaac MALIN and John HINKSON, Jr. #505.

MENDENHALL, MARGARET, Concord.
Feb 21, 1818 - Dec 8, 1818.
Speaks of four children: Phebe MENDENHALL, Ann MEREDITH, Rebeckah TRIMBLE and Robert MENDENHALL but names a son James and children Margaret and Stephen MENDENHALL, Ann and Rebeckah each has a minor son named Stephen. There is also a Margaret PEIRCE wife of Worral PEIRCE.
Wits: William MENDENHALL and Jacob PERDUE. #506.

HAMPTON, JOHN, Radnor.
Oct 16, 1818 - Dec 14, 1818.
Children: Woodward, Zillah CONNER wife of Timothy, Ann DONALD wife of William, Elizabeth, Jane, Rebecca CORNOGG and son John, Rachel STRINGFELLOW and son John and four minor children: Jane, John, Davis and Rudolph.
Exrs: Sd. son Woodward and Abner LEWIS.
Wits: Thomas TAYLOR and John OWENS. #507.

DIEHL, NICHOLAS, Tinicum.
Oct 9, 1811 - Dec 22, 1818.
Wife Mary, children: Adam, Nicholas, Thomas, William, John and Mary, granddaughter Mary EWING. Tracts in Centre County in names of sons Adam and Nicholas, other real estate to five sons. John's share being in trust for his children, annuity to daughter Mary and legacy to her children.
Exrs: Sd. sons.
Wits: William LAKE and Charles LLOYD. #508.

RUSSEL, SAMUEL, Sr., Birmingham.
May 22, 1817 - Jan 30, 1819.
Wife ____, children: James, Lettice, Elizabeth, Isabella, Martha and Samuel. Real estate bounded by lands of Robert FRAME, George HEYBURN and others.
Exrs: Son Samuel.
Wits: Benoni SHIELDS and Robert FRAME. #509.

POWELL, JOHN, Chester Township.
Dec 8, 1818 - March 17, 1819.
Wife Ann, children: Isaac, Margaret and six minors: George, John, Elizabeth, Sarah, Martin and James - mentions Isaac's settlement with Elizabeth PYLE's estate - mentions in connection with land, Isaac BARTON, Joseph SWAFFER, Joseph ENGLE and Samuel WEST. Division of estate not till youngest child is 14.
Codicil of Jan 30, 1819 refers to occupancy of part of homestead by Margaret so long as she stays single.
Exrs: Sd. wife, John SHARPLESS and Enos SHARPLESS.
Wits: Samuel WEST, Garrett EDWARDS and William SLAWTER. #510.

VERNON, WILLIAM, Concord.

Feb 8, 1819 - April 6, 1819.
Housekeeper and her heirs to have plantation in Concord bought of Joseph KERLIN, also to have other real estate in Concord and Bethel. Legacies to James ESPIN, George WALTER son of Thomas, James MARSHALL son of James, Vernon GRIFFEY, son of Joseph, Robert LOGAN son of Robert, niece Hannah VERNON daughter of brother Johnathan, nephew John WORROW'S three children Ann, Lydia and Zebulon, Thomas CASSON son of Luke and Ann.
Exrs: Moses PALMER and Rolph C. MARSH.
Wits: William PETERS and Samuel HANNUM. #511.

READ, JOHN, yeoman, Radnor.
Jan 14, 1818 - April 20, 1819.
Brothers and sisters: James, Ann GROVER and daughter Margret, William and his children John, Thomas and William, nieces Margret SCRIMGER and Eliza READ, nephew William BLACK. Legacies to William QUINN, Davis QUIN and John QUIN, Margret MULLING wife of Robert, Margret RAMAGE wife of Amer RAMAGE.
Exrs: James QUIN son of William.
Wits: Henry LEWIS and Enos LEWIS. #512.

WORRALL, THOMAS, Upper Providence.
April 9, 1819 - April 24, 1819.
Daughter Ann CASSIN, grandchildren Zebulon WORRALL, Ann KINSEY and Lydia JAMES, great grandchildren John, Luke and Thomas CASSIN sons of grandson Thomas.
Exrs: Grandson Thomas CASSIN.
Wits: Joseph WORRALL and Philip RUDOLPH. #513.

EVANS, MARY, Upper Providence.
Oct 24, 1814 - May 7, 1819.
Mother Rebecca sole legatee and executrix.
Exrs: Mother Rebecca.
Wits: Isaac COCHRAN, Lydia BIRCHALL and David PRATT. #514.

MORRIS, JONATHAN, physician, Darby.
March 18, 1818 - May 19, 1819.
Wife ___, children: Ann LYNN, Catherine SHALLCROSS, Alice Jackson wife of Joel, Samuel MORRIS, Evan MORRIS, grandchildren Jonathan Morris JACKSON, Mary Ann, Alice and Catherine JACKSON, John Ludon MORRIS and Maria MORRIS, friend James

MORRIS of Smyrna, a lot in Smyrna line of Mordica MORRIS to a road and line of James MORRIS.
Exrs: Samuel and Evan MORRIS and Joel JACKSON.
Wits: Jacob SERRILL and Joseph BUNTING.
Codicil April 6, 1818.
Wits: Jacob SERRILL and Morris C. SHALLCROSS.
Mentions Elizabeth CARSON and Phebe TIBOUT (OR TYBOUT) (children of my sister Mary) and Samuel MORRIS (son of son Evan MORRIS). #515.

READ, MARGERET, Radnor.
Oct 24, 1807 - June 10, 1819.
Children: John, Mary BLACK, James, Davis, Ann GROVER, nieces Martha QUINN and Margaret GROVER, nephew Thomas GROVER.
Exrs: Son John READ.
Wits: Esther LEWIS, Enos LEWIS and Henry LEWIS. #516.

MILLER, Rebecca, Ridley.
Nov 12, 1814 - July 20, 1819.
Sons John S. MORTON and Aaron MORTON - mentions Thomas SMITH, Esq., Samuel EVANS and Jacob SERRILL.
Exrs: Sd. sons John S. MORTON and Aaron MORTON.
Wits: William MARTIN and John CROSBY. #517.

CARPENTER, JOHN, Upper Chichester.
Aug 2, 1819 - Aug 25, 1819.
Wife Rachel, daughters: Jane and Rachel - mentions Silas GREEN and Nathan PENNELL.
Exrs: Sd. wife and brother Jacob CARPENTER.
Wits: George MARTIN, Jr. and Emmor J.NEWLIN. #518.

CROSS, JOSEPH, Upper Chichester.
July 15, 1819 - Aug 25, 1819.
Father (name not given), sisters Rachel and husband, Elizabeth and Sarah and brother John.
Exrs: Joseph WALKER.
Wits: Emmor J. NEWLIN and Silas GREEN. #519.

REVELL, PETER, Ridley Township.
Aug 18, 1819 - Aug 28, 1819.
Estate to wife Mary.

Exrs: James MADDOCK of Ridley.
Wits: Samuel LYTLE and Mary Ann REVELL. #520.

ROWAN, MARTHA, Upper Chichester.
Jan 25, 1799 - Sept 13, 1819.
Sons James ROWAN, grandsons John and James.
Exrs: Sd. son James.
Wits: William MILLER and Aaron HUSTON. #521.

WHITE, GEORGE, Radnor.
Aug 18, 1819 - Sept 13, 1819.
Children: Isaac, Jacob, Hannah GYGER and Nancy EDWARDS and her son Samuel EDWARDS.
Exrs: Son Isaac and neighbor Benjamin DAVIS.
Wits: Daniel Abraham and Edward SITER. #522.

BONSALL, ANN, Darby.
Aug 28, 1819 - Sept 16, 1819.
Mary BONSALL wife of Enoch, Elizabeth widow of Samuel BONSALL, niece Mary BONSALL daughter of Moses BONSALL, brother William.
Exrs: Brother Moses BONSALL.
Wits: Benjamin BONSALL and John PALMER. #523.

DAWES, RUMFORD, Springfield.
Dec 20, 1818 - Nov 1, 1819.
Names Books of Rumford and Abijah DAWES, first wife Mary and second wife Martha. Children: Jonathan, Mary W. HOWELL wife of Samuel E. and their children Samuel D., George, Mary D., Charles and his children; Elizabeth MASSEY wife of Thomas and their children Mary D., Charles R., Edward A., Thomas and William N., Mary and George WHITELOCK children of Charles WHITELOCK, dec'd., a brother of former wife. Legacies to Center and Springfield Meetings - mentions marriage contract with wife Martha as recorded at Chester. Nephew Samuel F. DAWES and wife Martha.
Exrs: Samuel E. HOWELL, son Jonathan and friend George Bolton LOWNES. Real estate belonging to second wife mentioned.
Wits: John OGDEN, Jr. and George LEWIS. #524.

PLANKINTON, SAMUEL, Edgmont.
Nov 11, 1819 - Nov 30, 1819
Wife Sarah sole legatee and executrix.

Exrs: Wife Sarah
Wits: Enos PAINTER and John YARNALL #525

MILLER, MARY, widow, Haverford.
May 4, 1818 - Jan 18, 1820.
Children: Jonathan, Deborah DOWNING wife of Hunt DOWNING; Patience MILLER wife of Robert MILLER; Ruth DUNWOODY; Mary Ann, Annetta, Theresa and Eliza children: of son Joseph I. MILLER, dec'd; and Mary wife of Samuel MILLER.
Exrs: Niece Deborah JORDAN, sd. son Jonathan.
Wits: William HALLOWELL and Jno. ELLIOTT. #526

SMEDLEY, AMBROSE, Middletown.
Nov 13, 1819 - June 24, 1820.
Wife Elizabeth; children: Ambrose, Samuel, Elizabeth KELLOGG, Mary, Ahinoam YARNALL and Sarah GRIFFITH - Mentions plantation "marked on Aaron MATSON'S draft" - also tract in Harrison Co. Va., to Sarah, Mary and Ahinoam, George MILLER, Samuel PANCOAST, Owen RHODES, Benjamin YARNALL, Enoch YARNALL and Jesse REECE to assist sons in settling line between them and heirs of Jacob MINSHALL and William SMEDLEY.
Exrs: Sd. wife, sons Samuel and Ambrose SMEDLEY.
Wits: George MILLER and James SMEDLEY #527.

DUTTON, JONATHAN, Upper Chichester.
Oct 9, 1819 - Feb 23, 1820.
Wife Marsha; children: John, Richard and his son Jonathan, Alice PAIST, Jonathan, Thomas and son Robert, and Rebecca - mentions land brought of Nicholas FAIRLAMB and of James DAY - mentions Nathan SUPLEE, Joseph TALBOT, John TAYLOR, Swen STAR, Isaac PENNELL, James CRAIGE, William GRAHAM - mentions property bought by father of John WILLIAMSON and wife with privileges mentioned in John COBURN'S Deed also of Isaac LAWRENCE and John COBOURN. Fishery on the Delaware to sons Jonathan and Thomas. Friends of John BROOMALL, Thomas DUTTON and Joseph TALBOT to appraise.
Exrs: Sons Jonathan and Thomas DUTTON.
Wits: Joseph FOX and Samuel F. HEWES. #528.

HUBBS, SARAH, widow, Springfield.
Sept 5, 1813 - Codicil Aug 4, 1818. Proved Mar 24, 1820.

Niece Clarissa LOWNES daughter of bro. Slater LOWNES - children
of niece Mary FORD wife of Anderson FORD. Sister Rebecca
LOWNES and sister in law Hannah LOWNES.
Exrs: Bro. George Bolton LOWNES and William PENNOCK.
Wits: George. B. LOWNES, Hannah LOWNES, William PENNOCK.
Exr: John LEWIS, Springfield, as executor in place of William
PENNOCK.
Wits: Hannah TOWNES and Rumford DAWES.
John LEWIS renounced. #529.

PEARSON, ELIZABETH, Ridley.
July 22, 1811 - May 30, 1820.
Five daughters: Hannah, Marsha, Ann, Elizabeth and Susanna.
Exrs: Cousin John PEARSON and his son Benjamin of Darby.
Wits: Anna B. GARRETT and Jane LEWIS. #530.

EDENTON, DINAH, Middletown.
April 14, 1818 - June 7, 1820.
Legacies to Jacob ARMSTRONG and Mary, his wife - Peter
WORRELL trustee for son Joseph HALL and lawful children should he
leave any. Four children of Rebecca a colored woman who was brought
up by the late Thomas WORRELL of Middletown namely George
STILL, John, Eliza and Prudence STILL.
Exrs: Abram SHARPLES of Aston.
Wits: Francis WISELY and Nathan YEARSLEY.
Adm. William MENDENHALL.
Abram SHARPLES renounced. #531.

BOTTOMLEY, JOHN, Aston.
Dec 9, 1815 - June 24, 1820.
Daughter Martha MURPHEY and surviving children. Granddaughter
Jane MURPHEY only one named.
Exrs: Brother Thomas BOTTOMLEY and James WOOD of Phila.
Wits: John PEIRCE and Jane PEIRCE. #532.

SIDDONS, WILLIAM, Chester.
May 12, 1815 - June 28, 1820.
Wife ____; children: John, Sarah, Ann and Joshua.
Exrs: Sd. wife.
Wits: William GRAHAM and Samuel J. WITHY. #533.

PENNELL, Joseph, Aston, Yeoman.
Feb 29, 1820 - July 3, 1820.
Wife Sarah; children: Robert and his son Joseph, Joseph and his children, Lewis, Mark, Alice and William; Mary CHURCHMAN wife of Owen and her children PENNELL and Edward; ___? PALMER and her children William, Eliza and PENNELL; ___? YARNALL daughter Priscilla; Meredith and his children Priscilla and Thamsin; Alice FRAZER no children named; Sarah MEREDITH wife of Joseph no children named, Richard? DILWORTH, children Mary and Hannah; Susanna HANNUM wife of Samuel, son PENNELL.
Exrs: Son Robert PENNELL and son in law Samuel HANNUM - mentions Thomas PENNELL, Mark WILLCOX, Jesse WALKER, A. & S. MENDENHALL - mentions house in Filbert St. Phila. and on 9th. Street Phila. previously Owen CUSHMAN'S also one in Wilmington. Lands in Randolph and Wood Counties, Va.
Wits: William FAIRLAMB and Jesse WALTER. #534.

LLOYD, JAMES, ___ Twp.
June 7, 1820 - Aug 25, 1820.
Mother Ann LLOYD, Mary HUMPHREYS daughter of William and Lowry HUMPHREYS, Bro. Isaac LLOYD to have stock in Farmers and Mechanics Bank and to be executor.
Exrs: Isaac LLOYD.
Wits: John HUNT and Abraham G. HUNT. #535.

RILEY, RICHARD, Lower Chichester.
Nov 28, 1818 - Sept 18, 1820.
Wife Mary, Daughter Margaret CONARROE. Each of nine grandchildren "a good family bible".
Exrs: Son in law Thomas CONARROE and wife Margaret.
Wits: Fredk. SHULL and Joseph WALKER, Jr. #536.

RUSSELL, JESSE, Edgmont.
Aug 2, 1820 - Sept 18, 1820.
Children: Mary (not 21) wife of Samuel LAMPLEY; Sarah Ann and William (both minors). Mentions deed to Obed RUSSELL for part ownership with Joseph RUSSELL in tract.
Exrs: John RUSSELL and Joseph REGESTER, also to be "guardeens" for William and Sarah Ann.
Wits: Daniel MEGEOWEN, George GREEN, Richard MEGOWEN and Obed RUSSELL. #537.

PENNELL, ISAAC, Upper Chichester.
June 18, 1816 - Oct 12, 1820.
Wife Esther and all the children when living, son John to have tract in Upper Chichester. Any deficiency in sharing with sisters Esther and Lydia to be paid out of real estate by son John, they, if single, to have occupancy of part of the homestead.
Wits: John BOOTH and Joseph BOOTH. #538.

BISHOP, MARY, Edgmont.
April 27, 1817 - Oct 17, 1820.
Children: Joseph, George, Thomas, Phebe PHAROH, Margaret FORWOOD, dec'd., wife of Robert and her children Sarah, Mary and Jane; Mary; Sarah HOWARD, dec'd., wife of Jonathan and her daughter Rebecca. Other grandchildren parents not named: Samuel B. GRUBB, Jane STEEL and William BISHOP.
Exrs: Grandson William BISHOP.
Wits: Thomas BISHOP and John RUSSELL. #539.

MINSHALL, LYDIA, Middletown.
July 1, 1817 - Dec 2, 1820.
Children Abel and John MINSHALL; Jesse REECE and Sarah BAKER wife of William BAKER.
Exrs: Jesse REECE and William BAKER.
Wits: George MILLER, Jr., Phebe MILLER and George MILLER. #540.

TALBOT, JOHN, Upper Chichester.
Jan 5, 1821 - Codicil: Jan 6, 1821. Proved Feb 3, 1821.
Wife Sarah, sister Martha BROOMALL, brother Jacob, nephews: Nathan PENNELL, John TALBOT, John DUTTON and son Jacob; Nehemiah BROOMALL and son John Talbot BROOMALL; David TOWNSEND and David BROOMALL, John Talbot LEVIS son of Joseph and Rebecca, and Sarah LARKIN daughter of Mishael ROGERS - mentions Ford tract in Bethel, James GRUBB tract, John BROOMALL'S, William MC CORP'S, George MARTIN'S, John SMITH'S, Rebecca and Ann HUSTON'S and William TALBOT'S land. Wills interest in mill at Westtown to Nathan PENNELL and Cyrus MENDENHALL in trust for education of poor children.
Exrs: Sd. wife, George MARVIN, nephew John BROOMALL and friend Nathan SHARPLESS, of Concord.
Wits: George MARTIN, Jr. and Joseph BOOTH.

Wits: George MARTIN, Jr. and Hannah LEED #541.

THOMPSON, ANN, Chester Twp.
Feb 3, 1817 - Feb 16 ,1817.
Children: Mordecai, Daniel and his daughters Ann, Ellen and Eliza; Mary, dec'd., daughter Sarah.
Exrs: Son Daniel.
Wits: Edward MENSHALL and Joseph WEAVER, Jr. #542.

HART, HANNAH, widow, Chester.
Feb 14, 1821 - Feb 26, 1821.
Grand daughter Hannah M. HART. Legacy to Mary Ann GRACE, of Phila.
Exrs: Grandson John D. HART, also to act as guardian of his sister Hannah.
Wits: William KERLIN and Z. W. FLOWER. #543.

CALEY, Samuel, Newtown.
April 26, 1820 - Mar 14, 1821.
Wife Hannah; sister Ann THOMAS; children Samuel, Mary wife of Phineas LEWIS, Ann and her children Jacob and Ann CALEY; grandson Samuel CALEY; Mary DUNN and John CHEYNY, Thomas WILLING for use of Ann MORRIS and John EVANS for use of Newtown Meeting. Lands in Radnor Twp.; lines of Lewis LEWIS, George BROOKES, Levi LEWIS, David PHILIPS, Benjamin DAVIS, James BAILY.
Exrs: Son Samuel CALEY.
Wits: Davis BEAUMONT and Edward HUNTER. #544.

PARSONS, MAHLON, Nether Providence.
April 15, 1818 - April 30, 1821.
Wife Mary, children Jemima, Nathaniel, Joseph, Mahlon H., George, Israel and Hannah.
Exrs: Sd. wife and son Nathaniel.
Wits: George MILLER and John SLAWTER. #545.

LOWNES, CURTIS, Ridley.
Nov 271, 1820 - April 18, 1821.
Children: John LOWNES, Agnes LEVIS, Elizabeth HUGINS and Esther LOWNES. Dwelling house Third below Market St. Phila. -

mentions George B. LOWNES, Joseph GIBBONS and THIMARY'S land. Names Samuel POTTS.
Exrs: Son John LOWNES and bro. George B. LOWNES.
Wits: Alice HIBBERD and Joseph LOWNES. #546.

CARTER, EDWARD, Chester.
Aug 14, 1819 - May 9, 1821.
Wife Catharine; daughters Ann ROBERTS and Hannah CULIN and heirs - mentions Nimrod MAXWELL, Joseph JOHNSON, Irwin ARMSTRONG, Thomas MALON and heirs of Abraham CARTER.
Exrs: John McMICHAEL and Dr. Job TERREL.
Wits: Peter DESHONG and Enoch TAYLOR. #547.

HEWES, SAMUEL, Aston, Yeoman.
Oct 20, 1817 - May 12, 1821.
Wife Sarah: children Samuel and Jemima.
Exrs: Sd. wife and son Samuel.
Wits: Joseph FOX and Isaac MASSEY. #548.

DAVIS, TACY, Newtown.
May 2, 1820 - May 16, 1821.
Brother Benjamin; sisters Ruth PIERCE, Hannah DAVIS and sister in law Frances; nieces Sarah and Tacy GUIGER, Anna CRAWFORD, minor, Lydia and Mary DAVIS children of Benjamin, David Jones DAVIS, Tacy GARRIGUES and daughter Sarah; Benjamin D. GARRIGUES.
Exrs: Sd. brother Benjamin.
Wits: Rebecca REECE and Elijah LEWIS. #549.

ASKEN, ELIZABETH, Upper Chichester.
May 9, 1818 - June 9, 1821.
Children: Joseph, Benjamin, Samuel, Mary HALL children Joseph A. and Elizabeth; also grandson Benjamin Asken.
Exrs: Sd. son Joseph.
Wits: Thomas MARSHALL and Joseph TALBOT. #550.

TRIMBLE, ESTHER, Thornbury.
____ - July 11, 1821.
Children: Joseph, Margaret PEIRCE and daughter Esther Ann, Samuel and daughter Esther, and Ann WILLIAMS.

Exrs: Thomas PEIRCE and Samuel TRIMBLE.
Wits: Abram SHARPLES and Eli D. PEIRCE.
Codicil of Nov 23, 1820 names Esther TRIMBLE daughter of Joseph, Phebe PEIRCE a granddaughter.
Wits: Eli D. PEIRCE and Samuel L. SMEDLEY. #551.

PRINCE, RACHAL, Brandiwine Hundred, New Castle County.
May 6, 1818 - June 21, 1821.
Legacies to the following: Joseph JOHNSON'S wife Amy, Samuel LAMPLUGH'S sister Lidia; Elizabeth MINTIRE, Hannah WILKINS daughter of Simon and Ann CRANSTON, dec'd., Mary wife of Joseph WORRELL, David CHANY son of Charles and Prudence CHANY, dec'd., Pheby LAMPLUGH wife of Beason LAMPLUGH, Thomas and Mary MACE and their three daughters Sarah PINKERTON, Elizabeth EBRIGHT and Rachal MACE, Davis OSLERE wife Selany and children: Job G. and Harriet S. OSLERE, Mary LAMPLUGH wife of Josiah, and Susannah LOYD wife of Jeremiah LOYD.
Exrs: Davis OSLERE and Samuel LAMPLUGH.
Wits: John DIXON and Richard CLAYTON. #552.

KIRK, PHILLIP, Upper Providence.
Dec 10, 1818 - Aug 4, 1821.
Sons Benjamin and John, grandson Phillip (under age) son of Benjamin.
Exrs: Friend George MILLER.
Wits: Benedict MALIN, Gideon Malin. #553.

BONSALL, GEORGE, Haverford.
April 22, 1821 - Aug 22, 1821.
Wife Mary and her mother Elizabeth MOORE, sister Mary PALMER widow of John PALMER and her sons Samuel, Isaac, John and Moses, Mary MOORE daughter of Eli MOORE - mentions Haverford Friends' Meeting and a bound child Parker BONSALL.
Exrs: Abraham LEWIS, Upper Darby and Israel W. MORRIS, Lower Merion.
Wits: Walker MOORE and Henry MORRIS. #554.

HAWORTH, PATIENCE, Haverford.
Aug 13, 1821 - Sept 27, 1821.

Children: John HAWORTH, Rebecca DAVIS, widow, Deborah
RUDOLPH and daughter Rebecca; Mary PYOTT and daughter
Patience.
Exrs: Rebecca DAVIS and Joseph WILSON, M.D.
Wits: Caleb BITTLE, Abraham FREE. #555.

HAHN, JOHN, Darby.
May 6, 1821 - Nov 20, 1821.
Children: Catherina wife of James RUDOLPH, Elizabeth BAKER, son
William PARRISH alias HAHN, John, Casper, Mary and Henry HAHN
and Rosina wife of James KINNEY, bound girl Matilda MEREDITH.
Exrs: John RIVELY and Halliday JACKSON.
Wits: George SERRILL and Thomas SEMANS. #556.

TALBOT, SARAH, Upper Chichester.
Oct 17, 1821 - Nov 26, 1821.
Brother Thomas LEVIS and his child Rebecca, Rebecca HENDERSON
and child Elizabeth HENDERSON, Sarah HUNTER, cousin Rebecca
MARTIN of Wilmington. Sarah wife of Mordicai LARKIN, and
Elizabeth BROBSON. Children of brother Thomas, and sister Mary.
Exrs: George MARTIN, Jr.
Written from notes taken by Sarah SHARPLESS and admitted on
testimony of same and George MARTIN, Nov 26, 1821. #557.

HUNTER, JOHN, Newtown.
Sept 6, 1813 - Dec 17, 1821.
Wife Ann, children: John, Sarah EVANS, Ann, Rebecca MATLACK,
Elizabeth HUNTER. Grandson Isaac VANLEER (a minor). Property in
Wilmington at Walnut and Third St.
Exrs: Sd. son John.
Wits: Elisha MOORE, Jesse BROOKE and John BROOKE. #558.

BALL, JOHN, Upper Darby.
March 12, 1818 - Dec 19, 1821.
Brothers, Joseph, Nathan and Thomas, sisters Mary LOBB, Elizabeth
BALL, Susanna EARL and Hannah POWELL. Children of Hannah:
John, Joseph, George, Abram, Thomas, Patience DICKINSON, Sarah
SNYDER, Hannah RUDOLPH, Mary POWELL. To brothers Joseph
and Nathan BALL property in Ohio.
Exrs: Brothers Joseph and Thomas and nephew Abram POWELL.
Wits: John W. BUNTING and Jehu MOORE. #559.

GRAHAM, WILLIAM, Chester.
March 4, 1820 - Jan 4, 1822.
Wife Jane, sisters Eleanor, Mary, Henrietta and Katharine.
Exrs: Sd. wife.
Wits: None.
Signature sworn to by Benjamin TILGHMAN and Preston EYRE.
#560.

BURNS, JOSEPH, Chester.
Dec 11, 1821 - Jan 2, 1822.
Wife Hannah, children Margaret and George.
Exrs: Brother John BURNS and nephew Gillead BURNS.
Wits: Joseph WEAVER and J. H. TERRILL. #561.

PENNELL, JAMES, Upper Chichester.
Nov 2, 1821 - Feb 9, 1822.
Wife Margaret PENNELL, she to educate and maintain my children during minority, Susanna the only one mentioned.
Exrs: George MARTIN, Jr.
Wits: John BROOMALL and John TALBOT. #562.

REDMAN, ELIZABETH, Springfield.
Dec 27, 1821 - Feb 11, 1822.
Sister Sarah CROXEN and nat. children Enos CROXEN and Mary BELL, Elizabeth LOWNES, Sidney LOWNES and Joseph LOWNES and his wife Rachel and their five children: Rebecca, Hugh, William, Phineas and Massey.
Exrs: Sd. Joseph LOWNES.
Wits: Owen RHOADS and George B. LOWNES. #563.

CROSBY, JOHN, Chester Boro.
July 18, 1813 - Feb 22, 1822.
Wife Ann, children: Eleanor HILL wife of John F. HILL; ---- MARTIN children William and Ann; Susanna MORTON husband, John S. Peirce and Robert P. CROSBY.
Exrs: Sons Peirce and Robert P.
Wits: Benjamin PEARSON and Joseph WEAVER. #564.

STEVENSON, JOHN, Haverford.
Feb 22, 1812 - March 8, 1822.

Frances WHITAKER, legacy "if living at time of my decease" residue to
children of brothers and sisters: William, James, Allen, Barbara, Jane
and Maria, and Jane THOMSON, the daughter of Jane STEVENSON;
the residue to be equally divided between my said brothers and sister's
children and said Jane THOMSON share and share alike."
Exrs: John ELLIOT of Lower Merion, Surveyor and Peter GASKELL
of Radnor.
Wits: Benjamin RITTENHOUSE and Joseph C. MORGAN. #565.

MARSHALL, SUSANNA, Darby.
June 8, 1818 - March 20, 1822.
Brother John MARSHALL and children: Joseph, Abram, Hannah
LUKINS, Margaret MARION, Nathan, sister Martha ---- and children:
Abram JOHNSON, Mary JOHNSON, Martha PASCHALL and Abigail
EVANS, dec'd., children of Abigail: Mary MOORE, Martha MOORE,
Elizabeth EVANS, Hannah EVANS, Abram EVANS, Joseph EVANS,
John EVANS and Susanna TYSON, dec'd., who is mentioned as having
left children, (their names not given). Hannah wife of Samuel MOORE,
William STEEL son of William and grandson of James STEEL.
Exrs: Friend Robert STEEL and nephew Abram JOHNSON.
Wits: John SELLERS and Nathan SELLERS. #566.

MATLACK, TACY, Radnor.
Feb 20, 1809 - March 26, 1822.
Children of brothers and sisters: Tacy LEWIS parents Dydemus and
Phebe, Tacy MATLACK parents Simeon and Elizabeth, Simeon
MATLACK, Hannah TRASEL (or TRACELL), Nathan MATLACK,
Thomas and Martha MATLACK of Virginia and George MATLACK.
Exrs: Eli LEWIS, Newtown.
Wits: Rachel MATLACK and Tacy MATLACK. #567.

HOWARD, ALICE, Edgmont.
May 26, 1821 - April 3, 1822.
Sister Martha YARNELL and daughter Omey, sister Hannah
YARNELL and children Hannah YARNELL and Deborah YARNELL
also three sons of Hannah HOWARD, Residue to Hannah's daughters.
Exrs: Cousin Everatt G. PASSMORE.
Wits: Everatt G. PASSMORE and Harper HOWARD. #568.

BEVAN, ISABELLA, Chester.
June --, 1820 - April 23, 1822.

Sister Tacy Ann STACY and children James G. and Davis Bevan
STACY. Brother David BEVAN and child Agnes C. BEVAN, cousin
Abigail TAYLOR. Legacy to Chester Meeting.
Exrs: Davis B. STACY.
Wits: S. EDWARDS and J. H. TERRILL. #569.

RICHARDSON, THOMAS, Chester.
Feb 5, 1816 - April 27, 1822.
Mentions housekeeper Maria REDDING; daughter Mary
RICHARDSON, minor.
Exrs: Ellis ROBERTS and John SHARPLESS, N. Providence.
Wits: Job H. TERRILL and Joseph WEAVER, Jr. #570.

GRIFFITH, GEORGE.
April 2, 1822 - May 27, 1822.
Wife Eunice, sister Mary S. GRIFFITH, son William S. GRIFFITH,
Joseph PENNELL of Middletown to act as guardian to sd. son.
Exrs: William MORGAN.
Wits: James EMLEN and Samuel L. SMEDLEY. #571.

EVANS, JOHN, Newtown.
May 16, 1822 - July 9, 1822.
Wife Phebe, brother Edward, brother in law Robert STEEL.
Exrs: Sd. brother and brother in law.
Wits: John PRATT and Samuel CALEY. #572.

HERMANY, JONATHAN, Chester.
June 24, 1822 - July 15, 1822.
Sister Rachel BAGGS wife of William and her heirs.
Exrs: Friend William KERLIN.
Wits: Samuel LONG and Joseph H. HORTON. #573.

BROOMALL, DANIEL.
Sept 10, 1821 - July 15, 1822.
Wife Rachel and her heirs, she to be executrix.
Exrs: Rachel.
Wits: J. H. TERRILL and S. EDWARDS. #574.

EDWARDS, JOSEPH, Chester.
Aug 17, 1822 - Aug 22, 1822.

Wife Mary, brothers Abner, Robert and James, dec'd., cousins Abigail
PRICE and Abraham TRIMBLE.
Exrs: Sd. wife and cousin Abraham TRIMBLE.
Wits: A. TRIMBLE and S. EDWARDS. #575.

YARNALL, ELIZABETH, Concord.
Aug 22, 1822 - Aug 28, 1822.
Brothers Nathan and Ellis and sister Rachel YARNALL.
Exrs: Sd. brother Ellis and cousin Nathan SHARPLES.
Wits: Samuel MARSHALL and Sarah MENDENHALL. #576.

WALTER, NATHANIEL, Concord.
Jan 4, 1822 - Sept 12, 1822.
Wife Susanna, children: Mary F., Ann M., Joseph (minor), Nathaniel
(minor), and Robert F. - niece Mary G. WALTER. Property joining that
of Benjamin MARTIN.
Exrs: Sd. wife.
Wits: Moses PALMER and John PALMER. #577.

WILLIAMS, MARGARET, Radnor.
Jan 12, 1819 - Sept 16, 1822.
Widow of William WILLIAMS. Wills to John GODFREY, Margaret wife
of D. DAVIS, Mary wife of James Smith, Margaret wife of Evan
ROBERTS, Margaret daughter of D. DAVIS, Wardens of Radnor
Church, Mary SHEAF wife of William, and Rachel FISHER wife of
Jacob. Property in Radnor left to her and heirs by act passed Jan 22,
1817.
Exrs: Evan ROBERTS and Joseph HOSKINS.
Wits: Daniel KINZIE and David EVANS. #578.

MOORE, ELIZABETH, widow of Richard, Lower Chichester.
Dec 15, 1811 - no date of probate.
Daughter Mary, wife of John BURNS, and her two children James and
Elizabeth. Other grandchildren William and Elizabeth MOORE.
Exrs: Richard RILEY.
Wits: Joseph WALKER, Jr. and Joseph MARSHALL.
Codicil June 12, 1821 mentions the death of Richard RILEY and
appoints Joseph WALKER, Jr. in his stead.
Wits: Phebe A. SEEDS and William BUCKNALL.
Inventory proved Nov 6, 1822. #579.

BEALE, JOHN, Bethel.
June 23, 1815 - Oct 21, 1822.
Wife Olive, children: Aaron, Ann CHAMBERLAIN, Phebe, Mary GRAVES, Lydia, John and Olive - mentions land purchased of Ezekiel PYLE.
Exrs: William TRIMBLE.
Wits: Levi MATSON and Abraham MATTSON. #580.

BURNS, JOHN, Lower Chichester.
Wife Mary, children: Gilliad, James and Eliza - mentions W. BURKNELL, Zachariah DERRICK, David TRAINOR, Dr. Gidein JAYKES as owning property.
Exrs: Son Gilliad BURNS and Thomas MARSHALL.
Wits: Mark ELLIOTT and Davis AFFLICK. #581.

LEWIS, HANNAH, Radnor. Nuncupative Will.
April 13, 1822 - Nov 7, 1822.
Mentions Rachel DAVIS, Elizabeth ESREY, Mary ROTHERFORD, Deberah WINDAL, Hannah GRIFFITH, Mary THOMAS, Enos LEWIS, Henry LEWIS, Evven JONES daughter, Joseph H. PRATT'S daughter, Richard GRIFFITH, three children, nieces Cicaly MENDENHALL, Mary THOMAS, Debrah WINDAL and Mary PRATT. To my sister Hannah BROOK and myself (Rebecca EVANS, party to whom she told what she wished done with property) - mentions William DAVIS.
Exrs: Enos LEWIS and Henry LEWIS.
Wits: Rebecca EVANS, Lydia EVANS and Hannah BROOKE. #582.

FAWKES, RICHARD, Newtown. Nuncupative Will.
Oct 19, 1822 - Dec 14, 1822.
Relatives Alice FAWKES and Elizabeth LITZENBERG, Thirza CANN, son Isaiah FAWKES.
Wits: Alice FAWKES and Elizabeth LITZENBERG.
December 7, 1822 approval of widow Mary FAWKES and asking that letters of administration be granted to son Isaiah FAWKES.
Wits: Joseph DAVIS and Simon LITZENBERG. #583.

DUNN, SARAH, ____ Twp.
Dec 29, 1822 - Feb 10, 1823.
Mother Mary, brother Mordecai DUNN, sisters Esther SANKEY and Mary DNT, sister Susanna DUNN.
Wits: Mary EDWARDS and Elizabeth SANKEY.

Letters granted to Susanna DUNN. #584.

MALIN, SAMUEL, ____ Twp.
Aug 22, 1820 - March 22, 1823.
Wife Susan P., brothers and sisters Abner*, Hannah MARTIN and her children: Joshua, Jehu, Hiram, Samuel, Caleb, Jacob and Orphy; George*; Pusey, Harvy and Samuel MALIN children of Joel; Thomas and his sons Minshall, William and Randle; Jacob MALIN*, and their three sisters Agnes, Ann and Elizabeth.
Exrs: Sd. wife.
Wits: James SMEDLEY and Sarah Ann KIRK.
*Classing of the three somewhat uncertain. #585.

MORTON, ERASMUS, Yeoman.
March 16, 1823 - May 5, 1823.
Mary MIDDLETON widow of Joseph MIDDLETON of Chester Twp. - mentions property on lines of David TREINOR, Jr. and Joseph COBURN.
Wits: Joseph CARTER, Wesley CARTER and Daniel LAMPLUGH. #586.

LEWELLIN, ANN, Newtown.
July 1, 1822 - May 14, 1823.
Step brother John HOWARD, three nieces Margaret DAVIS, Rebecca CONARD and Ann BEAVER, grandniece Elizabeth L. REECE, niece Rebecca REECE.
Exrs: Elijah Lewis.
Wits: Joseph LEWIS and William CRAWFORD. #587.

MC MICHAEL, JOHN, Chester.
Sept 17, 1822 - May 26, 1823.
Wife Ann and her daughter Hannah, brother Samuel and sister Mary MC ALISTER, niece Jersey THOMPSON - names friends George G. LEIPER, Esq., Dr. Job H. TERRILL and Thomas Kerns. Claim against estate of Edward TRENT, Richmond.
Exrs: George G. LEIPER.
Wits: Thomas MALIN and S. EDWARDS. #588.

HORNE, EDWARD, Darby.
July 3, 1823 - July 23, 1823.

Wife Mary, children: William D., Stephen, John, Davis, Elizabeth, Simon, Henry H., Martha M. GOODWIN. Property in Mercer County purchased of William GEESEMAN.
Exrs: Sd. sons Stephen and Henry H. HORNE.
Wits: George SERRILL and Margaret ENGLE. #589.

PITT, JOHN, Middletown.
Dec 31, 1819 - Aug 7, 1823.
Wife Hannah PITT, son Samuel, daughter Mary LINSHEED, son John's daughter Phebe.
Exrs: Samuel PITT and Nathan YEARSLEY.
Wits: William FAIRLAMB and Robert FAIRLAMB. #590.

BARNARD, SUSANNA, Chester Borough.
Dec 9, 1822 - Aug 18, 1823.
Sons Thomas, Isaac, daughter Elizabeth, dec'd.; granddaughters Susan Ann PRICE, Harriet D. PRICE and Elizabeth B. PRICE.
Exrs: Son Isaac D. BARNARD.
Wits: Jon. PENNELL and A. T. DICK. #591.

WORRALL, JANE, Marple Spinster.
Sept 13, 1823 - Sept 18, 1823.
Sisters Abigail WORRALL and Martha YARNALL - mentions Samuel BLACK.
Exrs: Sister Abigail WORRALL and kinsman Isaac W. YARNALL.
Wits: Samuel BLACK and Abel WORRELL. #592.

EDWARDS, JANE, widow, Chester.
Sept 26, 1823 - Oct 11, 1823.
Sons Garrett, Charles, George and Seth (a minor) - mentions judgement made against Jane VERNON and John HIBBERD. Friend John HIBBERD of N. Providence to be guardian of son Seth.
Exrs: Son Garrett and John HIBBERD.
Wits: Joshua HARRISON and Ann HARRISON. #593.

MARSHALL, JAMES, Darby.
June 24, 1820 - Oct 17, 1823.
To nephew Thomas MARSHALL, son of John MARSHALL, he to be sole executor.
Exrs: John MARSHALL.
Wits: Joseph BONSALL and Nicholas RICE. #594.

LOVEN, MELCHIOR, Lower Chichester.
July 8, 1820 - Oct 18, 1823.
Sole legatee and executrix, stepdaughter Lydia EBRITE.
Exrs: Lydia EBRITE.
Wits: Penelope BURNS and William MCGLAUGHLIN. #595.

BATTIN, SARAH, Lower Providence.
Sept 4, 1821 - Oct 23, 1823.
To Enos SHARPLESS in trust for purpose of schooling poor children, members of Chester preparative meeting.
Exrs: Sd. Enos SHARPLESS.
Wits: Nathan SHARPLES and Micajah SPEAKMAN. #596.

HOLLAND, ROBERT, (a coulared man), Darby.
Aug 31, 1823 - Nov 7, 1823.
Sister Sarah CHASE wife of Richard, of Phila, and her son Robert. Int of estate to sister and her children.
Exrs: Halladay JACKSON, signed Robert Holls.
Wits: Nathaniel NEWLIN and Martha COWGILL. #597.

PRATT, DAVID, Jr., Marple.
Oct 7, 1823 - Nov 7, 1823.
Brothers and sisters: Jane, Lydia, Christian, Orpha, Jeremiah, Henry, Randal, John, Abraham, and Joseph. Real Est. in Ohio - mentions Charles MULLEN.
Exrs: Father, Jeremiah and Henry.
Wits: Davis RICHARDS and Caleb D. WEST. #598.

LEWIS, JOHN, Springfield.
Oct 6, 1823 - Nov 1, 1823.
Children: William, Edward, Franklin, Mordecai, Jane, Mary, Sarah, Sidney, John and George.
Exrs: Sons John and George LEWIS.
Wits: Evan WALKER and J. L. PEARSON. #599.

WORRELL, AARON, Marple.
April 21, 1821 - Aug 16, 1823.
Nieces, Miriam WORRELL, Sidney LATCH wife of John, Hannah LATCH wife of Rudolph, Phebe WORRELL, nephew John LATCH.
Exrs: Mariam WORRELL and nephew John LATCH.
Wits: Benjamin LOBB, Enos LEWIS and William NUZUM. #600.

HAYMAN, WILLIAM, gentleman, Newtown.
Aug 8, 1816 - Nov 13, 1823.
Children: Anthony and his son William, William, Isaac Wayne, Elizabeth wife of George W. HOLSTEIN, Sophia wife of Matthias COATES and Ann wife of Aaron VOGDES. Property lines of John BROOKE, Joseph LEWIS, Elijah BROOKE, Jonathan THOMAS, Mordecai DAVIS - In Willistown and Edgemont, lines of Aaron SELL, Enoch YARNEL, Amos YARNEL, Aaron GARRET and others.
Exrs: George Washington HOLSTEIN, son William and nephew, Isaac WAYNE, Esq.
Wits: Levi PAWLING, Joseph CRAWFORD and David Henderson. #601.

FARR, ABRAHAM, Edgmont.
July 23, 1823 - Nov 26, 1823.
Grandchildren: Nathan, Mary, Phebe and Sarah WOOD. Girls to occupy home till marriage or youngest is twenty one.
Exrs: Son Abraham FARR and nephew John LEWIS.
Wits: George MILLER and Sarah MILLER. #602.

BOOTH, JOHN, Upper Chichester.
Nov 1, 1823 - Nov 26, 1823.
Wife Elizabeth, son Joseph and his five children: William, Caleb, Sarah, John and Elizabeth. Daughter Sarah McCAY dec'd. and children John McCAY and Elizabeth Cloud. Property lines of William HUSTON, Townsend THOMAS et al.
Wits: John BROOMALL and George MARTIN, Jr. #603.

PAINTER, Samuel, Thornbury.
Feb 1, 1818 - Dec 20, 1823.
Wife Esther, sister Lydia wife of Isaac BAILY and her sons James of Baltimore and Thomas of East Marlborough and Vincent of Mereland. Names four nieces: Betty MERCER; Lydia BENNETT, Esther CLEMSON and Hannah DICKENSON; a cousin Samuel Painter MERCER; Emy DIXON widow of brother in law Isaac DIXON of Wilmington; a stepson Jesse CHANDLER and his son Samuel Painter CHANDLER; niece Esther TATE and brother in law William TATE; Ruth and Hannah GILPIN daughters of Isaac G. GILPIN; Esther Painter JONES daughter of Benjamin and Ann JONES of E. Bradford; Samuel son of cousin Joseph PAINTER and Lydia his wife.

Exrs: Sd. wife and cousins Jesse MERCER, Thomas BAILY and James
BAILY sons of brother Isaac BAILY.
Wits: William CHEYNEY and Joseph James.
Codicil of Oct 27, 1823 mentions Joshua TATE, Martha TATE, Caleb J.
HOOPER and Daniel SPEAKMAN.
Wits: Abner HOOPER, Jesse MERCER and James BAILY. #604.

HEACOCK, PHEBE, Kingsessing.
June 20, 1814 - Dec 22, 1823.
Natural daughters Elizabeth HEACOCK and Eliza HORNE wife of
Thomas HORNE.
Exrs: Son in law of Thomas HORNE.
Wits: Edward GARRIGUES and Benjamin GARRIGUES. #605.

THOMAS, GIDEON, Newtown.
Nov 28, 1822 - Jan 21, 1824.
Wife Phebe, children: Robert M., Sarah LLEWELIN and Ann
SPEAKMAN.
Exrs: Sd. wife and son Robert M. THOMAS.
Wits: Uriah THOMAS and Phineas LEWIS.
Codicil Nov 28, 1823
Wits: Same. #606.

BOND, ISAAC, Haverford.
March 10, 1823 - Feb 6, 1824.
Wife Mary, children: Anna Maria, Sarah, Jonathan, Isaac and his
children Eliza, Mary and Thomas.
Exrs: Sd. wife and son Jonathan.
Wits: Reece HAYCOCK and Caleb BITTLE. #607.

BARKER, JACOB D., Chichester.
March 2, 1824 - March 9, 1824.
Eleven children: Eli, Lydia MARTIN, Susan HOWEL, Isabella
BIGART, Jacob, Eliza LEE, Thomas, James D., Sarah Ann, Evelina and
William. Sarah and William minors.
Exrs: Joseph WALKER, Jr., Jacob HOWEL and Jacob BARKER, Jr.
Wits: Isaiah HEISLER, James P. LEE and John TODD.
Codicil. ___
Wits: Isaiah HEISLER and James P. LEE. #608.

CLAYTON, JOSEPH, Lower Chichester.

Aug 12, 1807 - March 10, 1824.
Wife Rebecca, Cornelia the only child at time of making will. My good "friend" Rebecca CLAYTON sole executrix.
Exrs: Rebecca CLAYTON.
Wits: Nicholas FAIRLAMB and John FORD. #609.

BONSALL, SIDNEY, Darby.
Jan 1, 1824 - March 20, 1824.
Sister Hannah PALMER wife of Samuel, brothers Joshua and Joel BONSALL.
Exrs: Brother Joshua and brother in law Samuel PALMER.
Wits: Benjamin PEARSON and Joshua BONSALL. #610.

CHEYNEY, MARY, widow, Thornbury.
Feb 7, 1824 - March 20, 1824.
Children: William, Elizabeth (RAWN*) and Mary, grandchildren: Anna Maria HATCH wife of Jonathan, John CHEYNEY and David CHEYNEY. Land lines of Abraham SHARPLESS, Mary W. FRAZEN et. al.
Exrs: Son William and daughter Mary.
Wits: William YARNALL and Samuel LEWIS.
*Ad. acct. gives Elizabeth RAWN. #611.

LEWIS, MARY, Radnor.
Oct 17, 1823 - March 25, 1824.
Children: Esther LEWIS, Enos LEWIS and Mary PRATT and her children (not named).
Exrs: Son and daughter Enos and Esther LEWIS.
Wits: David GARRETT and James QUINN. #612.

BARTHOLOMEW, SARAH, widow, Chester.
May 6, 1814 - April 15, 1824.
Nieces and nephews, Ann LAWLER, Tacey Ann STACEY and children: James and David, Isabella BEVAN, Matthew L. BEVAN, Sarah MALIN, Mary daughter of John BARTHOLOMEW, dec'd., John son of Benjamin BARTHOLOMEW, dec'd., Isabella WEYMAN, Ann BRYANT and Sarah WHARTON a colored servant.
Exrs: Matthew L. BEVAN and Tacey Ann STACEY.
Wits: Ellen M. JUSTIS and William GRAHAM.
Codicil May 16, 1822 mentions death of Isabella BEVAN.
Wits: S. EDWARDS and J. H. SERRILL. #613.

TAYLOR, JOHN, Aston.
June 11, 1816 - April 26, 1824.
Wife Elizabeth, children: John, Charles and Elizabeth.
Exrs: Sd. sons John and Charles.
Wits: James CRAIG and Joseph TALBOT. #614.

MULLEN, WILLIAM, Newtown. Nuncupative Will.
April 6, 1824 - April 27, 1824.
Nephews William, Elijah and David ROBERTS. In trust with Uriah THOMAS for William, he dying before majority - the same to Elijah and on same conditions to David - brother in law Barney ROBERTS.
Wits: Uriah THOMAS and Mary THOMAS. #615.

WORRALL, PEIRCE, Middletown.
Feb 17, 1798 - April 27, 1824.
Legacies to parents Thomas and Mary. Thomas, Peter and George WORRALL (not mentioned whether brothers or sons) nephew Peirce WORALL, cousin Susan GILL. Preparative Meeting £50.
Exrs: Peter WORRALL.
Wits: John WORRALL and Amos SHARPLESS. #616.

BRATTEN, JAMES, Upper Chichester.
Dec 30, 1823 - May 6, 1824.
To guardians for education sons, John ___, James HUSTON and Ezra ELY.
Exrs: And guardians brother William BRATTEN, of Franklin County and friend James CRAIG of U. Chichester.
Wits: James HUSTON and Nathaniel BOOTH.
Codicil Jan 30, 1824 Land in town of New Philadelphia. Ohio.
Wits: Same. #617.

BULLOCK, THOMAS, Senior, Birmingham.
April 14, 1824 - May 12, 1824.
Wife Elizabeth, children: Thomas, Aaron, Robert, Jane, Marjory and Elizabeth. Grandchildren Thomas and Isaac. Land lines of George HEYBORN, Robert FRAMES, Moses BULLICK and Nathaniel SPEAKMAN.
Exrs: Sd. sons Thomas and Robert.
Wits: Robert FRAME and George HANNUM, Jr. #618.

SMITH, WILLIAM, Birmingham.

April 30, 1824 - June 1, 1824.
Wife Margaret, children: Robert, Elenor and Mary, minors.
Exrs: Sd. wife and Robert FRAME.
Wits: Noble BUTLER and Thomas JARMAN. #619.

MORRISON, JOSEPH, Birmingham.
Jan 2, 1824 - July 26, 1824.
Sons, Emmor, William, John and Joseph; daughters, Mary BULLOCK, Jane BAKER and her daughter Lydia ROGERS, Elizabeth FRAME. Lot purchased of Nehemiah BAKER in W. Caln Twp.
Exrs: Sd. sons Emmor, William and Joseph.
Wits: Isaac ARMENT and Robert N. GAMBLE. #620.

SHARPLES, CATHARINE F. Wife of Abraham SHARPLESS and one of the daughters of Caspar WISTAR dec'd., of Pennsbury in Chester County.
Feb. --, 1816 - July 28, 1824.
Brother Thomas WISTAR, sister Sarah PENNOCK, sons Caspar W. and Abraham W. (minors), Kinsman Isaac MORRIS, husband's children Robert SHARPLES and Rachel ASHBRIDGE and his half brother Joseph PALMER and his niece Edith PALMER. To children of cousins William ROBINSON and Catherine W. MORRIS. Names Hannah CHANDLER, Elizabeth wife of Jehu ROBERTS, also John WILLIAMS and Dorcas PHILIPS servants - mentions property in Yorktown and New York. Three children of sister Sarah. Mentions Aunt WISTAR'S legacy to Caspar.
Exrs: Stepson in law George G. ASHBRIDGE and friend John PEIRCE.
Wits: Francis WISELEY and Garrett LEWIS. #621.

MALIN, SUSANNAH, Nether Providence.
July 29, 1824 - Aug 6, 1824.
Sole legatee and executrix daughter Tacey Litzenberg.
Exrs: Tacey LITZENBERG.
Wits: Joseph WILSON and Philip RUDOLPH. #622.

WORRALL, ELISHA, Radnor.
Nov 24, 1823 - Aug 13, 1824.
Wife Ann, son Feddy (Freddy) and wife Sally. Grandchildren: Elisha, William, Patty Ann, Joseph LEWIS, John HUNTER and Elizabeth Lewis WORRALL. Property bought of William LEE and of Miles

ABBETT also of Peter HUNTER - mentions lawsuit with Hannah BARTLESON.
Exrs: Sd. wife and son Feddy.
Wits: Enoch RICHARDS and John RICHARDS. #623.

MARTIN, CALEB, Upper Providence.
Oct 10, 182 - Aug 16, 1824.
Children: Warrick, Hannah widow of Joseph and Caleb her son, Ruth NUZUM, George and his son Caleb, Elizabeth CARR - mentions Lydia ROBINSON and Hannah LONGACRE.
Exrs: Sd. son Warrick.
Wits: Thomas WILSON and Ann WILSON.
Codicil, July 5, 1824 mentions Hannah LONGACRE as a daughter and having purchased for her land of George ELKINS.
Wits: Luke CASSIN and George MILLER. #624.

FORD, LYDIA, Newtown.
July 14, 1824 - Aug 21, 1824.
Brothers and sisters: Mary MARKWARD, Jane FORD, Rebecca PARSONS, Sarah BISPAM, Abigal JACKSON, James FORD and his children: Rebeckca, William and John FORD; Caleb FORD and William FORD.
Exrs: Friends Enos WILLIAMSON and Edward Hunter, of Newtown.
Wits: John RUSSELL, William MOULDER and David PRATT. #625.

WALN, JOSEPH, of Darby Twp.
Aug 16, 1824 - Oct 1, 1824.
Wife Elizabeth and her father John STOKES, brothers and sisters Elizabeth WALN, Rebecca HARRISON, Nicholas WALN, Jacob S. WALN, Mary WISTAR and children of dec'd. sister Hannah RYERS. Property in Burlington, N. J. formerly of John STOKES dec'd., father of sd. wife. Wife Elizabeth WALN to be executrix and after her decease brothers Jacob S. and Nicholas WALN.
Exrs: Wife and after her decease Jacob S. and Nicholas WALN.
Wits: Isaac BARTRAM, Joseph DODG and John H. ANDREWS.
Codicil Aug 18, 1824 appoints nephew Joseph Waln RYERS as one of executors at death of sd. wife. #626.

PALMER, BENJAMIN, Aston.
Oct 2, 1824 - Oct 11, 1824.
Wife Ann, children not named to be educated by wife.

Wits: Rolph C. MARSH and Curtis JAMES. #627.

TRIMBLE, JOSEPH, Concord.
Jan 24, 1823 - Oct 26, 1824.
Brothers and sisters Richard TRIMBLE and Lydia BALDWIN and her son Joseph T. Children of dec'd. brother William not named, William son of dec'd. brother John, Phebe SHARPLES daughter of sister Ann, children of sister Hannah JACOBS, Lydia daughter of the late Joshua PUSEY, Frederick PIGON or PIGEON of London to be paid, his agent Thomas STEWARDSON.
Exrs: Moses PALMER and Nathan SHARPLES.
Wits: Rolph C. MARCH and Ellis YARNALL.
Codicil March 11, 1823. #628.

SHUSTER, JOHN, weaver, Marple.
Sept 27, 1824 - Nov 2, 1824.
Wife Prescilla; father Leonard SHUSTER.
Exrs: Sd. wife and father.
Wits: John SELLERS and George SELLERS. #629.

BALDWIN, LYDIA, widow, Concord.
Nov 3, 1824 - Nov 22, 1824.
Children: Joseph T., George, Thomas (minor), Catharine, Lydia (minor).
Exrs: Son Joseph T. BALDWIN.
Wits: Phebe MENDENHALL and Elizabeth C. CLOUD. #630.

GRIFFITH, ENOCH, Aston Twp.
Jan 6, 1825 - Jan 15, 1825.
Wife Rachel, children: John, Ann, William and Joseph.
Exrs: Son William GRIFFITH.
Wits: Thomas GRIFFITH and Caleb G. ARCHER. #631.

BALDWIN, JOHN, Bethell.
Sept --, 1818 - Jan 17, 1825.
Children: John, William, Elizabeth MASSEY and her sons Isaac and Samuel, Mary JOHNSON and Rebecca HOWARD. Plantation lines of John FAULK, Thomas BOOTHE, Caleb PERKINS, William WILLIS and Joseph PALMER.
Exrs: John BALDWIN and John PEIRCE.
Wits: Ezekiel PYLE and Wilson PALMER. #632.

HOLLAND, THOMAS, Marple.
Jan 11, 1825 - Feb 11, 1825.
Wife Phebe, children: John B., Nathaniel, Thomas, Sarah RHOADS wife of Joseph, Catharine, Mary Ann and Martha. Lot in Wilmington, Del., held with Edward FELL.
Exrs: Benjamin LOBB and Joseph RHOADS.
Wits: John GRIM and Philip RUDOLPH. #633.

BALL, JOSEPH, yeoman, Upper Darby.
Jan 4, 1825 - Feb 18, 1825.
Brothers and sisters, Susanna EARL wife of Isaac, Thomas, Nathan and Elizabeth BALL. Nephews and nieces, Abraham, Joseph, Thomas, George and Mary POWEL, Elizabeth EARL, Thomas and John LOBB, Patience DICKENSON, Sarah SNYDER and Hannah RUDOLPH. Land joining that of Benjamin BRANAN, A. LEWIS, Thomas KENNY, Joseph HIBBERD, heirs of Jonathan OWENS and Benjamin BRENNAN. In Kingsessing lines of A. ALBURGER, ____ GUIER and Nathaniel SMITH. Brother Thomas BALL of Columbianna Co., Ohio.
Exrs: Friend Halliday JACKSON and nephews Joseph and Abraham POWELL.
Wits: John H. BUNTING and James BUNTING. #634.

STUARD, WILLIAM, Darby Twp.
Nov 9, 1824 - Feb 19, 1825.
Wife Margaret, children: Henry, John, Mary, Sophia, Elizabeth, William, Margaret and Martha.
Exrs: John OAKFORD.
Wits: Benjamin PEARSON and Stephen HORN.
John OAKFORD renounced - letters of administration to John L. PEARSON. #635.

HOOPES, ABRAHAM, Newtown Twp.
Oct 28, 1820 - Feb 23, 1825.
Children: Mary, Sarah LEWIS wife of Jabez, John, Priscilla REGESTER, dec'd., her children: Abraham and Margaret REGESTER (others not named), Caleb HOOPES guardian of Priscilla's minor children.
Exrs: Son in law Jabez LEWIS and grandson Abraham REGESTER.
Wits: Daniel HOOPES and Caleb HOOPES. #636.

ROBERTS, ANN.

By date July 3, 1812 and also by agreement of March 21, 1823 the joint will of Ellis ROBERTS. Proved March 14, 1825.
Children: Jannet SHAW, Sarah SHAW and Joseph SHAW (by a former husband) - mentions personal property, hers before marriage to Ellis ROBERTS.
Wits: Isaac SHARPLES.
Letters of Adm. to John ENGLE. #637.

LINDSAY, JOHN, Haverford Twp.
Dec 24, 1817 - March 24, 1825.
Children: James, Andrew and his children Mary Ann, Jane and Elizabeth, John and his children William, James, John and Eliza Ann, Samuel, William, Margaret wife of Isaac CORNOG and children: Augustus, Isaac and Elizabeth, Elizabeth wife of William HOSKINS and children Robert LINDSAY and William, and Robert LINDSAY - mentions lands, lines of Philip SHEAF, Robert ANDREWS, John HEALMS, Robert McCLELLAN, John CORNOG, Samuel LINDSAY, Jonathan WILDAY and Jonathan MILLER - mentions Middletown Presbyterian Congregation.
Exrs: Sons Andrew and John LINDSAY.
Wits: J. ELLIOTT and Jonathan MILLER. #638.

WORRALL, JACOB, Ridley.
April 10, 1825 - May 25, 1825.
Children: Jesse and children Elizabeth, Jacob and Tacy, Susanna ___* and children Lewis, Elizabeth, Lydia, David, Susanna and Mahlon; Abigail* by John SMITH children John, William and Abigail; Elizabeth wife of Joseph OSBOURN children Mary, David, Jane and Peter; Rachel wife of Christopher NOBLE and children: Elizabeth, John, Jacob, Rachel, William and Jesse - mentions house in Chester.
Exrs: Son Jesse and friend James MADDOCK.
Wits: Israel THOMAS and Jonathan P. WORRALL.
*Inventory mentions Susanna MANCILL and Abigail BYERS. #639.

WILSON, HANNAH, Middletown.
April 7, 1815 - April 5, 1825.
Children: Richard DUTTON, Thomas DUTTON, Sarah HIBBERD, Hannah BROOMAL and daughter Hannah, and Susan STEEL. George MARTIN and John TALBOT to appraise personal estate.
Exrs: Sons Richard and Thomas DUTTON.
Wits: Jonathan DUTTON and Thomas DUTTON, Jr.

Samuel DUTTON aged 91 years (grandson of Hannah WILSON) living in Media at present, says her maiden name was ROUTH and that she was married twice - R. G. SWIFT. #640.

WORRALL, DANIEL, Marple.
Aug 24, 1808 - April 6, 1825.
Wife Ann and heirs.
Exrs: Sd. wife and neighbor William FRAME.
Wits: William FRAME and John CORKREY. #641.

HOOPES, JOSHUA, Thornbury.
Aug 15, 1814 - April 9, 1825.
Children: Abner, Joel, Mary MOORE, Hannah COVINGTON, Joshua, Rebecca BROBSON and Hannah HOOPES.
Grandson Francis HOOPES.
Exrs: Sons Abner and Joshua HOOPES.
Wits: Joseph JAMES (smith) and Ezra HOOPES. #642.

HOWARD, JAMES, Edgmont.
March 30, 1822 - April 18, 1825.
Children: Jonathan and son James, David, Phebe HAMOR, Mary YARNALL, Hannah dec'd., William and Harper. Lands, lines of John RUSSEL, Evan EACHUS, D. HOOPES and Joseph BISHOP.
Exrs: Sons Jonathan and William HOWARD.
Wits: Daniel HOOPES and Caleb HOOPES. #643.

REES, ISAAC, Marple Twp.
July 14, 1821 - April 21, 1825.
Children: Esther FARROW, Hannah GRIFFITH, Margaret JONES, daughter in law Phebe REES and her daughter Thamar, Ann FARROW. Property lines of JONES'S Mill, Richard GRIFFITH and Benjamin YARD - mentions William BOLTON.
Wits: William FRAME, Benjamin YARD and Jno. KERNS. #644.

BRANNAN, BENJAMIN, U. Darby.
Aug 8, 1822 - May 5, 1825.
Wife Eunice (dec'd.), children: Sarah BONSALL, Grace BRANNAN, Elizabeth BRANNAN, Eunice ASH and son Charles, John, Abigail McKINLEY, Mary REATH, Moses BRANNAN.
Exrs: Daughter Elizabeth BRANNAN, Samuel LEWIS and George SELLERS.

Wits: Thomas LOBB, John LOBB and John Talbot LEVIS. #645.

EDWARDS, ISAAC, Middletown.
April 4, 1825 - May 7, 1825.
Brother Issachar EDWARDS, children: Ann COILS and her children Alexander and Elizabeth, Isaac EDWARDS. Brother Issachar guardian for Ann's children.
Exrs: Issachar EDWARDS and Isaac EDWARDS.
Wits: William SMEDLEY, Samuel L. SMEDLEY and Jane EDWARDS. #646.

BUGLESS, JUDITH, Chester Twp.
Feb 20, 1825 - July 20, 1825.
Children: George BUGLESS and Elizabeth McGLOTHLAN, grandchildren Susanna HUNTLEY and Julian McGUIRE.
Exrs: Son George BUGLESS and friend Moses PALMER.
Wits: William SLAWTER and Joseph ENGLE. #647.

OGDON (OGDEN), JOHN, Springfield.
May 5, 1825 - July 25, 1825.
Children: James, John and son John W., Elizabeth, Mary, Eliza, Hannah, and Martha wife of David LONGSTRETH - mentions the George THOMAS tract also that bought of Martha DAWES, tracts purchased of James and David CALDWELL and Thomas HORNE.
Exrs: Sons James and John OGDEN.
Wits: George B. LOWNES and Joseph LOWNES. #648.

MARTIN, GEORGE, U. Chichester.
Nov 16,* 1825 - Aug 3, 1825.
Children: George, Beulah SHARPLESS dec'd., her children John and Hannah, Ann POWEL, Ruth SHARPLES, Elizabeth MARTIN, Sarah BROOMALL, dec'd., her children George, John and Elizabeth BROOMALL. Sister in law Rebecca MARTIN.
Exrs: Son George MARTIN and son in law John SHARPLESS.
Wits: Justua DUNOFF, John POWELL and Rolph C. MARSH.
*Will not correctly dated. Letters testamentary granted Aug 17, 1825.
#649

SITER, WILLIAM, Radnor township.
Feb 9, 1822 - Sept 1, 1825
Codicil March 24, 1824.

Sons William, Adam, John and David. Daughter Elizabeth (unmarried), grandchildren John and Mary DAVIS, children of daughter Ann deceased. (testator provides for his wife, but does not call her by name.)
Exrs: Sons William and Adam SITER.
Wits: Devault BEAVER, Ewd. SITER and Adam SITER.
This Will is a typed abstract by Charles Barker. The handwritten abstract is also included two wills later.

(Delaware County Will Book C p. 96.).

HEACOCK, NATHAN, Middletown.
---- - Aug 20, 1825.
Children: John, Enoch and his children Franklin and Mary Ann, Peter, Sarah* and her children . Also speaks of a wife - mentions land lines of TRIMBLE'S, DORAN'S, Daniel THOMSON'S, and Del. PENNELL'S.
Exrs: Wife and daughter Sarah.
Wits: Robert FAIRLAMB and Thomas DUTTON.
Ad. acct. of Nov 17, 1826 gives *Sarah JOYCE and Dec 8, 1828 gives Jane NICHOLSON late Jane HEACOCK. #650.

SITER, WILLIAM, Radnor.
Feb 9, 1822 - Sept 1, 1825
Codicil Mar 24, 1824.
Wife (Elizabeth?), children: Elizabeth, William, Adam, Ann dec'd., grandchildren John and Mary DAVIS*, John and David SITER - mentions John BROOK and Enoch ABRAHAM.
Exrs: Sons William and Adam SITER.
Wits: Devault BEAVER, Edward SITER and Adam SITER.
Ad. acct. *Mary ERBEN, husband Peter. #651.

GILPIN, GIDEON, Birmingham.
Feb 9, 1825 - Aug 26, 1825.
Children: Joseph, Bernard, Hannah wife of Moses PALMER, John and Sarah. Children of daughter Lydia SMITH dec'd., Albin, Sarah, Hannah, Joseph, Milton and Gideon SMITH, children of daughter Ann HEWES dec'd. Property lines of Isaac G. GILPIN, James BENNETT, Eli HARVEY, George FOX and William PAINTER.
Exrs: Sons in law Moses PALMER and Samuel HEWES - John PIERCE of Providence to be guardian of grandson Gideon SMITH.

Wits: Rolph C. MARSH, Alice TRAGO and William PAINTER.
Codicil same date mentions Elizabeth HICKMAN and wife Susanna GILPIN. #652.

SHOALTS, JOHN, U. Chichester.
Nov 26, 1810 - Sept 12, 1825.
Wife Marthaw.
Exrs: Sd. wife and Powell CLAYTON.
Wits: Robert JOHNSON and William SMITH. #653.

MARSHALL, THOMAS, U. Chichester.
Sept 26, 1825 - Oct 4, 1825.
Wife Mary Ann, child Sarah.
Exrs: Sd. wife and brother John MARSHALL.
Wits: Eli R. BURK, George HARVEY and Joseph HALL. #654.

PHILLIPS, DAVID, Radnor.
Aug 13, 1825 - Oct 8, 1825.
Wife Margaret, children: John, Margaret, Thomas, David, George, Ann CAWLEY, grandchildren named David, Ann, Margaret, Elizabeth, Cerwriah and Clementine PHILLIPS all children of son John PHILLIPS, Margaret CAWLEY and David CAWLEY. Jesse BROOKES, Daniel ABRAHAMS and Edward SITER to settle disputes.
Exrs: Son George PHILLIPS and son in law Samuel CAWLEY.
Wits: Benjamin DAVIS, Jesse BROOKE and Edward SITER. #655.

EYRE, ISAAC, Chester Borough.
Sept 21, 1825 - Oct 29, 1825.
Wife Abigail - house in Chester next to Mary ENGLE'S tavern. No executors and Abigail renounced the right to administer Oct 29, 1825, requesting that Jonas and William EYRE be appointed.
Wits: Jonathan PENNELL and Samuel SMITH. #656.

CARSON, MARTHA, Providence.
Oct 24, 1825 - Nov 5, 1825.
Cousin Joseph McMIN and oldest daughter, nephew William CARSON, nieces Ann and Jane CARSON of Baltimore, friend James EMLEN and his daughter Mary, John KING and indentured apprentice of James EMLEN. Joseph PENNELL intrust.
Exrs: James EMLEN and George SMEDLEY.
Wits: Jesse REECE and Davis REECE. #657.

BAKER, JOSEPH, yeoman, Middletown.
Oct 8, 1823 - Oct 25, 1825.
Brothers and sisters, Henry and wife Susannah their children: John, Henry, Joseph, Hannah JOHNSON, Margaret PLANKENTON, Mary BAKER, Susanna BAKER, and Martha BAKER, John BAKER, Peter BAKER, Mary NEWLIN, Martha "ARCHABOLD", Aaron BAKER and his son Aaron. Lines of Samuel SHARPLESS, Joshua SHARPLESS and Nathan BAKER. Lot now in possession of Cornelius WRIGHT. Appeal taken by Cyrus and Elizabeth BAKER Jan 17, 1825, Oct. Term 1825. Find for plaintiff Henry BAKER.
Exrs: William BAKER of Edgmont and Joshua "SHARPLES" of Middletown.
Wits: Nathan YEARSLEY and Joshua SHARPLES. #658.

TIPPENGS, RICHARD, Haverford.
Aug 23, 1814 - Nov 24, 1825.
Wife Abigail, nephew John GRIFFITH.
Exrs: Samuel DAVIS of Haverford.
Wits: John CORNOG and Andrew LINDSAY. #659.

LEWIS, ABRAHAM, Upper Darby.
April 14, 1825 - Dec 19, 1825.
Wife Rebecca, daughter Mary LEWIS, nieces Mary, Hannah, Sarah, Elizabeth and Ann, children of Rebecca FAWKES, James "HANUMS" tenement free for seven years. Davis RICHARDS farm for five years. John GRACEY and David LYWELLEN a trust fund for Haverford Meeting. Tract in Upper Darby lines of Benjamin BRENNAN, dec'd., and Abraham POWELL. Tract in Haverford joining Joseph DAVIS. Lands in U. Darby lines of Thomas, Nathan and Samuel GARRETT.
Exrs: Sd. wife, George B. LOWNS and Clement LAWRENCE.
Wits: Joel DAVIS and Joseph LLOYD. #660.

WASSON, HENRY, Birmingham.
Sept 17, 1825 - Dec 21, 1825.
Children: William WASSON, Henry WASSON and Sarah CHAFFIN, widow, and heirs. Property lines of "Cleb" RING and Nobel BUTTLER.
Exrs: Nephew William PIERCE.
Wits: Noble BUTLER and William L. BUTLER. #661.

BRINTON, JOSEPH.

April 5, 1821 - Feb 9, 1826.
This will is written in an old account book and only commands that a certain Tom DARLINGTON son of the Esq. shall have no part in his estate. Admitted on testimony to handwriting.
Wits: Joseph WEAVER, Jr. and George HEYBURN. #662.

CULIN, ISAAC, Ridley Twp.
Feb 11, 1826 - March 15, 1826.
To wife Hannah and all my heirs.
Exrs: Sd. wife.
Wits: William HILL and William WRIGHT. #663.

BARTRAM, BENJAMIN, Darby.
Jan 28, 1824 - March 29, 1826.
Children: Benjamin, Ann wife of Jacob SMITH, Elizabeth wife of Rubin BAILEY, Hannah wife of Stephen OGDEN, John and Isaac. Grandson Benjamin son of James, dec'd. Land lines of Samuel, Mathew and John ASH.
Exrs: Sons John and Isaac.
Wits: Hugh LLOYD and John SERRILL. #664.

HARLAN, E.C.
March 13, 1826 - May 13, 1826.
Wife Ann C. HARLAN - property in Lycoming County.
Renunciation of wife May 8, 1826 gives husband's name as Ellis C. HARLAN and requests letters of administration be granted to her father John S. MORTON.
Wits: Susan C. MORTON. #665.

THOMSON, WILLIAM, U. Darby.
Oct 14, 1820 - May 15, 1826.
Children: William, Margaret, Dilley and Thomas, nephew Edward "GRIBLE".
Exrs: Son William and daughter Margaret.
Wits: William KING, James GIBSON and Margaret GIBSON.
A valuable renunciation paper asks the appointment of Samuel GARRETT and is signed by Margaret THOMSON, William THOMSON, Elizabeth C. FLECK, Delia THOMSON, Joseph THOMSON, Mary NAYLOR, William E. GREBLE, Ann HANSEL.
#666.

BOOTH, THOMAS, Bethell Twp.
July 30, 1821 - May 24, 1826
Codicil April 19, 1823 mention Jonas EYRE'S land.
Wife Phebe, children: James, Joseph, Robert, Nathaniel, John, Isaac and Jemima (last two minors). Farm bought of Thomas BOOTH, Jr. Lines of John BALDWIN, John FOULK, John HUNTER, Nathaniel WILLIAMS and Isaac LARKIN. Home tract lines of Powel CLAYTON, ____ GUEST, Robert JOHNSON and Thomas MARSHAL. Son Robert to act as guardian.
Exrs: Sons James and Robert BOOTH.
Wits: Nathaniel WILLIAMS, John LARKIN and James BRATTEN. #667.

KERLIN, HENRY, Borough of Chester.
Aug 31, 1825 - June 3, 1826.
Sole legatee and executrix, wife Louisa.
Exrs: Louisa.
Wits: J. H. TERRILL and S. EDWARDS. #668.

FAIRLAMB, FREDERICK, Middletown.
Aug 30, 1821 - June 8, 1826.
Children: Robert, Joseph, William, Hannah ENGLE, Susannah WALTER, Nicholas FAIRLAMB, Ann HANNUM and Mary WALTER, granddaughter Susannah ENGLE daughter of Hannah ENGLE. Property lines of Jacob HIBBARD, John "HACOCK", Robert PENNELL, Dell PENNELL, Peter SKAVENDIKE and John PITT. Lands in Mercer Co. Pa.
Exrs: Sons Robert and William FAIRLAMB.
Wits: Samuel ANDERSON and Jacob HABBERSET. #669.

CALDWELL, MARY, Springfield.
Sept 17, 1820 - Aug 5, 1826.
Children: John, Joseph, Elizabeth and Sarah, grandchildren Rachel and Charles CALDWELL - mentions lands of Isaac WORRELL, David CALDWELL and John SHILLINGFORD.
Exrs: John LEWIS, Jr.
Wits: John LEWIS and John P. CROZER. #670.

DICKS, JOSEPH, Nether Providence.
July 29, 1826 - Aug 7, 1826.

Wife Mary, children: Joseph, James, William, Peter, Benjamin, Mary Ann and Sarah. Property occupied by Thomas Williams and by John WALKER - mentions HINKSON'S, WILLIAMS' and LEIPER'S lines - mentions Joseph WOODLAND. Brother Frederick Dicks. Guardians John PEIRCE and Enos SHARPLESS.
Exrs: Brother in law Joseph GIBBONS.
Wits: Jacob BYRE, Jr. and Thomas WILLIAMS, Jr. #671.

LARKIN, JOSEPH, Bethel.
May 1, 1821 - Aug 24, 1826.
Wife ___, children: John, Joseph, "Nathon", Salkeld, Elizabeth SHARPLES, Sarah EYRE, wife of Robert and her six children: Joseph, William, Nathen, Luis, Elizabeth and Ann. House in New Casel adjoining Samuel SHAW'S.
Exrs: Sons John, "Nathen" and Salkeld LARKIN.
Wits: William LARKIN and John LARKIN, Jr. #672.

MARSHALL, DAVID, Marcus Hook.
July 30, 1826 - Sept 9, 1826.
Wife Margaretta, children: Jesse and Mary, others not named. Children of daughter Mary ___.
Trustee son Jesse.
Exrs: Son Jesse.
Wits: Benjamin F. JOHNSON and John KERLIN. #673.

TAYLOR, ISRAEL, Aston.
Feb 17, 1826 - Oct 2, 1826.
Wife Ann, children: Joseph, Gideon, William, Bowman, Anna GARRETT - mentions lands of Thomas GRIFFITH, Amor WILLIAMSON, Joseph THATCHER, Thomas "THATTCHER".
Exrs: William YARNALL and son Joseph TAYLOR.
Wits: Thomas THATCHER, William GRIFFITH and Abraham PENNELL. #674.

McILVAIN, ANN, widow, Ridley.
May 16, 1826 - Nov 16, 1826.
Niece Mary PASSMORE, daughter of sister Mary PASSMORE, Lydia PENNOCK daughter of brother Abraham PENNOCK, Ruth PENNOCK daughter of brother John PENNOCK and Ruth PENNOCK daughter of brother Joseph PENNOCK. Legacy to Ann MILLER.

Exrs: Levis PASSMORE, Kingsessing.
Wits: Robert STEEL and Hannah P. STEEL. #675.

WALTER, BETTY, Christianna Hundred, County of New Castle, Delaware.
Nov 6, 1819 - Dec 7, 1826.
Lewis, William, John, Charles, Rachel, Hannah, Lydia and Beaulah children of John PALMER and wife Beaulah, dec'd.
Exrs: Son in law John PALMER.
Wits: Moses PALMER and Samuel HEWES. #676.

WORRALL, WILLIAM, Ridlay.
Nov 30, 1826 - Jan 9, 1827.
Codicil Dec 12, 1826.
Daughter in law Mary WORRALL daughter of Jonathan PAUL and her children Phebe and Elizabeth, granddaughter Edith PARRY (parents not given). Property on Springfield Rd., lines of James McILVAIN and Jacob WORRALL. Land bought of Richard CROSBY to grandson Jonathan B. WORRALL. Daughter Anne DOWNING and sons William W. DOWNING, Samuel and Charles.
Exrs: William W. DOWNING.
Wits: Jesse WORRALL and Patrick SEARY. #677.

WILLCOX, MARK, Concord.
Dec 27, 1826 - Feb 23, 1827.
Children: James, Ellena, dec'd., wife of son in law William JENKINS, of Baltimore and their six children: Elizabeth widow of son John, dec'd., and their two children.
Exrs: Son James and son in law William JENKINS.
Wits: Moses PALMER, William TRIMBLE and Samuel HEWES. #678.

TWADDLE (TWADDELL), WILLIAM. Birmingham.
Nov 23, 1823 - March 10, 1827.
Sons John P., James, Charles P., William. Land bought of Sheriff GIBBONS lines of Butler and William SMITH, also bought of Sheriff ADAMS, lines of "BELL, HARLAN AND BUSH." Names of Jonathan GRAVES, Sheriff MOODY'S Sale of land belonging to Joshua WILLIAMSON. Land purchased of Caleb BAILY in East Marlborough Twp. Chester Co. Daughter Rachel wife of Zachariah KIRK and children: Deborah, Ann, William, James, Rachel, Susanna, Mary and John. Daughter Sarah wife of George KLING, granddaughter Deborah

WILSON, Daughter Elizabeth BUTLER wife of Joshua BUTLER, daughter Ann wife of Elihu TALLY, daughter Hannah wife of Nathaniel NEWLIN, daughter Catharine OGLE wife of ___, daughter Susanna ___. Land at Centerville purchased of John MARSHALL. Daughter Rebecca wife of William TODD.
Exrs: Sons John P., James, William and Charles P. TWADDELL.
Wits: John Harlan and William MATSON. #679.

LAWRENCE, MORDECAI, Marple.
Feb 19, 1827 - April 4, 1827.
Brothers Joshua and "Clemment", daughter Ann LEWIS and children: Hannah, James, Eber, Lydia and Elizabeth - mentions Springfield Meeting.
Exrs: Sd. brothers Joseph and Clement LAWRENCE.
Wits: James MARIS and Richard FIMPLE. #680.

HUMPHREYS, REBECCA, Darby.
Jan 19, 1825 - April 5, 1827.
Children: William and his children Mary, William and Lowery HUMPHREYS, Charles HUMPHREYS, Elizabeth BROOKS, Mary HEACOCK (husband Joseph), Martha SERRILL (husband John), Samuel and John HUMPHREYS.
Exrs: Sons in law Joseph HEACOCK and John SERRILL.
Wits: Joseph BUNTING and George SERRILL. #681.

HILL, MARY, Middletown Twp.
Feb 25, 1826 - April 11, 1827.
Seven children: William HILL, Hannah PENNELL, Ann HIBBERD, Tacy YEARSLY, John HILL, Deborah MARSH and Sidney TEMPLE.
Exrs: Son William.
Wits: Jesse TAYLOR and James EMLEN. #682.

GARRETT, NATHAN, U. Darby.
April 3, 1826 - April 25, 1827.
Wife Elizabeth, children: Nathan, Ann wife of Samuel SWAYNE, Sarah wife of Samuel RHODES (or RHOADS), Elizabeth wife of John PRATT, James, dec'd. and children Gulielma and others *not named - mentions brother Thomas GARRETT and land of William LEVIS.
Exrs: Sd. wife, son Nathan GARRETT and nephew Samuel GARRETT.
Wits: Thomas WIDDOS and Edward GARRETT.
*Ad. acct. mentions *Davis GARRETT and Hannah GARRETT.* #683.

LARKIN, ISAAC, Bethel.
Sept 23, 1824 - May 5, 1827.
Children: William, John, Isaac and his children (not named), Margaret DUTTON and Lydia DUTTON - mentions lines of James LANCASTER, Caleb PERKINS, John BALDWIN, Thomas BOOTH and ____ HAMPTON.
Exrs: Sons William and John LARKIN.
Wits: John LARKIN, Sr. and Nathan LARKIN. #684.

HINKSON, JOHN, N. Providence.
May 10, 1827 - ____.
Father Thomas, dec'd., Mother Mary TRANOR, sister Sarah HINKSON.
Exrs: Neighbor Henry FORREST.
Wits: Jno. PEIRCE and Seth THOMAS. #685.

ELLIS, JONATHAN.
June 19, 1827 - June 28, 1827.
Friend and housekeeper Elizabeth HALL - mentions brothers and sisters, having children.
Exrs: Brother Amos ELLIS.
Wits: Samuel DAVIS and Dennis KELLY. #686.

BAKER, EDWARD, Edgment.
July 23, 1827 - Aug 15, 1827.
Wife (Jane), children: Anthony, George, Edward, Lidia and son Aaron BAKER, Abel, Abigail VOGDES wife of Israel, Mary ASHBRIDGE, Lidia BROOMHALL, Jane GARRETT. Names Anthony BAKER, Joseph SMITH, Thomas D. SMEDLEY.
Exrs: Brother William BAKER and son in law Israel VOGDES.
Wits: Israel MASSEY and Aaron MASSEY. #687.

DANIEL, DAVID, Newtown Twp.
Nov 21, 1823 - Aug 27, 1827.
To each of my five following named children: Ann MULLEN, John DANIEL, Jemima JENKINS, David DANIEL, Sarah HUGHES and Thomas DANIEL.
Exrs: Son Thomas DANIEL.
Wits: Elijah LEWIS and Thomas M. LEWIS. #688.

LEWIS, ALBAN H., Newtown Twp.

Aug 7, 1827 - Sept 4, 1827.
Wife "Hariot", son Evan, niece Sarah LEWIS daughter of brother Evan, Cloe BRADLEY a legacy.
Exrs: Jacob HORTON of Newtown and Daniel HOOPS of Eastown, Chester Co.
Wits: Elijah BROOKE and John HORTON. #689.

THOMAS, SETH, Nether Providence.
Sept 1, 1827 - Sept 5, 1827.
Children: Israel, David E., Seth C., Elizabeth DAVIS, Ann FELL, Sarah EDWARDS - mentions lines of William MILLER and HINKSON'S Corner.
Exrs: Three sons Israel, David E. and Seth C. THOMAS.
Wits: Henry FORREST and Jehu RICHARDS. #690.

GARRETT, HANNAH, Lower Providence.
Aug 17, 1821 - Sept 10, 1827.
Children: "Laticia" JOHNSON, James, Lewis, Noah and John GARRETT, granddaughters: Elizabeth TRENOR and Maria GARRETT.
Exrs: Son John GARRETT.
Wits: Joseph ELDRIDGE and Joseph ELDRIDGE, Jr. #691.

WILKINSON, MARY, Upper Providence.
June 10, 1824 - Oct 1, 1827.
Son Jon and his grandson John WILKINSON, William and his wife Hannah and their three daughters, Elizabeth COBOURN, Rachel SHEE and Mary LANE. Guardian Joseph GIBBONS.
Exrs: Robert and William FAIRLAMB.
Wits: Edward LEWIS and John F. VANLEER. #692.

BIRCHAL, ELIZABETH, Springfield.
June 23, 1825 - Sept 13, 1827.
Exr. and sole legatee sister Martha DAWES.
Exrs: Sister Martha DAWES.
Wits: Samuel E. HOWELL and Debby PRICE.
Martha DAWES renounced in favor of John OGDEN. #693.

MALIN, ISAAC, U. Providence.
Feb 20, 1820 - Oct 6, 1827.

Wife Hannah, three brothers Abner, George and Joel and sister
Hannah MARTIN - mentions Isaac HINKSON, Isaac MALIN son of
George MALIN, Isaac M. TAYLOR son of Ezra TAYLOR. To Society of
Friends for repairs to Grave Yard.
Exrs: Sd. wife and Woodward COSLEY.
Wits: Homer EACHUS and John HINKSON. #694.

MORGAN, RACHEL, Radnor.
May 27, 1826 - Oct 15, 1827.
Names heirs of John ROBERTS, dec'd., Jane LEWIS daughter of
Abner LEWIS.
Exrs: Abner LEWIS.
Wits: Enoch ABRAHAM and John HULL. #695.

LEWIS, MORDECAI, Radnor Twp.
Nov 7, 1826 - Oct 24, 1827.
Step brother Lewis L. WORRELL and his aunt Sarah SANDERS,
Cathorine DUNN wife of George DUNN, Mary BARTLESON wife of
Mark BARTLESON, uncle Evan EVANS, aunt Abigail EVANS.
Exrs: Sd. step brother Lewis L. WORRELL.
Wits: George DUNN and Joseph DUNN. #696.

LAMB, JOHN, Thornbury.
Sept 7, 1826 - Sept 27, 1826.
Wife Sidney, children: Elizabeth and Nelson (minors).
Exr and guardian Thomas PEIRCE of Thornbury.
Wits: John KING and Robert McCALL.
*Letter of renunciation written by a man calling himself Thomas
LITTLE but none from Thomas PEIRCE. The register says the
executor of the foregoing will having renounced, Sidney LAMB and
John KING were appointed under Act of 7th Day of April "1826".*
#697.

TWADDELL, ELIZABETH, Birmingham.
May 19, 1824 - Nov 7, 1827.
Children: Maris TAYLOR, Ezra TAYLOR, Ann SMITH, Mary
WALTER, Hannah LEACOCK, Jemimah ANDERSON, Julian TAYLOR
and grandsons Joseph CLOUD and Henry TAYLOR - mentions Land in
Springfield, lines of Elisha WORRELL, tract in Marple, lines of Thomas
HOLLAND.
Exrs: Son Maris TAYLOR.

Wits: William TWADDELL, Jr., George GEIGER and James DELAPLAIN. #698.

PYLE, PHEBE, Upper Chichester Twp.
July 17, 1827 - Nov 8, 1827.
Names Phebe MERCER (widdow) and Sarah McGRATTEN.
Exrs: Joseph A. HALL.
Wits: Cyrus MENDENHALL and Joseph ASKEW. #699.

MAXWELL, ROBERT, U. Chichester.
Nov 14, 1827 - Dec 6, 1827.
Wife Margaret, children: Martha McCLENTIC wife of Robert, grandchildren John and Hannah MAXWELL children of son James dec'd.
Exrs: Joseph WALKER, Jr. and Cyrus MENDENHALL.
Wits: Melchior L. EBRITE and William BUCKNALL. #700.

SHARPLESS, SAMUEL, Haverford.
Dec 3, 1827 - Dec 26, 1827.
Wife Mary and her heirs.
Exrs: Sd. wife and friend Clement LAWRENCE of Upper Darby.
Wits: Samuel DAVIS and Abraham FREE. #701.

PIPER, JOSEPH, Chester Borough.
Dec 3, 1827 - Dec 27, 1827.
To wife Sarah making her sole executrix. Exr: Wife Sarah.
Wits: Preston EYRE and E. DARLINGTON.
Sarah PIPER renounces in favor of her brother William KERLIN Dec 26, 1827. #702.

THOMAS, URIAH, Newtown Twp.
Feb 1, 1828 - Feb 23, 1828.
Wife Mary, children: David, Sarah and Margaret.
Codicil Feb 2, 1828 - mentions Seventh day Peoples burrying ground.
Wits: Elijah BROOKE and Richard GARDINER.
Exrs: Sd. wife and Elijah BROOKE of Newtown.
Wits: Samuel C. BRINKLE and Richard GARDINER. #703.

RICE, JACOB, Delaware County.
Jan 31, 1828 - Feb 25, 1828.

Wife Mary, nephews Daniel and Jacob RICE and nieces Hannah
GARDNER late RICE, Rachel RICE and Elizabeth RICE.
Exrs: Sd. wife and Samuel URIAN of Darby.
Wits: John ATTMORE and John SHAW. #704.

GRACEY, JOHN, Haverford Twp.
Dec 10, 1827 - Feb 25, 1828.
Wife Elizabeth, children: John Jr., Susanna, Thomas, Sarah,
grandchildren William and Mary RICHARDS children of daughter Jane,
dec'd. Sister Patience WILLIAMSON, land on West Chester Rd., lines
of George WILLING, Ludwick KNOLL, William BITTLE and Patience
WILLIAMSON.
Exrs: Son John GRACEY, Jr. and friend Joseph POWELL of
Springfield Twp.
Wits: Samuel DAVIS and Samuel SMITH. #705.

PENNELL, EDWARD, Chester Twp.
Feb 9, 1828 - March 13, 1828.
Children: Sarah Ann, Jane and Edward PENNELL.
Exrs: John DUTTON of Chester Twp.
Wits: John "SUPLEE" and Garrett EDWARDS. #706.

BISHOP, JESSE, Edgmont Twp.
March 8, 1828 - April 1, 1828.
Brothers and sisters: William, George, Joseph and Sarah BISHOP,
Phebe GREEN and Mary BISHOP.
Exrs: Brothers William and George BISHOP.
Wits: Amor BISHOP and Samuel PLANKINTON. #707.

TROTTER, THOMAS, Springfield.
June 8, 1819 - April 3, 1828.
Cousins: Joseph, Charles, David, Thomas, Samuel, Sarah and Mary
children of cousin Joseph BACON, Joseph, Nathan, Thomas and Mary
TROTTER children of Daniel TROTTER, dec'd., James OLDDEN,
Sarah ELFRETH daughter of Jeremiah ELFRETH, William and
Elizabeth TROTTER children of Joseph TROTTER, Jonathan, William
and Mary EVANS, Hannah RHOADS wife of Joseph RHOADS, Joel
EVANS, Thomas and Charles EVANS, Hannah EVANS wife of
Jonathan EVANS.
Exrs: Cousin Jonathan EVANS, of Philadelphia.
Wits: Charles CAREY, Jr. and Joseph LLOYD.

Codicil Nov 22, 1824 names children of Joseph SCATTERGOOD: Thomas, William, David, Joseph, Elizabeth, Samuel and Sarah SCATTERGOOD.
Wits: Charles CAREY and George B. ALLEN. #708.

CORNOG, JOHN, Haverford.
March 30, 1821 - April 16, 1828.
Wife Nancy, children Daniel and Thomas.
Exrs: Sons Daniel and Thomas CORNOG.
Wits: Andrew LINDSAY and John LINDSAY, Jr. #709.

CRAIG, JOHN, Marple Twp. (Will not signed.)
April 16, 1828 - May 15, 1828.
Wife Mary, children not named.
Agreement to accept will signed by Joseph ESREY, Margaret ESREY, J. F. VANLEER, Jane VANLEER, James CRAIG, John G. CRAIG, Maria CRAIG, Rebecca CRAIG, Robert B. CRAIG.
Exrs: Mary CRAIG and John LINDSAY, Sr.
Wits: Isaac HALDEMAN and John DUNWOODY. #710.

CLOUD, AGNES, Concord.
May 8, 1827 - May 16, 1828.
Nephew William MORRISON son of brother Joseph MORRISON, niece Mary BULLOCK wife of Aaron and daughter of brother Joseph MORRISON.
Wits: Moses PALMER and Joseph PALMER. #711.

BOOTH, JOSEPH, U. Chichester.
May 22, 1828 - July 8, 1828.
Wife Martha, children: William, Caleb, John, Sarah, Elizabeth and Martha BOOTH. Lands bounded by lines of Widow HUSTON, Salkeld LARKIN and Josua PYLE.
Exr. and guardian of children: Samuel EDWARDS.
Wits: John BROOMALL and Silas GREEN. #712.

HOWARD, JONATHAN, Edgmont.
May 6, 1828 - July 9, 1828.
Wife Hannah, minor sons Ellis P. and Joseph E. HOWARD, other children James, Rebecca and George B. HOWARD.
Exrs: Sons James and George B. HOWARD.

Wits: Joseph BISHOP and Evan EACHUS. #713.

RIVELEY, JOHN, Jr., Darby Twp.
April 21, 1828 - Sept 22, 1828.
Mother Elizabeth, speaks of brothers and sisters.
Exrs: Kinsman John RIVELY and John H. ANDREWS.
Wits: Israel BELTON and Oswald PATCHELL. #714.

DAVIS, JOSEPH, Haverford.
April 12, 1825 - Dec 17, 1828.
Children: Elizabeth wife of John HORNE, Lewis DAVIS and Hannah wife of Thomas HUNTER, Joseph, Hannah and Elizabeth children of son Nathan, dec'd. Plantation in Easttown occupied by John HORNE.
Exrs: Son Lewis.
Wits: Joel DAVIS, William DAVIS, Samuel RHOADS, Joseph ANDERSON. #715.

DAVIS, GEORGE, Ridley Twp.
Nov 30, 1819 - Jan 26, 1829.
Daughters: Rebecca, Sarah, Esther, Lewisa, Susana, Marget. Brother Caleb DAVIS. Property purchased by father, of Rebecca YARNALL and Michael SITZ, lines of Thomas SHIPLEY, Curtis LOWNES, George B. LOWNES and ___ BONSALL.
Exrs: Benjamin DAVIS and John OGDEN, Jr. of Springfield.
Wits: John LOWNES and Joseph HIBBERT, Jr. #716.

FIMPLE, MICHAEL, Haverford.
April 7, 1827 - Jan 30, 1829.
Wife Christiana FIMPLE, children: Rudolph, Mary, Michael, Jr., Richard, John and Isaac. Grandchildren Martha and Mary daughters of son George, dec'd.
Exrs: Sons Rudolph, Richard and John FIMPLE.
Wits: Thomas WILLIAMSON and Reece HAYCOCK. #717.

LAWRENCE, AMY, Springfield Twp.
April 28, 1817 - Feb 2, 1829.
Niece Margaret POWELL and nephew Isaac POWELL.
Codicil June 6, 1825 - mentions marriage of niece Margaret POWELL now FILBERD. Appoints Mordecai LAWRENCE and Clement LAWRENCE as executors. Clement LAWRENCE calls himself only surviving executor in his renunciation Feb 2, 1829.

Wits: John CALDWELL and Jesse J. MARIS.
Exrs: Friends Mordecai LAWRENCE and James RHOADS.
Wits: George RHOADS and Joseph RHOADS. #718.

PENNELL, MARTHA, Middletown.
Oct 12, 1828 - Feb 10, 1829.
Ann THOMPSON wife of Daniel, and daughters Mary and Emeline.
Exrs: Daniel THOMPSON.
Wits: Ambrose WILLIAMS and Joseph MANSILL. #719.

HOOPES, DANIEL, Edgmont Twp.
April 21, 1821 - Feb 12, 1829.
Codicil Aug 27, 1825.
Wife Hannah, children: Caleb, Sarah and Phebe.
Exrs: Sd. son Caleb.
Wits: William BISHOP and William HOWARD. #720.

LANE, EDWARD, gentleman.
Aug 21, 1828 - Nov 21, 1828.
Wife Elizabeth. Real Est. in Ridley and Springfield Twps. and in Philadelphia.
Exrs: Sd. wife and Daniel I. DESMOND, of the City of Philadelphia, Attorney at Law.
Wits: James MADDOCK and Jesse WORRALL. #721.

BONSALL, MARGARET, Upper Darby.
Feb 11, 1829 - April 10, 1829.
Brothers Joseph and James BONSALL, sisters Martha WELLS and Lydia PALMER and their children - mentions lines of Halliday JACKSON and John SERRILL.
Exrs: Brother Joseph BONSALL.
Wits: Charles GARRETT and John MYERS. #722.

TRIMBLE, HANNAH, Concord.
Dec 20, 1826 - May 9, 1829.
Nephew William TRIMBLE and wife Mary and children.
Exrs: William TRIMBLE and friend Rolph C.[?] MARSH.
Wits: Moses PALMER and Samuel MARSHALL. #723.

SHOULTS, MARTHA, U. Chichester.
April 21, 1826 - June 12, 1829.

Son William SMITH, daughters Margaret wife of Andrew DAVIS and
Ann HEWES. James SMITH and Martha BANNARD children of son
Aaron SMITH, dec'd., Margaret HUNTER, Jane HUNTER and
Elizabeth HUNTER children of daughter Elizabeth, dec'd., Robert
JOHNSTON trustee for James SMITH.
Exrs: Powel CLAYTON and Robert JOHNSTON.
Wits: John CLAYTON and Henry PEIRCE. #724.

PYLE, MARY, Thornbury Twp.
Feb 18, 1824 - July 6, 1829.
Children: Mary SMITH, Jane McAFEE, Jonathan, Abner, Moses and
his son Caleb, Sarah, widow of son Aaron and her children.
Exrs: Sons Abner and Moses PYLE.
Wits: Thomas PEIRCE and John KING. #725.

PENNELL, DELL, Darby.
Sept 9, 1822 - July 27, 1829.
Wife Hannah, children: Mary wife of James S. PETERS, Sidney wife of
Benjamin SERRILL and Hill PENNELL.
Codicil Feb 2, 1825.
Wits: John BARTRAM and Isaac BARTRAM.
Exrs: Sd. wife, son Hill and sons in law James S. PETERS and
Benjamin SERRILL.
Wits: Thomas STEEL and Hill PENNELL. #726.

TREVILLO, SUSANNA, Chester Twp.
Oct 10, 1825 - July 29, 1829.
Son Jonathan, daughters Sarah and Mary JOHNSON, granddaughter
Hannah P. JOHNSON. Samuel PENNOCK renounced and his son Joel
PENNOCK was appointed.
Exrs: Brother Samuel PENNOCK.
Wits: Joseph WALKER and Elizabeth C. WALKER. #727.

SHEAFF, PHILIP, Haverford Twp.
Jan 21, 1824 - Aug 24, 1829.
Wife Mary, children: William, Mary, Elizabeth, Sabinah, Deborah and
Catherine's five children: Catharine, Mary, William, John and Temaris,
son Philip's seven children.
Exrs: Son in law George BISHOP, daughter Deborah and grandson
Philip SHEAFF.

Wits: John BROOKE, Jesse BROOKE and Margaret D. BROOKE.
#728.

TRIMBLE, THOMAS, Middletown.
Sept 3, 1822 - Aug 28, 1829.
Children: Mary LEWIS, Phebe WILLIAMS, Hannah DOWNES and her children Thomas and John.
Exrs: Ambrose WILLIAMS and Phebe WILLIAMS. Disputes referred to Arbitrament of Friends Samuel TRIMBLE and James BRATTEN.
Wits: Samuel TRIMBLE and James BRATTEN. #729.

RUSSELL, WILLIAM, Jr., lawyer, Chester Boro.
Sept 1, 1829 - Sept 10, 1829.
Wife Lydia Ann, uncle John RUSSELL, sisters Sarah Ann RUSSELL and Mary LAMPLUGH and her children Jesse R. and Lydia LAMPLUGH, daughter Adeline.
Exrs: Sd. wife and friends Samuel EDWARDS and Archibald T. DICK.
Wits: Samuel A. PRICE and Jno. PENNELL. #730.

WEST, SARAH, Aston Twp.
Feb 5, 1825 - Sept 30, 1829.
Daughter Esther RILEY and son in law Isachar EDWARDS.
Exrs: Sd. daughter Esther RILEY.
Wits: Joshua WILLIAMSON, Thomas CASSIN and Rachel CASSIN.
#731.

NEWLIN, NATHANIEL, Darby Twp.
April 13, 1829 - Oct 13, 1829.
Father Nathaniel, children: Esther wife of Samuel SMITH of Chester, Ann P. JENKINS and her children Tabitha, Jabez and Martha N. JENKINS, Mary NEWLIN, Nathaniel and his children: William Parker NEWLIN, Hannah A. NEWLIN, Sarah L. NEWLIN, Mary and Hetty Ann NEWLIN, nephews Cyrus MENDENHALL and Nathaniel NEWLIN. Also daughter Martha COWGILL. Names Thomas SMITH, John RIVELY, J. BONSALL, Isaac PEARSON, Gibbons HUNT and Ann PUSEY in connection with property transactions.
Exrs: Nephew Cyrus MENDENHALL and friend Thomas SMITH, Esq. of Darby, also to be trustees and guardians of children of son Nathaniel NEWLIN.
Wits: John OAKFORD and William P. PUSEY. #732.

DUNN, JOSEPH.
Nov 13, 1829 - Nov 20, 1829.
Brothers William DUNN, George DUNN and Robert DUNN (dec'd.)
sister Martha DUNN - mentions Zebulon CROLL.
Exrs: Levi LEWIS.
Wits: Isaac WHITE and George SMITH. #733.

LEWIS, ELIZABETH, Edgmont.
Nov 8, 1829 - Nov 26, 1829.
Brothers Samuel, Abraham and his children: Josiah and his son Samuel A., also a grandson ____ BRANSON, nieces Martha wife of George GREEN, Jr. and Ann Maria wife of Jonathan HATCH, other nieces Hannah LEWIS and Alice LEWIS.
Exrs: Samuel L. SMEDLEY and Samuel A. LEWIS.
Wits: James YARNALL and Joseph MEREDITH, Jr. #734.

BIRCHALL, JAMES, Chester Borough.
Nov 14, 1829 - Dec 4, 1829.
Sarah BIRCHALL widow of brother Caleb. Property, lines of Jonas EYRE, Thomas ROBINSON and Ephraim PEARSON.
Exrs: William EYRE.
Wits: Samuel SHERRY and Mary Ann SHAW. #735.

HORNE, PHEBE, widow of William HORNE, Darby.
March 20, 1825 - Dec 31, 1829.
Children: Thomas, Mary THOMAS, Sarah PAPHALL [Paschall?], Edward HORNE and George HORNE - mentions dec'd. son Benjamin and his children.
Exrs: Sons Thomas and George HORNE.
Wits: Henry PASCHALL and John M. JUSTIS. #736.

WORRALL, ELISHA, Springfield.
Feb 2, 1829 - Jan 11, 1830.
Wife Mary, children: David, Mary LEEDOM wife of Joseph, Rebecca LEWIS, Joseph, Mordecai and David WORRALL. Grandchildren: Rebecca WHITE, Mary Ann KIRK, Sarah, George, Evan, Elisha and Maris LEWIS, Mirah TRIMBLE, Charles, Mary, Rebecca, Eleanor and Elizabeth JUSTIS. Names of properties of Eliza WORRALL, Esther LEVIS, Owen RHOADS and Joseph LEEDOM.
Exrs: Sons Joseph, Mordecai and David WORRALL.
Wits: George W. BARTRAM and S. EDWARDS. #737.

SMEDLEY, ELIZABETH, Middletown.
Dec 16, 1826 - Feb 3, 1830.
Children: Ahinoam and Samuel, granddaughters Elizabeth and Sarah YARNALL.
Exrs: Son Samuel SMEDLEY and George MILLER.
Wits: George MILLER, Jr. and Phoebe MILLER. #738.

CARTER, JOSEPH, Chester Twp.
July 16, 1828 - Feb 6, 1830.
Children: Abraham, William, Joseph, Robert, Cloud, Daniel, Edward, John Westley and Margaret GORBY. Property, lines James BARNARD, brothers Edward and Daniel CARTER.
Exrs: Sons Daniel and Robert CARTER.
Wits: E. DARLINGTON and George W. BARTRAM. #739.

HUSTON, REBECA, Upper Chichester.
Jan 3, 1830 - Feb 9, 1830.
Sister Ann HUSTON, heir and executrix.
Exrs: Ann HUSTON.
Wits: James CRAIG and Robert B. CRAIG. #740.

EDWARDS, MARGRET, Middletown.
Feb 4, 1830 - Feb 18, 1830.
Sister Sarah SUPLEE, heir and executrix.
Exrs: Sarah SUPLEE.
Wits: James TAYLOR and Ezekiel GRAY. #741.

DUTTON, MARTHA, Upper chichester.
March 12, 1823 - Feb 23, 1830.
Children: John, Richard, Alice wife of William PAIST, Jonathan, Thomas and Rebecca DUTTON, granddaughter Sarah daughter of Alice PAIST and grandson Jonathan PENNELL.
Codicil Feb 20, 1826.
Exrs: Richard and Rebecca DUTTON.
Wits: Thomas DUTTON and Amy DUTTON. #742.

SCHOFIELD, JAMES, Chester Twp.
Feb 1, 1830 - March 16, 1830.
Wife Lucy, brother John SCHOFIELD and friend Anthony DAVIS, of Philadelphia - mentions minor children.
Exrs: Sd wife, brother John and friend Anthony DAVIS.

Wits: John WHITEHEAD and S. EDWARDS. #743.

RHOADS, MARY, widow, Marple Twp.
Nov 1, 1824 - March 22, 1830.
Children: George, Joseph, Elizabeth, Rebecca, Phebe and William RHOADS.
Exrs: Sons George, Joseph and William.
Wits: Joseph EVANS and Joel EVANS. #744.

FRAZER, ALICE, Edgmont Twp.
March 23, 1830 - March 27, 1830.
Father Joseph PENNELL, dec'd., son Robert FRAZER.
Exrs: Friend William MENDENHALL.
Wits: Robert PENNELL and Mary CHURCHMAN. #745.

HINKSON, MORRIS, U. Chichester.
Feb 12, 1830 - April 5, 1830.
Mother Mary TRAINOR, half brother Lewis PARSONS.
Exrs: Charles L. SLEEPER.
Wits: E. DARLINGTON and Thomas WORRILOW. #746.

DUNWOODY, RACHEL, Marple Twp.
Aug 5, 1829 - April 6, 1830.
Sons: William, John and Joseph DUNWOODY and three daughters in law, great granddaughter Deborough Jain NEWLIN.
Exrs: Sd. three sons.
Wits: Jonathan WOOD and Isaiah FAWKES. #747.

HATTON, JAMES, Concord Twp.
March 8, 1830 - April 13, 1830.
Niece Sarah widow of Aaron PYLE.
Exrs: Sarah PYLE and friend Joseph HATTON, of Concord.
Wits: Rolph C. MARSH and Ellis YARNALL. #748.

TOWNSEND, CATHREN, spinster, U. Chichester.
Dec 1, 1829 - April 30, 1830.
To Rachel wife of Richard MILLER, she to be executrix.
Exrs: Rachel MILLER.
Wits: James CRAIG and Robert B. CRAIG. #749.

WORRALL, MARY, ___ Twp.

Feb 2, 1829 - May 10, 1830.
Husband ___, son Mordecai, his sisters Rebecca LEWIS, Mary LEEDOM, his niece Sarah LEWIS.
Exrs: Sd. son Mordecai WORRALL.
Wits: George W. BARTRAM and S. EDWARDS. #750.

PEIRCE, JOHN, Concord.
March 20, 1827 - May 31, 1830.
Wife Marget, children: Sarah PEIRCE, John and Henry PEIRCE - mentions Cauless and Tyson DURING.
Exrs: Son John PEIRCE.
Wits: Isaac ARMENT and Joseph PALMER. #751.

BURTON, JOHN, Germantown, County of Philadelphia but now residing with John MARSHALL, Upper Chichester.
June 6, 1830 - June 17, 1830.
Niece Anna wife of John EASTON, of Richmond, Va., brother Eli BURTON and sisters Anna wife of William CRAVEN and Lydia wife of Thomas CHAPMAN, all of Leeds, Yorkshire, England.
Exrs: William SHAW of Thornbury and John MARSHALL above named.
Wits: John ROBINSON and Samuel MARSHALL. #752.

RUSSELL, MOSES, Springfield.
May 9, 1830 - June 18, 1830.
Wife Mary, children: Edward, Aaron, Joseph and Catharine RUSSELL.
Exrs: Mary RUSSELL.
Wits: Charles CAREY and Joel EVANS. #753.

TAYLOR, VERNON G., Thornbury.
June 19, 1830 - June 30, 1830.
Mother Lydia TAYLOR.
Exrs: Friend William MENDENHALL, of Concord.
Wits: Rolph C. MARSH and Stephen V. MALIN. #754.

LEWIS, EVAN, Newtown.
Oct 9, 1824 - July 20, 1830.
Children: Jesse, James, Albin, George, Samuel LEWIS, children of daughter Hannah TREGO, dec'd., John and Phineas LEWIS children of son Evan, dec'd., grandson Phineas LEWIS.
Wits: Uriah THOMAS and Jehu GARRETT.

Codicil Sept __, 1829 - mentions John HUNTER, John WILLIAMSON, Miss HUNTER. #755.

MATLOCK, SARAH, single woman, Concord.
Oct 28, 1829 - July 24, 1830.
Mother Elizabeth NEWLIN, sister Mary Ann wife of William NELSON of East Caln Twp. Chester County, and their children Elizabeth M. NELSON, Emily D. NELSON and Caroline B. NELSON.
Wits: Martin PALMER and Marshall CLOUD. #756.

PENNELL, ANN, Concord.
April 4, 1829 - Aug 4, 1830.
Late husband Thomas PENNELL and their three children: Mary, Ann and Hannah - mentions another daughter Catharine.
Exrs: Daughter Mary PENNELL and friend William TRIMBLE, signed Anne PENNELL.
Wits: William MENDENHALL and William TRIMBLE. #757.

PENNELL, JONATHAN, Chester Borough.
Aug 13, 1829 - Sept 27, 1830.
Children: James, Sally Ann, Edmund, Henry H. and his children: Jonathan, Sarah and Rebecka, sister Rebecka and her daughter Phebe PROFOUNTAIN. Legacies to Susanna DUTTON late MENDENHALL and Margaret COLLINS.
Exrs: Son Edmund PENNELL. In property transactions mentions Jesse BROWN, Joseph LARKIN, Abraham LARKIN and Caleb COBOURN.
Wits: Preston EYRE and Samuel EDWARDS. #758.

LOWNES, REBECCA, Springfield.
April 14, 1829 - Sept 27, 1830.
Brother Slator and his daughter Clarissa LOWNES, sister Mary wife of Andrew REYNOLDS, brother Curtis and his children: Agness LEVIS, Elizabeth HUGGENS and Esther JONES, Kinsman Caleb LOWNES and son Edward, Moses RUSSELL, Susannah GARNER and her children: Drucilla, Susan, Kissiah, Henry and Sarah GARNER, nephew John LOWNES and children: Sarah and Hannah.
Exrs: Brother George B. LOWNES and kinsman Joseph LOWNES.
Wits: James NEELD and Hannah LOWNES. #759.

NEIDE, JOHN, farmer, Chester Twp.

Sept 24, 1830 - Oct 5, 1830.
Brother Jacob NEIDE and sister Ann EVANS.
Exrs: Sd. brother Jacob.
Wits: William G. FLOWER, Jacob EVANS and Isaac HENVIS. #760.

BROWN, THOMAS, Radnor Twp.
Nov 13, 1829 - Oct 17, 1830.
Brother James and daughter Emily DAVIS, sister Mary LOGAN, brother Samuel and wife (not named) and children Marget McAFEE and Sophia BROWN, brother John and his grandson Thomas WADE, brother Benjamin and children: Ann EVANS, Eliza BROWN and Samuel BROWN, Elijah BROOKE to be trustee for Benjamin's son Samuel.
Exrs: John EVANS, of Radnor.
Wits: Elijah BROOKE and Griffith McDERMOTT. #761.

SELLERS, NATHAN, Upper Darby.
June 5, 1827 - Oct 27, 1830.
Wife Elizabeth, children: Ann, Coleman, Nathan and Hannah HILL wife of Peter HILL, sister in law Margaret COLEMAN - mentions John DAVIS, George SELLERS, Amos ELLIS, Leonard SHUSTER, Abram JOHNSON, Benjamin BONSALL and Susan BLANKLEY.
Exrs: Nephew Samuel SELLERS, son Coleman and brother John SELLERS.
Wits: George SELLERS and Abraham JOHNSON and John SELLERS, Jr. #762.

MATTSON, ELIZA W., Aston Twp.
Feb 5, 1830 - Dec 7, 1830.
Sisters Mary Ann and Emaline L. MATTSON. Names Anne and Eliza TRAQUAIR and the Southwark Infant School Society. Property at John PALMER'S.
Exrs: Samuel HANNUM of Concord.
Wits: Isaac HALL, Thomas MATTSON and William W. PALMER. #763.

ALLEN, SARAH, Ridley Twp.
Sept 6, 1830 - Dec 14 ,1830.
Granddaughter Elizabeth wife of James BOTTOMLEY.
Exrs: None named.
Wits: George WARNER and Rachel ORMSBEY. #764.

WORRALL, JOHN, Nether Providence.
Sept 17, 1828 - Dec 21, 1830.
Wife Eliza WORRALL, children: Peter, John, Richard T., Eliza, Sarah (GARRETT), Abigail (GARRETT'S children), Edith (LEWIS), Hannah (OGDEN).
Exrs: Son Peter and sons in law John OGDEN and George LEWIS.
Wits: Abel GREEN and Jehu BROOMHALL. #765.

HART, JOHN D. Borough of Chester.
Oct 16, 1829 - Jan 13, 1831.
Mother ____, sister Hannah - mentions Mary B. FLOWER, Brinton I. DICK, Archibald T. DICK, Phebe Ann SPEER.
Exrs: And trustee Enos SHARPLESS and Archibald T. DICK.
Wits: H. R. DICK, Z. W. FLOWER and William KIRLIN. #766.

MOORE, NATHAN. Haverford.
April 21, 1827 - Jan 21, 1831.
Maskell E. MOORE, Nathan MOORE, Jr., sister in law Herreatta MOORE, Jesse MOORE'S son George, niece Marey MOORE.
Exrs: None.
Wits: George LEWIS and Samuel SMITH, Aug 29, 1830. #767.

SWAYNE, GEORGE, Darby.
March 18, 1824 - Feb 12, 1831.
Codicil Feb 5, 1830.
Children: Miriam, Mary LODGE, Moses, Aaron, Sarah MENDENHALL and Thomas dec'd., and his children: Mary, Phebe, Hannah, Miriam, George, John and Elizabeth SWAYNE.
Exrs: Son Aaron and friend John RIVELY.
Wits: Halliday JACKSON and John BUNTING.
Wits: Halliday JACKSON and Daniel HUMPHREYS. #768.

KNOLL, LUDWICK, Haverford.
Jan 11, 1831 - Feb 19, 1831.
Wife Mary, children: Sarah, Hannah WATKIN, Catharine WATKIN, dec'd., and her children and Mary BITTLE.
Wits: Samuel DAVIS and Samuel SMITH. #769.

TRENOR, DAVID, Ridley Twp.
July 7, 1829 - March 14, 1831.

Wife Margaret, children: David, George, James, Prudence BELL, Martha MILLER, Jane JORDAN, Lydia TRITES, Margaret ERSKINE, Mary HAMM and Daniel, dec'd., grandchildren David Trenor McCULLOUGH, Mary McCULLOUGH and Henry McCULLOUGH. Codicil of June 6, 1830 gives the McCULLOUGHS as children of Prudence BELL and includes children by present husband. Same witnesses, proved March 14, 1831.
Exrs: Sons David and George TRENOR.
Wits: William HILL and Christopher W. STEEL. #770.

EVANS, LYDIA. Radnor.
Feb 8, 1823 - April 6, 1831.
Est. to sister Rebecca EVANS, she to be executrix.
Exrs: Rebecca EVANS.
Wits: Owen BROOKE, Levi LEWIS and Mordecai LEWIS. #771.

HUNTER, SAMUEL, Bethel.
April 9, 1831 - April 18, 1831.
Wife Hannah, children: Susanna and Jane, children of brothers Andrew and William HUNTER.
Exrs: George PALMER and Nathan LARKIN.
Wits: Robert McCLURE and James M. MULLIN. #772.

WALTER, RACHEL, Middletown.
April 20, 1830 - May 25, 1831.
Susannah TALBOT, Samuel SHARPLESS (nephew), Joshua SHARPLESS and Rachel SHARPLESS wife of Samuel SHARPLESS, Beulah SHARPLESS, Hannah, Lydia and Joel SHARPLESS children of nephew Samuel SHARPLESS, Thomas IDDING son of sister Hannah IDDING, Phebe JOHN and her daughters Mira JOHN and Lydia RIGBY, and son William JOHN, Rachel SHARPLESS, Ruth SHARPLESS wife of Samuel SHARPLESS, Elizabeth MEREDITH, William and Sharpless YARNALL sons of Israel YARNALL, Phebe SMEDLEY.
Exrs: Nephew Samuel SHARPLESS.
Wits: Peter WORRALL, Jesse TAYLOR and Minshall PAINTER. #773.

BROWN, BENJAMIN, Radnor.
Feb 8, 1828 - June 2, 1831.
Wife Elizabeth, children: Samuel, Eliza and Ann BROWN, grandson William Cleaver BROWN.

Exrs: Sd. wife and friend Daniel ABRAHAMS.
Wits: Elijah BROOKE and Thomas BROWN. #774.

GYGER, MARGARET, Radnor.
Nov 15, 1824 - June 27, 1831.
Son Jacob GYGER and his children: George, Daniel and Mariann GYGER, daughter Mary WHITE and her daughter Susanna - mentions Isaac and David JAMES in business relations.
Exrs: Son Jacob GYGER.
Wits: James HUNTER and Robert B. SCOTT. #775.

LITZENBERG, SIMOND*, Newtown.
June 3, 1831 - July 21, 1831.
Wife Elizabeth and ten sons: John, George, Joshua, William, Rubin, Anthony Wayne, Simond, Hirum, Job and Perry.
Signed Simon* LITZENBERG.
Exrs: Isaiah FAWKES and son John LITZENBERG.
Wits: Isaac HALDEMAN and John JACOBS. #776.

GEORGE, LEMUEL, Radnor.
July 2, 1831 - Aug 13, 1831.
Wife Sarah GEORGE and children.
Exrs: Sd. wife Sarah.
Wits: Shepherd AYARS and Daniel ABRAHAM. #777.

COBOURN, THOMAS, U. Providence.
May 29, 1830 - Oct 8, 1831.
Wife Elizabeth COBOURN to have estate.
Exrs: Wife Elizabeth COBOURN.
Wits: Glouver BUCKINGHAM and Ann GEUST. #778.

PENNELL, ROBERT, Concord.
Sept 18, 1831 - Oct 15, 1831.
Wife Cidney, children: Sarah wife of Daniel THOMAS, Samml., Joseph, William, Elizabeth and Anna G., friend William MENDENHALL. Names Cyrus HOOPS, Joseph JAMES, Daniel TRIMBLE, Benjamin HICKMAN and Jacob PARKS.
Exrs: Sd. wife and William MENDENHALL.
Wits: Samuel TRIMBLE and Alexander McKEEVER. #779.

BRINTON, THOMAS H., Thornbury.

Oct 5, 1831 - Oct 22, 1831.
Wife Catharine, children: Hill, John, Henry, George H. BRINTON and Mary K. wife of son in law George BRINTON, William THATCHER.
Exrs: George H. BRINTON and George BRINTON.
Wits: Henry MYERS and Liba DARLINGTON. #780.

MAULE, BENJAMIN, Radnor.
May 14, 1831 - Oct 22, 1831.
Wife Ann, children: Thomas and Benjamin Maule, Mercy wife of Isaac CLENDENNON, Zillah wife of Nathan EVANS, Hannah wife of Isaac PHILLIPS and Ann MAULE.
Exrs: Sd. wife and sons Thomas and Benjamin MAULE.
Wits: Walker MOORE and Joseph R. HOSKINS. #781.

YARNALL, JANE, Edgmont.
Oct 8, 1825 - Nov 26, 1831.
Children: Isaac, Mary PENNELL, Sidney WOOD, Rachel YARNALL, James, Albin and Reuben YARNALL, granddaughters Jane YARNALL, Hannah YARNALL and Jane PENNELL.
Exrs: Sons Albin and Reuben YARNALL.
Wits: Samuel SHARPLESS and James EMLEN. #782.

BONSALL, WILLIAM, bachelor, Upper Darby.
Feb 14, 1826 - Dec 16, 1831.
Nephew David BONSALL and his son Samuel C. BONSALL.
Exrs: Sd. David BONSALL
Wits: Benjamin PEARSON and George SERRILL. #783.

YARNALL, WILLIAM, Thornbury.
Nov 20, 1826 - Dec 23, 1831.
Children: Peter, Jonas, Sarah, William, Bennet, Abnor, Thomas and Mary YARNALL and Elizabeth wife of Walker YARNALL.
Exrs: Sons Peter and Jonas YARNALL.
Wits: Waldron CHEYNEY. #784.

PYLE, MARTHA, Edgmont.
Dec 30, 1831 - Jan 12, 1832.
Daughters: Sarah Ann, Lydia and Melissa PYLE, friend and relation Jesse SHARPLESS of Goshen, trustee for three daughters.
Exrs: James YARNALL.
Wits: Samuel L. SMEDLEY and James YARNALL. #785.

OAKFORD, ANN, widow, Darby Twp.
July 24, 1824 - Jan 16, 1832.
Isaac OAKFORD only son named, daughters in law Grace OAKFORD and Hannah OAKFORD, granddaughters Ann CHAMPION and Eliza H. CLEMMENT. Legacies to Sarah URIAN and Elizabeth McGILTON.
Exrs: Son Isaac OAKFORD.
Wits: Halliday JACKSON and Jacob JACKSON. #786.

MERCER, ELIZABETH, Thornbury Twp.
March 10, 1831 - Feb 11, 1832.
Children: Euclid, Ann TAYLOR, Hannah TAYLOR, Sarah DILWORTH, Elizabeth COX, Richard and wife Hannah, Elizabeth MERCER daughter of son EUCLID.
Exrs: None.
Wits: Hiram BAILEY and George BUGLESS. #787.

SELLERS, ELIZABETH, widdow of Nathan deceased, U. Darby Twp.
Nov 21, 1831 - Feb 4, 1832.
Children: Coleman, Ann, Hannah wife of Peter HILL, and Nathan SELLERS, Nathan Sellers HILL, and Elizabeth Sellers HILL children of Peter and Hannah HILL, sister Hannah, Margaret and Ann COLEMAN, names colored girl Sarah TAYLOR and housemaid Ann KRIDER.
Exrs: Nephew Samuel SELLERS and husbands brother John SELLERS.
Wits: M. C. SHALLCROSS and Lewis WATKIN. #788.

PENNELL, CIDNEY, nuncupative.
Dec 25, 1831 - March 12, 1832.
Estate to daughters Elizabeth and Ann C. PENNELL.
Wits: William PAINTER and Phebe PAINTER. #789.

MALIN, ANN, Middletown Twp.
March __, 1830 - April 18, 1832.
Sister Phebe YARNALL and daughters Agnes WEBSTER and Phebe YARNALL, sister Mary THOMAS and daughters Agnes KING and Sarah KING, sister Grace MALIN and daughters Agnes HORTON, Ann PALMER and Elizabeth SMEDLEY. Names Hannah HARDCASTLE.
Exrs: Minshall PAINTER.
Wits: William FAIRLAMB and George W. FAIRLAMB. #790.

BULLOCK, JOHN, Concord Twp.
Dec 24, 1831 - April 16, 1832.
Wife Sarah BULLOCK, children: Isaac, Sarah WILDEN, Hannah SMITH, Margary PECK, Hester VERNON, Mary GRAY, Jane PEIRCE, Moses, John, and wife Sarah, and Thomas H. BULLOCK - mentions children of son John.
Exrs: Thomas H. BULLOCK.
Wits: Adam G. PALLEY and Lewis BULLOCK. #791.

WRIGHT, WILLIAM, Springfield.
Jan 27, 1832 - April 30, 1832.
Wife Mary, son Christopher Wilson WRIGHT, ___ PAINTER, children: Christianna, Mary and William.
Exrs: Son Christopher and friend George LEWIS.
Wits: Henry FORREST and James FORREST. #792.

BYRE, ELIZABETH, Chester.
April __, 1832 - May 21, 1832.
Brother Jacob BYRE and his daughter Jane BYRE, brother in law William KERLIN and Jane, Elizabeth and Henry KERLIN children of his son Henry.
Exrs: Brother Jacob and brother in law William KERLIN.
Wits: J. H. TERRILL and E. DARLINGTON. #793.

MYERS, JOHN, Concord.
Feb 26, 1832 - May 22, 1832.
Wife Margaret, children: Henry, John, Samuel, Jesse, Elizabeth, Margaret, Mary wife of John YARD and Eliza MYERS. Estate lines of Joseph PALMER, Robert M. GAMBLE, Charles BARRETT, Thomas MARSHALL and Joseph HATTON.
Wits: Joseph HATTON and Ellis YARNALL. #794.

MOORE, ABNER, Haverford.
May 22, 1831 - May 28, 1832.
Wife Leah, children: Benjamin, Isaac, Walker, Leah (husband's name not given) and her children Walker and Sarah ____?.
Exrs: Sons Benjamin and Walker MOORE.
Wits: Joseph RHOADS and James H. RHOADS. #795.

HALL, JOSEPH, Chester Twp.
July 8, 1832 - July 14, 1832.

Wife ___, brother Robert HALL, grandson James McGRATTON.
Exrs: His own son Isaac HALL.
Wits: Samuel LYTLE and William GRAY. #796.

MEGOWEN, JOHN, Concord Twp.
June 28, 1832 - Aug 16, 1832.
Brother James MEGOWEN, sister Mary GHEEN and children, sister Jane RICHARDS and children, half sister Mary MCCALL, nephew Richard MEGOWEN and wife. Others named Hannah ALTEMUS, Margaret JOHNSON (Wilmington, Del), widow, William MARSHALL (of Thornbury, an Englishman) and Sarah his wife, Rachel DENNIS, Mary BOOGER, widow, and Sarah NUTT. Names seven children of Samuel MARSHALL: Margaret, Ellis, Thomas, Samuel, William, Henry and Edward S. MARSHALL, Ann CLOUD, widow, of Concord, Elisha DAWSON, of Maryland, Rolph C. MARSH.
Exrs: Rolph C. MARSH and Samuel MARSHALL.
Wits: Ellis YARNALL and John PALMER. #797.

HEACOCK, JONATHAN, Darby Twp.
Jan 16, 1830 - Sept 17, 1832.
Children: Joseph, Jacob, Jonathan, Israel, Hannah, Phebe BARTRAM, John P. and Ann WILLIAMS - mentions lines of Calcon HOOK, John THOMPSON, Aaron OAKFORD, Isaac OAKFORD, Joshua BONSAL and John SERRILL.
Exrs: Hannah and John P. HEACOCK and Halliday JACKSON.
Wits: Isaac BARTRAM and John JACKSON. #798.

CROSBY, ROBERT P., Ridley Twp.
March 21, 1832 - Sept 19, 1832.
Wife Sarah Ann and children, brother Peirce CROSBY, Archibald T. DICK, William L. LEIPER and Samuel M. LEIPER - mentions as trustees and guardians, also with sd. wife to be executors.
Exrs: Sd. wife.
Wits: John L. CROSBY and Spencer McILVAIN.
Codicil of May 26, 1832 arranges for the marriage of older children during the trusteeship of the above named persons.
Wits: Susan MORTON and John L. CROSBY. #799.

PYOTT, ROSE, widow of James PYOTT, Upper Darby.
Feb 3, 1832 - March 13, 1832.

Daughter Elizabeth wife of George BLANKLY and daughter Mary, sons James, Richard, Alexander and Abram, dec'd., Mary and George PYOTT children of son James - mentions children of other dec'd. children.
Exrs: Sons James and Alexander PYOTT.
Wits: Samuel LEVIS and John H. NELLING. #800.

GARRETT, RACHEL, widow, Concord.
March 8, 1830 - Oct 12, 1832.
Brother William TRIMBLE and children: John, William and wife Mary, and Phebe (JACOBS), brother John and his son William, brother Daniel and his daughter Mary (T. PLEASANTS), brother Samuel and his children Joseph, Samuel and wife Rebecca, and Margaret (PEIRCE), Lydia BALDWIN, granddaughter of William TRIMBLE, Lydia KING and Jane KING and Grace EVANS, sister Ann SHARPLESS and daughter Phebe, Davis GARRETT son of Amos GARRETT.
Exrs: Nephew Samuel TRIMBLE.
Wits: Ennion COOK and Aaron SHARPLESS. #801.

EBRITE, LYDIA, Marcus Hook.
May 11, 1832 - Oct 19, 1832.
Children and grandchildren of brother Henry EBRITE, dec'd.: Ann EBRITE, Lydia EBRITE, Jacob EBRITE and his six children; Henry, Melchior, Elizabeth, Jacob, Joseph and Morgan, Melchior L. EBRITE and his five children, Sarah, Hannah, Zachariah, George W. and Lydia EBRITE; Rebecca, wife of Thomas TAYLOR and her three children: William Henry, George W. and Justice TAYLOR, Cyrus MENDENHALL and children, Jacob H., John, Cyrus and Esther; Jane MENDENHALL; nephew James FRANKLIN; and son Benjamin.
Legacies also to Barbara BOSS of Philadelphia. Catharine PHILIPS, S. S. UNION and Episcopal A. M. E. SOCIETY. Also St. Martin's Church at Marcus Hook.
Exrs: Cyrus MENDENHALL.
Wits: Frederick SHULL and Joseph WALKER, Jr. #802.

VERNON, SARAH, Thornbury.
Nov 16, 1832 - Nov 28, 1832.
Names James HICKMAN, son of her friend James HICKMAN as heir. Legacies to Elizabeth HICKMAN and to Baptist Meeting near Gideon GILPIN'S.

Exrs: Elizabeth HICKMAN.
Wits: John PARKS and Hiram BAILEY.

LEVIS, ELIZABETH, Upper Darby.
Aug 7, 1818 - Nov 26, 1832.
Children: William LEVIS, Ann LEVIS daughter Elizabeth LEVIS, Mary and Margaret LEVIS, Sarah Ann CLEMENT daughter Elizabeth, Henrietta GARRETT, Samuel LEVIS and Oborn LEVIS.
Grandchildren: Ann C., Margaretta, Elizabeth P., Abigail Ann and Margaret LEVIS.
Exrs: Sons William, Samuel and Oborn LEVIS.
Wits: Thomas GARRETT and Robert E. JONES.
Codicil Oct 3, 1824 mentions death of son William and appoints brother in law Robert E. JONES.
Exrs: Robert E. JONES.
Wits: Abby Ann LEVIS and John Talbot LEVIS. #804.

TALBOT, JOSEPH, Upper Chichester.
Nov 11, 1832 - Nov 28, 1832.
Brother John TALBOT and his children John and Elizabeth, sisters Ruth NEIDA and Rachel ELLIOT. Legacies to Melchior EBRITE and William CRESSON, son of John H. CRESSON, of Philadelphia and to George MARTIN in trust for Chichester Meeting.
Exrs: Mark ELLIOT and George MARTIN.
Wits: Salkeld LARKIN and Isaac MORGAN. #805.

DUTTON, RICHARD, Aston.
July 30, 1831 - Nov 19, 1832.
Wife Margaret DUTTON, brother in law John LARKIN, children: Thomas (dec'd.), Isaac (dec'd.), John Larkin DUTTON and John Brinton DUTTON. Children of ad. sons Thomas and Isaac DUTTON.
Exrs: Son J. Larkin DUTTON and brother in law John LARKIN.
Wits: Thomas DUTTON and Samuel R. HALL. #806.

VANNEMAN, JOHN S., Lower Chichester.
Sept 10, 1827 - March 11, 1833.
Wife Mary, children Anna S. WHITE and Mary D. VANNEMAN. In property transactions Simon CRANSON, Hewe's Lane, Daniel LIKENS, William BEEM, Zachariah DERRICK, Hannah BEEMS and Francis ENNIS.
Wits: John D. WHITE and John MITCHELL.

Codicil Aug 11, 1829 mentions St. Martin's Church Yard, Marcus HOOK.
Wits: Piercey POSTILL and Cyrus MENDENAHLL. #807.

HOOPES, SUSANNA, Newtown.
Sept 7, 1828 - March 23, 1833.
Children: Rees, Daniel and Alice HOOPES.
Exrs: Sons Rees and Daniel.
Wits: Caleb HOOPES and Joseph DAVIS. #808.

PYLE, DANIEL, Concord.
Dec 22, 1823 - March 27, 1833.
Wife Prudence, children: John, Joseph, Robert, Rebecca PETERS wife of Pennell PETERS, and Dutton PYLE, dec'd.
Exrs: Son John PYLE and James BRATTEN of U. Chichester.
Wits: R. M. HUSTON and Aaron HUSTON.
Codicil Feb 25, 1826 mentions death of son Joseph, wife name Mary, appraisers, Joseph PALMER, blacksmith and Nathaniel NEWLIN, storekeeper.
Wits: Rolph C. MARSH and Joseph PALMER, B.S. #809.

BISHOP, THOMAS, Upper Providence.
Feb 23, 1833 - April 6, 1833.
Wife Priscilla, grandson Thomas son of Amor, nephew Phineas PRATT. Provides for educations of Thomas by sale of ground in Marcus HOOK.
Exrs: Wife, Priscilla BISHOP and nephew Phineas PRATT.
Wits: George MILLER and Evans EACHUS. #810.

HANNUM, RUTH, widow, Concord.
March 8, 1833 - April 9, 1833.
Daughters, Elizabeth GRUBB and Jane HANNUM, sons William, Joseph, Evan P., Aaron and Norris HANNUM.
Exrs: Sons Aaron and Norris.
Wits: George PALMER and S. EDWARDS. #811.

CHEYNEY, EDITH, Thornbury.
Dec 29, 1832 - April 13, 1833.
Children: Mary GREEN, Phebe CHEYNEY, Curtis CHEYNEY and Waldron CHEYNEY.
Exrs: Sons Curtis and Waldron CHEYNEY.
Wits: Rufus T. CHEYNEY and William H. CHEYNEY. #812.

DILWORTH, JAMES, Birmingham.
Oct 19, 1829 - April 23, 1833.
Wife Mary, sons Thomas and Ziba DILWORTH. (*Ruth wife of Henry MERSHON, Hannah wife of Jessy PARRY, Ann wife of Isaiah DYSON, Rachel BAKER, James DILWORTH, Joseph DILWORTH) - mentions line of Edward DARLINGTON also Thomas BEYERS as a tenant.
Exrs: Sd. son Ziba DILWORTH.
Wits: Cheyney WESTON, Cyrus DARLINGTON and William H. TAYLOR.
*All these probably children but not so designated. #813.

LINCH, MICHAEL, U. Darby.
March 12, 1832 - May 2, 1833.
Children: Samuel LINCH and Elizabeth wife of John FREDERICK.
Exrs: Samuel GARRETT.
Wits: Thomas WIDDOS and John HOOFSTITLER. #814.

RIVELY, JOHN, Darby.
July 10, 1832 - June 10, 1833.
Children: Mary wife of John C. ANDREWS and Sarah C. RIVELY, nieces Mary HUTTON, Elizabeth PEDRICK and Ann RIVELY wife of Daniel RIVELY - mentions in connection with property Thomas MITCHELL, John JUSTICE, John HUNT and Samuel BUNTING, also property in Philadelphia.
Exrs: John C. ANDREWS and Sarah C. RIVELY.
Wits: William SUPLEE and Samuel BUNTING, Jr. #815.

OAKFORD, DEBORAH, Darby.
April 18, 1833 - June 14, 1833.
Sister Mary OAKFORD, heir and executrix.
Exrs: Mary OAKFORD.
Wits: M. C. SHALLCROSS and James SERRILL. #816.

RICE, RACHEL, Darby Twp.
March 5, 1832 - Jan 3, 1833.
Mother ____, brother Daniel RICE and his son William, brother Jacob and sisters Elizabeth RICE and Hannah GARDNER.
Exrs: Brother Jacob RICE.
Wits: Thomas JARMAN and Mifflin S. FRAME.
Codicil March 20, 1832.
Wits: Thomas JARMAN and Eliza GARDINER. #817.

RICE, DANIEL, Darby Twp.
May 8, 1833 - Aug 15, 1833.
Wife Deborah, children: ____ DANIEL, William and Ann RICE, all minors.
Exrs: And guardians brother Jacob RICE and Dr. Morris C. SHALLCROSS.
Wits: John STROOPS and John L. PEARSON. #818.

ROBINSON, DEBORAH.
June 3, 1833 - Aug 26, 1833.
Niece Sarah WILLIAMS wife of Nathaniel WILLIAMS.
Exrs: Sd. Nathaniel WILLIAMS.
Wits: John LARKINS and Joseph BOOTH. #819.

RYAN, MARY, seamstress, Nether Providence.
Nov 8, 1830 - March 29, 1833.
Daughters: Dinah GANEY and Elizabeth CARRELL.
Exrs: Sd. two daughters.
Wits: Jane ANNESLEY and Annesley NEWLIN. #820.

BOWLEN, JOHN, Marcus Hook.
Aug 10, 1833 - Sept 12, 1833.
Estate to wife Mary, she to be executrix.
Exrs: Wife Mary.
Wits: Frederick SHULL and John LARKIN, Jr. #821.

BALL, ELIZABETH, Upper Darby.
June 24, 1832 - Sept 19, 1833.
Brothers, Thomas BALL, of Ohio, and Nathan BALL, sister Susanna EARL and daughter Elizabeth STROOPES and her daughter Elizabeth STROOPS, nephew John LOBB, Phebe MORRIS a colored woman.
Codicil Jan 28, 1833 mentions Sarah POWEL.
Exrs: Haliday JACKSON.
Wits: John H. ANDREWS and Jonathan OWEN. #822.

HIBBERD, JOSEPH, Brandywine Hundred, N. Castle County, Delaware.
March 11, 1833 - May 6, 1833. Registered in Del. Co. Oct 5, 1833.
Wife Elizabeth, right to land in U. Darby, lines of Norris and Isaac HIBBERD, Matthew ASH, Owen RHODES and Samuel DAVIS.
Exrs: Sd. wife Elizabeth HIBBERD.

Wits: Harry WILLIAMSON and John BIRD. #823.

QUIG, FANNEY, Ridley Twp.
Jan 28, 1823 - Oct 8, 1833.
Eliza WRIGHT widow of nephew James WRIGHT and her minor son Alexander WRIGHT.
Exrs: Eliza WRIGHT.
Wits: James MADDOCK, Christopher NOBLE and Joseph LAWSON. #824.

CARTER, DANIEL, Chester Twp.
Oct 4, 1833 - Oct 10, 1833.
Children: Gillied, John Wesley, Abraham, Ann LOYD, Eliza TRITES, Agnes MORRISON, Eleanor WARD and Mary PEIRCE. Property lines of Edward and Daniel CARTER, Jr. - mentions Elijah WARD.
Exrs: Sons John Wesley CARTER and Abraham CARTER.
Wits: Samuel LYTLE and Amor SMITH. #825.

BOYD, JOHN, Brandywine Hundred, New Castle County, Delaware.
April 11, 1833 - April 26, 1833.
Wife Elizabeth, brother David BOYD, children: William, Matthew, Mary, Sarah Jane, John Summerfield and James BOYD. Property in Wilmington, lines of Samuel NEWLIN and Jane GRIFFIN, land in U. Chichester bought of Nehemiah BROOMALL, lines of Peirce CROSBY and Ann HARVEY; land in village of Brandywine, lines of James PRICE, Alex. McGEE and others. Names uncle James CRAIG as guardian of oldest three children.
Exrs: Wife Elizabeth and friend James PRICE.
Wits: John RICE, Edward TATNALL and Lea PUSEY. #826.

LOBB, THOMAS, Upper Darby.
Nov 12, 1833 - Nov 28, 1833.
Five sons: Samuel, Benjamin, John, James and Jesse LOBB.
Exrs: Friend Samuel DAVIS, of Haverford.
Wits: Isaac LOBB and Thomas WIDDOS. #827.

THOMAS, PRISCILLA, Newtown Twp.
Dec 6, 1833 - Dec 16, 1833.
Thomas and Priscilla SPEAKMAN children of niece Ann, Thomas LLEWELLYN son of niece Sarah, Martha and Selina THOMAS

daughters of nephew Robert M. THOMAS - mentions Mary RUSSEL and Eliza THOMAS.
Exrs: Elijah BROOKE, of Newtown.
Wits: Jehu GARRETT and Henry PRATT. #828.

EVANS, SAMUEL, Aston Twp.
April 29, 1832 - Dec 16, 1833.
Mentions Samuel as on of the children of Joseph and Sidney FAIRLAMB, William, John, Samuel, Joseph, Evan P., Aaron and Norris sons of sister Ruth HANNUM, sister Jane, Hannah E. and Samuel E. children of John and Lydia DUTTON, Edwin HANNUM, Betsey TREE, of Philadelphia, Betsey KERLIN, housekeeper, John DUTTON, Stephen OTTY, Frederick STIMMEL and John BUTLER.
Exrs: Samuel HANNUM and John HANNUM.
Wits: Robert HALL and S. EDWARDS. #829.

PEIRCE, JOHN, Nether Providence.
July 6, 1833 - Dec 28, 1833.
Children: Sarah D. and Eli D. PEIRCE, grandchildren John D. PEIRCE, Sarah D. PEIRCE and Jane ____ - mentions wife ____.
Codicil Oct 15, 1833.
On testimony of George MILLER and Preston EYRE.
Exrs: Sd. son Eli D. PEIRCE.
Wits: None. #830.

HEACOCK, PETER, Middletown Twp.
Nov 7, 1833 - Jan 18, 1834.
Four minor children: Jacob, George, Susanna and Margaretta HEACOCK - mentions lines of Joseph JOHNSON, Jr. and Dell PENNELL, Thomas DUTTON, tanner, of Aston, and Dr. Jesse YOUNG, of Chester to be executors and guardians.
Exrs: Thomas DUTTON and Dr. Jesse Young.
Wits: John MOORE and J. YOUNG.
Exrs. refuse to act; Daniel THOMAS granted letters of administration Jan 22, 1834. #831.

DAVIS, BENJAMIN, Radnor Twp.
Dec 9, 1830 - Jan 24, 1834.
Daughters: Anna CRAWFORD and her daughter Lydia, Lydia DAVIS, Mary DAVIS, Tacy GARRIGUES and her children: Hannah relict of son David I. DAVIS, and son Ralph DAVIS, neighbors Elijah LEWIS,

Abner LEWIS, William JONES and Samuel CAWLEY to arbitrate
disputes. Home estate lines of Isaac LEDEM, Jesse BROOKE, Phineas
LEVIS and David PHILLIPS, also plot lines of Jacob MAULE, Friends
Meeting House and old Lancaster Rd.
Filed Aug 30, 1833.
Exrs: Sd. son Ralph and Edward SITER.
Wits: Abner LEWIS, Adam SITER and Simeon M. LEWIS. #832.

BALDWIN, WILLIAM, Borough of Chester.
Jan 30, 1834 - Feb 17, 1834.
Wife Sarah BALDWIN and her son J. P. HATTON, children: Hatton
BALDWIN, Jerome BALDWIN, Sarah Ann BALDWIN and Mary Ann
BALDWIN. Sd. wife and Giliad BURNS, guardians.
Exrs: Sd. wife and Peter Hill ENGLE.
Wits: I. O. DESHONG and Evans WAY. #833.

ENNISE, MARY, Bethel Twp.
March 28, 1833 - Feb 22, 1834.
Son Francis, daughter Mary SHADE and her sons Ennise SHADE and
James P. SHADE, six children of dec'd. daughter Marget MARSHALL
formerly Marget PENNELL, namely, Mary BROOMALL wife of John
T. BROOMALL, Sarah SMITH wife of James A. B. SMITH, Beulah
PENNELL, Margaret PENNELL, Emaline PENNELL and Ennise
MARSHALL. Property in Brandywine Hundred, in Bethel, in
Zeansville, O., and Westmoreland.
Exrs: Son Francis ENNISE.
Wits: Stephen CLOUD, John BARLOW and Nathaniel CLOUD. #834.

HOOPES, ABNER, Thornbury Twp.
Feb 5, 1834 - Feb 28, 1834.
Children: Caleb I. HOOPES, Marshall HOOPES, Mary M. wife of
Thomas G. GARRETT. Grandchildren: Sarah HOOPES, Benjamin F.
HOOPES, Rebecca HOOPES and Mary HOOPES.
Exrs: Son Caleb I. HOOPES.
Wits: Joshua HOOPES and Charles BALDWIN. #835.

LOWNES, GEORGE B., Springfield.
May 8, 1833 - March 13, 1834.
Wife Hannah, brother Curtis LOWNES and daughter Agnes LEVIS,
brother Slater LOWNES and his daughter Clarissa LOWNES and his
grandsons Slater Lownes FORD and Curtis Lownes FORD, nephew

Joseph LOWNES and children George B., William B., Phineas, Hannah and Sarah; Caleb LOWNES and son Edward R. and his daughter Hannah. George B. LOWNES (3) son of John of the Western Country dec'd., William R. LOWNES. Other names Preston EYRE and son I. Ashmead EYRE, Curtis LEVIS son of Edward LEVIS, Joel EVANS, John LEVIS, Thomas WEST, Jehu Curtis CLAY, Richard M. MORGAN, William BROWN son of Capt. William BROWN, Peter Curtis CLAY son of Rev. Slater CLAY, James NEAL, Evalina and Susan CAUFFMAN, Louisa GREEN daughter of Adam DRIVER, Susan GARNER and children; George B. L. CLAY son of Jehu CLAY, Samuel PANCOAST, John THOMSON, Isaac NEWTON.
Exrs: Joseph LOWNES, Joel EVANS of Springfield and William P. LAWRENCE.
Wits: Charles CAREY and William CAREY.
Codicil Dec 2, 1833 mentions tenant John SAFFER and wife Dolly and their sons John, Frederick and William SAFFER, also Joseph RUSSELL.
Wits: Ira BURDSALL and Frnk. WILKINSON. #836.

PANCOAST, SAMUEL, Marple.
Oct 30, 1832 - March 17, 1834.
Children: John, Samuel, William, Seth and Rebecca PANCOAST.
Property in Marple, Providence and Springfield Twps.
Exrs: Sd. four sons.
Wits: Esther LEVIS and William RHOADS. #837.

GRIFFITH, THOMAS, Aston.
Aug 31, 1833 - April 9, 1834.
Brother Joseph, brother Enoch and his children: Joseph, Ann and William and his son Thomas, Edith FOX and Naomi WOOLMAN daughters of James FOX, Hannah WOOLMAN daughter of Naomi WOOLMAN, niece Sarah GRIFFITH, nephew Jeffry GRIFFITH, nieces Mary JOHNSON and Deborah PETERS.
Exrs: William GRIFFITH and Abram HIBBERD, Sr.
Wits: George THOMPSON and Robert R. JOHNSON. #838.

KING, WILLIAM, weaver, Bethel Twp.
Feb 21, 1834 - April 10, 1834.
Provides for wife ____ and child____.
Exrs: Sd. wife ____.
Wits: George PALMER and Jesse WALTER. #839.

THOMAS, ISRAEL, Providence Twp.
Feb 28, 1834 - May 2, 1834.
Wife Sarah, eight children: Elizabeth, Ann, Louisa, Edward, Seth, David, Mary and Sarah THOMAS.
Exrs: Jonathan P. WORRALL.
Wits: Jehu RICHARDS and Charles WILLIAMSON. #840.

HEMPHILL, ANN, Thornbury.
___, 1825 - May 21, 1834.
Children: Joseph, Christian (a daughter), Thomas, Ann, Mary, Elizabeth and Susanna HEMPHILL.
Exrs: Christian, Ann, Mary and Elizabeth HEMPHILL.
Wits: James BROOMALL and Henry BAKER. #841.

GREEN, SILAS, U. Chichester.
Aug 1, 1833 - May 26, 1834.
Mentions his mother, and his sister Sarah. Three minor children: Mary, Eliza Ann and Silas GREEN.
Exrs: and guardian, George MARTIN, of Upper Chichester.
Wits: John BROOMALL and John TALBOT. #842.

VERNON, JOSEPH, Thornbury.
Feb 1, 1831 - June 2, 1834.
Sister Lydia TAYLOR (probably widow of Vernon G. TAYLOR) and her children: Cidney TAYLOR, John TAYLOR, Huldah HUNT and Drusilla T. ENTREKIN.
Exrs: William MENDENHALL.
Wits: Stephen O. MALIN. #843.

PUGH, JOHN, Radnor.
March 3, 1824 - June 10, 1834.
Wife Mary, children: Edward, John, Amelia BAUGH and Mary BURNS. David PUGH son of dec'd. son Joseph. Property lines of Edward SITER, Enoch, Abraham and Robert KENNEDY.
Exrs: Sons Edward and John PUGH.
Wits: Edward SITER and D. WILSON, Jr. #844.

GARNER, SUSAN, widow, Ridley.
May 23, 1834 - June 20, 1834.
Children: George HUNTER, Drusilla DAVIS, Susan MILLER, Keziah GARNER and Sarah GARNER.

Exrs: John S. MARTIN of Springfield.
Wits: Sketchley MORTON and Joel EVANS. #845.

OAKFORD, ELIZABETH C., Darby.
June 16, 1834 - Aug 13, 1834.
Estate to sister Mary OAKFORD.
Exrs: Benjamin TILGHMAN, Esq, (renounced).
Wits: Benjamin PEARSON and James SERRILL. #846.

EVANS, BENJAMIN, U. Providence.
March 22, 1820 - Aug 25, 1834.
Wife Mary, children: Joseph, Mary, Ann, Nathan, Peter and Jacob EVANS.
Exrs: Wife Mary and son Joseph EVANS.
Wits: Thomas HAWS and John MILLER. #847.

IRWIN, JOHN, Borough of Chester.
Sept 2, 1834 - Sept 15, 1834.
Estate to wife Jane IRWIN, she to be sole executrix.
Exrs: Jane IRWIN.
Wits: J. H. TERRILL and J.[I?] 0. DESHONG. #848.

BEALE, OLIVE, Bethel.
Oct 4, 1822 - Sept 15, 1834.
Children: Aaron BEALE, Rachel FILAR, John BEALE, Olive GRIFFITH and Lydia BEALE. Property lines of Mary JONES and William VERNON.
Exrs: Levi MATTRON and James M. MARTIN.
Wits: William BALDWIN and Andrew HUNTER. #849.

BURK, ELI R., Aston.
Sept 9, 1834 - Oct 3, 1834.
Mother Rachel BURK, wife Rachel BURK.
Exrs: Robert HALL, Esq. and Thomas DUTTON, tanner.
Wits: J. YOUNG and Edmund DUTTON. #850.

MOONY, JOHN, Concord.
Sept 30, 1834 - Oct 28, 1834.
Wife Elizabeth, children: Marier, Thomas, Sarah, Eliza, Mark, John, William and Ellen - mentions Eliza as wife of Peter JONES. Rolph C. MARSH guardian of sons Mark and John.

Exrs: Ralph C. MARSH.
Wits: William BOWERS and Mary EVANS. #851.

SMEDLEY, SAMUEL L., Edgmont.
Oct 18, 1834 - Nov 4, 1834.
(Nuncupative) I give to my wife ___ to bring up the children.
Wits: Isaac YARNALL, Israel HOWELL and James YARNALL. #852.

SHARPLES, JOHN, farmer, Concord.
June 27, 1833 - Nov 8, 1834.
Wife Hannah, children: Jesse, Susanna HICKMAN, Sarah wife of Jesse SEAL, Hannah LEWIS, John, Jr., Smith and Samuel SHARPLESS. Deceased daughter Edith TAYLOR, John and Elizabeth Sharpless, children of deceased son Nathan SHARPLES, sister Jane, widow of John HAINES. Land in Goshen, Chester County. An Ashridge tract lines of Abraham PRATT, Edward HICKS and Thomas GOODWIN.
Exrs: Sons Jesse SHARPLES and Smith SHARPLES.
Wits: Caleb I. HOOPES, Abraham W. SHARPLES and Robert MENDENHALL.
Codicil ___ 1834, mentions grandsons Harvy SHARPLES, son of Jesse SHARPLES and Thomas son of Samuel SHARPLES.
Wits: Stephen PYLE, Abraham W. SHARPLES and William JONES. #853.

WILLING, GEORGE CHARLES.
June 12, 1833 - Nov 10, 1834.
Two aunts Mary HEMPHILL and Elizabeth HEMPHILL to have estate, they to be executrices.
Exrs: Mary and Elizabeth HEMPHILL.
Wits: Thomas HEMPHILL and Susanna LUNGREN. #854.

CAMPBELL, WILLIAM, Chester Borough.
Sept 8, 1834 - Nov 13, 1834.
Estate to mother Fanny CAMPBELL in Ireland.
Letters of administration to Robert CHURCHMAN.
Wits: G. DARLING, Owen MULLIN and Thomas McGARVEY. #855.

WORRELL, ISAAC, Ridley Twp.
July 30, 1832 - Nov 14, 1834.
Wife Ann, step grandson Isaac D. WORRELL, son of Abraham WORRALL, daughter Jemima WATSON and children: Isaac, George, Daniel and Ann WATSON, other grandchildren Rebecca and Sarah

WORRELL. Land in Ridley and Springfield, lines of Thomas HORNE, Jonathan THOMAS and Jesse WORRALL.
Exrs: Stepson Abram WORRELL and friends George LEWIS and Joseph LOWNES who renounced same day.
Wits: J. H. TERRILL and A. T. DICK. #856.

SMEDLEY, SUSANNA, widow, Radnor.
June 22, 1830 - Dec 5, 1834.
Daughter Susanna HOOD wife of Jonathan, daughter Mary LAMBORN wife of George LAMBORN, Esther and Jacob ROGERS children of daughter Esther ROGERS, dec'd., other grandchildren Sarah HARRISON and Elizabeth COX and great granddaughter Susanna LITZENBERG.
Exrs: Son Jacob SMEDLEY.
Wits: Benjamin SMEDLEY, Sarah C. HOOD. #857.

BOND, JOSEPH, Haverford.
Sept 1, 1831 - Dec 27, 1834.
Children: Thomas, Joseph, David, Jesse, Sarah, Mary EACHUS and John BOND dec'd. and his children.
Exrs: Sons Thomas and Joseph, both of Philadelphia.
Wits: Walker MOORE and Jonathan BOND. #858.

WILLS NOT RECORDED

BARTHOLOMEW, BENJAMIN, gentleman, Chester, Chester County.
Sept 9, 1784 - Dec 22, 1784.
Wife Sarah, Joseph son of nephew John BARTHOLOMEW, brother Edward, nephews John and Benjamin sons of brother Joseph, nephew Joseph son of brother Thomas, sister Rachel DAVIS, niece Hannah THOMSON widow of Archibald THOMSON, sister in law Catharine widow of brother Thomas, dec'd. and her daughter Elizabeth GRIFFITH, Sarah BOGGS former housekeeper, nephews John and Joseph BARTHOLOMEW, sons of brother Andrew, dec'd., nephew John DAVIS and niece Elizabeth DAVIS children of sister Elizabeth, niece Sarah WILSON daughter of ____.
Codicil Oct 18, 1784, legacy to Baptist Meeting in Tredyferrin.
Wits: Benjamin NORRIS, Henry ODENHEIMER and E. PRICE.
Codicil Nov 4, 1784.
Wits: Jacob TOBIN, Elizabeth JOHNSON and Ed. PRICE.
Exrs: Brother Edward and nephew John son of brother Joseph.

Wits: John ODENHEIMER, Henry ODENHEIMER and E. PRICE.

SMITH, ANTHANY, Radnor.
July 29, 1802 - ____
Judith MILLER, (relationship not mentioned) and her son Antay MILLER (a minor) she to choose an executor.
Exrs: ____ Wits: Isaac DAVIS and Jonathan RIGBY.

HUNTER, PETER, Radnor.
March 26, 1812 - ____.
Wife Hannah, grandmother Hannah HUNTER.
Exrs: John RUDOLPH and Bartlet BARTLESON.
Wits: John TALFORD and Samuel C. BOWELL.

WORRALL, ISAIAH, U. Providence.
Feb 4, 1817 - ____
Children and grandchildren: John WORRALL and his son Edward, Rachel wife of Jonas MOORE and her son Isaiah, Martha wife of John CRAIG, Jane and Abigail WORRALL.
Caveat entered Feb 6, 1817 by Jonah MOORE.
Citation issued Feb 10, 1817.
Exrs: Son John and daughters Jane and Abigail WORRALL.
Wits: Edward HUNTER and Isaac COCHRAN.

EYRE, REBECCA, Aston,
Feb 13, 1818 - Nov 21, 1826.
Sisters Sarah PALMER wife of George PALMER, Beulah E. THOMAS wife of Townsend THOMAS and her six children: Rebecca, Mary, Beulah, Elma, Townsend and Sarah THOMAS.
Exrs: Brother in law Townsend THOMAS, sister Beulah his wife and friend Enos SHARPLESS of Lower Providence.
Wits: Isaac SHARPLESS and Henry SHARPLESS.

WORRALL, SETH, Marple.
Oct 4, 1818 - ____.
Wife Mary, children: Lot, Phebe BURNIGHT, Mary, Rachel WEST, Job WORRALL and Sarah JONES.
Exr: Friend Enos Lewis.
Wits: Ham WORRALL and Thomas CASSIN.
Will revoked Aug 8, 1821. Caveat entered Oct __, 1822.
Wits: Samuel BLACK and Samuel BLACK, Jr.

HAMPTON, JOHN, Radnor.
Oct 16 ,1818 - ____.
Children: Woodward HAMPTON, Zillah CONNER wife of Timothy CONNER, Ann DONALD wife of William DONALD, Elizabeth HAMPTON, Jane HAMPTON and Rebecca CANOGY and her son John and her other children not named - mentions four of his children as minors, Jane, John, Davis and Rudolph HAMPTON.
Exrs: Son Woodward HAMPTON and Abner LEWIS.
Wits: Thomas TAYLOR and John OWENS.

BONSALL, SIDNEY, Darby.
Nov 19, 1821 - ____.
Brother Joel BONSALL heir and executor.
Exrs: Joel BONSALL.
Wits: Tyson H. LANARES and Jacob LINCOLN.

SMITH, ELIZA ANN, Borough of Chester.
July 28, 1826 - ____.
Sisters Margaret TERRILL and Kitty E. SMITH, nieces Emeline TERRILL and Ann Louisa TERRILL daughters of doctor Job H. TERRILL.
Caveat Sept 16, 1826.
Exrs: Sd. Job H. TERRILL.
Wits: Henry MYERS and S. EDWARDS.

LEWIS, AZARIAH, Newtown Twp.
Dec 12, 1828 - ____
Wife Hanah, children: Robert LEWIS, Hannah LEWIS, Unity GARRETT, Sarah WILLIAMSON, dec'd., and Margaret MAULE, children of sd. daughters Unity, Sarah and Margaret.
Exrs: Son Robert LEWIS and son in law Enos WILLIAMSON.
Wits: William CRAWFORD, Eli LEWIS and William LEWIS.

INDEX

-A-

ABBETT, Miles, 153
ABRAHAM, Daniel, 131, 185; Enoch, 159, 169
ABRAHAMS, Daniel, 160, 185
ADAMS, Jonathan, 64; Sheriff, 165
AFFLICK, Davis, 144
ALBURGER, A., 155
ALEXANDER, David, 1
ALLEN, Aaron, 112; Alfred, 112; Elizabeth, 112; George B., 172; Harriet, 112; Mary, 112; Orasher, 112; Sarah, 20, 182; Thomas, 20, 23, 112
ALLISON, William, 79
ALSTON, Jonathan, 120; Osborn, 120
ALTEMUS, Hannah, 189
AMBER, Catharin, 90
ANDERSON, Abraham, 80; James, 13; Jemimah, 169; Joseph, 173; Robert, 105; Samuel, 163; William, 70
ANDREWS, Hannah, 59; James, 58, 59; John, 59; John C., 193; John H., 153, 173, 194; Josiah, 59; Martha, 59, 101; Mary, 193; Rebecca, 59; Robert, 156; Sarah, 59
ANNELSEY, Robert, 51
ANNESLEY, Jane, 194; Robert, 51
ARCHABOLD, Martha, 161
ARCHER, Caleb G., 154
ARMENT, Cathren, 43; Elizabeth, 43; Hannah, 43; Isaac, 43, 152, 180; John, 43; Nansy, 43; William, 43
ARMER, Samuel, 49
ARMETT, Isaac, 80; Rachel, 80
ARMSTRONG, Irwin, 137; Jacob, 133; James, 34; Mary, 133; Susan, 87
ARNOLD, James, 42; Martha, 42
ART, Ann, 68; James, 68; William, 68
ASH, Alice, 3; Elizabeth, 4; Eunice, 157; James, 45; John, 5, 162; Mary, 30; Mathew, 162; Matthew, 30, 32, 79, 109, 194; Samuel, 70, 162; Widow, 124
ASHBRIDGE, Aaron, 18; Ann, 18; George G., 9, 83, 152; Mary, 63, 167; Rachel, 152
ASHFORD, Susan, 87; William, 87
ASKEN, Benjamin, 137; Elizabeth, 137; Joseph, 137; Mary, 137; Samuel, 137
ASKEW, Benjamin, 60; Elizabeth, 60; Hannah, 39, 83; John, 60; Joseph, 45, 60, 75, 170; Mary, 60; Parker, 60; Samuel, 60; William, 60
ASKREW, Joseph, 95
ASTON, Samuel, 37
ATKINSON, Elizabeth, 86; Rachel, 92
ATMORE, Rachel, 87
ATTMORE, John, 75, 82, 171
AYARS, Shepherd, 185

-B-

BABB, Grace, 67
BABE, George, 80; John, 80; Kitty, 80; Mary, 80
BACKHOUSE, Isabella, 45
BACON, Charles, 171; David, 171; Joseph, 171; Mary, 171; Samuel, 171; Sarah, 171; Thomas, 171
BAGGS, Rachel, 142; William, 142
BAILEY, Elizabeth, 162; Hiram, 187, 191; Rubin, 162
BAILY, Caleb, 165; Isaac, 148; James, 136, 148, 149; Lydia, 148; Thomas, 148, 149; Vincent, 148
BAKER, Aaron, 115, 161, 167; Abel, 167; Abigail, 34, 167; Anthony, 79, 167; Cyrus, 161; Dilworth, 115; Edward, 34, 79, 167; Elizabeth, 108, 139, 161; Elizeth., 121; Esther, 35, 107, 108; George, 167; Hannah, 115, 161; Henry, 161, 199; Jane, 34, 152, 167; Jesse, 35; John, 72, 161; Joseph, 35, 89, 108, 121, 161; Lidia, 167; Margaret, 161; Margret, 108; Martha, 121, 161; Mary, 89, 97, 106, 161, 167; Nathan, 108, 121, 161; Nehemiah, 108, 121, 152; Peter, 161; Phebe, 35; Rachel, 193; Richard, 115; Ruth, 50; Sally Ann, 108; Samuel, 108; Sarah, 103, 135; Susanna, 126, 161; Susannah, 108, 161; William, 97, 103, 135, 161, 167
BALDWIN, Catharine, 10, 154; Charles, 197; Elizabeth, 8, 154; George, 53, 154; Hatton, 197; Jerome, 197; John, 4,

10, 22, 29, 154, 163, 167; Joseph T., 154; Lydia, 154, 190; Martha, 10; Mary, 10, 154; Mary Ann, 197; Rebecca, 154; Robert, 10; Sarah, 197; Sarah Ann, 197; Sophia, 10; Thomas, 154; William, 154, 197, 200
BALL, Elizabeth, 139, 155, 194; Hannah, 139; John, 41, 49, 72, 139; Joseph, 41, 49, 139, 155; Mary, 139; Nathan, 139, 155, 194; Rebecka, 28; Susanna, 139, 155; Thomas, 139, 155, 194
BALLARD, Elisa, 46
BANNARD, Martha, 175
BARDE, John, 13
BARKER, Charles, 159; Eli, 149; Eliza, 149; Evelina, 149; Isabella, 149; Jacob D., 28, 71, 149; James D., 149; John, 110; Lydia, 149; Sarah Ann, 149; Susan, 149; Teacy, 110; Thomas, 149; William, 149
BARLOW, John, 197
BARNARD, Elizabeth, 71, 146; Isaac, 71, 146; Isaac D., 146; James, 24, 28, 40, 55, 71, 178; James D., 71; Richard, 21; Susanna, 71, 146; Thomas, 71, 146
BARR, Ann, 82; Joanna, 82; Mary, 82; Tacy, 82
BARRET, Charles, 64
BARRETT, Ann, 64; Charles, 78, 188; Lydia, 78
BARRINGTON, Charles, 19, 47, 72; Henry, 115; Martha, 19, 47, 72; Rebecca, 115
BARTELSON, Henry, 73
BARTEN, Isaac, 123
BARTHOLOMEW, Andrew, 202; Benjamin, 150, 202; Catharine, 202; Edward, 202; Elizabeth, 202; John, 150, 202; Joseph, 202; Mary, 150; Rachel, 202; Sarah, 150, 202; Thomas, 202
BARTLESON, Ann, 104; Bartlet, 104, 203; Cephas, 104; George, 104; Hannah, 153; Hannah Lee, 104; Jonathan, 104; Lydia, 104; Mark, 104, 169; Mary, 169; Rachel, 104
BARTON, Abner, 73, 85; Adam, 72; Eden, 73, 85; Edon, 79; Elizabeth, 37, 73; Isaac, 72, 128; James, 13, 72; Jane, 72; Sarah, 52, 73, 85; Ziba, 72
BARTRAM, Ann, 162; Benjamin, 162; Elisabeth, 7; Elizabeth, 162; George W., 177, 178, 180; Hannah, 162; Isaac, 153, 162, 175, 189; James, 123, 162; John, 162, 175; Phebe, 189
BARTROM, Benjamin, 7
BATES, Richard, 78
BATTIN, Sarah, 147
BAUGH, Amelia, 199
BAYLEY, Hannah, 106; James, 106
BEALE, Aaron, 144, 200; Ann, 144; John, 75, 144, 200; Lydia, 144, 200; Mary, 144; Olive, 144, 200; Phebe, 144; Rachel, 200; Susanna, 60
BEATTY, Joseph, 67
BEATY, Enkurius, 79
BEAUMONT, Ann, 113; Davis, 113, 136; Elizabeth, 113; George W., 36; George Washington, 113; Hannah, 113; Joseph, 36; Margaret, 36; Mary, 113; Sarah, 113; William, 112, 122
BEAVER, Ann, 145; Devault, 159
BECKERTON, Elizabeth, 38; Jesse, 38
BEEM, William, 191
BEEMS, Hannah, 191
BEERY, Jacob, 103
BELFORE, Ann, 40; Hannah, 40; James, 40
BELL, Mary, 140; Prudence, 184
BELTON, Israel, 173
BENNETT, Caleb T., 54; Catherine, 54; Elizabeth, 93; James, 159; Joseph, 75, 115; Lydia, 148; Thomas, 89
BENTLEY, Mary, 10; Ruth, 99
BENTLY, Catharine, 10
BERCHAL, Elizabeth, 42
BERRY, Esther, 22; Jane, 59; John, 59, 92; Levallin, 59; Mary, 59; Richard, 59; Standish, 59
BETTLE, Charles, 60
BEVAN, Agnes C., 142; Ann, 126; Charles, 70; David, 62, 66, 142; Davis, 34, 126; Isabella, 126, 141, 150; Matthew L., 126, 150; Tacy Anna, 126
BEVEN, David, 29
BEYERS, Thomas, 193
BICKERTON, Elizabeth, 38; Jesse, 20, 38; Joseph, 38; Samuel, 38
BIGART, Isabella, 149
BIGLAR, Ann, 40
BINGHAM, William, 45
BIOREN, Elizabeth, 107;

Elizabeth Ewin, 84; Hannah, 84; John, 84; Mary, 84; Polly, 84; Sarah, 84
BIRCHAL, Elizabeth, 168
BIRCHALL, Caleb, 42, 115, 177; Elizabeth, 93; James, 42, 55, 67, 115, 177; Lydia, 129; Sarah, 177
BIRD, Jane, 125; John, 195; Maria, 125
BISHOP, Amor, 103, 171, 192; George, 16, 54, 81, 95, 135, 171, 175; Jane, 16; Jesse, 81, 171; Joseph, 11, 16, 30, 54, 76, 79, 81, 95, 135, 157, 171, 173; Margaret, 16, 76, 135; Mary, 16, 81, 135, 171; Nansy, 43; Phebe, 16, 81, 135, 171; Priscilla, 192; Sarah, 16, 30, 76, 81, 171; Thomas, 16, 27, 51, 64, 72, 81, 135, 192; William, 81, 135, 171, 174
BISPAM, Sarah, 153
BITTLE, Caleb, 105, 139, 149; Demaris, 127; Mary, 183; William, 65, 171
BLACK, Ann, 76; Catherine, 112; Christian, 64; Eliza, 64; Elizabeth, 116, 126; Isabella, 12; James, 64; Joseph, 64; Mary, 64, 130; Samuel, 12, 71, 76, 146, 203; Sarah, 116; Thomas, 64; William, 129
BLACKHAM, Richard, 31
BLACKMAN, David McCall, 120; Samuel Osburn, 120
BLANKLEY, Susan, 182
BLANKLY, Elizabeth, 190; George, 190
BLUNSTON, ---, 101
BOGGS, Sarah, 202
BOLTON, Deborah, 2; William, 157
BOND, Abraham, 37; Amos, 37; Anna Maria, 149; Benjamin, 37; David, 202; Eliza, 149; Elizabeth, 37; Esther, 43; Isaac, 118, 149; Jesse, 202; John, 202; Jonathan, 149, 202; Joseph, 12, 43, 202; Mary, 149, 202; Rosanna, 37; Sarah, 149, 202; Thomas, 149, 202
BONSAL, Elizabeth, 25; Hannah, 25; Jane, 25; Joseph, 25; Joshua, 189; Obadiah, 25; Rebecah, 25; Samuel, 25; Sarah, 25; Tacy, 25
BONSALL, ---, 101, 173; A. C., 5; Abraham, 15; Ann, 5, 119, 131; Benjamin, 5, 7, 67, 72, 78, 131, 182; Caleb, 12; Charles, 5, 119; David, 186; Edward, 78; Elenor, 12; Elizabeth, 5, 131; Enoch, 5, 131; Esther, 5, 78; George, 5, 77, 93, 138; Hannah, 5, 44, 49, 150; Isaac, 5, 12; J., 176; James, 5, 78, 117, 174; Joel, 5, 150, 204; John, 125; John Caleb, 5; Jonathan, 5, 34, 70, 117, 119; Joseph, 5, 7, 44, 48, 117, 146, 174; Joshua, 5, 119, 150; Levi, 5; Lydia, 5, 117; Margaret, 5, 117, 174; Margret, 119; Martha, 5, 117; Mary, 5, 12, 49, 131, 138; Moses, 5, 131; Obadiah, 44; Parker, 138; Phillip, 12; Rachel, 5; Rebeckah, 44; Rebekah, 44; Reuben, 5, 119; Robert, 44; Samuel, 5, 44, 131; Samuel C., 186; Sarah, 5, 117, 157; Sidney, 5, 150, 204; Susannah, 5, 117; Tacy, 44; Vincent, 12; William, 5, 131, 186
BOOGER, Mary, 189
BOON, Andrew, 63; Elen, 90; Elizabeth, 47; Hans, 63; John, 60, 63; Joseph, 59, 60, 63; Lydia, 47; Mary, 90; Rebecca, 47, 60, 63; William, 47, 90
BOONE, Mary, 90; Swan, 90
BOOTH, Caleb, 148, 172; Elizabeth, 148, 172; Isaac, 163; James, 163; Jemima, 163; John, 135, 148, 163, 172; Joseph, 57, 135, 148, 163, 172, 194; Martha, 98, 172; Nathaniel, 151, 163; Phebe, 163; Robert, 163; Sarah, 148, 172; Thomas, 61, 88, 163, 167; William, 148, 172
BOOTHE, Thomas, 154
BOSS, Barbara, 190
BOSTICK, James, 98; John, 98; Joseph H., 98; Mary, 98; Sarah, 98
BOTTOMLEY, Elizabeth, 182; James, 182; John, 133; Martha, 133; Thomas, 133
BOWELL, Samuel C., 203
BOWERS, John, 22; William, 201
BOWLEN, John, 194; Mary, 194
BOWMAN, Ann, 114; Henry, 83; Thomas, 49
BOYD, Ann, 105; David, 195;

Elizabeth, 195; James, 195; Jane, 195; John, 195; John Summerfield, 195; Martha, 105; Mary, 195; Matthew, 195; Sarah, 195; William, 195
BOYERS, Elizabeth, 110; John, 110
BOYLE, Hugh, 52
BOYS, Nancy, 98
BRADFORD, Mary, 84
BRADLEY, Cloe, 168; Mary, 68
BRAINARD, Mary, 50
BRANAN, Benjamin, 155
BRANNAN, Abigail, 157; Benjamin, 72, 157; Charles, 157; Elizabeth, 157; Eunice, 157; Grace, 157; John, 157; Mary, 157; Moses, 157; Sarah, 157
BRANNEN, George, 127
BRANNER, Sarah, 67
BRANNON, Benjamin, 24, 49, 70
BRANON, Mary, 50
BRANSON, ---, 177
BRATTEN, James, 151, 163, 176, 192; William, 151
BRATTON, James, 102
BRENNAN, Benjamin, 155, 161
BRIGGS, Isaac, 96; Mary, 96; Samuel, 96
BRINKLE, Samuel C., 170
BRINTON, Amos, 14; Ann, 120; Caleb, 36, 119; Catharine, 186; Christiana, 36; Christianna, 119; Edward, 14; Esther, 14; George, 14, 36, 119, 186; George H., 186; Hannah, 36; Harriet, 120; Henry, 186; Hill, 119, 186; James, 89; Jane, 14, 36; John, 36, 101, 115, 119, 186; Joseph, 14, 36, 82, 88, 101, 119, 120, 161; Margaret, 101; Mary, 36, 88, 101; Mary K., 186; Phebe, 36, 94, 120; Rebecca, 36, 119; Sarah, 119; Thomas, 36, 119, 120; Thomas H., 185; William, 14
BRITTON, Amy, 54; Ann, 54; Catherine, 54; Ezekiel, 54; Mary, 54; Rebecah, 83; Richard, 53, 54; Sarah, 54
BROBSON, Elizabeth, 139; Rebecca, 157
BROMALL, Hannah, 100
BROMWELL, Beulah, 61; William, 61
BROOK, Hannah, 144; Lydia, 106
BROOKE, Alexander, 106; Benjamin, 110; Charles, 32; David, 89; Elijah, 32, 148, 168, 170, 182, 185, 196; Hannah, 144; James, 89, 110; Jehu, 32; Jesse, 10, 32, 106, 125, 139, 160, 176, 197; John, 32, 38, 59, 80, 92, 95, 106, 112, 139, 148, 176; Jones, 110; Margaret, 32, 89; Margaret D., 176; Mark, 110; Mary, 110; Nathan, 89, 110; Owen, 184; Rachel, 89; Ruth, 89; Samuel, 32; Sarah, 89; William, 109
BROOKES, George, 136; Jesse, 160
BROOKS, Elizabeth, 166; Hannah, 61; John, 59, 70
BROOM, Jacob, 8
BROOMAL, Hannah, 156
BROOMALL, Daniel, 111, 121, 126, 142; David, 121, 135; Elizabeth, 121, 158; Enoch, 121; George, 158; Hannah, 111, 121, 126; Isaac, 121; Jacob, 121; James, 69, 121, 199; Jane, 121; John, 98, 121, 132, 135, 140, 148, 158, 172, 199; John T., 197; John Talbot, 135; Joseph, 69, 121; Martha, 121, 135; Mary, 197; Nathan, 121; Nehemiah, 121, 135, 195; Rachel, 121, 142; Sarah, 121, 126, 158
BROOMEL, Isaac, 13
BROOMER, Phebe, 10
BROOMHALL, Jehu, 183; Lidia, 167
BROWN, Agnes, 28; Ann, 182, 184; Archibald, 80; Benjamin, 182, 184; Caleb, 28; Daniel, 28; Eliza, 182, 184; Elizabeth, 28, 95, 184; Emily, 182; Esther, 95; George, 79; George Washington, 80; Hannah, 28; James, 182; Jane, 80; Jeremiah, 28; Jesse, 181; John, 182; Joseph, 23, 28, 116; Marget, 182; Maria, 80; Mary, 80, 182; Nancy, 80; Nathaniel, 95; Rebekah, 95; Samuel, 182, 184; Sarah, 28, 95; Sophia, 182; Susannah, 28, 95; Thomas, 182, 185; William, 28, 71, 80, 198; William Cleaver, 184
BRYAN, Sarah, 19
BRYANT, Ann, 150
BUCKINGHAM, Glouver, 185
BUCKLEY, Adam, 21; Ann, 42
BUCKNALL, William, 143, 170
BUCKNELL, William, 102

BUGLESS, Elizabeth, 158; George, 158, 187; Judith, 158
BULLICK, Moses, 151
BULLOCK, Aaron, 151, 172; Elizabeth, 151; Hannah, 188; Hester, 188; Isaac, 56, 151, 188; Jane, 56, 151, 188; John, 122, 188; Lewis, 188; Margary, 188; Margery, 56; Marjory, 151; Mary, 56, 152, 172, 188; Moses, 56, 188; Robert, 151; Sarah, 188; Thomas, 56, 122, 151; Thomas H., 188
BUNTING, Ann, 101; Elizabeth, 101, 123; Hannah, 7, 101; James, 101, 155; John, 59, 96, 123, 183; John H., 91, 155; John W., 139; Joseph, 101, 130, 166; Joseph M., 123; Josiah, 6, 7, 15, 59, 101; Mary, 123; Samuel, 7, 101, 193; Sarah, 6, 101; William, 101
BURD, Maria, 80
BURDSALL, Ira, 198
BURK, Benjamin, 17, 100; Eli, 200; Eli R., 160; Rachel, 200
BURKNELL, W., 144
BURN, Ann, 11, 58; Isaac, 11, 58; Jane, 11, 58; Joseph, 11, 58; Rachel, 58; William, 11, 58
BURNIGHT, Phebe, 203
BURNS, David, 108; Eliza, 144; Elizabeth, 143; George, 140; Giliad, 197; Gillead, 140; Gilliad, 144; Hannah, 108, 140; Henrietta, 108; James, 57, 77, 108, 143, 144; John, 140, 143, 144; Joseph, 68, 140; Kerlin, 67; Margaret, 68, 84, 140; Margret, 34; Mary, 143, 144, 199; Mathias, 67, 84; Penelope, 147; Shaw, 38; William, 26, 38, 57, 108
BURNSIDE, William, 121
BURTNITT, Daniel, 2
BURTON, Anna, 180; Eli, 180; John, 180; Lydia, 180
BURY, Jacob, 34
BUSH, ---, 165; David, 7; Elisabeth, 7
BUTLER, Elizabeth, 166; John, 66, 196; Joshua, 166; Nobel, 152; Noble, 161; William L., 161
BUTTLER, Nobel, 161
BYERS, Abigail, 156; Elizabeth, 22
BYRD, Richard W., 35; Richard Willing, 35
BYRE, Elizabeth, 188; Jacob, 164, 188; Jane, 188

-C-

CADWELL, Hugh, 126
CALDWELL, Charles, 163; David, 36, 43, 158, 163; Edmond, 125; Elizabeth, 43, 93, 125, 163; Henry, 21; Hugh, 66, 71; James, 16, 37, 93, 158; Jane, 125; Jeames, 42; John, 36, 41, 42, 79, 93, 163, 174; Joseph, 163; Mary, 36, 42, 93, 163; Rachel, 163; Robert, 117; Samuel, 93; Sarah, 43, 93, 163
CALEY, Hannah, 22, 84, 136; Jacob, 136; Mary, 136; Samuel, 36, 85, 136, 142
CALVART, Ann, 27; Daniel, 27
CALVERT, Abraham, 30; Ann, 71; John, 33; Thomas, 11
CALVERTE, Thomas, 46
CALVIN, Robert, 60, 63
CAMPBELL, Fanny, 201; Margaret, 95; William, 201
CANN, Patrick M., 67; Thirza, 144
CANOGY, John, 204; Rebecca, 204
CAREY, Charles, 171, 172, 180, 198; William, 198
CARPENTER, Hannah, 113; Jacob, 130; Jane, 130; John, 130; Mary Ann, 125; Rachel, 130
CARR, Elizabeth, 153; Samuel, 117
CARRELL, Elizabeth, 194
CARSON, Ann, 160; Elizabeth, 130; James, 47; Jane, 160; Martha, 160; Mary, 47; William, 160
CARTER, Abraham, 137, 178, 195; Agnes, 195; Ann, 137, 195; Catherine, 137; Cloud, 178; Daniel, 26, 178, 195; David, 26; Edward, 67, 137, 178, 195; Eleanor, 195; Eliza, 195; Gillied, 195; Grace, 67; Hannah, 137; Jane, 67; John Wesley, 195; John Westley, 178; Joseph, 26, 145, 178; Lydia, 26; Margaret, 26, 178; Martin, 67; Mary, 195; Moses, 67; Nineveh, 45; Prudence, 67; Robert, 178; Sarah, 67; Theron, 67; Thomas, 67; Wesley, 145; William, 178
CARY, Phins., 56
CASSIN, Ann, 129; John, 129; Luke, 57, 60, 81, 129, 153;

Rachel, 176; Thomas, 129, 176, 203
CASSON, Ann, 129; Luke, 129; Thomas, 129
CAUFFMAN, Evalina, 198; Susan, 198
CAWLEY, Ann, 160; David, 160; Margaret, 160; Samuel, 160, 197
CAZZEL, Sarah, 84
CECIL, Algernoon, 110; Alice, 110; Charles, 110; Julian, 110; Keziah, 110; Liza, 110
CHADDS, Elizabeth, 8, 10
CHADS, Elizabeth, 8
CHAFFIN, Sarah, 161
CHALFANT, Margaret, 4
CHALFONT, George, 90; Phebe, 90; Philip, 90; Robert, 90; Thomas, 90
CHALLIS, John, 52
CHAMBERLAIN, Ann, 75, 144; Hannah, 75; James, 75; John, 75; Joseph, 75; Mary, 75; Robert, 75; William, 75
CHAMBERLIN, Abel, 65; Ann, 65; Elizabeth, 65; Hannah, 65; Jane, 65; Jesse, 65; Phebe, 65; Samuel, 65; Susannah, 1; Waldron, 65
CHAMPION, Ann, 187
CHANDLER, Amor, 108; Amos, 8, 10; Elizabeth, 108; Hannah, 152; Jesse, 148; Joseph, 108; Phebe, 45; Samuel Painter, 148; Thomas, 4, 108
CHANY, Charles, 138; David, 138; Prudence, 138
CHAPMAN, Lydia, 180; Thomas, 180
CHARLES, Elizabeth, 100
CHASE, Richard, 147; Robert, 147; Sarah, 147
CHERRY, James, 68; Rachel, 17
CHEW, Benjamin, 36
CHEYNEY, Abel, 73; Alice, 73; Ann, 73; Betsy, 73; Charles, 8; Curtis, 65, 73, 89, 192; David, 150; Edith, 192; Elizabeth, 8, 150; Esther, 73; Hannah, 73; Jane, 8, 73; Jesse, 73; John, 8, 73, 150; John H., 66, 108, 109; Joseph, 48, 65, 73, 89; Lucy, 73; M., 73; Mary, 8, 73, 150, 192; Phebe, 73, 192; Richard, 8, 73; Rufus T., 192; Samuel, 73; T., 73; Thomas, 73; Waldron, 73, 186, 192; William, 8, 65, 73, 109, 149, 150; William H., 192

CHEYNY, John, 136
CHURCHMAN, Edward, 27, 134; Hannah, 111; Joseph, 111; Mary, 134, 179; Mord., 51; Owen, 134; Pennell, 134; Rebecca, 110; Robert, 201
CITER, Adam, 58; Edward, 58; Mary, 58; Sarah, 58
CITERS, Adam, 58; Ann, 58; Elizabeth, 58; Mary, 58
CLARK, Abisha, 109; Rebecca, 109
CLARKSON, Sarah, 109
CLAUGUS, Joseph, 63
CLAXTON, Elizabeth, 41; James, 45
CLAY, George B. L., 198; Jehu, 198; Jehu Curtis, 198; Peter Curtis, 198; Slater, 198
CLAYTON, Abigail, 94; Adam, 55; Cornelia, 150; Elizabeth, 94; Hannah, 94; John, 175; Joseph, 149; Joshua, 50; Lydia, 50; Powel, 163, 175; Powell, 94, 160; Rebecca, 150; Richard, 138; Thomas, 55
CLEMENT, Aaron, 95, 114; Ann, 55, 95; Eliza, 95; Elizabeth, 95, 114; Isaac, 95, 114; John, 55, 95; Sarah Ann, 191
CLEMMENT, Eliza H., 187
CLEMMONS, Catharine, 89
CLEMSON, Esther, 148
CLENDENNON, Isaac, 186; Mercy, 186
CLIME, Philip, 48
CLINE, Henry, 18
CLOUD, Agnes, 49, 172; Ann, 49, 79, 189; Benjamin, 49; Elizabeth, 148; Elizabeth C., 154; Harlin, 49; James, 79; Jeremiah, 27; John, 55; Joseph, 15, 61, 68, 79, 169; Joshua, 79; Lydia, 71, 118; Marshall, 181; Martha, 79; Mary, 15, 79; Mordicai, 49; Nathaniel, 197; Rachel, 61; Sarah, 79; Stephen, 197
COATES, Matthias, 148; Sarah, 88; Sophia, 148
COBORN, Rachel, 18; Thomas, 18
COBOURN, Aaron, 42; Abraham, 115; Caleb, 73, 115, 181; Eliza, 115; Elizabeth, 168, 185; Esther, 115; John, 132; Lazarus, 115; Susannah, 115; Thomas, 87, 115, 185
COBURN, Caleb, 50; Israel, 18; Joseph, 145; Thomas, 73
COCHRAN, Isaac, 114, 129, 203; John, 127; Mary, 64; Sarah,

127; Thomas, 127
COFFMAN, Abigail, 53
COILS, Alexander, 158; Ann, 158; Elizabeth, 158
COLBERT, John, 65; Margaret, 65
COLEMAN, Ann, 187; Hannah, 187; Margaret, 182, 187
COLINS, Phillip, 62
COLLINS, Margaret, 181
COLVIN, Alexander, 94; Jane, 94; Mary, 94; Robert, 94
CONARD, Rebecca, 145
CONARROE, Margaret, 134; Thomas, 134
CONNELL, Eliza, 98; Joseph R., 97
CONNER, Timothy, 128, 204; Zillah, 128, 204
CONNOLLY, Heini, 99
CONRO, John, 73; Margaret, 73
COOK, Ennion, 190
COOPER, Benjamin, 3; Sarah, 123
CORBITT, Daniel, 14; Edward, 14; Jemima, 14; John, 14; Mary Ann, 14; Pennell, 14; Thomas, 14
CORKREY, John, 157
CORNOG, Allice, 122; Augustus, 156; Daniel, 172; Elizabeth, 156; Isaac, 156; John, 156, 161, 172; Margaret, 156; Nancy, 172; Thomas, 123, 172
CORNOGG, Rebecca, 128
COSLEY, Woodward, 169
COTTER, Mary, 115
COUBOURN, John, 23
COURTNEY, Ann, 46; Thomas, 46
COVINGTON, Hannah, 157
COWEN, Ann, 11; Ephraim, 11; Jonas, 11; Mary, 11; William, 11
COWGILL, Martha, 147, 176
COWPLAND, Caleb, 57; David, 57, 121; Sarah, 57
COX, Andrew, 120; Elizabeth, 97, 187, 202; Isaac Newton, 120; Thomas, 97; Tristin, 3; William, 120
CRAIG, James, 115, 151, 172, 178, 179, 195; John, 100, 112, 172, 203; John G., 172; Maria, 172; Martha, 203; Mary, 172; Rebecca, 172; Robert B., 172, 178, 179; Ruth, 121
CRAIGE, Ann, 105; Elizabeth, 105; George, 55; James, 105, 132; John, 105; Martha, 105
CRANSON, Simon, 191
CRANSTON, Ann, 138; Hannah, 138; Simon, 138

CRAVEN, Anna, 180; William, 180
CRAWFORD, Ann, 91; Anna, 137, 196; Hannah, 5; John, 5; Joseph, 148; Margaret, 5; Samuel, 5; William, 145, 204
CRESSON, John Elliott, 82; John H., 191; William, 191
CRIPS, Jacob, 28; Sarah, 28; William, 28
CROLL, Zebulon, 177
CROMWELL, Ann, 86; James C., 86; Martha, 57
CROS, Elizabeth, 43
CROSBY, Ann, 56, 65, 140; Charles, 56; Eleanor, 18, 20, 140; Eliza, 65; Elizabeth, 18; John, 18, 21, 34, 42, 107, 130, 140; John L., 189; Joseph, 65; Peirce, 118, 140, 189, 195; Rebecca, 65; Richard, 18, 165; Robert P., 140, 189; Ruth, 56; Sarah, 65; Sarah Ann, 189; Susanna, 18; William, 17; Woodward, 118
CROSLEY, James, 28; Mary, 46
CROSS, Elizabeth, 130; James, 45; John, 130; Joseph, 130; Margaret, 45; Rachel, 130; Sarah, 130
CROWLEY, James, 73
CROXEN, Enos, 140; Mary, 140; Sarah, 140
CROZER, Elizabeth, 36, 116; Esther, 36, 42; James, 11, 36; John, 15, 36, 37, 42, 43, 55, 117; John P., 163; Martha, 36, 42, 93; Mary, 36, 93; Rachel, 36, 37, 42, 43, 93; Rebecca, 36; Sarah, 36, 117
CROZIER, John, 7, 20; Mary, 7
CULIN, Alice, 98; Ann, 105; Daniel, 98; Hannah, 137, 162; Isaac, 125, 162; Israel, 105; John, 47, 54, 94, 105; Justis, 105; Margaret, 98; William, 98
CULLIN, John, 98
CUMMINGS, Elizabeth, 99, 116; James, 99; Thomas, 99
CURRIE, William, 32
CUSHMAN, Owen, 134

-D-
DANIEL, Ann, 167; David, 167; Jemima, 167; John, 17, 167; Sarah, 167; Thomas, 167
DARBY, George, 2; John, 2; Seeneth, 88
DARLING, G., 201

DARLINGTON, Amy, 30, 97; Cyrus, 193; E., 170, 178, 179, 188; Edward, 14, 193; Esther, 56; Jesse, 30, 69, 93; John, 56; Liba, 186; Martha, 97; Rhoda, 97; Samuel, 97; Thomas, 162
DAUGHERTY, Susannah, 43
DAVID, Amer, 37; Amos, 37; David, 103; George, 37; Isaac, 103; John, 37; Joseph, 37; Mary, 37; Morgan, 2; Samuel, 37; Sarah, 37
DAVIS, Abigail, 111; Abraham, 17, 111; Amey, 8; Andrew, 175; Ann, 45, 63; Anna, 196; Anthony, 178; Benjamin, 8, 32, 43, 63, 87, 91, 131, 136, 137, 160, 173, 196; Caleb, 173; Catherine, 17; D., 143; David, 91, 103; David I., 196; David Jones, 137; Dorothy, 17; Drusilla, 199; Edith, 43, 71; Edward, 43, 70, 71; Eleanor, 17; Eliza, 123; Elizabeth, 8, 17, 25, 32, 168, 173, 202; Emily, 182; Ephraim, 62; Esther, 173; Frances, 91, 137; George, 173; Hannah, 43, 63, 71, 137, 173, 196; Isaac, 10, 22, 23, 32, 102, 103, 203; Jane, 45; Joel, 161, 173; John, 18, 32, 35, 95, 159, 182, 202; Jonathan, 110; Joseph, 7, 8, 36, 37, 62, 63, 68, 83, 90, 111, 113, 125, 144, 161, 173, 192; Lewis, 2, 47, 63, 72, 111, 173; Lewisa, 173; Lydia, 47, 91, 137, 196; Margaret, 8, 103, 143, 145, 175; Marget, 173; Mary, 17, 63, 91, 137, 159, 196; Mordecai, 86, 92, 106, 148; Moredcai, 98; Nathan, 32, 96, 173; Nathaniel, 21; Nehemiah, 17; Owen, 111; Perthenia, 8; Rachel, 23, 144, 202; Ralph, 91, 196, 197; Rebecca, 35, 70, 139, 173; Ruth, 43; Ruth Ann, 91; Samuel, 70, 87, 91, 96, 99, 102, 116, 123, 125, 161, 167, 170, 171, 183, 194, 195; Sarah, 8, 17, 39, 93, 173; Susana, 173; Susanna, 17; Tacey, 91; Tacy, 43, 78, 137, 196; Timothy, 17; William, 8, 17, 72, 144, 173
DAWES, Abijah, 131; Elizabeth, 131; Jonathan, 131; Martha, 131, 158, 168; Mary, 131; Mary W., 131; Rumford, 131, 133; Samuel D., 131; Samuel F., 131
DAWSON, Elisha, 189; Jennis, 94
DAY, James, 77, 132; John, 77; Margaret, 77; Samuel, 77; Sarah, 28
DEHAVEN, Edith, 14; H., 18; Hannah, 14; Peter, 14; Sarah, 18
DELAPLAIN, James, 170
DEMSEY, John, 107
DENNIS, Jane, 46; Rachel, 189; Tabitha, 59, 92
DERIBERKER, Eli, 24; Jacob, 24
DEROBARLER, Jacob, 24
DERRAH, Elizabeth, 15
DERRICK, Mary, 15; Zachariah, 144, 191
DESHONG, I. O., 197; J. I., 200; J. O., 200; Peter, 126, 137
DESMOND, Daniel I., 174
DICK, A. T., 146, 202; Archibald T., 176, 183, 189; Brinton I., 183; H. R., 183; Phebe, 89; Roger, 35; Thomas, 57, 89, 98; Thomas B., 68, 71, 77, 80; Valentine, 67
DICKENSON, Mary, 45; Patience, 155
DICKERSON, Hannah, 148; Patience, 41
DICKINSON, Patience, 139
DICKS, Abraham, 32, 34, 42; Benjamin, 164; Elizabeth, 42; Frederick, 57, 164; James, 164; John, 56; Joseph, 163, 164; Mary, 164; Mary Ann, 164; Peter, 17, 56, 164; Rebecca, 81; Roger, 12, 17, 27, 43, 57, 61, 81, 110; Sarah, 164; William, 164
DIEHL, Adam, 128; John, 128; Mary, 128; Nicholas, 3, 128; Thomas, 128; William, 128
DILWORTH, Brinton, 119; Charles, 20; Christiana, 119; Elizabeth, 119; James, 5, 14, 20, 193; Joseph, 193; Mary, 193; Phebe, 119; Richard, 134; Sarah, 77, 187; Thomas, 193; William, 115; Ziba, 193
DINGEE, Charles, 35, 38; Jacob, 9
DINNELL, Sarah, 109
DIXON, Emy, 148; Isaac, 148; John, 138
DIZER, Abigale, 127; James, 23
DNT, Mary, 144
DOBSON, Thomas, 116
DODG, Joseph, 153

DONALD, Ann, 128, 204; William, 128, 204
DONNE, Charlotte, 100; Evelina, 100; John, 100; John A., 100; Nathan, 100
DOUGHERTY, John, 73
DOWNES, Hannah, 176; John, 176; Thomas, 176
DOWNING, Anne, 165; Deborah, 132; Elizabeth, 22, 84, 90; Hunt, 132; Richard, 22, 84, 90; William W., 165
DOYLE, Barnaby, 23; Sarah, 80; William, 23, 80, 81, 114
DRIVER, Adam, 198
DUFF, Samuel Mucl., 19
DUNBAR, David, 105
DUNN, Andrew, 121; Catharine, 121, 169; David, 123; Esther, 144; George, 21, 71, 169, 177; Joseph, 169, 177; Martha, 71, 177; Mary, 71, 121, 136, 144; Mordecai, 144; Phebe, 123; Robert, 71, 121, 124, 177; Sarah, 144; Susanna, 44, 123, 124, 144, 145; Thomas, 121; William, 123, 177
DUNOFF, Justua, 158
DUNWOODY, David, 111; James, 58, 102, 111; Jane, 58; John, 111, 172, 179; Joseph, 111, 179; Rachel, 11, 58, 111, 179; Ruth, 132; William, 111, 179
DURING, Cauless, 180; Tyson, 180
DUTTEN, Margarett, 101
DUTTON, Alice, 132, 178; Amy, 178; Edmund, 200; Hannah, 23, 24; Hannah E., 196; Hibbard, 24; Isaac, 191; J. Larkin, 191; Jacob, 135; John, 44, 132, 171, 178, 196; John Brinton, 191; John Larkin, 191; Jonathan, 23, 44, 49, 50, 60, 75, 119, 132, 156, 178; Jonatn., 60; Lydia, 167, 196; Margaret, 167, 191; Marsha, 132; Martha, 178; Mary, 105; Rachel, 119; Rebecca, 132, 178; Rebeckah, 24; Richard, 23, 24, 34, 98, 100, 132, 156, 178, 191; Robert, 132; Samuel, 157; Samuel E., 196; Sarah, 23, 24; Susanna, 24, 181; Susannah, 23; Thomas, 23, 24, 34, 100, 132, 156, 159, 178, 191, 196, 200
DUTTS, Jeremiah, 35

DYLE, Loas, 88
DYSON, Ann, 193; Isaiah, 193

-E-

EACHES, Virgil, 66
EACHUS, Evan, 54, 157, 173; Evans, 192; Hannah, 54; Homer, 169; Mary, 202; Virgil, 99
EARL, Elizabeth, 155; Isaac, 155; Susanna, 139, 155, 194
EASTON, Anna, 180; John, 180
EAVENSON, George, 83; Joseph, 125; Richard, 36
EBRIGHT, Elizabeth, 138
EBRITE, Ann, 190; Elizabeth, 190; George W., 190; Hannah, 190; Henry, 190; Jacob, 190; Joseph, 190; Lydia, 147, 190; Melchior, 190, 191; Melchior L., 170, 190; Morgan, 190; Rebecca, 190; Sarah, 190; Zachariah, 190
EDDINS, Hannah, 6; William, 6
EDENTON, Dinah, 133
EDWARDS, Abner, 143; Ann, 158; Charles, 146; Elizabeth, 99; Garrett, 128, 146, 171; George, 146; Isaac, 158; Isachar, 176; Issachar, 158; Issacher, 99; Jacob, 52, 79, 88; James, 52, 99, 143; Jane, 98, 146, 158; John, 27, 28, 121; Joseph, 142; Margaret, 52, 178; Mary, 143, 144; Nancy, 131; Prudence, 52; Robert, 143; S., 142, 143, 145, 150, 163, 177, 179, 180, 192, 196, 204; Samuel, 107, 126, 131, 172, 176, 181; Sarah, 52, 168; Seth, 146; William, 52
EFFINGAR, Agnes, 29; Henry, 29
EFFINGER, Agnes, 83; Agness, 42; Henry, 42, 83; Jacob, 42, 83; Malachi, 83; Margaret, 42, 83; Rachel, 42, 83; Rebecca, 42, 83; Sarah, 42, 83
EGBERT, Laurence, 89
ELDRIDGE, Joseph, 168
ELFRETH, Jeremiah, 171; Sarah, 171
ELKINS, George, 153
ELLIOT, Ann, 80; Hugh Linn, 80; Israel, 123; John, 141; Mark, 191; Mary, 80; Rachel, 191; Sarah, 80, 91; William, 80
ELLIOTT, Benjamin, 119; Christian, 5; Enoch, 119; Israel, 5, 81; J., 156;

James, 91; John, 43, 73, 91, 103, 132; Mark, 144; Mary, 5, 81; Ruth, 5; Sarah, 119

ELLIS, Amos, 17, 34, 167, 182; Ann, 17; Bridget, 43, 91; David, 34; Elizabeth, 16, 17; Griffith, 43, 91; Guinn, 43; Hannah, 17, 43, 86, 102; Hester, 34; Humphrey, 16; Isaac, 17, 34; Jesse, 43, 86; Jonathan, 34, 167; Margaret, 91; Mary, 16, 34, 43; Rachel, 17; Rebecca, 43, 70, 91; Sarah, 34; Tacey, 70; Tacy, 43; Thomas, 34, 71; William, 17

ELLY, Esther, 57

ELY, Esther, 56, 57, 69; Ezra, 151; George, 69; Joshua, 27, 52, 56, 69; Sarah, 56

EMLEN, James, 7, 22, 30, 39, 46, 66, 111, 142, 160, 166, 186; Joshua, 111; Mary, 160; Phebe, 111; Samuel, 111

ENGLE, Abigail, 110; Frederick, 27; Hannah, 163; Isaac, 26, 52, 110; John, 27, 156; Joseph, 69, 84, 126, 128, 158; Margaret, 146; Mary, 84, 160; Peter Hill, 197; Susannah, 163

ENNIS, Francis, 191

ENNISE, Francis, 197; Marget, 197; Mary, 197

ENOCHS, Collet, 95; Jerremiah, 95; Rebekah, 95

ENTREKIN, Drusilla T., 199; George, 90

ENTRIKIN, Ann, 98; Samuel, 121; Sarah, 121

ERBEN, Mary, 159; Peter, 159

ERSKINE, Margaret, 184

ERSREY, Elizabeth, 144

ERWIN, Elizabeth, 19, 47; Nathaniel, 19, 47

ESBEN, Alice, 107

ESPIN, James, 129

ESREY, Joseph, 172; Margaret, 172

EVAN, David, 103; Joel, 198; Thamer, 103

EVANS, Abigail, 84, 90, 141, 169; Abraham, 57; Abram, 141; Acquilla, 20, 106; Alice, 57; Amey, 20; Amy, 3; Ann, 57, 120, 182, 200; Anne, 57; Benjamin, 66, 200; Cadwalader, 57, 73; Cadwalleder, 57; Cadwaller, 126; Catherine, 74; Charles, 171; Daniel, 103; David, 12, 20, 73, 106, 125, 143; Deborah, 4; Edward, 75, 142; Elizabeth, 41, 66, 141; Eunice, 120; Evan, 31, 59, 169; Grace, 190; Hannah, 2, 3, 66, 73, 106, 141, 171; Jacob, 182, 200; Jane, 6, 196; Joel, 171, 179, 180, 198, 200; John, 3, 20, 73, 74, 90, 136, 141, 142, 182; Jonathan, 39, 70, 120, 171; Joseph, 66, 74, 141, 179, 200; Lydia, 50, 97, 144, 184; Margaret, 20, 110; Martha, 120, 141; Mary, 4, 12, 66, 73, 74, 129, 141, 171, 200, 201; Musgrave, 51; Nathan, 3, 16, 23, 106, 109, 186, 200; Peter, 39, 200; Phebe, 142; Rebecca, 97, 129, 144, 184; Robert, 57, 74; Ruth, 20, 66; Samuel, 51, 60, 66, 130, 196; Sarah, 2, 3, 120, 139; Susanna, 141; Thomas, 4, 6, 112, 171; William, 106, 116, 120, 171; Zillah, 186

EWING, Mary, 128

EYRE, Abigail, 160; Ann, 55, 164; Caleb, 49, 60, 95; Elizabeth, 164; I. Ashmead, 198; Isaac, 5, 6, 33, 66, 67, 109, 160; Isabella, 95; John, 60, 67, 95; Jonas, 40, 67, 84, 109, 160, 177; Joseph, 164; Lewis, 34; Luis, 164; Maryann, 95; Nathen, 164; Preston, 97, 118, 140, 170, 181, 196, 198; Rebecca, 203; Robert, 55, 164; Sarah, 164; William, 49, 57, 109, 160, 164, 177

EYRES, Beaulah, 35; John, 35; Jonas, 163; Rebecca, 35; Sarah, 35

-F-

FAIRLAMB, Ann, 163; Catherine, 15; Eleanor, 51; Francis, 15; Frederick, 13, 15, 28, 50, 58, 69, 78, 163; George W., 187; Hannah, 163; John, 13, 15, 27, 47, 51; Joseph, 163, 196; Maria, 15; Mary, 1, 40, 58, 77, 163; Nich., 73; Nicholas, 28, 50, 58, 78, 132, 150, 163; Richard, 50; Robert, 146, 159, 163, 168; Samuel, 15, 196; Sidney, 196; Susanna, 15; Susannah, 163; William, 110, 116, 126, 134, 146, 163, 168, 187

FARMER, Ferdinand, 23
FARR, Abraham, 16, 30, 148; Abram, 90
FARRA, Samuel, 29
FARROW, Ann, 157; Esther, 157
FAULK, John, 154
FAWKES, Alice, 108, 144; Ann, 47, 87, 114, 161; Elise, 1; Elizabeth, 114, 161; Hannah, 161; Isaiah, 87, 144, 179, 185; John, 1, 36, 87; Joseph, 2, 87, 108; Mary, 87, 114, 144, 161; Nathaniel, 87, 114; Rebacah, 1, 2; Rebeca, 114; Rebecca, 87, 161; Rebeccah, 1; Richard, 1, 2, 23, 47, 48, 51, 87, 88, 144; Samuel, 87; Sarah, 1, 87, 114, 161; Thomas, 1
FAWKS, Richard, 11
FELL, Ann, 168; Edward, 11, 12, 13, 29, 46, 47, 111, 155; Hannah, 11; William, 11
FENTHAM, Ann, 75; Priscilla, 75; Sarah, 75
FERGUSON, Elizabeth, 16; Mary M., 25; Robert, 16
FERMAN, Amy, 54; John, 54
FERRIS, Edith, 97
FETTERMAN, George, 20
FEW, Ann, 75; Eli, 14, 40
FIELD, Elizabeth, 43, 115; Nathan, 43
FILAR, Rachel, 200
FILBERD, Margaret, 173
FIMPLE, Christiana, 173; George, 35, 173; Isaac, 173; John, 173; Martha, 173; Mary, 173; Michael, 35, 173; Richard, 166, 173; Rudolph, 173
FINCH, Joseph, 29
FISHER, Jacob, 103, 143; Miers, 39; Rachel, 143; Thomas, 39
FISS, Ann, 82, 86
FLECK, Elizabeth C., 162
FLETCHER, Daniel, 81
FLOWER, Henrietta, 36, 40, 41, 124; Henry Hale, 6; Mary B., 183; Richard, 6; Sarah, 57; William G., 182; Z. W., 136, 183
FLOWERS, John, 77
FOLK, Jan, 103; Jane, 103
FORD, Anderson, 133; Benjamin, 57; Caleb, 153; Curtis Lownes, 197; James, 153; Jane, 153; John, 150, 153; Lydia, 153; Mary, 133; Mathias, 57; Philip, 57; Rebeckah, 153; Slater Lownes, 197; William, 57, 153
FOREMAN, Amy, 105; John, 105; Thomas, 105
FORREST, Andrew, 53; Elizabeth, 53; Henry, 53, 86, 112, 167, 168, 188; James, 53, 188; Jane, 53; Nancy, 53; William, 53
FORRESTER, Ralph, 95; Sarah, 95
FORTNER, Uriah, 22
FORWOOD, Margaret, 135; Mary, 135; Robert, 135; Sarah, 135
FOULK, Ann, 126; Charles, 126; Edith, 125; Elennor, 125; George, 126; Isaac, 126; Jane, 126; John, 163; Joseph, 126; Morris, 126; Stephen, 56; William, 56, 126
FOX, Alice, 111; Ann, 19; Edith, 198; George, 159; James, 198; John, 126; Joseph, 111, 123, 132, 137; Joshua, 45, 111; Richard, 19; Sarah, 111; Thomas, 124
FRAME, Eleanor, 121; Elenor, 82; Elizabeth, 121; Enos, 99; James, 99, 122; Jane, 121; John, 82, 99; Margaret, 121; Mary, 121; Mifflin S., 193; Orpah, 121; Rebecca, 82, 86, 99, 121, 122; Robert, 56, 99, 121, 122, 128, 152; Ruth, 121; Sarah, 121; Thomas, 99; William, 157
FRAMES, Robert, 151
FRANCIS, Charles, 35; Henrietta Maria, 51; John, 35, 51; Maria, 51; Philip, 51; Tench, 35; Thomas, 35
FRANKLIN, Anne, 111; Benjamin, 190; James, 190; Walter, 111
FRAZEN, Mary W., 150
FRAZER, Alice, 134, 179; Robert, 179
FREDERICK, Elizabeth, 193; John, 193
FREE, Abraham, 20, 44, 63, 71, 86, 87, 139, 170; David, 86; John, 43, 44, 86; Mary, 43; Ruth, 20; Samuel, 86, 87
FREED, Hugh, 34
FRY, William, 116
FUSSELL, Solomon, 4

-G-

GAMBLE, John, 49; Mary, 6; Patrick, 49; Peter, 49; Robert M., 188; Robert N., 152; Robert Nossit, 49
GANEY, Dinah, 194
GARDINER, Eliza, 193; Mary,

125; Richard, 170
GARDNER, Archibald, 112; Hannah, 112, 171, 193; Sheriff, 28
GARNER, Drucilla, 181; Henry, 45, 181; Keziah, 199; Kissiah, 181; Sarah, 181, 199; Susan, 181, 198, 199; Susannah, 181
GARRET, Aaron, 148; Ruth, 108; William, 39
GARRETSON, Hannah, 11; Joseph, 11
GARRETT, Aaron, 35; Abigail, 183; Amos, 19, 190; Ann, 24, 58, 63, 70, 166; Anna, 164; Anna B., 90, 133; Charles, 174; David, 150; Davis, 166, 190; Dorthea S., 124; Edward, 166; Eliza, 69; Elizabeth, 22, 24, 25, 69, 70, 166; Ester, 22, 68; Esther, 69, 97; Gulielma, 166; Hannah, 25, 166, 168; Henrietta, 191; James, 25, 166, 168; Jane, 58, 167; Jehu, 46, 90, 180, 196; John, 24, 70, 74, 75, 168; Jonah, 68, 69; Laticia, 168; Lewis, 168; Lydia, 70, 74; Maria, 168; Mary M., 197; Nathan, 25, 51, 58, 161, 166; Noah, 168; Oborn, 24, 31, 70; Rachel, 190; Samuel, 21, 58, 70, 120, 161, 162; Sarah, 51, 91, 166, 183; Thomas, 51, 58, 70, 76, 78, 91, 120, 161, 166, 191; Thomas G., 197; Unity, 46, 204; William, 19, 24, 31, 70
GARRETTSON, Hannah, 70; Lydia, 70
GARRIGUES, Benjamin, 149; Benjamin D., 137; Edward, 91, 149; Margaret, 91; Samuel, 96; Sarah, 137; Tacy, 137, 196; William, 96
GASKELL, Peter, 141
GEESEMAN, William, 146
GEIGER, George, 170
GEORGE, Amos, 90; Ann, 54; David, 103; Edward, 90; Franklin, 90; John, 18; Lemuel, 185; Mary, 103; Mordecai, 90; Rebecca, 90; Sarah, 185; Thomas, 2, 3; William, 54, 90
GEST, Abraham, 61; Alice, 61; Benjamin, 61; Hannah, 61; Henry, 61; John, 61; Joseph, 36; Mary, 61; Rachel, 61; Samuel, 61; Sarah, 61;

Susanna, 61; William, 61
GEUST, Ann, 185
GHEEN, Mary, 189
GIBBONS, Ann, 30; Elizabeth, 30; George W., 30, 109; Hannah, 30; Jacob, 112; James, 27, 53, 66, 80; James M., 109; James Mifflin, 30; Jane, 30, 109; Jesse, 68; John Haysham, 30; Joseph, 29, 30, 37, 137, 164, 168; Margery, 109; Mary, 30; Mary Ash, 109; Mifflin, 30; Rebecca, 30, 109; Sarah, 30, 109; Sherriff, 165; William, 14, 19, 53, 80
GIBSON, Lydia, 6; Nathan, 74, 82, 86, 87, 96, 100, 102, 114, 117, 124; Thomas, 25
GILES, Jacob, 17
GILL, Joseph, 67; Susan, 151; Susannah, 49
GILLINGHAM, Sarah, 88
GILPIN, Abigail, 46; Ann, 159; Bernard, 159; Gideon, 14, 39, 75, 86, 159, 190; Hannah, 148, 159; Isaac G., 39, 70, 74, 75, 86, 148, 159; John, 159; Joseph, 159; Lydia, 46; Mary, 46; Ruth, 148; Sarah, 45, 159; Susanna, 160
GLASCOE, Thomas, 114
GLEAVE, James, 7
GODFREY, Jane, 103; John, 103, 143; Mary, 103
GOODING, Rachel, 6
GOODLY, Samuel, 95
GOODWIN, John, 84; Martha M., 146; Thomas, 201
GORBY, Margaret, 178
GOSSET, Ann, 68; Elizabeth, 68; Hannah, 68; Pompey, 68
GOVELL, William, 51
GRACE, Mary Ann, 136
GRACEY, Elizabeth, 171; Jane, 171; John, 92, 161, 171; Patience, 92; Samuel, 92; Sarah, 171; Susanna, 171; Thomas, 171
GRACY, Hannah, 5; John, 2, 76; Samuel, 2
GRAHAM, Abigail, 14, 27, 36, 45; Catharine, 40; Catherine, 18, 36; Dorothea, 15, 36; Dorothy, 40; Eleanor, 27, 36, 140; H. H., 5; Henrietta, 36, 140; Henry Hall, 27; Jane, 140; Katharine, 140; Margaret, 87; Mary, 14, 36, 40, 140; W. M., 6, 84; Widow, 97; William, 14, 15, 16, 18,

36, 40, 41, 42, 45, 52, 55, 84, 90, 104, 107, 109, 118, 132, 133, 140, 150; Zedekiah Wyatt, 6, 40; Zedkiah W., 40
GRANTHAM, Charles, 29, 42, 65, 125; George, 29
GRAVES, Jonathan, 165; Mary, 144
GRAY, Ezekiel, 178; Mary, 188; William, 189
GREBLE, William E., 162
GREEN, Abel, 19, 34, 48, 72, 183; Amos, 4; Daniel, 10; Eliza Ann, 199; Esther, 34; George, 19, 34, 45, 54, 98, 99, 126, 134, 177; Hannah, 100; Jane, 34; Jesse, 4, 53, 68, 108; Joseph, 12; Lot, 4, 29; Louisa, 198; Lydia, 12, 34; Martha, 177; Mary, 65, 75, 192, 199; Phebe, 171; Priscilla, 19; Rachel, 4; Rebecca, 4; Robert, 4, 34, 45, 94; Sarah, 34, 199; Silas, 4, 29, 130, 171, 199; William, 74
GREENWAY, Sallie, 35
GREGG, Elizabeth, 25; Mary, 94
GREGORY, Alexander, 66; Elizabeth, 66; John, 66; Joseph, 66
GRIBLE, Edward, 162
GRIBONS, James, 162; Margaret, 162
GRIFFEY, Joseph, 129; Vernon, 129
GRIFFIN, Jane, 195
GRIFFITH, Abner, 124; Amos, 102; Ann, 154, 198; Castle, 95; Edith, 198; Elizabeth, 102, 113, 202; Enoch, 154, 198; Eunice, 142; George, 142; Hannah, 102, 123, 144, 157; Jeffry, 198; John, 102, 154, 161; Joseph, 95, 154, 198; Llewelin App, 95; Lydia, 102; Margaret, 95; Mary, 102; Mary S., 142; Naomi, 198; Olive, 200; Priscilla, 124; Rachel, 154; Richard, 144, 157; Robert E., 126; Sarah, 95, 102, 132, 198; Thomas, 123, 124, 154, 164, 198; William, 95, 102, 154, 164, 198; William S., 142
GRIFFITHS, Amy, 83; Cassell, 72; Evan, 83; Hannah, 45, 72; Lewellin, 72; Lydia, 43; Mary, 43
GRIFFITS, Abigail, 26; William, 27

GRIM, John, 155; Joseph, 68
GRIME, Elizabeth, 3
GRIMM, Ann, 106
GRISCOM, Deborah, 2; Rachel, 2; Samuel, 2; Sarah, 2; William, 2
GRISSEL, Edward, 23
GRISSELL, Edward, 49
GRIZEL, Thomas, 6
GRIZLE, Hannah, 56
GROVER, Ann, 129, 130; Christopher, 15; Elizabeth, 15, 119; George, 15; Hannah, 119; Hugh, 15; John, 15; Margaret, 15, 130; Mary, 15; Robert, 15; Sarah, 119; Thomas, 130
GRUB, Mary, 66; Sarah, 84
GRUBB, Aaron, 6; Adam, 6; Elizabeth, 192; George, 6; Hannah, 6; Isaac, 6; James, 135; John, 6; Margaret, 5; Mary, 6, 45, 66; Nathaniel, 3, 22; Richard, 6; Samuel, 6; Samuel B., 135; Samuel Bishop, 16; Sarah, 22; Susannah, 6, 57; Thomas, 5; William, 6, 21
GRUBER, Catharine, 48; Elizabeth, 48; George, 48, 60; John, 48; Margaret, 48; Mary, 48
GUEST, ---, 163; Daniel, 94
GUIER, ---, 155
GUIGER, Sarah, 137; Tacy, 137
GUIRE, Adam, 6
GUYGER, George, 60, 92; Jacob, 60, 92; Jesse, 43; Margaret, 60; Mary, 60; Sarah, 43; Susanna, 60
GYGAR, Jesse, 104
GYGER, Daniel, 185; George, 185; Hannah, 131; Jacob, 185; Margaret, 185; Mariann, 185; Mary, 185

-H-
HABBERSET, Jacob, 163
HACOCK, John, 163
HAHN, Casper, 139; Catherina, 139; Elizabeth, 139; Henry, 139; John, 139; Mary, 139; Rosina, 139; William, 141
HAINES, Jane, 201; John, 201
HALDEMAN, Isaac, 172, 185
HALEY, Patrick, 123; Susanna, 123
HALL, Andrew, 35; Ann, 49, 113; Beulah, 61; David, 2, 12, 61, 106, 119; Deborah, 12; Edward, 61; Elizabeth, 47,

49, 113, 137, 167; George, 113; Hannah, 31, 43, 119; Isaac, 182, 189; John, 21, 31, 89; Joseph, 49, 61, 133, 160, 188; Joseph A., 137, 170; Margaret, 89; Martha, 90; Mary, 31, 49, 51, 56, 60, 113, 137; Norris, 89; Phebe, 113; Rebeckah, 111; Robert, 19, 33, 34, 49, 66, 89, 123, 189, 196, 200; Ruth, 114; Ruth M., 114; Samuel R., 191; Sarah, 33, 49, 61; Stephen, 50, 56, 88, 113; Susannah, 113; Thomas, 48, 73, 89; William, 89, 114
HALLOWAY, Sarah, 2
HALLOWELL, Lydia, 53; William, 132
HALTON, Peter, 26
HAM, John L., 70
HAMBLETON, Ann, 114
HAMET, Phebe, 30
HAMM, James, 27; Mary, 184
HAMMEL, Phebe, 76, 81
HAMMILL, Phebe, 48
HAMMILS, Phebe, 76
HAMOR, Phebe, 157; Thomas, 33
HAMPTON, ---, 167; Ann, 128, 204; Davis, 128, 204; Elizabeth, 117, 128, 204; James, 117; Jane, 128, 204; John, 128, 204; Rachel, 128; Rebecca, 128, 204; Rudolph, 128, 204; Woodward, 128, 204; Zillah, 128, 204
HAND, Mary, 90
HANNON, Hannah, 77
HANNUM, Aaron, 192, 196; Edwin, 196; Evan P., 192, 196; George, 151; Jane, 192; John, 196; Joseph, 116, 192, 196; Norris, 192, 196; Pennell, 134; Ruth, 66, 192, 196; Samuel, 129, 134, 182, 196; Sarah, 25, 44; Susanna, 134; William, 49, 53, 66, 78, 113, 192, 196
HANSEL, Ann, 162
HANSELL, Sarah, 4; William, 20
HANUM, Ann, 163
HANUMS, James, 161
HARDCASTLE, Hannah, 187
HARDEN, Phebe, 71
HARDIN, Phebe, 27
HARDING, Joseph, 68
HARE, Charles, 35; Robert, 35
HARLAN, ---, 165; Ann C., 162; E. C., 162; Ellis C., 162; Hannah, 109; John, 166; Joshua, 118

HARLON, Enock, 30; Hannah, 30
HARMON, John, 60
HARPER, James, 13
HARREY, Alice, 44; Mary, 44; Sarah, 44
HARRISON, Ann, 40, 86, 146; Caleb, 12, 13, 15, 46; Eleanor, 12; Eliza, 46; Elizabeth, 40; Hannah, 12; John, 13, 40; Joseph, 40; Joshua, 12, 50, 146; Kitty, 46; Mary, 12, 15, 40; Rebecca, 153; Sarah, 202; Tacey, 82, 86
HARRY, Hannah, 51; Samuel, 20
HART, Hannah, 136, 183; Hannah M., 136; John D., 136, 183; William, 19
HARTLEY, Hannah, 28
HARVERY, Alice, 44
HARVEY, Amos, 10; Ann, 195; David, 44; Eli, 159; Ely, 68; George, 160; Job, 10; Joseph, 94; Kaziah, 10; Mary, 44; Peter, 94; Sarah, 44; William, 5
HASKINS, Joseph, 73
HASTINGS, Sarah, 38
HATCH, Ann Maria, 177; Anna Maria, 150; Jonathan, 150, 177
HATTEN, Elizabeth, 83; Hannah, 83; Joel, 93; Joseph, 83; Peter, 83; Rachel, 83; Sarah, 83; Thomas, 83
HATTON, Elizabeth, 39, 121; Hannah, 39, 121; J. P., 197; James, 105, 179; James Prior, 121; Joseph, 39, 179, 188; Peter, 39; Rachel, 39; Sarah, 39, 121; Thomas, 39
HAVISTER, James, 109
HAVORD, Samuel, 37
HAWES, John, 111; Mary, 111, 126
HAWORTH, Ann, 51; Deborah, 139; George, 2, 59; Hannah, 2; John, 2, 139; Lydia, 51; Mary, 2, 139; Patience, 138; Rachel, 51; Rebecca, 139
HAWS, John, 98; Thomas, 200
HAY, William, 23
HAYCOCK, Hannah, 1; Jonathan, 1, 114; Reece, 149, 173
HAYES, Ann, 4; Nathan, 8; Sarah, 8
HAYMAN, Ann, 148; Anthony, 148; Elizabeth, 148; Isaac Wayne, 148; Sophia, 148; William, 35, 86, 148
HAYS, Elizabeth, 3; Sarah, 116,

HAYWORTH, Deborah, 76; George, 22, 76; John, 76; Mary, 76; Patience, 76; Rebeccah, 76
HAZARD, Ely, 30; Jane, 30; Joel, 30; Mary, 30; Oram, 30; Phebe, 30
HEACOCK, ---, 101; Ann, 22, 189; Eliza, 149; Elizabeth, 149; Enoch, 159; Franklin, 159; George, 196; Hannah, 22, 189; Israel, 189; Jacob, 189, 196; Jane, 159; John, 22, 159; John P., 189; Jonathan, 22, 189; Joseph, 166, 189; Margaretta, 196; Mary, 166; Mary Ann, 159; Nathan, 22, 159; Peter, 159, 196; Phebe, 149, 189; Sarah, 159; Susanna, 196
HEALMS, John, 156
HEATH, Beau Clark, 85
HEISLER, Isaiah, 149
HELMN, Israel, 83; Rebecah, 83
HELMS, Martha, 125
HEMPHILL, Ann, 199; Christian, 199; Elizabeth, 199, 201; Joseph, 199; Mary, 199, 201; Susanna, 199; Thomas, 121, 126, 199, 201
HENCOCK, Ann, 11
HENDERSON, David, 148; Elizabeth, 139; James, 24; Joseph, 95; Rebecca, 139
HENRY, John, 106
HENVIS, Deborah, 37; Isaac, 182
HERBISON, Ann, 116; Jane, 116
HERMANY, Jonathan, 142
HEWES, Ann, 159, 175; Charles, 39; Jemima, 137; John, 98; Samuel, 126, 137, 159, 165; Samuel F., 132; Sarah, 137; William, 38
HEYBORN, George, 151
HEYBURN, George, 128, 162
HIBBARD, Jacob, 163; John, 28
HIBBERD, Abraham, 101; Abram, 198; Alice, 92; Ann, 101, 166; Benjamin, 19; Caleb, 19, 22; Elizabeth, 2, 32, 69, 101, 194; Hezekiah, 2, 5, 58, 78; Isaac, 30, 32, 194; Jacob, 100, 101; Jane, 69; John, 2, 16, 30, 32, 35, 49, 79, 100, 105, 117, 146; Joseph, 2, 32, 49, 58, 62, 65, 77, 78, 155, 194; Martha, 101; Mary, 2, 49, 92, 101; Rachel, 101; Samuel, 101; Sarah, 44, 100, 156; Thomas, 100; William, 69

HIBBERT, Joseph, 173
HIBBS, Sarah, 16
HICKLEN, William, 4
HICKMAN, Benjamin, 185; Elizabeth, 160, 190, 191; Hannah, 75; James, 59, 190; John, 74; Lucy, 73; Mary, 121; Susanna, 113, 201; Thomas, 74
HICKS, Edward, 201
HIGHFIELD, Martha, 78
HILL, Ann, 166; Catherine, 15; Deborah, 166; Eleanor, 140; Elizabeth Sellers, 187; Hannah, 166, 182, 187; John, 93, 104, 166; John F., 140; John Howard, 104; Lowry, 81; Mary, 104, 166; Nathan Sellers, 187; Peter, 15, 54, 182, 187; Rachel, 104; Sidney, 166; Tacy, 166; William, 83, 162, 166, 184
HIND, John, 49
HINGLE, George, 103
HINKLE, George, 111
HINKSON, Isaac, 169; James, 57, 80; John, 57, 127, 169; John N., 167; Mary, 167; Morris, 179; Sarah, 167; Thomas, 167
HOBBERD, John, 32
HOBSON, Phebe, 40
HOFFMAN, Barbary, 100; Daniel, 100; David, 100; Joseph, 100; Samuel, 100
HOLLAND, Catharine, 29, 155; Henry, 11, 12; Ithamar, 12; Johannah, 29; John B., 155; Martha, 155; Mary, 11, 29; Mary Ann, 155; Nathan, 29; Nathaniel, 13, 29, 155; Phebe, 155; Robert, 147; Samuel, 29; Sarah, 29, 155; Thomas, 12, 29, 155, 169
HOLLINGSWORTH, Aaron, 4; Abigail, 4; Hannah, 4; Phebe, 113; Robert, 4
HOLLOWAY, Thomas, 7
HOLLS, Robert, 147
HOLMAN, Margret, 14
HOLMES, Richard, 67; Susannah, 67; Thomas, 67
HOLSTEIN, Elizabeth, 148; George W., 148; George Washington, 148
HOLSTON, Ann, 27; Benjamin, 27; George, 27; John, 27; Joseph, 27; Martha, 27
HOOD, John, 7; Jonathan, 109, 202; Joseph, 51, 88, 122; Sarah C., 202; Susanna, 202
HOOF, John, 11

HOOFSTITLER, John, 193
HOOK, Calcon, 189; Marcus, 15, 20, 57, 192
HOOPER, Abner, 149; Caleb J., 149; Enos, 69; Joseph, 64
HOOPES, Abigail, 27; Abner, 157, 197; Abraham, 27, 45, 54, 58, 76, 155; Alice, 192; Benjamin, 27; Benjamin F., 197; Caleb, 155, 157, 174, 192; Caleb I., 197, 201; D., 157; Daniel, 27, 155, 157, 174, 192; Eli, 46, 58; Elizabeth, 45, 76; Ezra, 157; Francis, 157; George, 27; Hannah, 157, 174; Isaac, 27, 46, 58; Jacob, 27; Jane, 27; Joel, 157; John, 27, 155; Joshua, 157, 197; Lydia, 28; Marshall, 197; Mary, 155, 157, 197; Mary M., 197; Phebe, 174; Priscilla, 45, 76, 155; Rebecca, 157, 197; Rebeckah, 24; Rees, 192; Sarah, 155, 174, 197; Susanna, 192
HOOPS, Abigail, 87; Abraham, 58, 81; Cyrus, 185; Daniel, 168; Eli, 58; Elizabeth, 2, 65, 87; Enos, 65, 87; Isaac, 58; James, 87
HOOVER, Margret, 127
HOPPERSETT, Agnes, 83
HORN, Edward, 42; Martha, 42; Stephen, 155
HORNE, Davis, 146; Edward, 63, 145; Eliza, 149; Elizabeth, 146, 173; Henry H., 146; John, 24, 146, 173; Joseph, 62; Martha M., 146; Mary, 146; Phebe, 15; Simon, 146; Stephen, 146; Thomas, 149, 158, 202; William, 15; William D., 146
HORNER, Benjamin, 177; Edward, 177; George, 177; Mary, 177; Phebe, 177; Sarah, 177; Thomas, 177
HORTON, Agnes, 187; Emily, 2; Jacob, 168; John, 168; Joseph H., 142; Rebecca, 91; Thomas, 91
HOSKIN, Caleb, 98; Elizabeth, 98; Frances, 98; Hannah, 98; John, 98; Joseph, 98; Martha, 98; Nathaniel, 98; Rebecca, 98; William, 98
HOSKINS, Dolly, 124; Dorothea, 124; Eleanor, 36, 40, 41; Elizabeth, 156; Joseph, 60, 73, 124, 143; Joseph R., 186; Mary, 36, 40, 41, 124; William, 156
HOULSTEIN, Peter, 17
HOULSTON, Mary, 17
HOUSE, Amos, 10; Benjamin, 10; Jehu, 10; Martha, 10; Mary, 10; Sarah, 10; Susanna, 10
HOUSLTON, Ann, 71; Benjamin, 71; George, 71; John, 71; Joseph, 71; Martha, 71; Mary, 71; Phebe, 71; Sarah, 71
HOUSTON, Benjamin, 48
HOWARD, Alice, 141; David, 157; Ellis P., 172; George B., 172; Hannah, 157, 172; Harper, 141, 157; James, 16, 30, 54, 76, 157, 172; John, 145; Jonathan, 76, 81, 135, 157, 172; Joseph E., 172; Mary, 157; Phebe, 157; Rebecca, 33, 135, 154, 172; Sarah, 135; William, 157, 174
HOWEL, Jacob, 149; Susan, 149
HOWELL, Charles, 131; George, 131; Israel, 201; Mary D., 131; Mary W., 131; Rebacca, 6; Ruth, 6; Samuel E., 131, 168; Thomas, 1
HUBBERD, Hezekiah, 70
HUBBERT, Thomas, 3
HUBBS, Sarah, 132
HUEY, John, 88; Phebe, 88; William, 92
HUGGENS, Elizabeth, 181
HUGHES, Sarah, 167
HUGINS, Elizabeth, 136
HULL, John, 169
HUMPHREY, Daniel, 81; Jacob, 110; John, 105; Mary, 105
HUMPHREYS, Ann, 55; Charles, 110, 166; Clement, 80; Daniel, 6, 17, 48, 183; David, 103; Elizabeth, 166; Hannah, 17; Jacob, 17, 34; John, 15, 166; Joshua, 55; Lowrey, 166; Lowry, 134; Margeret, 110; Martha, 166; Mary, 134, 166; Phebe, 17; Rebecca, 6, 110, 166; Samuel, 55, 166; Sarah, 55, 110; Solomon, 91; William, 82, 119, 134, 166
HUNT, Abraham G., 134; Gibbons, 119, 176; Huldah, 199; John, 6, 7, 82, 95, 119, 134, 193; Mary, 113; Phebe, 27; Rebecca, 113; Susanna, 113; William, 113
HUNTER, Albert Gallatin, 61; Allice, 122; Andrew, 184, 200; Ann, 60, 61, 139;

Edward, 21, 22, 33, 46, 58, 59, 61, 71, 72, 83, 88, 90, 92, 95, 113, 122, 136, 153, 203; Elizabeth, 60, 90, 92, 122, 139, 175; Emily, 61; George, 19, 47, 61, 72, 90, 105, 122, 199; George Morgan, 61; Hannah, 60, 61, 92, 122, 173, 184, 203; James, 21, 60, 61, 125, 185; Jane, 175, 184; John, 21, 22, 61, 72, 87, 90, 92, 122, 125, 139, 152, 163, 181; Jonathan, 19, 47, 72; Joseph, 69, 125; Margaret, 92, 122, 175; Martha, 21, 60, 61, 125; Mary, 60, 61, 92; Miss, 181; Morgan, 60; Peter, 19, 47, 60, 153, 203; Rachel, 60; Rebeca, 122; Rebecca, 139; Richard, 19, 47; Robert, 125; Samuel, 60, 184; Sarah, 60, 61, 125, 139; Sidney, 60; Susanna, 184; Tamzin, 92; Thomas, 92, 173; Thompson, 125; William, 59, 92, 122, 125, 184
HUNTLEY, Susanna, 158
HUSTON, Aaron, 102, 131, 192; Ann, 135, 178; Ann James, 124; James, 151; Mary, 124; R. M., 192; Rebeca, 178; Rebecca, 135; Samuel Jones, 124; Thomas, 124; Thomas Steel, 124; Widow, 172; William, 148
HUTTON, Mary, 107, 193

-I-

IDDING, Hannah, 69, 184; Phebe, 69; Samuel, 69; Thomas, 184
IDDINGS, Hannah, 93, 111; James, 7; Mary, 110; William, 93, 111
INSLEY, Martha, 96
IRETON, Anthony, 77; Mary, 77
IRWIN, Elizabeth, 72; George, 72, 118; Jane, 200; John, 200; Nathaniel, 72; Richard, 72

-J-

JACKSON, Abigal, 153; Alice, 129; Catharine, 107; Catherine, 129; Haliday, 114, 194; Halladay, 147; Halliday, 114, 139, 155, 174, 183, 187, 189; Jacob, 187; Joel, 129, 130; John, 189; Jonathan Morris, 129; Mary, 68; Mary Ann, 129

JACOBS, Hannah, 26, 39, 154; Isaac, 26, 40; Jesse, 40; John, 39, 185; Lydia, 39, 58; Mary, 36, 119; Phebe, 190; Thomas, 39, 58
JAMES, Aaron, 74; Caleb, 74; Curtis, 154; Daniel, 17; David, 185; Eleanor, 88; Frederick, 69; Hannah, 107, 110; Isaac, 185; James, 110; Jesse, 74; John, 28, 82; Joseph, 28, 65, 125, 149, 185; Joshua, 157; Lydia, 129; Mary, 28, 29; Samuel, 110
JARMAN, John, 16; Thomas, 152, 193
JAYKES, Gidein, 144
JEFFERIES, James, 29
JEFFERIS, Cheyney, 81
JEFFREYS, Samuel, 111
JENKINS, Ann P., 176; Elizabeth, 120; Ellena, 165; Jabez, 120, 176; Jemima, 167; Jonathan, 120; Joseph, 120; Joshua, 120; Martha N., 176; Tabitha, 120, 176; William, 165
JESS, Rebecca, 7; Walter, 9; Zachariah, 7
JINNINGS, Martha, 120
JOBSON, Hannah, 117; John, 117; Joseph, 117; Mary, 117; Samuel, 69, 117; Susannah, 117
JOHN, Mira, 184; Phebe, 184; William, 184
JOHNSON, Abraham, 63, 68, 73, 182; Abram, 141, 182; Amy, 64, 65, 101, 138; Ann, 65, 101; Benjamin, 68; Benjamin F., 164; Cato, 61; David, 23; Elizabeth, 202; Hannah, 161; Hannah P., 175; Henry, 10; James, 10; Joseph, 40, 61, 65, 117, 123, 137, 138, 196; Laticia, 168; Magdalen, 110; Margaret, 189; Martha, 10; Mary, 73, 141, 154, 175, 198; Peter, 61; Robert, 160, 163; Robert R., 198; Sarah, 40; Thomas, 35; William, 10, 86, 105, 116, 127
JOHNSTON, Andreas, 9; Joseph, 64; Robert, 175
JONES, Abigail, 17; Alice, 59, 71, 92; Ann, 32, 70, 148; Benjamin, 56, 148; Brinton, 124; David, 2; Edward, 17; Elinor, 3; Eliza, 200; Elizabeth, 49, 94; Esther, 181; Esther Painter, 148;

Evven, 144; Hannah, 56, 59, 125; Hugh, 16; James, 54, 61, 78; Jane, 58; Jehu, 7; Jennis, 78, 94; John, 20, 23, 59, 71, 94; Margaret, 157; Martha, 94; Mary, 61, 200; Mary Ann, 70; Mathue, 101; Matthew, 7; Peter, 200; Robert E., 191; Sarah, 17, 92, 203; William, 56, 70, 197, 201
JORDAN, Deborah, 132; Jane, 184; Rachel, 57
JOYCE, Sarah, 159
JUSTICE, John, 193
JUSTIS, Charles, 120, 177; Eleanor, 177; Elizabeth, 177; Ellen M., 150; John M., 120, 177; Mary, 177; Rebecca, 177

-K-

KELLOGG, Elizabeth, 132
KELLY, Dennis, 167
KENDLE, Mary, 6
KENNEDY, Abraham, 199; Enoch, 199; Robert, 199
KENNEY, William, 80
KENNY, Betty, 53; Mary, 45; Thomas, 53, 155
KERLIN, Abraham, 67, 84; Ann, 57; Betsey, 196; Catharine, 67, 84; Elizabeth, 188; George, 84; George Henry, 84; Hannah, 57; Henry, 163, 188; Jane, 188; John, 84, 109, 164; Joseph, 67, 129; Louisa, 163; Margaret, 84; Mathias, 60, 77; Matthias, 57; Rebeccah, 57; Sarah, 57; Susannah, 57; William, 41, 45, 57, 67, 84, 136, 142, 170, 188
KERN, Ann, 34
KERNS, Ann, 8; Benjamin, 8, 9; Elizabeth, 8; George, 8, 9; Hugh, 8; John, 8, 9, 117, 157; Margaret, 8; Martha, 8; Thomas, 145; William, 9
KERR, Mary, 9
KERSEY, Brinton, 119; Elizabeth, 119; Phebe, 119
KERSON, Luke, 80
KIBLER, Daniel, 100; Elizabeth, 100; Jacob, 100; John, 100; Mary, 100
KILLE, Thomas, 107
KIMBER, Emmore, 96; Isaac, 38; Richard, 87
KING, Agnes, 187; Ann, 108; Jane, 190; John, 97, 124, 160, 169, 175; Joseph, 1; Lydia, 190; Sarah, 187; William, 83, 161, 198
KINLEY, William, 45
KINNEY, James, 139; Rosina, 139
KINSEY, Ann, 129
KINZIE, Daniel, 143; John, 103
KIRK, Ann, 165; Benjamin, 10, 118, 138; Deborah, 165; Elizabeth, 77, 116; Ester, 10; Hannah, 77; Isaac, 31; Isaiah, 91; James, 165; John, 10, 31, 76, 77, 138, 165; Joseph, 31, 76, 77; Joshua, 10; Lydia, 77; Martha, 77; Mary, 165; Mary Ann, 77, 177; Phillip, 138; Rachel, 165; Samuel, 31, 70, 76, 120; Sarah Ann, 145; Susanna, 165; Thomas, 31, 76, 77, 116; William, 76, 77, 165; Zachariah, 165
KIRLIN, George Henry, 68; William, 183
KITTS, Jacob, 125; John, 125; Michael, 125
KLING, Sarah, 165
KNIGHTS, Hannah, 99
KNOLL, Catharine, 183; Hannah, 183; Ludwick, 123, 171, 183; Mary, 183; Sarah, 183
KNOWLES, J., 7
KRIDER, Ann, 187
KUHNS, Dr., 45

-L-

LAD, Jane, 57
LAKE, William, 128
LAMB, Elizabeth, 169; John, 169; Nelson, 169; Sidney, 169
LAMBLUGH, Biasor, 95
LAMBORN, George, 202; Mary, 202
LAMPLEY, Mary, 134; Samuel, 134
LAMPLUG, Beason, 138; Pheby, 138
LAMPLUGH, Bezer, 96, 105, 116; Bozer, 115; Daniel, 145; Jesse R., 176; Josiah, 138; Lidia, 138; Lydia, 116, 176; Mary, 138, 176; Phebe, 116; Samuel, 116, 117, 138
LANARES, Tyson H., 204
LANCASTER, James, 167
LANE, Edward, 62, 174; Elizabeth, 174; Mary, 168; Sarah, 1
LANGUIN, Susannah, 43
LARKIN, Abraham, 181; Elizabeth, 164; Esther, 101; Isaac, 61, 163, 167; John, 78, 93, 163, 164, 167, 191, 194; Joseph, 49, 164, 181;

223

Lydia, 167; Margaret, 167; Mordecai, 119; Mordicai, 139; Nathan, 167, 184; Nathon, 164; Salkeld, 119, 164, 172, 191; Sarah, 119, 135, 139, 164; William, 164, 167
LARKINS, John, 194
LATCH, David, 102; Hannah, 147; John, 147; Rudolph, 147; Sidney, 147
LATTY, William, 106
LAWLER, Ann, 150
LAWLES, Ann, 126; Matthew, 126
LAWRENCE, Amy, 173; Ann, 166; Clement, 59, 96, 104, 106, 161, 166, 170, 173; Clemment, 166; Henry, 3, 76, 96, 104, 110; Isaac, 23, 77, 132; Joseph, 96, 104, 166; Joshua, 96, 104, 123, 166; Mary, 37, 104, 123; Mordecai, 59, 63, 76, 87, 96, 104, 166, 173, 174; Richard, 55; Samuel, 96; Thomas, 104; William, 2, 104; William P., 198
LAWSON, Joseph, 195
LAYCOCKS, ---, 123
LEA, Thomas, 14
LEACOCK, Hannah, 169
LEDEM, Isaac, 197
LEE, Eliza, 149; James, 9; James P., 149; Mary, 9; William, 152
LEED, Hannah, 136
LEEDAM, Edmund, 116
LEEDOM, Daniel, 116; Edmund, 116; Elizabeth, 116; Hannah, 116; John, 116; Joseph, 177; Mary, 177, 180; Samuel, 116
LEIPER, George G., 121, 145; Samuel M., 189; Thomas, 110; William L., 189
LEONARD, Ezekiah, 14; Ezekiel, 23, 28; Mary, 84
LEVES, Anne P., 46
LEVIS, Abby Ann, 191; Abigail Ann, 191; Agnes, 136, 197; Agness, 181; Ann, 191; Ann C., 191; Curtis, 198; Edward, 198; Elizabeth, 21, 24, 70, 191; Elizabeth P., 191; Esther, 177, 198; Hannah, 21; Henrietta, 70, 191; Isaac, 21; John, 21, 70, 198; John Talbot, 135, 158, 191; Joseph, 21, 81, 135; Joshua, 21; Margaret, 70, 191; Margaretta, 191; Martha, 21; Mary, 21, 70, 191; Nancy, 70; Oborn, 70, 191; Phineas, 197; Rebecca, 135, 139; Samuel, 21, 70, 76, 190, 191; Sarah, 61, 70; Sarah Ann, 191; Thomas, 70, 139; William, 21, 70, 166, 191
LEWELLIN, Ann, 145
LEWELYN, William, 96
LEWIS, A., 155; Abel, 59, 92; Abner, 47, 77, 78, 87, 107, 128, 169, 197, 204; Abraham, 32, 35, 77, 96, 111, 138, 161, 177; Abram, 72, 104; Agnes, 58, 61; Alban H., 167; Albin, 180; Alice, 177; Allixander, 23; Ann, 43, 63, 166; Anthony, 72; Azariah, 95, 204; Catharine, 127; David, 1, 11, 23, 85, 97; Demaris, 127; Didimus, 90; Dydemus, 37, 141; Eber, 166; Edith, 183; Edward, 147, 168; Eli, 105, 141, 204; Elijah, 78, 94, 106, 107, 137, 145, 167, 196; Elisha, 152, 177; Elizabeth, 16, 19, 35, 59, 90, 127, 166, 177; Enoch, 78, 107; Enos, 102, 124, 129, 130, 144, 147, 150; Esther, 19, 35, 46, 124, 130, 150; Evan, 2, 58, 61, 77, 78, 102, 107, 112, 168, 177, 180; Franklin, 147; Garrett, 152; George, 131, 147, 177, 180, 183, 188, 202; Hannah, 11, 23, 47, 58, 61, 72, 95, 97, 113, 114, 144, 166, 177, 180, 201, 204; Hariot, 168; Henery, 102; Henry, 3, 23, 47, 58, 62, 64, 74, 102, 112, 129, 130, 144; Hester, 102; Isaac, 13, 80; Isaiah, 19; Jabez, 155; James, 97, 166, 180; James Jones, 78; James Mifflin, 109; Jane, 23, 47, 78, 90, 107, 127, 133, 147, 169; Jenkin, 78; Jesse, 108, 180; John, 37, 43, 46, 59, 90, 133, 147, 148, 163, 180; Joseph, 54, 59, 78, 94, 107, 145, 148, 152; Josia, 48; Josiah, 16, 19, 35, 44, 177; Levi, 95, 112, 136, 177, 184; Levy, 46; Lewis, 11, 23, 47, 58, 62, 64, 71, 90, 136; Lydia, 61, 166; Margaret, 204; Maris, 177; Mary, 11, 23, 47, 58, 80, 96, 97, 102, 136, 147, 150, 161, 176; Mordecai, 3, 22, 31, 90, 127, 147, 169, 184; Mordecai Reece, 90; Mordicai, 58; Nathan, 105; Patty Ann, 152;

Phebe, 13, 35, 37, 141; Phineas, 90, 136, 149, 180; Rachel, 23, 47; Rebecca, 96, 161, 177, 180; Reuben, 86; Robert, 98, 106, 204; Samuel, 35, 44, 77, 150, 157, 177, 180; Samuel A., 177; Sarah, 13, 61, 78, 107, 127, 147, 155, 168, 177, 180, 204; Sidney, 127, 147; Simeon M., 197; Siscela, 23; Susanna, 78; Tacy, 141; Thomas, 13, 31, 70, 78, 107, 120, 127; Thomas M., 167; Unity, 204; William, 31, 35, 46, 78, 147, 152, 204
LIKENS, Daniel, 115, 191
LINCH, Elizabeth, 193; Michael, 193; Samuel, 193
LINCOLN, Jacob, 204
LINDASY, Samuel, 156
LINDSAY, Andrew, 102, 112, 156, 161, 172; Christianna, 112; Eliza Ann, 156; Elizabeth, 13, 15, 156; James, 13, 71, 85, 156; Jane, 156; John, 112, 156, 172; Joseph, 108; Margaret, 13, 156; Mary Ann, 156; Robert, 156; Samuel, 156; William, 156
LINDSEY, Ann, 38; Elizabeth, 105; John, 18; Joice, 38; Martha, 102; Samuel, 38; William, 105
LINN, Prudence, 67
LINSHEED, Mary, 146
LITTLE, Thomas, 169
LITZENBERG, Adam, 50; Anthony Wayne, 185; Elizabeth, 144, 185; George, 114, 185; Hirum, 185; Jacob, 18; Job, 185; John, 185; Joshua, 185; Perry, 185; Philip, 50; Rubin, 185; Simon, 102, 144, 185; Simond, 185; Susanna, 202; Tacey, 152; William, 185
LITZENBERGER, Adam, 52; Dorothy, 52; George, 52; Jacob, 52; John, 52; Simon, 52
LLEWELIN, Sarah, 149
LLEWELLYN, Sarah, 195; Thomas, 195
LLEWELYN, William, 22
LLOYD, Ann, 134; Charles, 128; Elizabeth, 109; Hannah, 4; Hugh, 3, 4, 7, 25, 95, 119, 127, 162; Isaac, 134; James, 134; Joseph, 161, 171; Levi, 55; Martha, 101; Mary, 4, 134; Mary Ash, 109; Richard, 42, 55, 96, 101; Richard P., 127; Sarah, 4; Thomas, 4
LOBB, Amy, 62, 104; Ann, 62; Benjamin, 31, 58, 86, 122, 147, 155, 195; Edward, 65; Elizabeth, 62; Ephraim, 62, 65; Esther, 62; Esthor, 104; George, 31; Hannah, 31, 122; Isaac, 21, 62, 101, 104, 105, 122, 195; Israel, 62, 101, 104, 105; James, 195; Jane, 62; Jesse, 122, 195; John, 122, 155, 158, 194, 195; Josiah, 62, 104; Martha, 122; Mary, 122, 139; Phebe, 62; Samuel, 195; Sarah, 31, 65; Thomas, 122, 155, 158, 195
LODGE, Isaac, 60
LOGAN, Deborah, 45; George, 45; Mary, 182; Robert, 129
LONG, Elizabeth, 19; Samuel, 142
LONGACRE, Hannah, 153; Peter, 47, 72; Sarah, 73
LONGSTRETH, David, 158; Jane, 51; Martha, 158
LOVEN, Melchior, 5, 147
LOWAIN, Mary, 50
LOWELLIN, Elizabeth, 106; Rebecca, 106
LOWNES, Agnes, 136, 197; Agness, 181; Benanwell, 116; Burns, 16; Caleb, 181, 198; Clarisa, 16; Clarissa, 133, 181, 197; Curtis, 16, 136, 173, 181, 197; David, 32; Edward, 181; Edward R., 198; Elizabeth, 16, 116, 136, 140, 181; Esther, 136, 181; George, 16; George B., 96, 116, 137, 140, 158, 173, 181, 197, 198; George Bolston, 16; George Bolton, 131, 133; George R., 137; Hannah, 133, 181, 197, 198; Hugh, 12, 100, 116, 140; Jane, 16; John, 136, 137, 173, 181, 198; Joseph, 25, 116, 137, 140, 158, 181, 198, 202; Mary, 16, 181; Massey, 140; Phineas, 140, 198; Rachel, 140; Rebecca, 133, 140, 181; Rebeckah, 16; Sarah, 16, 181, 198; Sidney, 116, 140; Slater, 16, 133, 197; Slator, 181; William, 140; William B., 198; William R., 198
LOWNS, George B., 161
LOYD, Ann, 195; Jeremiah, 138; Susannah, 138
LUKENS, Amos, 41, 44, 76, 87,

93
LUKINS, Hannah, 141
LUNGREN, Charles, 114, 116, 126; Edwin, 126; Elizabeth, 116, 126; Harriot, 126; John, 85, 116, 126; Joseph, 68; Samuel, 114, 116, 126; Sarah, 116, 126; Susan, 126; Susanna, 201; William, 85, 116, 126
LYKIN, Eliza, 79
LYNN, Ann, 129
LYON, William, 18
LYONS, David, 86, 116; Elizabeth, 86; James, 86; William, 86
LYTLE, Samuel, 89, 131, 189, 195
LYWELLEN, David, 161

-M-

MCAFEE, Joseph, 35, 39; Marget, 182
MCAFFEE, Jane, 175
MCALISTER, Mary, 145
MCCALL, George, 5; Isabel, 41; James, 41; John, 5; Joseph, 5, 29, 41; Mary, 41, 189; Robert, 169; Thomas, 4, 5; William, 5, 41
MCCARTY, Sarah, 27, 71; William, 9, 71
MCCAY, John, 148; Sarah, 148
MCCLEAVE, Lettice, 124
MCCLEES, Rebecca, 6; Rebeckah, 7
MCCLELLAN, Ann, 120; Joel, 120; Robert, 156
MCCLENAN, Samuel, 11
MCCLENE, James, 13
MCCLENTIC, Martha, 170; Robert, 170
MCCLESTER, Hannah, 76
MCCLURE, Elizabeth, 104; Martha, 104; Nancy, 104; Robert, 184; Samuel, 104; Thomas, 104; William, 73
MCCONNELL, Joseph, 85; Martha, 85
MCCORP, William, 135
MCCULLOUGH, David Trenor, 184; Hannah, 9; Henry, 184; Mary, 184; Thomas, 9
MACCULLUM, Persifor, 73
MCCULLY, Hannah, 34; Thomas, 34
MCDERMOTT, Griffith, 182
MACE, Ann, 82; Elizabeth, 138; Mary, 138; Rachal, 138; Sarah, 138; Thomas, 138
MACEY, Samuel, 10
MCGARVEY, Thomas, 201

MCGEE, Alex., 195
MCGILTON, Elizabeth, 187
MCGLAUGHLIN, William, 147
MCGLOTHIAN, Elizabeth, 158
MCGOWING, Daniel, 34; Esther, 34
MCGRATTEN, Sarah, 170
MCGRATTON, James, 189
MCGUIRE, Hester, 82; Julian, 158
MACHEMSON, Elizabeth, 7
MCILVAIN, Ann, 164; Hugh, 20; James, 21, 165; Spencer, 189; Susanah, 88
MCKEE, David Kerlin, 57; Hannah, 57; Sarah, 86
MCKEEVER, Alexander, 185
MACKEMSON, Elizabeth, 6
MCKINLEY, Abigail, 157; Rebecca, 121
MCKINLY, Rebecca, 99
MCLAUGHLIN, Margaret, 54; Robert, 66; William, 54
MCLEER, Arthur, 117; Catarine, 117; Daniel, 117; Eleanor, 117; Hugh, 117; Jane, 117; Margaret, 117; Patrick, 117
MCMICHAEL, Ann, 145; Charles, 9; Hannah, 145; John, 137, 145; Mary, 145; Samuel, 145
MCMIN, Joseph, 160; Joshua, 102; Mary, 76
MCMINN, Ann, 12; Isabella, 12; James, 12; John, 12; Joseph, 65, 79; Martha, 12; Mary, 12; Thomas, 12
MCMULLIN, Deborah, 12; William, 12
MCNULTY, Daniel, 52
MADDOCK, Eunice, 62; Eunis, 32; George, 29; James, 48, 65, 119, 125, 131, 156, 174, 195; Jesse, 62; Sarah, 106; Unis, 88; William, 29
MADDOX, Rebecca, 45
MALCOM, Jane, 30, 109; Robert, 30
MALIN, Abner, 82, 109, 145, 169; Agnes, 109, 145; Ann, 99, 109, 145, 187; Benedict, 85, 138; David, 30; Elizabeth, 109, 145; George, 145, 169; Gideon, 85, 138; Grace, 99, 187; Hannah, 82, 145, 169; Harvy, 145; Isaac, 99, 112, 127, 169; Isaac U., 168; Jacob, 109; Joel, 82, 145, 169; Mary, 85; Minshall, 109, 145; Phebe, 85; Pusey, 145; Randel, 109; Randle, 145; Samuel, 82, 145; Sarah,

150; Stephen O., 199; Stephen V., 180; Susan P., 145; Susanna, 85; Susannah, 114, 122, 152; Tacey, 85, 152; Tacy, 114; Thomas, 109, 145; William, 82, 109, 145
MALINE, George, 89
MALON, Thomas, 137
MANCILL, John, 28; Susanna, 156
MANLEY, James, 83
MANLOVE, Margaret, 89
MANLY, Benjamin, 124; Charles, 124; Elizabeth, 124; Lydia, 124; Susanna, 124; Thomas, 124; William, 124
MANSILL, Joseph, 174
MARCH, Rolph C., 154
MARION, Margaret, 141
MARIS, Ann, 82; Eliza, 37, 123; Elizabeth, 37, 123; Hannah, 92; Hester, 82; Isaac, 37, 123; J., 2; James, 37, 123, 166; Jesse, 13, 21; Jesse J., 174; John, 82; Jonathan, 86; Joseph, 82, 86; Levis, 72; Mary, 37, 123; Owen, 126; Rebecca, 82; Richard, 61; Tacey, 82; William, 82, 86
MARKWARD, Hannah, 112; Mary, 153; Mordicai, 25
MARKWORTH, William, 26
MARLOW, Rachel, 127
MARSH, Deborah, 166; Perthenia, 5, 8; Ralph, 104; Ralph C., 201; Rolph C., 108, 129, 154, 158, 160, 174, 179, 180, 189, 192, 200; Rolph E., 104
MARSHAL, Thomas, 163
MARSHALL, Abram, 141; Amor, 98; Ann, 98; David, 77, 98, 164; Edward S., 189; Ellis, 189; Ennise, 197; Hannah, 98, 141; Henry, 189; J., 73; James, 61, 87, 129, 146; Jesse, 164; John, 8, 75, 98, 141, 146, 160, 166, 180; Joseph, 98, 141, 143; Margaret, 99, 141, 189; Margaretta, 164; Marget, 197; Martha, 141; Mary, 164; Mary Ann, 160; Nathan, 141; Samuel, 7, 143, 174, 180, 189; Sarah, 77, 160, 189; Stephen, 74; Susanna, 141; Thomas, 24, 26, 44, 68, 78, 92, 95, 98, 137, 144, 146, 160, 188, 189; William, 12, 98, 189
MARTIN, Abraham, 19, 50, 88; Alice, 61; Ann, 140, 158; Benjamin, 88, 113, 143; Beulah, 158; Caleb, 145, 153;

Eliza, 61; Elizabeth, 88, 153, 158; George, 38, 75, 130, 135, 136, 139, 140, 148, 153, 156, 158, 191, 199; Hannah, 82, 88, 145, 153, 158, 169; Hiram, 145; Jacob, 145; James M., 200; Jehu, 145; John, 38, 61, 158; John S., 200; Jonathan, 50; Joseph, 82, 153; Joshua, 145; Lewis, 61; Lydia, 50, 149; Mary, 50, 88; Orphy, 145; Phebe, 88; Rebecca, 139, 158; Ruth, 153, 158; Samuel, 145; Sarah, 158; Susan, 88; Susanna, 100; Susannah, 28; Thomas Welch, 85; Warrick, 153; William, 33, 130, 140
MARVIN, George, 135
MASSEY, Aaron, 167; Charles R., 131; Edward A., 131; Elizabeth, 131, 154; George, 25; Hannah, 94; Isaac, 19, 22, 30, 137, 154; Israel, 167; Mary D., 131; Rachel, 107; Samuel, 154; Thomas, 131; William, 131; William N., 131
MATHER, Deborah, 9; Elizabeth, 9; Jane, 9; John, 9; Joseph, 9; Mary, 9; Robert, 9, 73; Sarah, 9
MATLACK, Elizabeth, 141; George, 19, 37, 47, 141; Hannah, 37; Isaiah, 47, 105; Jesse, 19, 47; Jonathan, 19, 47, 48; Josiah, 105; Martha, 141; Mary, 19, 47; Nathan, 37, 86, 105, 141; Phebe, 37; Rachel, 105, 141; Rebecca, 139; Reuben, 105; Simeon, 25, 32, 38, 78, 141; Susanna, 105; Tabitha, 80; Tacy, 37, 141; Thomas, 37, 38, 141; William, 37
MATLOCK, Sarah, 181
MATSON, Aaron, 23, 132; Abraham, 144; Arron, 12; George, 21; Isaac, 14; John, 22; Levi, 13, 22, 94, 121, 144; Levis, 17; Mary, 79; Nehemiah, 17; Peter, 21; Rachel, 14, 17, 94; Sarah, 17, 22, 94; Susannah, 10; William, 166
MATTHEWS, William, 117
MATTRON, Levi, 200
MATTSON, Eliza W., 182; Emaline L., 182; Mary Ann, 182; Thomas, 182
MAUL, Mary, 6

MAULE, Ann, 186; Benjamin, 78, 87, 107, 186; Caleb, 87; Daniel, 87; Elizabeth, 87; Hannah, 186; Jacob, 91, 197; Jonathan, 87; Lydia, 87; Margaret, 87, 204; Mercy, 186; Thomas, 186; Zillah, 186
MAULSBY, Samuel, 89
MAXWELL, David, 106; Hannah, 170; James, 170; John, 170; Margaret, 170; Martha, 170; Nimrod, 137; Robert, 170; William, 10
MAY, Arthur, 55; Sarah, 29
MECTEER, Martha, 122; Samuel, 122
MEGEOWEN, Daniel, 134
MEGOWEN, Daniel, 54; James, 189; John, 189; Richard, 134, 189
MEGOWN, John, 27
MEHAFFY, Elizabeth, 13; James, 13
MENDENHALL, A., 134; Aaron, 79; Ann, 84, 127; Benjamin, 53; Betty, 53; Beulah, 53; Cicaly, 144; Cyrus, 135, 170, 176, 190, 192; Edward, 90; Elijah, 53; Esther, 190; Jacob H., 190; James, 84, 127; Jane, 190; Joel, 53; John, 45, 50, 93, 96, 190; Lydia, 6, 30; Margaret, 90, 127; Mary, 53, 90; Orpha, 53; Phebe, 84, 90, 127, 154; Philip, 90; Rachel, 79; Rebecca, 84; Rebekah, 127; Robert, 1, 84, 90, 127, 201; Ruth, 53; S., 134; Sarah, 79, 143, 183; Stephen, 1, 29, 80, 84, 127; Susanna, 181; Thomas, 90, 91; William, 84, 113, 127, 133, 179, 180, 181, 185, 199
MENSHALL, Edward, 136
MERCER, Abigail, 35; Ann, 97, 187; Betty, 148; Caleb, 97; David, 83; Elizabeth, 39, 97, 187; Euclid, 97, 187; Hannah, 97, 187; Isaac, 97, 113; Jesse, 115, 149; Mary, 97; Phebe, 35, 113, 170; Richard, 97, 187; Samuel Painter, 148; Sarah, 97, 187; Zacheriah, 97
MEREDITH, Ann, 84, 127; David, 44; Elizabeth, 184; John, 44, 74, 75, 77, 84; Joseph, 44, 74, 77, 133, 177; Mary, 44, 77; Matilda, 139; Moses, 44; Pennell, 77; Sarah, 44, 77, 133; Simon, 78

MEREDITHS, Moses, 35
MERIDITH, Hannah, 12; John, 12
MERIN, Abigail, 64; Joseph, 64; Mary, 64; Rebecca, 64; Ruth, 64; Thomas, 64
MERRION, Abigail, 5; Joseph, 5; Ruth, 5; Thomas, 5
MERSHON, Henry, 193; Ruth, 193
MESSENGER, Martin, 96
MESTON, Mary, 101; William, 101
MICKLEDUFF, Martha, 47; Samuel, 47
MIDDLETON, Joseph, 145; Mary, 145
MIDDLTON, John, 10
MIERS, Elizabeth, 24; Henry, 24; John, 24; Phebe, 24; Rebeckah, 24; Sarah, 24
MIFFLIN, Sarah Ann, 92
MILES, Abigail, 17; Elizabeth, 121; Evan, 18; George, 114; John, 18; Nathaniel, 59, 92; Richard, 17, 18; Samuel, 18
MILEY, Mary, 32
MILLER, Ahinoam, 132; Ann, 164; Annetta, 132; Antay, 203; Benjamin, 47; Deborah, 132; Eliza, 132; Elizabeth, 94; George, 7, 11, 30, 33, 64, 89, 95, 98, 103, 132, 135, 136, 138, 148, 153, 178, 192, 196; James, 47, 71; Jane, 47; John, 47, 200; Jonathan, 132, 156; Joseph I., 132; Judith, 203; Margaret, 47; Martha, 71, 184; Mary, 71, 132; Mary Ann, 132; Patience, 132; Phebe, 33, 135; Phoebe, 178; Rachel, 179; Rebecca, 130; Richard, 179; Robert, 71, 132; Ruth, 132; Samuel, 132; Sarah, 7, 132, 148; Susan, 199; Theresa, 132; William, 71, 131, 168
MINDINGHALL, Robert, 122
MINEAR, Michael, 17; Phebe, 17
MINSHALL, Abel, 64, 103, 135; Agnes, 45, 46, 98, 110; Ann, 46, 99, 110; Grace, 46, 99; Jacob, 7, 22, 27, 33, 46, 48, 57, 74, 76, 99, 103, 110, 132; Jane, 51; John, 19, 103, 135; Lydia, 34, 103, 126, 135; Margaret, 46, 99; Mary, 46, 51, 99; Phebe, 46, 99; Sarah, 19, 51, 103; Thomas, 51, 103
MINTIRE, Elizabeth, 138
MITCHELL, Hannah, 25; John, 25, 125, 191; Thomas, 193
MODLIN, Joseph, 62

MOLDON, John, 124
MOLYNEAUX, Robert, 23
MONRO, Dr., 44
MOODY, Sheriff, 165
MOONY, Eliza, 200; Elizabeth, 200; Ellen, 200; John, 200; Marier, 200; Mark, 200; Sarah, 200; Thomas, 200; William, 200
MOOR, Mary, 100
MOORE, Abner, 86, 188; Alice, 25; Ann, 113; Benjamin, 188; Eli, 138; Elisha, 80, 139; Elizabeth, 77, 80, 100, 138, 143; Ely, 77; George, 32, 183; Hannah, 15, 20, 119, 141; Henry, 100; Herreatta, 183; Isaac, 188; Isaiah, 203; Jacob, 77; James, 25, 80, 86; Jehu, 139; Jennis, 78, 80; Jesse, 77, 183; John, 15, 78, 100, 196; Jonah, 203; Jonas, 80; Jonathan, 78; Leah, 188; Marey, 183; Martha, 141; Mary, 3, 77, 80, 100, 112, 138, 141, 143, 157; Maskell E., 183; Mifflin, 80; Mordecai, 32, 80; Moses, 3, 55; Nathan, 77, 183; Phebe, 100; Philip, 58, 100; Rachel, 203; Richard, 143; Sampson, 40; Samson, 77; Samuel, 25, 78, 80, 94, 141; Sarah, 188; Thomas, 15, 20, 80; Walker, 138, 186, 188, 202; William, 77, 100, 143
MORE, Benjamin Elliott, 119; Eliza, 119
MOREY, Lewis, 67
MORGAN, ---, 101; Elizabeth, 123; Hannah, 40, 91; Isaac, 191; Isarel, 87; James, 59; John, 37, 40, 102; Joseph, 101, 123; Joseph C., 141; Joshua, 87; Lillah, 87; Magdalene, 40; Mary, 102, 123; Rachel, 40, 169; Rebecca, 102; Richard M., 198; Ruth, 40; Sarah, 123; Thomas, 72; William, 142
MORIS, Caleb, 2
MORRIS, Abraham, 114; Alice, 57, 129; Ann, 4, 57, 64, 129, 136; Anna, 103; Anthony C., 103; Cadr., 20; Cadwalder, 103; Catharine, 57, 90; Catharine W., 152; Catherine, 129; David, 1, 63, 90; Elizabeth, 11, 72, 114; Evan, 28, 57, 129, 130; George, 64, 74; Hannah, 100, 103; Henry, 138; Isaac, 152; Israel W., 138; James, 130; John, 23, 74, 90; John Ludon, 129; Jonathan, 12, 28, 33, 57, 70, 103, 129; Joseph, 64; Lewis, 82, 102, 114; Margaret, 103; Maria, 129; Mary, 4, 64, 90, 103; Mordica, 130; Phebe, 64, 100, 194; Samuel, 57, 90, 129, 130; Samuel R., 103; Sarah, 74; Susannah, 90
MORRISON, Agnes, 195; Elizabeth, 98, 152; Emmor, 152; Jane, 152; John, 152; Joseph, 43, 49, 53, 56, 68, 85, 152, 172; Lydia, 152; Mary, 152; William, 152, 172
MORTON, Aaron, 54, 130; Elizabeth, 47; Erasmus, 145; George, 7; Israel, 48; John, 21; John S., 130, 140, 162; Mary, 48; Sketchley, 200; Susan, 189; Susan C., 162; Susanna, 140
MOUDLER, Joseph, 20
MOULDER, John, 39; Margaret, 39; Rebecca, 98; William, 153
MOUNTAIN, James M., 100
MUCKELDUF, Samuel, 48
MULLEN, Ann, 167; Charles, 147; William, 151
MULLIN, James M., 184; John, 72; Owen, 201
MULLING, Margret, 129; Robert, 129
MULVANEY, Patrick, 69
MURPHEY, Jane, 133; Mary, 133
MUSGRAVE, A., 38
MYERS, Eliza, 188; Elizabeth, 188; Henry, 186, 188, 204; Jesse, 188; John, 174, 188; Margaret, 188; Mary, 188; Samuel, 188

-N-

NAYLOR, Mary, 162
NEAL, Ann, 114; Elizabeth, 114; James, 114, 198; Lydia, 114; William, 114
NECOR, Mary, 100
NEELD, James, 181
NEGRO, Bazin, 126; Ceazar, 13; Cloe, 40; Jin, 13; Lemon, 21; Milleigh, 13; Sylvia, 66; Tom, 41
NEIDA, Ruth, 191
NEIDE, Abegal, 41; Amelia, 79; Ann, 182; Benjamin, 41; Elizabeth, 41; Jacob, 41, 182; John, 41, 181; Joseph, 41, 79; Mary, 41; Orpah, 79;

Rebecka, 41; Sarah, 41, 79
NEILER, Jacob, 115
NELLING, John H., 190
NELSON, Caroline B., 181;
  Elizabeth M., 181; Emily D., 181; Mary Ann, 181; William, 181
NEW, Thomas, 20
NEWBOLD, George, 111; Mary, 111
NEWLAN, Sarah, 40
NEWLAND, Abigail, 40
NEWLIN, Abigail, 58; Abraham, 80; Ann, 80; Anna P., 176; Annesley, 194; Benjamin, 92; Deborough Jain, 179; Eliza, 92; Elizabeth, 80, 124, 181; Emmor J., 130; Esther, 176; Hannah, 166; Hannah A., 176; Hetty Ann, 176; Jane, 80, 90, 122; John, 80, 92, 108, 124; Joseph, 57, 80; Margret, 108; Martha, 92, 176; Mary, 108, 161, 176; Mary Ann, 181; Nathal, 114; Nathaneel, 85; Nathaniel, 25, 84, 101, 122, 147, 166, 176, 192; Nicholas, 40, 92; Rachel, 80; Richard, 80; Robert, 58; Samuel, 66, 93, 195; Sarah Ann, 92; Sarah L., 176; Thomas, 44, 68, 71, 80, 84, 92, 93; William Parker, 176
NEWTON, Isaac, 198
NICHOLSON, Jane, 159
NICKLIN, Joseph, 26
NOBBIT, Elizabeth, 63; Joseph, 63
NOBLE, Christopher, 121, 156, 195; Elizabeth, 156; Jacob, 156; Jesse, 156; John, 156; Rachel, 156; William, 156
NOBLIT, Joseph, 14, 24; Mary, 14; Thomas, 98; William, 14
NORRIS, Benjamin, 202; Brinton, 119; Charles, 45, 55; Christianna, 119; Deborah, 45; Hannah, 119; Isaac, 45; Joseph P., 45; Maria Jane, 119; Mary, 45
NORTON, Ann, 38
NOWLIN, Samuel, 66
NUTT, Sarah, 189
NUZUM, Hannah, 10; John, 10; Margaret, 99; Phebe, 10; Richard, 9, 10, 23; Ruth, 153; Sarah, 10, 99; Thomas, 9; William, 147

—O—
OAKFORD, Aaron, 7, 55, 59, 114, 189; Ann, 55, 114, 187;
Anthony, 114; Benj. W., 59; Benjamin W., 114, 119; Benjamin Webber, 55; Charles, 126; Deborah, 193; Elizabeth, 114, 126; Elizabeth C., 200; Grace, 187; Hannah, 55, 187; Isaac, 55, 95, 112, 114, 187, 189; John, 114, 126, 155, 176; Mary, 193, 200
ODENHEIMER, Henry, 202, 203; J. W., 109; John, 84, 203; Joseph, 68; William, 68, 84
OGDEN, Eliza, 93, 158; Elizabeth, 93, 158; Hannah, 93, 158, 162, 183; James, 93, 158; James M., 109; John, 42, 93, 131, 158, 168, 173, 183; John W., 158; Martha, 93, 158; Mary, 93, 158; Rachel, 42; Sarah, 93; Stephen, 162
OGDON, John, 158; Sarah, 42
OGLE, Catharine, 166
OGLEBE, Sarah, 89
OGLEBY, Sarah, 89; William, 89
OLDDEN, James, 171
OLIVER, Martha, 96; Mary, 96; Samuel, 96
ORMSBEY, Rachel, 182
ORMSBY, George, 75; Sarah, 75
ORR, Elizabeth, 94; Thomas, 94; William, 94
OSBOURN, Abigail, 156; David, 156; Elizabeth, 156; Jane, 156; John, 156; Joseph, 156; Peter, 156; Mary, 156; William, 156
OSLERE, David, 138; Davis, 138; Harriet S., 138; Job G., 138; Selany, 138
OSWALD, Eleazer, 67
OTTEY, Ann, 48; Eli, 48; Hannah, 48; John, 48, 58; Lydia, 48; Philip, 48; Richard, 48, 75; Sarah, 48; Thomas, 48
OTTY, Stephen, 196
OVERLY, Hannah, 4
OWEN, Abraham, 49; Elizabeth, 49; John, 17; Jonathan, 2, 49, 78, 194
OWENS, Jesse, 25; John, 128, 204; Jonathan, 155

—P—
PAINTER, ———, 188; Christiana, 188; Elizabeth, 60; Enos, 99, 104, 132; Esther, 148; Joseph, 148; Lydia, 148; Mary, 188; Minsahll, 187; Minshall, 184; Phebe, 187; Samuel, 39, 59, 148; William,

159, 160, 187, 188
PAIST, Alice, 132, 178; Sarah, 178; William, 29, 178
PALLEY, Adam G., 188
PALMER, Aaron, 124; Abigail, 53; Abraham, 53; Allice, 122; Ann, 153, 187; Asher, 43, 53, 64; Ashur, 122; Beaulah, 165; Benjamin, 51, 53, 66, 153; Charles, 165; Edith, 152; Eliza, 125, 134; George, 40, 122, 184, 192, 198, 203; Hannah, 53, 88, 150, 159, 165; Isaac, 125, 138; John, 53, 56, 88, 113, 114, 122, 131, 138, 143, 165, 182, 189; Joseph, 43, 49, 64, 71, 114, 122, 124, 125, 152, 154, 172, 180, 188, 192; Joshua, 150; Lewis, 165; Lydia, 53, 165, 174; Martin, 181; Mary, 5, 113, 125, 138; Morris, 122; Moses, 53, 62, 92, 93, 111, 124, 129, 138, 143, 154, 158, 159, 165, 172, 174; Norris, 53; Pennell, 134; Rachel, 165; Samuel, 138, 150; Sarah, 203; Susannah, 122; Thomas, 53; William, 134, 165; William W., 182; Wilson, 154
PANCAST, Samuel, 46
PANCOAST, Ann, 46; Anne, 46; Ester, 46; Hannah, 46; John, 46, 198; Rebecca, 198; Rebekah, 46; Samuel, 47, 132, 198; Seth, 46, 198; Stephen, 46; William, 198
PANCOST, Elisa, 13; Ester, 13; Hannah, 13; Phebe, 13; Samuel, 13; Sarah, 13; Seth, 13
PAPHALL, Sarah, 177
PARCLE, Ann, 31
PARISH, Abigail, 2
PARK, John, 9
PARKER, Abraham, 10, 50; Betty, 10; Elizabeth, 50; Evins, 50; John, 10, 50; Mary, 50; Ralph, 50; Robert, 50; Thomas, 50
PARKS, Hannah, 59; Jacob, 59, 185; John, 191; Richard, 59; Sarah, 59; Vernon, 59
PARRISH, William, 139
PARRY, Edith, 165; Hannah, 193; Jessy, 193
PARSON, Thomas, 42
PARSONS, George, 136; Hannah, 136; Israel, 136; Jemima, 136; Joseph, 136; Lewis, 179; Mahlon, 33, 136; Mahlon H., 136; Mary, 33, 88, 136; Nathaniel, 136; Rebecca, 153
PASCHALL, Ann, 25, 58; Benjamin, 25; Henry, 177; Martha, 141; Sarah, 177
PASSMORE, Abigail, 83; Abijah, 83; Everatt G., 141; Everet, 83; Levis, 165; Mary, 83, 164; Phebe, 83; Richard, 83; Sarah, 83
PATCHELL, Oswald, 173
PAUL, Jonathan, 165; Mary, 165; Thomas, 60; William, 40
PAWLING, Levi, 148
PEARCE, Ann, 115; Cromwell, 115; Edward, 115; Frances B., 115; John, 115; Joseph, 115; Margaret, 115; Rachel, 115
PEARSON, Ann, 62, 133; Benjamin, 120, 122, 133, 140, 150, 155, 186, 200; Bevan, 77; Charles, 25, 48; Elizabeth, 62, 90, 133; Ephraim, 55, 177; Hannah, 62, 133; Isaac, 176; J. L., 77, 94, 105, 147; John, 4, 20, 25, 31, 41, 48, 55, 61, 63, 77, 90, 114, 119, 133; John L., 62, 94, 155, 194; Jonathan, 4; Joseph, 62; Levi, 62; Margaret, 4; Marsha, 133; Martha, 62, 90; Nathan, 55; Sarah, 4; Susanna, 62, 90, 133; Thomas, 4
PECHIN, Peter, 123; Rebeca, 122; Rebecca, 92
PECK, Margary, 188
PEDRICK, Ann, 15; Daniel, 42; Elizabeth, 42, 115, 193; John, 6, 15; Susanna, 15; Susannah, 6; Thomas, 41, 42
PEIRCE, Ann, 111; Caleb, 29, 49, 110; Charles, 53; Edward, 111; Eli D., 138, 196; Eli Dicks, 81; Elizabeth, 24; Esther Ann, 137; George, 89; Hannah, 61, 111; Henry, 53, 175, 180; Isaac, 89; Jacob, 53; Jane, 17, 133, 188, 196; John, 17, 28, 29, 49, 53, 61, 81, 85, 92, 111, 115, 118, 133, 152, 154, 164, 167, 180, 196; John D., 196; Joseph, 102, 111; Joshua, 111; Margaret, 127, 190; Marget, 180; Margret, 53; Mary, 28, 29, 53, 61, 110, 195; Mires, 29; Nathan, 118; Phebe, 138; Rebecca, 110; Ruth, 43; Sarah, 29, 81, 180; Sarah D.,

196; Thomas, 91, 110, 111, 117, 125, 138, 169, 175; William, 53; William T., 117; Worral, 127; Worrall, 29
PEIRCY, Thomas, 22
PENEGAR, Amos, 67
PENNALL, Joseph, 75
PENNALLS, Joseph, 28
PENNEL, Evan, 9; Joseph, 1, 40; Mary, 39; Robert, 40; Susannah, 1, 113; Thomas, 39, 40
PENNELL, Aaron, 124; Abigail, 1, 36, 58; Abraham, 39, 48, 61, 69, 96, 104, 121, 164; Alice, 134; Ann, 14, 181; Ann C., 187; Anna G., 185; Anne, 181; Beulah, 197; Catharine, 181; Catherine, 15; Charles, 88, 113; Cidney, 185, 187; Deborah, 114; Del., 159; Dell, 163, 175, 196; Edmund, 181; Edward, 134, 171; Eleanor, 15; Eliza, 134; Elizabeth, 185, 187; Emaline, 197; Ester, 124; Esther, 97, 135; Hannah, 119, 134, 166, 175, 181; Henry H., 181; Hervey, 32; Hill, 175; Isaac, 49, 60, 97, 105, 106, 117, 132, 135; James, 32, 56, 119, 140, 181; Jane, 97, 171, 186; Jesse, 104, 124; John, 6, 15, 27, 97, 119, 135, 146, 176; Jonathan, 31, 67, 71, 84, 97, 103, 160, 178, 181; Joseph, 14, 26, 36, 44, 51, 58, 66, 87, 91, 97, 108, 117, 119, 134, 142, 160, 179, 185; Ledah, 1; Lewis, 37, 134; Lydia, 56, 58, 97, 135; Margaret, 140, 197; Marget, 197; Mark, 134; Martha, 174; Mary, 15, 27, 58, 120, 124, 134, 175, 181, 186, 197; Meredith, 134; Nathan, 119, 130, 135; Nicholas, 15; Priscilla, 96, 134; Rachel, 119, 124; Rebecka, 181; Robert, 4, 15, 23, 27, 48, 58, 59, 84, 124, 134, 163, 179, 185; Sally Ann, 181; Samml., 185; Samuel, 124; Sarah, 44, 87, 96, 109, 119, 134, 181, 185, 197; Sarah Ann, 171; Sidney, 175; Susann, 15; Susanna, 119, 134, 140; Thamsin, 134; Thamzin, 96; Thomas, 1, 4, 58, 88, 92, 113, 134, 181; William, 84, 119, 123, 124, 134, 185
PENNIL, Hannah, 1; Joseph, 1
PENNINGTON, Paul, 74
PENNOCK, Abraham, 164; Joel, 175; John, 164; Joseph, 164; Lydia, 164; Ruth, 164; Samuel, 175; William, 14, 21, 45, 80, 93, 109, 116, 117, 133
PENROSE, Joseph, 1
PERDUE, Jacob, 127
PERKINS, Caleb, 154, 167; Hannah, 93
PETERS, Ann, 49; Deborah, 198; James S., 175; Mary, 175; Pennell, 192; Rebecca, 192; William, 122, 129
PEW, Mary, 111
PHARO, Jane, 16; Oliver, 16; Phebe, 16
PHAROH, Phebe, 135
PHILIPS, Catharine, 190; David, 136; Dorcas, 152
PHILLIPS, Ann, 160; Cerwriah, 160; Clementine, 160; David, 71, 160, 197; Elizabeth, 160; George, 160; John, 160; Margaret, 160; Thomas, 63, 160
PHIPPS, Caleb, 18; Elisha, 18, 94; Susanna, 18
PIERCE, George, 4; John, 39, 55, 98, 159; Joseph, 36; Margaret, 127; Mary, 98; Ruth, 137; William, 161
PIGEON, Frederick, 154
PIGON, Frederick, 154
PILKINGTON, Rebekah, 24
PILKINTON, Sarah, 32
PINESET, Eliza, 108
PINKERTON, Sarah, 138
PIPE, Sarah, 84
PIPER, Joseph, 68, 170; Sarah, 67, 170
PIRA, Joseph, 10
PITT, Hannah, 146; John, 146, 163; Mary, 146; Phebe, 146; Samuel, 146
PLANKENTON, Margaret, 161
PLANKINTON, Samuel, 102, 131, 171; Sarah, 131, 132
PLEASANTS, Mary, 190; T., 190
PLOWMAN, Hannah, 24, 44
POLLING, Hannah, 31; Nathan, 31
POOLE, Sarah, 30, 97; William, 30
PORTER, Lydia, 46; Margaret, 13
POSTILL, Piercey, 192
POTTS, Joannah, 29; Samuel, 29
POWEL, Abraham, 155; Ann, 158; George, 155; Joseph, 155;

Mary, 155; Sarah, 194; Thomas, 155
POWELL, Abraham, 41, 155, 161; Abram, 139; Ann, 128; Elizabeth, 128; George, 41, 128, 139; Hannah, 41, 139; Isaac, 118, 128, 173; James, 128; John, 12, 13, 41, 45, 46, 73, 94, 115, 128, 139, 158; Joseph, 41, 63, 139, 155, 171; Margaret, 128, 173; Martin, 128; Mary, 41, 139; Nathan, 41; Patience, 41; Samuel, 35; Sarah, 41, 128, 139; Thomas, 41, 139
POWER, Thomas, 5
POWERS, Pearce, 41
PRATT, Abraham, 69, 147, 201; Christian, 147; David, 36, 46, 83, 113, 123, 129, 147, 153; Elizabeth, 166; Henry, 147, 196; Jane, 147; Jeremiah, 147; John, 142, 147, 166; Joseph, 54, 102, 147; Joseph H., 144; Lydia, 147; Mary, 102, 144, 150; Orpha, 147; Phineas, 192; Randal, 147; Sarah, 22, 69
PRESTON, Abigail, 14; Hannah, 14; John Jonas, 16; Jonas, 14, 33, 45, 84, 90, 96; Joseph, 90; Mary, 14, 27; Orpah R., 84
PRICE, Abigail, 143; Abijah, 54; Ann, 55, 91; Benjamin, 91; Charles, 70, 91; Charlotte, 70; Debby, 93, 168; E., 38, 202, 203; Ea., 38; Ed., 202; Elisabeth, 7; Elisha, 55, 126; Elizabeth, 38, 55, 91; Elizabeth B., 146; Hannah, 55, 70, 91; Harriet D., 146; Henry, 91; Isaac, 91; James, 195; John, 7, 18, 34, 37, 45, 55; Joseph, 65; Lydia, 44; Mary, 65, 75, 91; Peter, 70; Philip, 75, 91; Rachel, 91; Sammuel, 91; Samuel, 55; Samuel A., 176; Sarah, 19, 55, 91; Susan Ann, 146; William, 19, 54, 91
PRICHETT, Elizabeth, 76
PRINCE, Adam, 61; Isaiah, 61; Rachal, 138; Sarah, 61
PRITCHARD, Elizabeth, 54
PRITCHET, Elizabeth, 30, 76, 81; Jesse, 30; John, 30; Phebe, 30; William, 30
PRITCHETT, William, 33
PROFOUNTAIN, Phebe, 181; Rebecka, 181
PUGH, Amelia, 18, 199; David, 199; Edward, 66, 199; Edwin, 17; Elijah, 18; John, 17, 18, 199; Joseph, 18, 199; Mary, 18, 199
PUSEY, Ann, 176; Hannah, 14, 81; Joshua, 154; Lea, 195; Lydia, 154; William P., 176
PYLE, Aaron, 175, 179; Abner, 53, 175; Caleb, 1, 82, 175; Daniel, 192; David, 56; Dutton, 192; Elizabeth, 56, 128; Ezekiel, 144, 154; Hannah, 56; Israel, 28; Jacob, 90; Jane, 175; John, 192; Jonathan, 175; Joseph, 8, 53, 79, 113, 192; Josua, 172; Levi, 82; Lydia, 113, 186; Malissa, 113; Martha, 113, 186; Mary, 53, 82, 90, 175; Melissa, 186; Moses, 113, 175; Nathan, 14; Phebe, 53, 113, 170; Prudence, 192; Ralph, 10, 56; Rebecca, 192; Robert, 94, 192; Ruth, 99; Sally Ann, 113; Samuel, 56; Sarah, 56, 179; Sarah Ann, 186; Stephen, 113, 201; Susannah, 56; William, 56
PYOTT, Abram, 190; Alexander, 190; Elizabeth, 190; George, 190; James, 31, 70, 120, 189, 190; Mary, 139, 190; Patience, 139; Richard, 190; Rose, 189
PYWELL, William, 34

-Q-
QUARLL, John, 104
QUIG, Fanney, 195
QUIGG, Fanny, 119; John, 118
QUIGLEY, Christopher, 18
QUIGLY, Hannah, 93; Joseph, 93; Margaret, 93; Mary, 93; Moses, 93; Sarrah, 93
QUIN, Martha, 62
QUINN, Davis, 129; James, 129, 150; John, 129; Martha, 130; William, 129

-R-
RAMAGE, Amer, 129; Margret, 129
RANDEL, Abraham, 80; Jane, 80
RATTAW, Morris, 22
RAWN, Elizabeth, 150
RAY, Hannah, 28
READ, Ann, 129, 130; David, 61; Davis, 130; Eliza, 129; James, 129, 130; John, 102, 129, 130; Margeret, 130;

Margret, 129; Mary, 130;
Thomas, 129; William, 129
REATH, Mary, 157
REDDER, Ann, 34
REDDING, Maria, 142
REDMAN, Elizabeth, 140
REDMOND, Elizabeth, 116
REECE, David, 22, 97; Davis,
160; Debby, 97, 106;
Elizabeth, 22, 80, 90;
Elizabeth L., 106, 145; Enos,
90, 106; Hannah, 22; Jesse,
3, 22, 92, 97, 106, 132, 135,
160; Lewis, 22, 97, 98, 106;
Mary, 89, 93; Mordecai, 3;
Orpha, 3; Rebecca, 43, 106,
137, 145; Sarah, 22; Sidney,
3; William, 3, 22, 90
REED, Ann, 62; Davis, 62;
Elizabeth, 56; Hannah, 56;
Hugh, 97, 125; James, 62;
John, 62; Margaret, 62; Mary,
56, 62; Rachel, 56; Susannah,
62; Thomas, 62
REEDER, Ann, 49
REES, Ann, 157; Esther, 157;
Hannah, 157; Isaac, 157;
Margaret, 157; Phebe, 157;
Tharmar, 157
REESE, Rebecca, 70
REGESTER, Abigail, 27; Abraham,
155; Daniel, 47; Joseph, 134;
Margaret, 155; Priscilla,
155; William, 27
REGISTER, Daniel, 34; David, 44
REID, Clotoworty, 18;
Elizabeth, 18; Frances, 18;
Hannah, 18; Paul, 18
REJESTER, Joseph, 54; Sarah, 54
RETTEW, Aaron, 85; Eleanor, 85;
James, 85; John, 85
REVELL, Mary, 130; Mary Ann,
131; Peter, 130
REY, David, 67
REYNOLDS, Andrew, 181;
Benjamin, 38; David, 10;
Elizabeth, 10; Jane, 38;
Lydia, 10; Margaret, 38;
Mary, 10, 181; Phebe, 38;
Samuel, 38
RHOADS, Elizabeth, 24, 25, 83,
179; George, 25, 82, 174,
179; Hannah, 24, 25, 171;
James, 82, 106, 123, 174;
James H., 188; John Owen, 24;
Joseph, 9, 12, 13, 24, 25,
33, 37, 42, 46, 59, 61, 82,
83, 123, 155, 171, 174, 179,
188; Leah, 46; Mary, 31, 82,
179; Owen, 24, 31, 83, 116,
140, 177; Phebe, 83, 179;
Rebecca, 179; Rebeckah, 24,
83; Samuel, 166, 173; Sarah,
63, 155, 166; Tacy, 24;
William, 83, 179, 198
RHODES, Owen, 132, 194; Samuel,
166; Sarah, 166
RICARD, Mary, 49
RICE, Ann, 194; Daniel, 41, 63,
171, 193, 194; Deborah, 194;
Elizabeth, 41, 171, 193;
Hannah, 171, 193; Jacob, 41,
63, 170, 171, 193; John, 195;
Mary, 171; Nicholas, 146;
Rachel, 171, 193; William,
193, 194
RICHARD, David, 16; Jonathan,
60
RICHARDS, Abigail, 43;
Benjamin, 5; Dannie1, 91;
Davis, 147, 161; Dutton, 44,
118; Edward, 23; Enoch, 153;
Hannah, 24, 44, 118, 127;
Isaiah, 77; Jacob, 75, 124;
Jane, 171, 189; Jehu, 24, 44,
118, 168, 199; John, 124,
153; Jonathan, 24, 44, 118;
Joseph, 24, 44, 118, 127;
Josiah, 24, 44, 118; Lucey,
44; Lucy, 24; Lydia, 24, 30,
44, 118, 127; Margaret, 77;
Mary, 17, 94, 127, 171; Mary
Ann, 44; Nathan, 112;
Nathaniel, 127; Richard, 24,
44, 118; Samuel, 17, 91;
Sarah, 127; Sarah Ann, 44;
Susanna, 44; Thomas, 24, 44,
118; William, 171
RICHARDSON, Frances, 126;
Francis, 126; Kesiah, 108;
Mary, 126, 142; Thomas, 108,
142
RICKABOUGH, Adam, 106
RICKER, John, 116
RIDGWAY, Daniel, 25
RIGBY, Hannah, 127; James, 38;
Jonathan, 203; Lydia, 184
RIGHT, Orpha, 42
RILEY, Esther, 176; John, 32;
Margaret, 134; Mary, 73, 134;
Richard, 55, 73, 97, 134, 143
RINALS, Jacob, 1
RINEHART, Samuel, 24; Simon, 24
RING, Ann, 86, 94; Caleb, 86,
94; Chambles, 86; Chamless,
94; Cleb, 161; Hannah, 94;
James, 86, 94; Joseph, 86,
94; Julian, 94; Lesson, 94;
Mary, 86, 94; Nathaniel, 86;
Rachall, 110; Susanna, 108;
William, 86, 94
RITTENHOUSE, Benjamin, 141;

Hannah, 39
RIVELEY, Elizabeth, 173; John, 173
RIVELY, Ann, 193; Daniel, 193; John, 96, 101, 139, 176, 183, 193; Mary, 193; Sarah, 193
ROADS, James, 101; Joseph, 101
ROBERTS, Abigail, 110, 127; Alice, 110; Ann, 109, 110, 137, 155; Barney, 151; David, 103, 151; Davis, 103; Elijah, 151; Elizabeth, 109, 152; Ellinor, 109; Ellis, 35, 86, 110, 118, 142, 156; Evan, 58, 59, 74, 103, 125, 143; Hannah, 109; Israel, 127; Jacob, 74; Jehu, 152; John, 109, 110, 169; Margaret, 143; Margret, 103; Mary, 103; Moses, 32; Reuben, 52, 110, 118; Susanna, 103; Susannah, 103; Sussanna, 103; Teacy, 110; William, 99, 151
ROBESON, Samuel, 111
ROBINS, Jane, 27; Joseph, 27; Mary, 27
ROBINSON, Catharine, 40; Catherine, 36, 41; Deborah, 194; Elizabeth, 99; Esther, 99; Hannah, 12, 99; John, 99, 180; Joseph, 99; Lydia, 153; Margaret, 99; Rachel, 115; Sarah, 99; Susannah, 12; Thomas, 85, 177; William, 53, 99, 152
RODGERS, Lyda, 64
ROGAN, Sophia, 10
ROGERS, Abner, 113; Abnor, 101; Alse, 101; Deborah, 64; Esther, 202; Jacob, 202; John, 113; Lydia, 152; Mischael, 135; Sarah, 135
ROGGERS, Joseph, 64; Lidya, 64; Thomas, 64
ROSS, Elizabeth, 31; John, 31
ROTHERFORD, Mary, 144
ROUTH, Hannah, 157
ROWAN, Ann, 102; James, 55, 102, 131; John, 95, 102, 131; Martha, 102, 131; Rebecca, 102
RUDOLPH, Ann, 25; Catherine, 139; Deborah, 139; Hannah, 25, 139, 155; Jacob, 25; James, 139; John, 203; Joseph, 25; Mary, 25; Philip, 118, 129, 152, 155; Rebecca, 139
RUSSEL, Elizabeth, 128; Isabella, 128; James, 99, 128; John, 157; Lettice, 128; Martha, 128; Samuel, 99, 128
RUSSELL, Aaron, 180; Adeline, 176; Catharine, 180; Edward, 180; Ephram, 10; George, 34; Gideon, 112; Hannah, 54; Isabella, 10; James, 10, 38, 41, 122; Jamima, 66; Jane, 10; Jesse, 54, 95, 134; John, 10, 54, 76, 135, 153, 176; Joseph, 33, 66, 134, 180, 198; Lydia, 54, 69, 93; Lydia Ann, 176; Martha, 10; Mary, 66, 134, 176, 180, 196; Moses, 180, 181; Obed, 54, 134; Samuel, 10, 38, 41, 122; Sarah, 54; Sarah Ann, 134, 176; William, 16, 54, 93, 134, 176
RUTHERFORD, Phebe, 64
RYAN, Dinah, 194; Elizabeth, 194; Mary, 194
RYERS, Hannah, 153; Joseph Waln, 153
RYLE, Benjamin, 1

-S-

SAFFER, Dolly, 198; Frederick, 198; John, 198; William, 198
SALYARDS, Sarah, 71
SANDELAND, James, 45
SANDERLAND, David, 45
SANDERS, Sarah, 169
SANKEY, Elizabeth, 144; Esther, 144; Margaret, 43; Martha, 43; William, 43, 110
SAUNDERS, Rachel, 6
SAVERY, Sarah, 57
SAWYER, Elizabeth, 39
SAYRES, Dr., 44
SCATTERGOOD, David, 172; Elizabeth, 172; Joseph, 172; Samuel, 172; Sarah, 172; Thomas, 172; William, 172
SCHOFEL, Hanna, 19; Nathaniel, 19
SCHOFIELD, James, 178; John, 178; Lucy, 178
SCHOPHEL, Hannah, 19; Mary, 19
SCHOPHELL, Hannah, 47; Nathan, 47
SCHOPPELL, Hannah, 47; Nathan, 47
SCOT, Ann, 19
SCOTT, Ann, 47, 48, 72; Elizabeth, 72; John, 47, 48, 72; Richard, 72; Robert B., 185
SCRIMGER, Margret, 129
SEAL, Jesse, 201; John Polis, 83; Mary, 85, 113; Sarah, 113, 201

SEARY, Patrick, 165
SEEDS, Alice, 38; Phebe A., 143
SELL, Aaron, 148
SELLARS, Ann, 182; Coleman, 182; Elizabeth, 182; Hannah, 182; Nathan, 182
SELLERS, Ann, 63, 187; Coleman, 187; David, 63, 70; Elizabeth, 187; George, 63, 70, 154, 157, 182; Hannah, 187; Jane, 4; John, 141, 154, 182, 187; Joseph, 63; Nathan, 63, 70, 82, 141, 187; Samuel, 63, 182, 187
SEMANS, Thomas, 139
SERILL, Jacob, 130
SERRILL, Benjamin, 175; George, 91, 139, 146, 166, 186; Hannah, 4; J. H., 150; Jacob, 4, 25, 130; James, 193, 200; John, 162, 166, 174, 189; Martha, 166; Rebecca, 4; Sidney, 175; Thomas, 120
SEYES, Abraham, 69
SHADE, Ennis, 197; Ennise, 197; James P., 197
SHAKESPEAR, William, 102
SHALLCROSS, Catherine, 129; Joseph, 42, 67, 82; M. C., 187, 193; Morris C., 130, 194
SHARPLES, Aaron, 97; Abigail, 69; Abraham, 152; Abraham W., 152, 201; Abram, 133, 138; Amy, 97; Ann, 113, 154; Benjamin, 97; Caspar W., 152; Catharine, 152; Daniel, 69; Davis, 113; Edith, 97, 113, 201; Elizabeth, 164, 201; Esther, 97, 113, 201; George, 118; Hannah, 93, 97, 113, 201; Harvy, 201; Isaac, 97, 156; Jane, 201; Jesse, 113, 201; Joel, 69, 93; John, 93, 113, 201; Jonas, 118; Joseph, 69; Joshua, 69, 93, 97, 161; Lydia, 69, 93, 97; Martha, 97; Mary, 93, 113, 115; Nathan, 69, 93, 97, 111, 113, 127, 143, 147, 154, 201; Phebe, 93, 154; Rachel, 93, 152; Robert, 152; Ruth, 158; Samuel, 93, 97, 111, 201; Sarah, 97, 113, 201; Smith, 201; Susanna, 113, 201; Thomas, 69, 93, 201
SHARPLESS, Aaron, 30, 190; Abigail, 6, 35; Abraham, 26, 96, 150; Abram, 81, 102, 111; Amos, 13, 81, 151; Amy, 30; Ann, 190; Benjamin, 30; Beulah, 118, 158, 184; Caleb, 35; Cidney, 94; Daniel, 6, 17, 19, 35, 37, 43, 86, 110, 118; Edith, 6; Emeline, 118; Enos, 35, 118, 128, 147, 164, 183, 203; Ester, 30; Esther, 30; Grace, 118; Hannah, 6, 118, 184; Henry, 118, 203; Isaac, 30, 35, 118, 124, 203; Jane, 6; Jesse, 186; Joel, 6, 69, 118, 184; John, 6, 30, 35, 50, 86, 118, 128, 142; Jonas, 79, 89, 100, 107; Joshua, 30, 161, 184; Lydia, 6, 184; Martha, 33, 91; Mary, 6, 50, 101, 170; Morris C., 119; Nathan, 104, 105, 118, 135; Phebe, 6, 118, 190; Rachel, 6, 104, 184; Ruth, 184; Samuel, 6, 13, 30, 69, 118, 161, 170, 184, 186; Sarah, 30, 35, 110, 118, 139; Susannah, 6; Thomas, 6, 17, 30, 33, 50, 67; William, 6, 28, 33, 50, 67
SHAW, James, 38, 41, 42, 54; Jane, 33; Jannet, 86, 156; John, 38, 171; Joseph, 156; Margaret, 48; Martha, 33, 55; Mary, 45, 46; Mary Ann, 177; Preston, 33; Samuel, 38, 48, 55, 164; Sarah, 86, 156; William, 180
SHEAF, Deborah, 92; Mary, 143; Philip, 3, 92, 156; William, 143
SHEAFF, Catherine, 175; Deborah, 175; Elizabeth, 175; John, 175; Mary, 175; Philip, 175; Sabinah, 175; Temaris, 175; William, 175
SHEE, Parke, 52, 53; Rachel, 168
SHELDRON, William, 100
SHELLEY, Rebeccah, 57
SHELLINGTON, John, 26
SHELLY, Frances, 98
SHEPHERD, William, 53
SHERRY, Samuel, 177
SHIELDS, Benoni, 122, 128; Marcey, 10
SHILLINGFORD, John, 163
SHIPLEY, Thomas, 101, 173
SHIPPEN, Priscilla, 93; Robert, 83
SHOALTS, John, 160; Marthaw, 160
SHOEMAKER, William, 49
SHOTTEN, Bream, 34; Mary, 34
SHOULTS, Martha, 174
SHULL, Frederick, 190, 194; Fredk., 134

SHUSTER, John, 154; Leonard, 154, 182; Prescilla, 154
SIDDONS, Ann, 133; John, 133; Joshua, 133; Sarah, 133; William, 38, 133
SIDERS, Adam, 37; Elizabeth, 37; George, 37; Jacob, 37; John, 37; Mary, 37; Sarah, 37; William, 37
SILL, Aaron, 39; Ann, 39; Elizabeth, 39; James, 27, 39; Mary, 27, 71; Michael, 74; Nehemiah, 39; William, 39
SILLS, James, 35
SIMMONS, Benjamin, 67; Isaac, 67; Jacob, 67; Levi, 67; Margaret, 67; Mathias, 67; William, 67
SIMONSON, Edward, 8; Martha, 10; William, 10
SIMPSON, Richard, 102
SITER, Adam, 159, 197; Ann, 159; David, 159; Ed, 160; Edward, 66, 104, 131, 159, 160, 197, 199; Elizabeth, 159; John, 66, 73, 159; William, 158, 159
SITERS, Adam, 17, 54; Clerica, 54; Edward, 17; George, 54; Hannah, 18, 54, 59; John, 54; Joseph, 54; Nathaniel, 54; Sarah, 54
SITZ, Michael, 173
SKAVENDIKE, Peter, 163
SKELTON, Owen, 23
SKOT, Ann, 19; John, 19
SLATER, Ann, 51; Elizabeth, 51; James, 51; John, 51; Libby, 51; Mary, 51; Prudence, 51; Sibby, 51; Thomas, 51
SLATERY, Thomas, 23
SLAWTER, John, 26, 136; Samuel, 85; William, 128, 158
SLEEPER, Charles L., 179
SLETER, ---, 51
SMEDLEY, Ahinoam, 132, 178; Ambrose, 31, 76, 103, 132; Ann, 19; Benjamin, 202; Clinton, 99; Daniel, 19; Elizabeth, 132, 178, 187; Francis, 19, 99; George, 7, 19, 160; Hannah, 19; Hunter, 72; Isaac, 99; James, 82, 85, 132, 145; Jesse, 19, 47, 72; Joseph, 7, 19; Mary, 7, 19, 47, 72, 132, 202; Mary Ann, 99; Peter, 6, 7, 93; Phebe, 6, 93, 184; Samuel, 7, 132, 178; Samuel L., 138, 142, 158, 177, 186, 201; Sarah, 7, 19, 99, 132; Susanna, 202; Thomas, 19, 121; Thomas D., 167; William, 7, 99, 100, 132, 158
SMEDLY, Mary, 57; Sarah, 34
SMEDLEY, Mary, 57; Phebe, 69
SMITH, Aaron, 175; Abigail, 156; Agnes, 28; Albin, 159; Amor, 195; Ann, 3, 90, 162, 169, 175; Anthany, 203; Benjamin H., 59, 61, 70, 71, 92; Benjamin Hayes, 44, 65; Butler, 165; David, 10, 156; Davis, 79; Dorothy, 36, 40, 41, 45; Dr., 44; Elenor, 152; Eliza, 79; Eliza Ann, 204; Elizabeth, 20, 40, 156, 175; Esther, 176; George, 82, 177; Gideon, 159; Hannah, 79, 85, 98, 121, 126, 159, 188; Henry Hays, 3; Jacob, 162; James, 66, 85, 103, 122, 143, 175; James A. B., 197; Jamima, 66; John, 55, 60, 62, 105, 121, 135, 156; Jonathan, 62; Joseph, 98, 159, 167; Keziah, 10; Kitty E., 204; Lewis, 156; Luke, 1; Lydia, 79, 156, 159; Mahlon, 156; Margaret, 1, 70, 71, 121, 152, 175, 204; Martha, 40, 49, 175; Mary, 103, 143, 152, 175; Milton, 159; Nathan, 74; Nathaniel, 30, 79, 82, 103, 155; Phebe, 10; Rachel, 3; Rebecah, 83; Rebecca, 1, 79; Rebecka, 29; Robert, 152; Samuel, 20, 79, 160, 171, 176, 183; Samuel Sharp, 3; Sarah, 79, 159, 197; Susanna, 108, 156; Susannah, 85; Thomas, 1, 64, 83, 84, 85, 108, 130; Tristram, 42; William, 11, 25, 74, 85, 107, 122, 151, 156, 160, 165, 175
SNEATH, Elizabeth, 73; George, 115; Robert, 73
SNEIDER, Catherine, 59; David, 59; Elizabeth, 59; John, 59; Leonard, 59; Margaret, 59; Mary, 59; Mathias, 59; Sarah, 59; Thomas, 59
SNYDER, Sarah, 139, 155
SOLEY, Edward, 106; Jane, 106
SPAKMAN, M., 24
SPARKS, James, 67
SPEAKMAN, Ann, 149, 195; Daniel, 149; Esther, 68; John, 68; Mary, 3; Micaijah, 8; Micajah, 29, 127, 147; Michajah, 68; Nathaniel, 68, 151; Phebe, 68; Priscilla,

195; Thomas, 56, 68, 102, 195
SPECKMAN, Micajah, 68; Phebe, 68
SPEEKMAN, Micaijah, 8
SPEER, Phebe Ann, 183
SPRAY, James, 21
SQUIB, Nathaniel, 26
STACEY, David, 150; James, 150; Tacey Ann, 150
STACY, Davis B., 126; Davis Bevan, 142; James G., 126, 142; Tacy Ann, 142; Tacy Anna, 126
STANDLEY, Jacob, 52
STANDLY, Martha, 50
STAPLER, John, 86
STAR, Swen, 132
STARKES, Samuel, 87
STARR, ---, 103; Ann, 71; Aquilla, 31; Eliza, 88; Isaac, 4; Joseph, 31, 88; Joseph James, 88; Margaret H., 49; Margaret Hall, 34; Sarah, 19, 51
STEEL, Andrew, 100, 125; Ann, 125; Christopher W., 184; Hannah, 125; Hannah P., 165; James, 63, 141; Jane, 135; Margaretta, 125; Mary, 104, 125; Robert, 63, 141, 142, 165; Susan, 156; Susanna, 100, 125; Thomas, 125, 175; William, 141
STEELE, Peter, 67; Thomas, 51
STEPHENSON, James, 26; John, 52
STEVENSON, Allen, 141; Barbara, 141; Isaac, 61; James, 141; Jane, 141; John, 140; Maria, 141; William, 141
STEWARD, Martha, 10
STEWARDSON, Thomas, 154
STEWART, Ann, 10; George, 10; John, 10
STIDHAM, Isaac, 54; Mary, 54
STILL, Eliza, 133; George, 133; John, 133; Prudence, 133; Rebecca, 133
STILLE, Sarah, 107; Thomas, 107
STIMMEL, Frederick, 196
STOKES, John, 153
STREET, Providence, 52
STRINGFELLOW, Rachel, 128
STRODE, Esther, 65
STROOPES, Elizabeth, 194
STROOPS, John, 194
STUARD, Elizabeth, 155; Henry, 155; John, 155; Margaret, 155; Martha, 155; Mary, 155; Sophia, 155; William, 155
STUARTSON, Thomas, 39
STURGIS, Jonathan, 122; Sarah, 122
SULLENDER, Isaac, 123
SULLINDER, Isaac, 101
SUPLEE, John, 171; Nathan, 115, 132; Sarah, 178; William, 193
SUPPLEE, Sarah, 113
SUTTON, Bartholomew, 22; Deborah, 23, 114
SWAFER, Joseph, 31
SWAFFER, Abigail, 17, 94; Joseph, 128; Mary, 94; Rachel, 94; William, 17, 41
SWAN, Catharine, 90
SWAYN, Mary, 38
SWAYNE, Aaron, 183; Ann, 166; Elizabeth, 183; George, 15, 48, 63, 183; Hannah, 183; John, 183; Mary, 183; Miriam, 183; Moses, 183; Phebe, 15, 183; Samuel, 166; Sarah, 183; Thomas, 15, 183
SWIFT, R.G., 157

-T-

TAGGERT, Phebe, 123
TALBERT, Jacob, 6; Susannah, 6
TALBOT, Elizabeth, 191; Hannah, 75; Jacob, 69, 135; John, 38, 49, 75, 119, 135, 140, 156, 191, 199; Joseph, 35, 60, 75, 95, 105, 117, 132, 137, 151, 191; Rachel, 75; Ruth, 75; Sarah, 135, 139; Susanna, 69; Susannah, 184; William, 135
TALFORD, John, 203
TALLEY, Elizabeth, 28, 116
TALLY, Ann, 166; Elihu, 166
TATE, Esther, 148; Joshua, 149; Martha, 149
TATNALL, Edward, 195; Joseph, 8
TAYLOR, Abigail, 142; Abraham, 126; Ambrose, 57; Amy, 50; Ann, 97, 103, 164, 187; Anna, 164; Benjamin, 12, 61, 106; Bowman, 164; Bulah, 106; Charles, 151; Cidney, 199; Deborah, 65; Drusilla T., 199; Edith, 113, 201; Eliza, 52; Elizabeth, 52, 65, 115, 151; Enoch, 50, 52, 137; Evan, 50; Ezra, 52, 53, 60, 169; Francis, 57; George W., 190; Gideon, 164; Grace, 57; Gula, 52; Hannah, 50, 52, 97, 187; Henry, 169; Huldah, 199; Isaac, 9; Isaac M., 169; Isarel, 33; Israel, 1, 7, 11, 33, 164; James, 178; Jane, 25, 44; Jemima, 52; Jesse, 166, 184; John, 9, 50, 56, 57, 65, 75, 87, 118, 132,

151, 199; Jonah, 58; Joseph, 57, 164; Julian, 169; Justice, 190; Lydia, 180, 199; Maris, 52, 169; Martha, 58; Mary, 9, 52, 57, 65; Moses, 57; Nathan, 50, 52, 53; Peter, 33, 50, 57; Rebecca, 113, 190; Robert, 9; Ruth, 50; Samuel, 43; Samuel H., 65; Sarah, 12, 106, 187; Stephen, 97; Susannah, 85, 113; Thomas, 9, 128, 190, 204; Vernon G., 180, 199; William, 97, 164; William H., 193; William Henry, 190
TELTON, James, 44
TEMPLE, Caleb, 36, 121; Edward, 36; Rachel, 121; Sidney, 166; Thomas, 20, 36
TEPPINGS, Richard, 52
TERRALL, George, 91
TERREL, Job, 137
TERRILL, Ann Louisa, 204; Emeline, 204; George, 91; J. H., 119, 140, 142, 163, 188, 200, 202; Job H., 142, 145, 204; Margaret, 204
THATCHER, Abigail, 17, 94; Beulah, 94, 118; Deborah, 109; Elizabeth, 74; Hannah, 74; Jane, 14; John, 14; Joseph, 12, 17, 22, 74, 79, 94, 164; Phebe, 74; Richard, 74; Robert, 74; Sarah, 74, 94; Thomas, 97, 164; William, 74, 75, 118, 186
THATTCHER, Thomas, 164
THIMARY, ---, 137
THOMAS, Amos, 40; Ann, 112, 136, 149, 168, 199; Benjamin, 23, 44, 125; Beulah E., 88, 203; Daniel, 185, 196; David, 63, 170, 199; David E., 168; Edward, 199; Eliza, 196; Elizabeth, 168, 199; Elma, 203; Ezra, 112; George, 44, 100, 117, 158; George W., 123; Gideon, 112, 149; Hezekiah, 112; Israel, 156, 168, 199; James, 44; Jonathan, 44, 148, 202; Joshua, 25, 43, 57; Louisa, 199; Margaret, 170; Martha, 195; Mary, 99, 144, 151, 170, 177, 187, 199, 203; Owen, 23, 44; Phebe, 149; Priscilla, 112, 195; Prudence, 52; Rebecca, 44, 203; Rees, 86; Richard, 111; Robert, 112; Robert M., 149, 196; Sarah, 57, 112, 149, 168, 170, 185,

199, 203; Selina, 195; Seth, 44, 52, 167, 168, 199; Seth C., 168; Solomon, 112; Susanah, 23; Susanna, 44; Thomas, 54, 78, 112, 122, 125; Townsend, 84, 88, 148, 203; Uriah, 112, 149, 151, 170, 180; William, 40, 90
THOMPSON, Amor, 93; Ann, 14, 136, 174; Daniel, 136, 174; Eliza, 136; Elizabeth, 93; Ellen, 136; Emeline, 174; George, 198; Hannah, 45; Isaac, 14, 93; James, 93; Jersey, 145; John, 14, 189; Jonah, 14; Joshua, 14, 65; Mary, 45, 93, 117, 136, 174; Mordecai, 136; Moses, 33; Priscilla, 93; Robert, 93; Sarah, 93, 136; William, 93, 120
THOMSON, Ann, 125; Archibald, 202; Daniel, 159; Delia, 162; Dilley, 162; Esther, 125; Hannah, 202; Hester, 125; Jane, 141; John, 81, 125, 198; John E., 125; Jonah, 125; Joseph, 162; Levis P., 125; Margaret, 162; Mary, 125; Mary A., 125; P., 81; Thomas, 162; William, 162
THORNBURY, Hannah, 106
THORPE, Elizabeth, 80; Thomas, 80
TIBOUT, Phebe, 130
TILGHMAN, Benjamin, 104, 140, 200; Edward, 36, 52
TIPPENGS, Abigail, 161; Richard, 161
TIPPINGS, Richard, 18
TOBIN, Jacob, 202
TOD, Alexander, 52
TODD, John, 149; Rebecca, 166; William, 166
TORTON, John, 5
TOWNSEND, Ann, 82; Benjamin, 4; Catharen, 115; Cathren, 179; David, 135; Esther, 4; Hannah, 38; Isaac, 38; John, 10, 115; Joseph, 38; Lydia, 4; Rachel, 179; William, 10
TRACEL, Hannah, 37; Jacob, 37
TRACELL, Hannah, 141
TRAGO, Alice, 160
TRAINOR, David, 144; Mary, 179
TRANOR, Mary, 167
TRAQUAIR, Anne, 182; Eliza, 182
TRASEL, Hannah, 141
TREE, Betsey, 196
TREGO, Hannah, 180
TREINOR, David, 77, 145

John, 45, 111, 152; Joseph, 111; Lydia, 45, 111; Margaret, 103, 143; Margret, 103; Nathaniel, 163, 194; Phebe, 83, 176; Samuel, 45; Sarah, 194; Thomas, 164; William, 143
WILLIAMSON, Abigail, 65, 87; Abraham, 8, 27, 74; Adam, 21, 69; Amor, 79, 164; Ann, 22, 69; Charles, 199; Cheyny, 74; Daniel, 21, 68; Elizabeth, 21, 22, 65, 66, 69, 87; Emor, 65, 66, 87; Enos, 21, 22, 69, 90, 153, 204; Ester, 22; Esther, 69, 74; Eunice, 120; George, 65, 69, 87; Gidion, 65, 87; Harry, 195; James, 31, 87; Jane, 22; John, 16, 21, 23, 69, 132, 181; Joshua, 87, 165, 176; Passmore, 74; Patience, 92, 171; Phebe, 74; Rebecca, 69; Sarah, 21, 22, 74, 120, 204; Sidney, 127; Thomas, 65, 74, 87, 173; Walter, 21, 69; William, 65, 74
WILLIANG, Richard, 31
WILLING, Charles, 19; George, 171; George Charles, 201; James, 35; Margaret, 35; Richard, 35; Thomas, 1, 35, 136; Thomas M., 35
WILLINGS, Ann, 35; Charles, 35
WILLIS, Ruth, 89; Susanna, 61; William, 154
WILLS, Jane, 89
WILSON, Ann, 153; Christiana, 29; D., 199; Deborah, 166; Dinah, 29; Elizabeth, 83; Ester, 29; Ezekiel, 98, 117; George, 98; Hannah, 100, 156, 157; John, 19; Joseph, 139, 152; Margaret, 29; Mary, 19; Mary M., 117; Rachel, 39, 83; Sarah, 99, 117, 156, 202; Susan, 156; Thomas, 19, 98, 117, 153
WINDAL, Deborah, 144; Debrah, 144
WINING, Harriot, 91; Mary Ann, 91
WINNEY, Elizabeth Wyatt, 40
WISE, Martin, 18, 112
WISELEY, Francis, 27, 97, 152
WISELY, Francis, 133
WISTAR, Caspar, 152; Catharine, 152; Mary, 153; Sarah, 152; Thomas, 152
WITHY, Elizabeth, 107; James, 67, 107; Samuel J., 133;
Sarah, 107
WITTY, Betsey, 84; James, 84, 85; Mary, 84
WOLLEY, Sarah Ann, 111
WOOD, Aaron, 88; Ann, 4; Cornelius, 6, 93; Elizabeth, 123; George, 4; Hannah, 4; Henry, 4; Jacob, 88; James, 52, 88, 133; John, 32, 63, 88, 123; Jonathan, 4, 179; Joseph, 2; Margaret, 4; Mary, 6, 69, 88, 93, 148; Mathew, 88; Matthew, 63, 90; Nathan, 148; Phebe, 148; Rebeckah, 88; Sarah, 4, 63, 88, 148; Septimus, 88; Sidney, 186; Tacey, 4; Thomas, 13; William, 63, 88
WOODLAND, Joseph, 164
WOODWARD, Alice, 46, 69; Betty, 69; Edward, 46, 69; Jean, 69; Mary, 46, 69; Sarah, 46, 69
WOOLLAS, John, 79; Mary, 79; Nicholas, 79; Phebe, 79; Rachel, 79; Sarah, 79; William Hart, 79
WOOLLEY, Ann, 46; Jane, 46; Sarah, 46
WOOLLY, Ann, 46
WOOLMAN, Hannah, 198; Naomi, 198
WORALL, Prissila, 111
WORRAL, Curtis, 88; Isaiah, 88; Tecy, 87
WORRALL, Abel, 32; Abigail, 17, 146, 183, 203; Ann, 88, 129, 152, 157; Benjamin, 10, 33; Charles, 127, 165; Daniel, 28, 157; David, 89, 156, 177; Edith, 183; Edward, 203; Eleanor, 31, 32, 88; Elias, 127; Elija, 33; Elisha, 9, 72, 89, 152, 177; Eliza, 32, 88, 177, 183; Elizabeth, 28, 156, 165; Elizabeth Lewis, 152; Ellenor, 61; Enos, 127; Eunice, 32; Feddy, 152, 153; Frances, 33; Frazer, 127; Freddy, 152; George, 66, 151; Ham, 203; Hannah, 10, 28, 126, 183; Isaac, 28, 45; Isaiah, 9, 203; J., 99; Jacob, 32, 34, 61, 156, 165; James, 28; Jane, 146, 156, 203; Jesse, 33, 156, 165, 174, 202; Job, 203; John, 9, 12, 17, 28, 45, 93, 94, 99, 111, 151, 183, 203; Jonah, 127; Jonathan, 10, 32, 88; Jonathan B., 165; Jonathan P., 156, 199; Joseph, 9, 25,

32, 33, 62, 89, 129, 177;
Loas, 88; Lois, 32; Lot, 203;
Lydia, 28, 45, 126, 127;
Margaret, 9; Maris, 26;
Martha, 10, 32, 88, 203;
Mary, 17, 45, 126, 127, 151,
156, 165, 177, 179, 180, 203;
Mordecai, 177, 180; Owen, 9,
89; Peirce, 66, 151; Peter,
66, 81, 93, 94, 96, 104, 111,
127, 151, 156, 183, 184;
Phebe, 12, 165, 203; Phoebe,
1; Rachel, 17, 28, 156, 203;
Rebecca, 177, 180; Rebecka,
28; Richard T., 183; Sally,
152; Samuel, 31, 32, 45, 88,
126, 165; Sarah, 17, 32, 45,
88, 111, 126, 183, 203; Seth,
32, 203; Susanna, 126, 156;
Tacy, 88, 156; Teacy, 88;
Thomas, 10, 45, 66, 89, 129,
151; Unis, 88; William, 1,
33, 62, 80, 88, 165; Zebulon,
129
WORRELL, Aaron, 147; Abel, 111,
146; Abraham, 201; Abram,
202; Ann, 201; Daniel, 29;
Elisha, 169; Isaac, 163, 201;
Isaac D., 201; Jemima, 201;
Joseph, 138; Lewis L., 169;
Maris, 111; Mary, 138;
Miriam, 147; Peter, 133;
Phebe, 147; Rebecca, 201;
Sarah, 201; Thomas, 133
WORRILOW, Thomas, 179
WORROW, Ann, 129; John, 129;
Lydia, 129; Zebulon, 129
WORTHINGTON, Sarah, 107
WRIGHT, Alexander, 195;
Christopher Wilson, 188;
Cornelius, 161; Eliza, 195;
James, 195; John, 45; Mary,
188; Samuel, 50; William, 70,
162, 188
WRIGLEY, Nancy, 80

-Y-

YARD, Benjamin, 157; John, 188;
Mary, 188
YARNALL, Abigail, 83; Abnor,
186; Agnes, 48; Ahinoam, 132;
Alben, 120; Albin, 186;
Alice, 107, 108; Allice, 91;
Amos, 72; Ann, 34; Benjamin,
72, 75, 77, 79, 107, 132;
Bennet, 186; Caleb, 22, 28,
48; Edith, 6; Eli, 6, 45, 72,
96, 108; Elizabeth, 105, 110,
143, 178, 186; Ellis, 6, 96,
105, 143, 154, 179, 188, 189;
Enoch, 76, 83, 99, 107, 132;
Ephraim, 6; Ezekiel, 33, 64,
76, 92, 106; George, 48, 76,
83, 107; Hannah, 6, 30, 99,
186; Isaac, 74, 75, 117, 120,
121, 186, 201; Isaac W., 146;
Israel, 78, 107, 184; James,
120, 121, 177, 186, 201;
Jane, 19, 120, 186; Jesse,
107; John, 6, 48, 76, 107,
132; Jonas, 186; Joshua, 6,
97; Lydia, 27; Margaret, 89;
Martha, 146; Mary, 76, 105,
107, 120, 157, 186; Mordecai,
30; Nathan, 105, 143; Owen,
48, 72; Peter, 62, 186;
Phebe, 48, 51, 99, 107, 187;
Rachel, 105, 120, 143, 186;
Rebecca, 173; Reuben, 186;
Rheuben, 120; Samuel, 6, 105;
Sarah, 51, 59, 88, 92, 96,
107, 108, 178, 186;
Sharpless, 184; Sidney, 120,
186; Thomas, 120, 186;
Walker, 96, 108, 186;
William, 19, 28, 48, 65, 73,
76, 102, 107, 120, 124, 150,
164, 184, 186
YARNEL, Amos, 148; Enoch, 148
YARNELL, Deborah, 141; Hannah,
141; Martha, 141; Omey, 141
YEARDSLEY, Isaac, 36
YEARLEY, Nathan, 93
YEARSLEY, Jacob, 113; Nathan,
39, 93, 111, 133, 146, 161
YEARSLY, Jacob, 113; Tacy, 166
YEATES, John, 45
YOKUM, Sarah, 37
YOUNG, Cunrod, 3; George, 52;
J., 200; Jesse, 196